RENEWALS 458-4574

DATE DUE			
GAYLORD			PRINTED IN U.S.A.

Allegories of Dissent

Allegories of Dissent

The Theater of
Agustín Gómez-Arcos

Sharon G. Feldman

Lewisburg
Bucknell University Press
London: Associated University Presses

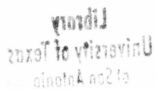

Associated University Presses
440 Forsgate Drive
Cranbury, NJ 08512

Associated University Presses
16 Barter Street
London WC1A 2AH, England

Associated University Presses
P.O. Box 338, Port Credit
Mississauga, Ontario
Canada L5G 4L8

The paper used in this publication meets the requirements
of the American National Standard for Permanence of Paper
for Printed Library Materials Z39.48-1984.

Library of Congress Cataloging-in-Publication Data

Feldman, Sharon G., 1962–
    Allegories of dissent : the theater of Agustín Gómez-Arcos /
Sharon G. Feldman.
        p.   cm.
    Includes bibliographical references and index.
    ISBN 0-8387-5377-9 (alk. paper)
    1. Gómez-Arcos, Agustín—Dramatic works.   I. Title.
PQ6657.O425Z64   1998
842'.914—dc21   98-19648
                                                                        CIP

PRINTED IN THE UNITED STATES OF AMERICA

In memory of Robert

Yo te enseñaré el mundo como es, que tú no alcanças a ver sino lo que parece.
—*Francisco de Quevedo*, "El mundo por de dentro"

The theater restores us all our dormant conflicts and all their powers, and gives these powers names . . .
—*Antonin Artaud*, El teatro y su doble

He who tells too much truth shall surely be hanged.
—*George Bernard Shaw*, Saint Joan

Contents

Preface

C'est le moment. Ce voyage, tu dois l'entreprendre dignement, sans peur. Avec l'espoir que moi, je ne serai pas aussi mesquine avec toi que la Vie.[1]

—*Agustín Gómez-Arcos*, Ana Non

OF ABSENCE, MEMORY, AND REDISCOVERY

"THE case of this writer is in great measure irreparable."[2] This somber affirmation, written by the venerable Spanish theater critic Moisés Pérez Coterillo, appeared in his introduction to the 1991 edition of Agustín Gómez-Arcos's one-act farce *Interview de Mrs. Muerta Smith por sus fantasmas* (Mrs. Dead Smith's interview with her phantoms). Indeed, the case of Gómez-Arcos (b. Almería, 1933) represents an extraordinary paradox for those prone to observe the ebb and flow of European literary history. In France, where he has lived in self-imposed exile since 1968, he has garnered preeminent status as a prolific award-winning writer. He is the author of fourteen novels written directly in French, and in 1985, he became one of only four Spanish artists (along with Rafael Alberti, José Bergamín, and Pablo Picasso) ever to be decorated by the French Legion of Honor as *Chevalier de l'Ordre des Arts ès Lettres*.

Yet, in Spain, the mere mention of the name "Agustín Gómez-Arcos" is bound to inspire a pensive stare or bewildered gaze.[3] Curiously, in his native country, he is still regarded by many as a kind of phantom figure of Spanish theater history, a member of a lost generation of playwrights whose work was censored and prohibited during the years of the Franco dictatorship and whose rebellious cries have all but since been forgotten. He attributes his enigmatic condition to a persistent rejection and erasure of his historical memory, of the remembrances and allegorical evocations of authoritarian Spain that have always been a constant in his literature. He commented on this situation in a 1990 lecture, presented at the Dia Art Foundation in New York City:

In some cases, like mine, memory is the key to this general rejection. The freedom to remember and recount is converted automatically into

9

libertarianism. And if this freedom is practiced in exile, or in an exiled language, the memories that it reveals loose legitimacy, are transferred into aggressive acts aimed towards the new order, an order which, if we judge its desire to hide history, to minimize it and even to erase it, looks like a twin brother of the older order. . . . The rebellious work, the work in constant rebellion, continues without having rights to citizenship.[4]

To be scorned and cast aside by one's homeland is perhaps the most tragic form of rejection that one could possibly endure. It is analogous to the experience of an orphaned child, abandoned by his mother. The scars do not heal easily, and the damage is likely to be, in Pérez Coterillo's words, "irreparable." Over time, the artistic freedom and success that Gómez-Arcos was able to achieve through exile may have offered him a semblance of compensation for this rejection and even a feeling of revenge. Nevertheless, I personally recall a particular summer evening in which I wandered through the streets of Madrid with my friend Agustín, and as we strolled passed the hallowed Teatro Español, a site of his former battles with censorship, he confessed to me that for many years, during his occasional visits to Spain, he would feel an overwhelming sense of sorrow and anguish each time he walked by a theater. The sight of the marquee bearing a name that was not his own was a painful reminder of his absence from the Spanish stage. Despite his international acclaim as a novelist, Gómez-Arcos has always considered himself to be first and foremost a dramatist.

It was only recently that signs of a change in attitude toward his work and toward his memories began to emerge in the so-called "new democratic Spain." A prominent young director, Carme Portaceli, was invited to stage his plays, and the Spanish Ministry of Culture followed with economic support. Opportunities such as these, which he had only dreamed of as a young playwright in Madrid, continued to unfold, prompting him to embark upon the difficult journey home, to return to the scene of prior battles and publicly confront his enemies after an indeterminately prolonged absence.

Presently, as I compose this preface, Gómez-Arcos's theater is undergoing a renaissance on the stages of his native Spain, where seemingly overnight he has succeeded in reestablishing his prestige as a dramatist. The culmination of this process of renewal and rediscovery came in 1994, when he was selected as a finalist for Spain's Premio Nacional de Literatura Dramática. Between 1991 and 1994, Spanish spectators witnessed the premières of three of his plays at major Madrid theaters: the María Guerrero (Centro Dramático Nacional) and the Sala Olimpia (Centro Nacional de Nuevas Tendencias Escénicas). All three of these productions received large subventions from the Spanish Ministry of Culture. The staging of *Los gatos* under Portaceli's direction during the 1992–93 theater season was so successful that it was selected for a national tour of Spain. It prompted theater critic María Francisca Vilches de Frutos to call Gómez-Arcos one of the "great renovators" of the contemporary Spanish stage.[5] Portaceli and the cast, which included the distinguished Argentinean actor Héctor Alterio, also accepted an invitation to stage *Los gatos* in Buenos Aires. Each of these three recent premières coincided with the publication of the corresponding dramatic text. As a result, more of Gómez-Arcos's theater is now available in print than ever before, and interest in his work continues to grow on both sides of the Atlantic.

Allegories of Dissent is a case study of the artistic strategies employed by a single playwright in his ongoing struggle against censorship and oppression. In this study, I draw upon theoretical discussions of contemporary culture in order to situate Gómez-Arcos's theater in terms of the historical trajectory of twentieth-century Spanish drama, establish the relevant correlations that exist between his theater and the allegorical strategies of postmodernist art, and trace the structural and thematic transformations that emerge in the course of his radical move from censored artist to bilingual *exilé*.

This book begins with a two-part introduction. The first part, "From Censorship to Exile to Bilingualism," is a biobibliographical profile, which navigates Gómez-Arcos's labyrinth of plays and novels in Spanish and French, maps out the fundamental stages of his literary career, and summarizes his connections with Spanish theater history. The second introductory section, "A Poetics of Expanse and Enclosure: The Allegorical Way of Seeing," proposes a critical framework for the treatment of postmodernist allegory and, more specifically, considers the unique implications of allegorical imagery as expressed both visually and verbally in Gómez-Arcos's theater. The chapters that follow proceed in chronological order and treat seven of Gómez-Arcos's most important plays. For historic as well as thematic reasons, I have grouped the first six plays into pairs. Generally, I open my discussion of each play with a summary of the circumstances surrounding its performance, reception, and/or censorship. I then offer a detailed analysis of the dramatic text. Part I, "Spectacles of Sacrifice," examines two pre-exilic works, *Diálogos de la herejía* (Dialogues of heresy, 1962) and *Los gatos* (The cats, 1965), in relation to the notion of sacrificial ritual.[6] Part II, "Allegory and the Absurd," presents analyses of *Mil y un mesías* (One thousand and one Messiahs, 1966) and *Queridos míos, es preciso contaros ciertas cosas* (My dear friends, it's time we get certain things straight, 1966) and demonstrates how Gómez-Arcos's absurdist allegorizing functions as a strategic camouflage for an underlying critique of political oppression. Part III, "The Language of Exile," focuses on *Adorado Alberto* (Adored Alberto, 1968) and *Pré-papa* (1969), two plays written at the beginning of Gómez-Arcos's residence in France, and looks at how his treatment of the themes of sexuality, gender, and bilingualism translates into an allegorical quest for freedom of expression. Finally, Part IV, "Sanctifying the Scatological and Debasing the Divine," explores Gómez-Arcos's postmodern conception of the sacred as manifested in one of his most defiant works *Interview de Mrs. Muerta Smith por sus fantasmas* (Mrs. Dead Smith's interview with her phantoms, 1972).

In addition to the previously mentioned sections, I have also included two appendices in this study. The first is an alphabetical listing of premières and performances, including information on actors, directors, places, dates, and theaters. The second is a comprehensive interview with Mr. Gómez-Arcos, conducted in Spanish, in which he discusses his work as both playwright and novelist, and his situation as a bilingual writer living in exile

Allegories of Dissent is the first book-length study of the theater of Gómez-Arcos. His work has received lavish attention from the popular press in the form of articles, book reviews, and play reviews, and I have included an extensive selection of these articles and reviews in my bibliography. However, to date, Gómez-Arcos's literature has received only scarce mention in critical anthologies and academic journals. On the whole, most standard histories of modern Spanish theater devote very limited attention, or no attention at all, to his work as a dramatist. María Pilar Pérez-Stansfield (*Teatro español de postguerra*, 1983), José García Templado (*El teatro español actual*, 1992), and Alberto Miralles (*Aproximación al teatro alternativo*, 1994) allude momentarily to his theater in their discussions of the playwrights of the realist generation, and Juan Emilio Aragonés (*Teatro español de postguerra*, 1971) cites his name as part of a list of *novísimos*.

The exceptions to these fleeting glimpses of his drama can be found in the works of César Oliva, L. Teresa Valdivieso, and Phyllis Zatlin. In *El teatro desde 1936* (1989), Oliva offers a short commentary on Gómez-Arcos and his activities in Spain with specific reference to *Diálogos de la herejía* and *Los gatos*. In her essay "El intertexto como principio configurativo en el teatro de Fernando Arrabal y Agustín Gómez Arcos" [*sic*] (1995), Valdivieso focuses on *Diálogos de la herejía* and *Interview de Mrs. Muerta Smith por sus fantasmas*, observing a series of biographical and stylistic parallels in the work of Gómez-

Arcos and Arrabal. In *Cross-Cultural Approaches to Theatre: The Spanish-French Connection* (1994), Zatlin devotes her attention to Gómez-Arcos's ties with the French stage, offering brief commentaries on the productions of *Et si on aboyait* and *Pré-papa* in Paris, and *Diálogos de la herejía* and *Interview de Mrs. Muerta Smith por sus fantasmas* in Madrid. In addition, Zatlin's essay "The Return of the Prodigal: The Theatre of Gómez-Arcos" (1995) provides a fascinating overview of Gómez-Arcos's recent return to the Spanish stage.

With regard to the treatment of Gómez-Arcos's narrative work, I am aware of the publication of only two scholarly articles: Elena Gascón-Vera's psychoanalytic study "Los reflejos del yo: Narcisismo y androginia en Agustín Gómez-Arcos" (1991), and Ann Duncan's comprehensive essay titled "Agustín Gómez-Arcos" in *Beyond the Nouveau Roman: Essays on the Contemporary French Novel* (1990).[7]

Allegories of Dissent considers published and unpublished, performed and never-performed plays. If I were to cite a precedent for this type of study it would be George E. Wellwarth's *Spanish Underground Drama* (1972; Spanish translation, 1978). Wellwarth attempted to resuscitate the theater of more than twenty Spanish dramatists whose work had been suppressed by Francoist censorship. Although he perceived the first wave of realist playwrights (e.g., Antonio Buero Vallejo, Carlos Muñiz, Lauro Olmo, and Alfonso Sastre) as undoubtedly pertaining to the Spanish "underground," he chose not to include them in his study and, instead, devoted his attention to what he considered to be a younger "lesser-known" generation of dramatists, often referred to as the "new" Spanish theater and/or the "symbolist" generation (e.g., Jerónimo López Mozo, Manuel Martínez Mediero, Miguel Romero Esteo, and José Ruibal). Wellwarth eventually encountered abundant criticism for his overall selection of dramatists and his omission of the realists—who considered themselves to be just as far "underground" as the younger generation.[8] Nevertheless, his study, written during the period of the Franco dictatorship, was significant in its endeavor to uncover and rescue these muted voices. He did not include Gómez-Arcos in his book, although he conceivably might have done so.

With regard to this process of resuscitation and redemption of once-prohibited works, it is also important to recognize the crucial endeavors of José Monleón, editor of the leading Spanish theater journal *Primer Acto*. In 1980, during the democratic transition, Monleón organized a Spanish theater series at the Teatro María Guerrero, known as "El ciclo de los lunes," which was devoted to the revival of plays by several dramatists whose works had been prohibited under Franco. Monléon subsequently published the work of many of these playwrights, such as Alberto Miralles, Jerónimo López Mozo, and José Ricardo Morales, in *Primer Acto*.

Over the course of the past two decades—with the exception of Buero Vallejo, Sastre, and Fernando Arrabal—very few monographic studies of individual playwrights from the Spanish post–Civil War period have appeared in print. Some relatively recent departures from this norm include Jesús Barrajón on Francisco Nieva (1987), Ángel Cabo on José Martín Recuerda (1993), Elda María Phillips on José Ruibal (1984), Virtudes Serrano on Domingo Miras (1991), Juan Tebar on Fernando Fernán Gómez (1984), and Zatlin on Jaime Salom (1982). There are also various studies that take up the work of several playwrights from the postwar and/or post-Franco period within a single volume. Some noteworthy examples are Gwynne Edwards's *Dramatists in Perspective: Spanish Theatre in the Twentieth Century*, 1985; Martha Halsey and Phyllis Zatlin's anthology *The Contemporary Spanish Theater: A Collection of Critical Essays*, 1988; Marion P. Holt's *The Contemporary Spanish Theater* (1949–1972), 1975; Oliva's *Disidentes de la generación realista (Introducción a la obra de Carlos Muñiz, Laura Olmo, Rodríguez Méndez and Martín Recuerda)*, 1979; and Alfonso de Toro and Wilfried Floeck's anthology *Teatro español contemporáneo: Autores y tendencias*, 1995. Only this last volume treats the theater of Gómez-Arcos: in Valdivieso's essay on his theater and that of Arrabal.[9]

It is my hope that the present study will serve to uncover the work of yet another playwright from the postwar period and thereby contribute to the process of recuperation and reconsideration that can be traced back to Wellwarth and Monleón. I am concerned with not only how Gómez-Arcos's allegories of dissent may have been perceived in the past, in totalitarian Spain; but also, how they can be interpreted in the present, in a contemporary world where oppression and intolerance have become universal notions, indelibly inscribed in the headlines of our daily newspapers. In the program notes for the 1994 production of *Queridos míos, es preciso contaros ciertas cosas*, director Carme Portaceli wrote that the voice of Gómez-Arcos is that of "someone who, unfortunately like so many others, had to leave this country because he was not permitted to speak, to work, or to live." That same voice that was once silenced is now able to speak, even to scream, and if we refuse to listen to it today, in the present, then we run the risk of validating the censorship that was once imposed upon it in the past. Perhaps the moment has finally arrived in which Gómez-Arcos's memories can and should be heard.

I wish to express my sincere appreciation to Lee Fontanella, who introduced me to the work of Agustín Gómez-Arcos and encouraged me to take on this project. I shall always be grateful for his generosity and mentoring. My gratitude extends as well to Andrew P. Debicki, Roberta Johnson, Douglass Rogers, W. B. Worthen, and especially Phyllis Zatlin for their thoughtful insights and suggestions and their unyielding encouragement. I am grateful to Moisés Pérez Coterillo, Director of the Centro de Documentación Teatral, and to Ana Jelín of Producciones Teatrales Contemporáneas for providing me with the photographs that are reprinted in this study. I also wish to express my gratitude to Agustín Gómez-Arcos for his friendship and kindness in graciously providing me with unpublished manuscripts and sharing with me his thoughts on his life, his work, and the creative process. I am grateful to my family for their endless enthusiasm, and finally, a special thanks goes to my friend Javier Guitart, whose passion for detective fiction facilitated my first encounter with Agustín in Madrid.

Partial funding of this project was provided by grants from the General Research Fund and the Center of Latin American Studies of the University of Kansas.

Abbreviations

ALL English translations are my own with the following exceptions: the translated passages from Gómez-Arcos's *L'agneau carnivore* pertain to William Rodarmor's published translation of this novel, and the translated passages from *Los gatos* and *Queridos míos, es preciso contaros ciertas cosas* were prepared by Lee Fontanella. In citing passages from Gómez-Arcos's works, I have preserved the original French/Spanish version in a series of corresponding notes. Within these notes, I employ the following abbreviations:

DH	*Diálogos de la herejía*
LG	*Los gatos*
MM	*Mil y un mesías*
QM	*Queridos míos, es preciso contaros ciertas cosas*
AA	*Adorado Alberto*
PP	*Pré-papa*
IMM	*Interview de Mrs. Muerta Smith por sus fantasmas*
MR	*Maria Republica*
PPR	*Pré-papa ou Roman des fées*

Allegories of Dissent

Introduction

1

From Censorship to Exile to Bilingualism

*Parce que mes souvenirs, qui pourrait les effacer? Surtout main-
tenant que j'ai enfin trouvé le moyen de m'en servir. Comme des
bombes pour vous annihiler. . . . Mais enfin je comprends. Vous ne
voulez pas de mes souvenirs. Mes souvenirs sont aussi votre histoire. Sale histoire. C'est bon. Il est peut-être trop tard, mais . . .
le temps qui me reste est un temps précieux. Le temps de régler
nos comptes.*[1]

—*Agustín Gómez-Arcos*, Maria Republica

On the evening of 26 February 1991, Agustín Gómez-Arcos's one-act
absurdist farce *Interview de Mrs. Muerta Smith por sus fantasmas*
(Mrs. Dead Smith's interview with her phantoms) premiered at Madrid's Sala Olimpia. Although it was staged as a coproduction of two
of Spain's prestigious state-run theater entities, the Centro Dramático
Nacional (CDN) and the Centro Nacional de Nuevas Tendencias Escénicas (CNNTE), Gómez-Arcos's play, directed by Carme Portaceli,
may have gone largely unnoticed due to an undeservedly meager
allotment of seventeen performances. Nevertheless, the production of
Interview de Mrs. Muerta Smith marked an extraordinarily noteworthy occasion in recent Spanish theater history in that, with the première of this play, the voice of one of Europe's most distinguished
living writers triumphantly returned to the Spanish stage after an
absence that had endured nearly twenty-six years.

The story of this absence really begins as far back as 1933. On 15
January of that year, Gómez-Arcos was born in Enix, a village perched
high above of the sea in the Andalusian province of Almería.[2] There
he spent his childhood, laboring at times as village goat herd, while
always remaining faithful to his passion for literature. While his parents were illiterate, he and his six siblings shared a love of books and
would often read to each other into the late hours of the night. Sadly,
the outbreak of the Spanish Civil War in 1936 brought an end to the
optimistic innocence of his youth. His family, sympathizing with the
vanquished Republicans, endured significant hardship and misfor-
tune during the war and the years that followed. Even at a very early

age, Gómez-Arcos was keenly aware of the role that literature could play in his life as a way of fulfilling his desire to transcend the limits of oppression. In a 1990 interview, he commented, "For me, having been born into a practically illiterate family, reading gave me access to freedom. I will always remember that I am indebted to it."[3] His literature professor at an *instituto* in Almería played a key role in cultivating his interest in writing, drama, and the French language. His fondness of Russian literature and his readings of Franz Kafka, Nikolai Gogol, and Feodor Dostoyevsky eventually would influence the course of his own writing, particularly with regard to his employment of allegory and his treatment of morally ambiguous themes.

As for many writers of Gómez-Arcos's generation, the experience of having lived through such a tragic period in Spain's history undoubtedly left a lasting imprint on his literature and his overall view of the world. The origins of his theater thus can be traced to his memories of the Civil War and the somber postwar period in which looming clouds of oppression cast a sweeping shadow across the Spanish cultural landscape. Although in the future, Gómez-Arcos would leave behind both *patria* and native language, these dark clouds would continue to serve under varying guises as the backdrop for his allegorical expressions of dissent. Throughout nearly three decades of exile, having distanced himself spatially, temporally, and linguistically from the realities of totalitarian Spain, he would never completely forgo his memories of the past, never turn his back on history, and never abandon his vision of the theater as a place where one must strive to uncover the truth. He declared, in a 1985 interview with Rosa Montero, "I do not believe that society should be at the service of the artist. But that the artist should be at the service of society, and moreover, in the most difficult way in the world, that is, like Cassandra, making them see what they do not want to see."[4]

The evolution of Gómez-Arcos's career entails four principal stages, summarized in table 1, which are marked by a labyrinthine progression of changes in residence, literary genre, and language.

Table 1   Principal Stages of Gómez-Arcos's Literary Trajectory

Stage	Dates	Country	Genre	Principal Language
1	1955–1966	Spain	Theater	Spanish
2	1968–1975	France	Theater	Spanish / French
3	1973–1991	France	Novel	French
4	1991–Present	Spain/France	Theater/Novel	Spanish/French

The first stage of his artistic trajectory began during the 1950s when, having completed secondary school in Almería, he left the pastoral life of Andalusia for the more cosmopolitan surroundings of Barcelona. While studying law for three years at the University of Barcelona, he found himself continually drawn to the world of literature. During this period, he won a national prize for his short story "El último Cristo," published a collection of poetry titled *Ocasión de paganismo*, and contributed to the literary review *Poesía Española*. Also during this time of residence in Barcelona, he became increasingly involved in University theater productions, writing, directing, and performing in several plays. Ultimately, he completely abandoned his legal studies and traveled to Madrid with the intention of realizing his dream of a life in the theater.

Throughout the early part of the 1960s, Gómez-Arcos worked in Madrid as a playwright, actor, director, and translator. His experience as a performer would serve as a cornerstone in his formation as a dramatist, for it helped him to expand his awareness of the subtleties involved in writing dramatic dialogue. In his theater, the word has always played a weighty role; hence, the ability to write dialogue was for him an important skill and one that he would later integrate into his work as a novelist. He wrote a total of fifteen plays during this early period, listed here in order of composition: *Doña Frivolidad* (Madame Frivolity); *Unos muertos perdidos* (Some lost deaths); *Verano* (Summer); *Historia privada de un pequeño pueblo* (Private story of a small village); *Elecciones generales* (General elections); *Fedra en el Sur* (Phaedra in the south); *El tribunal* (The tribunal); *El rapto de las siamesas* (The rapture of the Siamese), in collaboration with Enrique Ortenbach and Adolfo Waitzman; *Balada matrimonial* (Matrimonial ballad); *El salón* (The drawing room); *Prometeo Jiménez, revolucionario* (Prometheus Jiménez, revolutionary); *Diálogos de la herejía* (Dialogues of heresy); *Los gatos* (The cats); *Mil y un mesías* (One thousand and one Messiahs); and *Queridos míos, es preciso contaros ciertas cosas* (My dear friends, it's time we get certain things straight).

Gómez-Arcos's public debut as a dramatist took place in 1960 when his *Elecciones generales*, a "farsa político-disparatada" based on Gogol's *Dead Souls*, won a prize at the Primer Festival Nacional de Teatro Nuevo (First National Festival of New Theater). The play premiered in Madrid on 3 April at the theater of the university residence of Santa María de la Almudena. It featured renowned stage and screen actor Alfredo Landa and even the playwright himself performed in a minor role. The première of *Elecciones generales* was an occasion that inspired great hope and excitement, and the reviews appearing in the popular press unequivocally confirmed the emergence of a promising new Spanish dramatist. Critic-playwright Alfredo Marquerie made the following pronouncement in the daily *ABC:*

> *Elecciones generales* heralds the emergence of a full-fledged author who could perfectly stage his plays in any theater and not limit himself to exclusive circles. . . . He has a wide and noble vision of scenic architecture, of character development, of harmony, and of the resolution of performance issues, of irony and fantasy, and above all an absolute mastery of dialogue and language, between the popular and the poetic, which many of the "famous ones" would envy.[5]

During these early years in Madrid, Gómez-Arcos also translated and adapted three French plays for the Spanish stage: Jean Giraudoux's *La folle de Chaillot* and *Intermezzo* (both of which premiered at the Teatro María Guerrero in 1962), and René-Jean Clot's *La révélation* (which premiered at the Teatro Goya in 1963). His translation-adaptation of Giraudoux's *La folle de Chaillot* (The madwoman of Chaillot) has come to be regarded as the definitive Spanish version, and in 1989, it was restaged at the María Guerrero by its original director José Luis Alonso. Gómez-Arcos's other activities during this period include his adaptation of a Norwegian children's musical by Thorbjorn Egner titled *La villa de los ladrones* (The city of thieves), staged in 1963 by the Títeres de la Sección Femenina.

In 1962, he was selected as a finalist for the Calderón de la Barca National Prize and was awarded the Lope de Vega National Prize for *Diálogos de la herejía*, a historical drama in which the Inquisition is invoked as a metaphor for twentieth-century Spanish fascism. The Lope de Vega is a major accolade that typically would have guaranteed him a *mise en scène* of his play at one of Spain's "official" (or, "national") theaters, such as the María Guerrero or the Teatro Español.[6] However, almost immediately following conferral, the prize was swept from his hands in a wave of controversy, annulled in a blatant gesture of censorship that represented the Franco regime's official response to his unorthodox choice of thematic material. Consequently, the play was banned from the stages of the state-supported national theaters. He gives the following account of the circumstances surrounding the annulment of this Lope de Vega Prize:

> The jury for the prize was composed of a series of people that included José Tamayo, who was at that time the director of the Teatro Español, which was then a national theater. Today, it is still a national theater but it depends on the government of Madrid for support, and at that time it was directly dependent on the Ministry. And so, they gave me the prize,

and since the play had a lot of censorship problems, they put pressure on Tamayo to retract his vote. He called me, we had lunch together, and he explained to me what was happening. He said, "Well, either I retract my vote or they will take the theater away from me. So, I have no choice but to retract my vote."[7]

In 1964, Gómez-Arcos finally saw a censored rendition of *Diálogos de la herejía* premier to conflicting reviews at Madrid's Teatro Reina Victoria. Also that year, a severed version of the dramatic text appeared in the Spanish theater revue *Primer Acto*, along with a series of articles addressing the play's powerful thematic material. The retraction of the prize and the subsequent debate aroused by Gómez-Arcos's heretical dialogues did not represent an isolated episode in his career; but rather, the struggle for freedom of expression is an issue that would unceasingly prevail as a central theme in both his literature and his life. Indeed, the controversy surrounding *Diálogos de la herejía* was merely a prelude to a series of combative encounters with Francoist censorship that eventually would prompt his voluntary exile from Spain.

Following the *Diálogos* episode, a censored version of his "bourgeois *esperpento*" *Los gatos* premiered in September 1965 at the Teatro Marquina. By this time, he had already begun to suspect that this première might very well be his last, although he never imagined that another twenty-five years would pass before his return to the Madrid stage. Beginning in 1962, when Franco appointed Manuel Fraga Iribarne to the position of Minister of Information and Tourism, censorship practices supposedly had loosened somewhat as part of a general initiative of *apertura*, designed to open Spain to increased cultural and economic communication with the rest of western Europe and the United States. (In 1969, in the wake of a scandal, Franco removed Fraga from office and replaced him with the extremely conservative Alfredo Sánchez Bella, who once again instituted rigorous censorship standards and reduced the frequency of government subsidies for the arts.) Fraga's presence, nevertheless, was of little consolation and consequence to Gómez-Arcos. The theater—perhaps, even more so than any other literary genre of this postwar period—was still extremely vulnerable to the sacrificial flames of censorship. Not only was the written dramatic text subject to the inquisitorial and capricious scrutiny of the Spanish censors; but also, the performance was forcibly laid open for inspection prior to its presentation before a general audience. Furthermore, even when a play had gained approval at all the necessary levels, its scheduled run suddenly could be canceled for mysterious reasons.[8] Gómez-Arcos had dealt with these stifling and enigmatic "rules of the game" for quite some time, and in light of the intensely defiant attitude that permeates each of his plays, it is in some respects astounding that he had managed to see any of his theater staged at all.

By the mid-1960s, it was clear to him that the performance and publication of his works would remain a difficult and uncertain aspiration, and that censorship would continue to prevail as an opposing force with regard to his artistic endeavors in Spain. Like other Spanish dramatists of this period who engaged in the creation of a politically-charged theater of protest, he faced a series of alternatives that included self-censorship, *posibilismo*, and *imposibilismo*. Here, I have in mind the well-known debate waged in 1960 on the pages of *Primer Acto* between Antonio Buero Vallejo, Alfonso Paso, and Alfonso Sastre over the polemical issue of a "possible"—as opposed to an "impossible"—theater. In brief, Buero proposed that playwrights work within the artistic constraints of the Franco dictatorship in order to do what was possible to avoid censorship and stage their plays. Paso, who like Buero, enjoyed a relatively large degree of commercial success, assumed the position that playwrights should work within the system in order to contribute to its downfall. In contrast, Sastre criticized the privileging of commercial interests over political and ideological commitments, suggesting that a complacent acceptance of the artistic boundaries designated by Francoist censorship would only serve to endorse and strengthen the existence of such limitations.[9] Sastre's theater, as well as that of Gómez-Arcos, would remain virtually invisible and "impossible" throughout the period of the dictatorship. For Gómez-Arcos (again, like Sastre), any sort of self-censorship or *posibilismo* was absolutely inconceivable. Moreover, another alternative—that of exile—began to hover in his path, enticing him at every step of the way.

In 1966, he reached an important turning point in his career, one that marked the beginning of his absence from the Spanish stage. This was the year in which he wrote two absurdist allegories, *Mil y un mesías* and *Queridos míos*. Curiously, in both plays, he intertwined the themes of censorship and exile in a way that seemed to foreshadow his own impending situation. He received a second Lope de Vega Prize for *Queridos míos*; however, once again, the censoring authorities prevented the play from being staged.[10] Upon receiving the award, he cashed in his winnings to purchase a plane ticket to London and with this dramatic gesture made a decisive break with his Spanish past and a definitive leap into exile. He would not return to his homeland until the summer of 1977, when Spain was already veering in the direction of democracy.

Gómez-Arcos originally thought that he would be able to establish a career in London. At one point, London's National Theatre organized a reading of his work, but eventually Kenneth Tynan, who was then adjunct director of the theater, informed Gómez-Arcos, rather prophetically, that his was a theater that would be more appropriate in twenty years.[11] After two years in London, Gómez-Arcos decided that his artistic prospects would be greater in France. He arrived in Paris in June 1968—just one month after the May upheaval that shook the French universities and the Gaullist government. The barricades had long since been removed from the city streets, but the scent of protest continued to linger in the air. This was an extremely exciting time to be a young playwright in Paris. The artistic climate was imbued with anti-authoritarianism, anti–institutionalism, and innovation, and these conditions provided Gómez-Arcos with fertile ground in which to search for new directions for his theater.

The events of May 1968, in effect, motivated many artists living and working in France to reflect upon the nature of theater as an instrument of social, cultural, and political agitation. As Marvin Carlson points out, "The student and worker uprisings of 1968 stimulated fresh consideration of the relationship between theatre and the social order, especially in Paris, where the Living Theatre's participation in the student occupation of the national theatre, the Odéon, made it a somewhat reluctant symbol of the defiance of the old order."[12] Throughout Europe, Latin America, and the United States, a series of parallel events, which included the Parisian May and the war in Vietnam, inspired new conceptions of the theater as an allegorical site of political and ideological confrontation. Communitarian radical theater groups, such as the Living Theater (est. 1951) and the Théâtre du Soleil (est. 1964), flourished during this age of insurrectionism. The iconoclastic politics that characterized their performances would translate into an analogous interrogation of the conventional hierarchy of theatrical invention that typically assigned separate roles to actors, directors, playwrights, and spectators. Spanish theater also witnessed a reconsideration of performance as a means of opposition and resistance with the genesis of several experimental "independent" theater groups that were considered nonofficial alternatives to commercial and/or government-subsidized theater. Els Joglars (est. 1962) and Tábano (est. 1968) are but two examples of this *teatro independiente*. However, in Spain, unlike the France in which Gómez-Arcos chose to remain, censorship was still an influential force that continued to determine the course of theatrical invention.

The Paris of the late 1960s was alive with both foreign and domestic theater productions. Gómez-Arcos, an enthusiastic spectator, was able to see the works of many Paris-based artists, as well as several international touring companies. One of his most memorable experiences as a theatergoer was the monumental *mise en scène* of *Orlando furioso* under the direction of Luca Ronconi in 1968. He was also able to attend performances of Bertolt Brecht's theater and plays by major dramatists associated with the theater of the absurd, such as Samuel Beckett, Eugène Ionesco, Arthur Adamov, and most importantly, Jean Genet. Gómez-Arcos had been an avid reader of Genet even prior to his departure from Spain, and while it is difficult to estimate the extent to which his contact with Genet's theater and narrative works may have had an impact upon his own, there are undoubtedly notable points of correspondence between the two writers; above all, in their employment of ritual as a way of challenging conventionally accepted notions of the sacred, identity, and authenticity.

The second stage of Gómez-Arcos's career began amid the *café-théâtres* of the Parisian Latin Quarter. The *café-théâtre* scene, which was especially animated during the mid-1960s, offered an attractive and rather eclectic alternative to the more conventional and commercial theaters that tended to cater to bourgeois tastes. It provided a relaxed atmosphere where playwrights were encouraged to experiment and where many young dramatists were afforded their first opportunities to stage their plays. A 1969 issue of the French theater review *L'Avant-Scène Théâtre* (the issue in which Gómez-Arcos published *Pré-papa*) chronicles the activities at several café-theaters. At the Café-Théâtre de l'Absidiole, for instance, one could view a variety show presented by Yves-Robert Viala; at the Café de la Gare, Romain Bouteille presented a series of "sketches insensés, joués, chantés et dansés"; and at the Théâtre de la Lucernaire, one could witness Alfred Panou's *Black Power*, a spectacle devoted to black music and poetry. In the same issue of *L'Avant-Scène*, André Camp offers the following description of the *café-théâtre* scene, which he perceives as already having begun to wane:

> Three years ago, they flourished on every corner of the Latin Quarter, Montparnasse, and even the Marais. In narrow smoke-filled rooms, small groups of enthusiastic actors interpreted sketches and sainetes, often interspersed with poems and songs, in front of spectators seated at tables, among whom they would then make an appeal to help "defray the artists." In these intermittent cafés—they didn't open, most of the time, until nightfall—performers and authors were born. Often they were one and the same.[13]

Corresponding with the scenario portrayed in Camp's description, Gómez-Arcos, in effect, worked at several café-theaters as a playwright, director, actor, and sometimes even a waiter. Soon after his arrival in France, he met another Spanish *exilé*, Miguel Arocena, who was then the manager of the Café-Théâtre de l'Odéon. Arocena commissioned him to write two one-act plays, thus providing him with the opportunity to present his theater to a French audience. Gómez-Arcos wrote the texts in Spanish, and his Belgian friend, actress Rachel Salik, translated them for performance in French. His Parisian debut took place at the Odéon in February 1969 with a dual-program consisting of two absurd farces *Pré-papa* and *Et si on aboyait?* (And if one were to bark?)—originally titled *Adorado Alberto* (Adored Alberto). Following this debut, he continued to work at the café-theaters for four more years. His activities included the presentation in 1972 of *Dîner avec Mr & Mrs Q* (Dinner with Mr. and Mrs. Q) at the Café-Théâtre Campagne and a restaging in 1973 of *Pré-papa* and *Et si on aboyait?* It was arduous and exhausting work, but he derived great pleasure from the fact that he was finally able to express himself freely, without apprehension, and without the burden of censorship. This was, consequently, the period in which he wrote his most intensely defiant and denunciatory theater pieces *Sentencia dictada contra P y J* (The sentencing of P and J, 1970) and *Interview de Mrs. Muerta Smith por sus fantasmas* (Mrs. Dead Smith's interview with her phantoms, 1972).

The third stage in Gómez-Arcos's literary trajectory began one evening at the Odéon in 1973 following a performance of *Et si on aboyait?* An unsuspecting editor from éditions Stock, impressed with what he had witnessed on stage, asked his unsuspecting waiter if the playwright happened to be in the house. The waiter responded, "C'est moi!" and with this fortuitous encounter, Gómez-Arcos's career as a novelist was launched. The editor proposed that he write a novel in French—an idea that at the time seemed absolutely absurd to the Spaniard—but he nevertheless embraced the challenge. After his meeting with the editor, Gómez-Arcos promptly purchased another plane ticket, this time to Athens, where he sought solitary refuge in a city of anonymous faces. When he returned to Paris months later with the manuscript for *L'agneau carnivore* (The carnivorous lamb) under his arm, he hardly imagined that it would win the Prix Hermès for France's best first novel of 1975 (ironically, the year of Franco's death). Nor did he ever dream that this novel and others that he would later write would become required reading at many French *lycées*.

Since 1975, Gómez-Arcos has published fourteen novels, written directly in French, which have earned him international acclaim and a succession of highly coveted accolades. His narrative works have

been translated into at least fourteen languages. He has been twice
a finalist for the Prix Goncourt—in 1978 for *Scène de chasse (furtive)*
([Furtive] hunt scene), and in 1984 for *Un oiseau brûlé vif* (A bird
burned alive)—and in 1985, he was decorated by the French Legion
of Honor. His novel *Ana Non* (Ana no, 1977) is one of his most
celebrated works, considered by many to be his masterpiece.[14] Situated during the postwar period, it recounts with bare simplicity the
story of an Andalusian widow's picaresque journey to the north of
Spain in search of her son, a political prisoner who has been incarcerated by the Francoists. The novel won the Prix de Livre Inter 1977,
the Prix Roland Dorgelès 1978, and the Prix Thyde-Monnier de la
Société des Gens de Lettres 1978. During the early 1980s, it was converted into a film for French television.

Gómez-Arcos's narrative voice in French, his language of exile, expresses a cry of defiance, freedom, and openness. It is an innovative
narrative discourse, filled with inventive linguistic twists and turns,
offering a unique contrast with more orthodox French writing. At
the same time, despite his experimentation with various narrative
structures and techniques, the realism and the lyricism of his novels
are characteristics that distance him from the practitioners of the
nouveau roman.[15]

From a thematic as well as structural standpoint, his novels are
closely aligned with his theater. In effect, he writes very "theatrical"
narratives, in which dialogue plays a key role and characters often
create their own metaliterary *mises en scène* that blur the distinctions
between reality and fiction. Paula Pinzón, for example, in *Un oiseau
brûlé vif*, creates a grotesque spectacle on the first story of her house
using mannequins who represent the other characters in the novel.
When asked about this relationship between theater and narrative,
Gómez-Arcos affirms that the theatricality of his novels is derived
from what he perceives as a fusion of the notions of spectatorship
and readership: "For me, the reader of the novel is systematically
confused with the audience of the theater. Thus, when I write novels,
I do not make a distinction between the theater audience and the
reader of the novel. For me it is the same interlocutor, and so, what
I like to do is take advantage of the two possibilities within the novel
specifically . . . so that the reader can enter as in a spectacle."[16]

His narrative works contain a parade of ideas, characters, and
themes that originally surfaced in his plays in embryonic form. The
novel *Pré-papa ou Roman de fées* (Pré-Papa or A fairy tale, 1979),
based on *Pré-papa*, the play, is the most obvious example of this
correlation between theater and narrative. Gómez-Arcos incorporated
into this novel segments of dramatic dialogue drawn not only from

Pré-papa, the play, but also from his once prohibited work *Queridos míos*. Another striking example of this affiliation between genres can be detected in the novel *Maria Republica* (written 1975, published 1983). Maria Republica's name, her corresponding left-wing ideology, and her ambiguous status as a prostitute/syphilitic nun are all distinguishing characteristics that link her personage to a vast lineage of rebels and outcasts—many of them, women—found throughout the trajectory of Gómez-Arcos's theater. In essence, Maria Republica is of the same pedigree as Tristeza de Arcos of *Diálogos de la herejía*, Teresa la Roja of *Mil y un mesías*, and Casandra of *Queridos míos*, each of whom personifies a resounding cry for freedom within the context of Gómez-Arcos's dramatic works.

In a similar manner, the characterizations of the Ubuësque governors appearing in the plays *Mil y un mesías* and *Queridos míos* can be considered precursors of the grotesque figure of German Enriquez, the police chief who protagonizes the novel *Scène de chasse (furtive)*. Enriquez, one of Gómez-Arcos's most disturbing literary inventions, is a sadistic torturer who violently rapes and devours the life out of his victims by sucking their bodily orifices. His assault on the most vulnerable regions of the human body is a metaphoric representation of his attack on the dangerous and (according to his view) impure forces that stem from society's margins. Because of its graphic portrayal of torture, *Scène de chasse (furtive)* received an uneven reception from the French press. Amnesty International was so alarmed by the some of the images in the novel that it sent a letter to Gómez-Arcos expressing its concerns. (Amnesty apparently had misinterpreted the author's intentions, which were to protest the violation of human rights.) *Scène de chasse (furtive)*, nevertheless, earned him the honor of finalist for the prestigious Prix Goncourt.

L'aveuglon (The little blind one, 1991), one of his most recent novels, chronicles a blind child's quest for sight. The quest motif that emerges in this novel, and in many others, is an extension of the search for truth that is so intrinsic to Gómez-Arcos's theater. In 1991, he was awarded the first annual Prix du Levant, one of France's most opulent literary prizes for *L'aveuglon* and his complete works. In addition, three of his novels have been published in English translation: *The Carnivorous Lamb* (1986), *Ana No* (1986), and *A Bird Burned Alive* (1988).

The fourth and current stage of Gómez-Arcos's career can be described as a "tale of two cities," in which he divides his time between Paris and Madrid. Since the 1991 staging of *Interview de Mrs. Muerta Smith*, Spanish spectators have witnessed the seemingly miraculous revival of two more Gómez-Arcos plays. *Los gatos*, in its original, uncensored version, opened at the Teatro María Guerrero (CDN) in November 1992 and was promptly selected for a national tour of Spain. In December 1994, Gómez-Arcos finally witnessed the long overdue première (also, at the María Guerrero) of *Queridos míos*, twenty-eight years after having obtained the Lope de Vega Prize for this play. The recent resurrection of his voice as a dramatist is in part due to the enthusiastic interest and admiration of Carme Portaceli, the director of all three productions, who has long been a champion of his work. In 1994, Gómez-Arcos was selected as a finalist for Spain's Premio Nacional de Literatura Dramática (National Prize for Dramatic Literature).[17] Ironically, his life appears finally to have come full circle in that the Spanish Ministry of Culture that once denigrated his work, with the advent of democracy, is finally promoting it.

SITUATING GÓMEZ-ARCOS

Gómez-Arcos pertains to a second wave of Spanish artists who chose to live and work in exile during the Franco years. This second wave includes playwrights Francisco Nieva, José Martín Elizondo, and Fernando Arrabal. The first wave, immediately following the Civil War, includes playwrights Max Aub, Jacinto Grau, Rafael Alberti, Pedro Salinas, and Alejandro Casona.[18]

In defining Gómez-Arcos's theater and its place in Spanish theater history, the predominant tendency of critics, such as María Pilar Pérez-Stansfield, José García Templado, Alberto Miralles, José Monleón, and César Oliva, is to situate him within the so-called "realist generation" of the post–Civil War period. Two important premières, Buero's *Historia de una escalera* in 1949 and Sastre's *Escuadra hacia la muerte* in 1953, are often cited as crucial pillars in the construction of this "realist aesthetic," which posed a radical alternative to the politically and ideologically evasive bourgeois comedies that dominated the Spanish stage and enjoyed widespread commercial success during the decades immediately following the Civil War. In his 1962 review of Lauro Olmo's *La camisa*, titled "Nuestra generación realista," Monleón situates Gómez-Arcos within a group of playwrights (Olmo, Carlos Muñiz, Ricardo Rodríguez Buded, José María Rodríguez Méndez, José Martín Recuerda, and Alfredo Mañas) who took part in the realist tradition that was established by Buero and Sastre.[19] Their theatrical discourse was critical and "committed" in its endeavor to oppose, resist, subvert, and/or protest the dominant discourse of the regime. The dramatists of this "generation," like their counterparts in poetry and narrative, were not afraid to sully their hands in the treatment of themes that alluded to the social, political, and cultural realities of this period in Spain's history. They also set out to induce the spectator into confronting these realities. As Olivia observes, if there truly exists one unifying factor among these dramatists it is that they were all forced to struggle with the burdens of censorship.[20] In so doing, many of the realists employed an allegorical system of dual meaning as a way of disguising their critiques.

The emergence of the realist generation is aligned with the advent of neorealism in Italian postwar cinema (which, influenced in significant ways the development of Spanish film during 1950s). However, the term *realist*, when applied to this group of playwrights, is somewhat problematic, for it is a thematic rather than an aesthetic designation. Indeed, the "realism" of the realist generation quite often has very little to do with the traditional nineteenth-century conception of theatrical realism. Oliva correspondingly notes that the term *realist*, when used to describe this heterogeneous group of dramatists, is almost always accompanied by some other adjective: "We see how, depending upon the author and the period, the term *realist* is always accompanied by another qualifier, which defines—according to the playwright's own vision—the aesthetic that he or she employs. Thus Buero casts his *realism* as symbolist; Sastre, social; Martín Recuerda, and the first Gómez-Arcos, poetic and Iberian; Laura Olmo and Alfredo Mañas, popular; Muñiz, expressionist, etc."[21]

Despite this prevalent tendency to classify Gómez-Arcos as a "realist," there have been occasions, particularly following his exile to France, in which his name has been linked to the next "generation" of dramatists known as the "new" Spanish theater (or the "symbolist" generation). Indeed, the fact that Oliva, in the previously cited declaration, refers to a "first" Gómez-Arcos suggests that there must be a "second": hence, in *Teatro Español de Posguerra*, Juan Emilio Aragonés includes Gómez-Arcos among a group of playwrights that he calls the *novísimos* (Maria Aurèlia Capmany, Antonio Martínez Ballesteros, Manuel Martínez Mediero, Luis Matilla, and José Ruibal).[22] In 1972, Gómez-Arcos was invited to take part in a series of events at the Sorbonne, organized around the theme of the new Spanish theater. Among the participants were Arrabal, Manuel Azaña, Josep Maria Benet i Jornet, Francisco Nieva, Alfredo Crespo, Martín Elizondo, José Guevara, and Miguel Romero Esteo.[23] By association with this Sorbonne group, many of whom were close to his age and were also living in exile in France, Gómez-Arcos can be perceived as having distanced himself temporally and spatially from the realists.[24]

This distance is also apparent in terms of style and technique. As Oliva explains, the playwrights of the new Spanish theater abandoned realism in favor of alternative modes of representation, such as the theater of the absurd, the *farsa esperpéntica*, and "post-Brechtian" drama. Frequently, these antirealist forms were employed as a seemingly innocent mask for an intensely critical subtext.[25] Oliva's description is easily applicable to the type of theater that Gómez-Arcos was creating even prior to his departure from Spain. While maintaining his politically committed stance, he has always expressed a profound awareness of the hazards and limitations involved in employing an overtly realistic aesthetic that might reduce the overall sphere of reference in his theater to a very specific time and place (e.g., Francoist Spain). In exile, he became even more conscious of the need to expand this sphere of reference so that his theater would be accessible to a non-Spanish audience. As I shall demonstrate in subsequent chapters, the employment of allegory, combined with the aforementioned anti-classical/antirealist modes of representation provided him with the tools necessary to achieve this expansion.

To summarize, there are two prevailing attitudes with regard to the placement of Gómez-Arcos's theater within the trajectory of Spanish theater history. His interest in critiquing the oppressive realities of Francoist Spain situates him within the realist generation, while his desire to open up his theater to a more global audience positions him within the category of the new Spanish theater. I would, therefore, suggest that his theater be viewed as a point of transition between these two generations.

A Theater of Transgression

Gómez-Arcos seems to have been born with a strong sense of outrage and indignation. He once told a reporter for the Spanish daily *Diario 16*, "When I write theater, I wage war."[26] His theater is colored with accusatory tones and denunciatory hues. It is a place where defiance and dissent are converted into an aesthetic. In keeping with the tradition of Ramón María del Valle-Inclán's *esperpentos*, his plays often straddle a very fine line between dark comedy and grotesque tragedy. Yet, above all, Gómez-Arcos's literature is about freedom. He candidly declares, "In reality, what I always defend is freedom of the individual."[27] His theater, as well as his narrative fiction, is "committed" in the sense that it is never oblivious to history and sociocultural circumstance, while, at the same time, it resists identification with any particular political-ideological designation. Propelled by an underlying discourse of transgression, his plays employ an allegorical language of the stage as a tropological weapon in the irreverent violation of taboos and other sacred emblems of sociocultural order.

In the essay "A Preface to Transgression" (written in honor of Georges Bataille), Michel Foucault describes the relationship between taboo and transgression as a "play of limits," with the "limit" constituting the unstable, indeterminate boundary that flows between these two terms. As transgression continually questions the limit, the limit is propelled forward in the creation of an inexhaustible spiral. By interrogating the limit, transgression is able to defy the world of order and reason, opening the way to a universe of excess, free of denial. "Transgression," declares Foucault, "opens onto a scintillating and constantly affirmed world, a world without shadow or twilight, without that serpentine 'no' that bites into fruits and lodges their contradictions at their core."[28] For Foucault, this interrogation represents a search for totality. In Gómez-Arcos's writing, it manifests itself as the pursuit of individual freedom, whereby allegory is used to interrogate the limits of authority. Transgression is an illuminating gesture disclosing the passageway to limitless being. Gómez-Arcos comments:

> Freedom. Not libertinage. Freedom. I believe that in my works this is always the case. I try to find the protagonist a moral, ethical, or philosophical justification, even for the individual who rebels against the system. I transform that individual into personage, into somebody who can be a metaphor not only for a single individual, but for a whole series of individuals, and that "whole series of individuals" even could become humanity itself.[29]

This is the essence of his discourse of transgression. The sacred institutions of religion, systems of government, censorship, the family, marriage—Gómez-Arcos interrogates the limits of these institutions which stand as pillars of an established order, and it is through allegory that he is able to knock them down. Through this discourse of transgression, he is able to interrogate and violate all limits, including the limits of language itself.

CENSORSHIP/EXILE/BILINGUALISM

Gómez-Arcos's pre- as well as his post-exilic literature reveals an implicit sense of self-consciousness with regard to his status as a censored artist. Images of censorship, literal and metaphoric, surface throughout his novels and plays, and his works are populated by characters who are repeatedly stifled, suppressed, castrated, silenced, or severed. In *Diálogos de la herejía*, the Peregrino is burned at the stake for engaging in heretical dialogues, while in *Queridos míos*, Casandra's tongue is removed because she speaks the truth. In *Scène de chasse (furtive)*, fascist police chief German Enriquez castrates, eviscerates, and cannibalizes his Republican victims.

Intricately tied to the thematic motif of censorship is that of exile. The idea of banishment is essentially a grand-scale form of censorship, a rite of purification performed with the intention of expelling human pollutants and societal ills from a given community and thereby bringing about a stabilization of order. The censorship of works of art also can be viewed as derivative of this concept of expiation. Censorship is a sort of *sacrifice of the text*, designed to exorcise transgressive impulses from a particular community of readers or spectators and thereby reinforce the social structure.[30] As several historians and critics have observed, the history of Spain can be construed as one long trajectory of self-purgation and censorship carried out by the Spanish state. In his introduction to the work of Spanish exile writer Blanco White, Juan Goytisolo summarizes this historical process in biological terms as "an arduous ascetic-depurative process, destined to carry out the suppression of antibodies (Jews, *moriscos*, Lutherans, enciclopedists, Masons, etc.)."[31]

In *Shifting Ground*, Michael Ugarte conceives of the history of Spain as one continuous exilic process, for it is a country whose identity paradoxically has been defined by the successive traversals of its borders. Spain's unity in 1492, Ugarte argues, was a function of a series of simultaneous exilic movements: Granada fell and the Moors were banished, Aragon and Castile became unified (relinquishing their borders), and Spanish Jews (technically, already in exile) were forced to choose between conversion or expulsion. The Cid's banishment was also an early example of exile that in the future would serve as a paradigm in literature and throughout Spanish history.[32]

Diasporic crossings and images of displacement surface even in Gómez-Arcos's earliest plays which were written prior to his departure from Spain. In *Los gatos*, Pura and Angela banish their sexual urges to the other side of a door, while Lucio of *Mil y un mesías* and Casandra of *Queridos míos*—both incarnations of chaos and disorder—are expelled from the Governor's tyrannical realm. As Paul Ilie demonstrates in his study of Spanish "inner exile," it is not necessary for a writer to engage in a physical form of departure in order to be considered exiled; rather, exile is also a state of mind that can reveal itself through literature, even though the writer may not have physically shifted ground.[33] Such plays as *Queridos míos* and *Mil y un mesías* disclose signs of inner exile occurring well before Gómez-Arcos's departure from Spain. However, the exile theme becomes even more pronounced in the plays written after 1966. Adorado Alberto, the protagonist of *Et si on aboyait?*, is able to find freedom and happiness in Paris, while in *Pré-papa*, John, the pregnant father-to be, embarks upon an exilic voyage into outer space. Likewise, in *Interview de Mrs. Muerta Smith por sus fantasmas*, Mrs. Muerta Smith attempts to establish a home in the heavens.

In May 1990, Gómez-Arcos was invited to New York City to participate in the Dia Art Foundation's "Critical Fictions" symposium.[34] At Dia's exhibition space in Soho, he was given the opportunity to cast a retrospective gaze, in a public milieu, upon his personal struggle for artistic freedom. In his speech, published as an essay in 1991 under the title "Censorship, Exile, Bilingualism: A Long Road to Freedom of Expression," he gives a provocative account of his own exilic journey, offering an intriguing series of meditations on the relationship between freedom, oppression, and the creative process. He begins with the following statement: "In sum: censorship creates exile, exile creates bilingualism, and bilingualism, freedom of expression."

Throughout his life, Gómez-Arcos's three-fold experience with censorship, exile, and bilingualism has functioned as a catalyst with regard to his literary production. His flight from Spain and his employment of a second language have afforded him the opportunity to speak his mind *en revanche*, to wage his own literary form of retaliation against oppression. In the Dia essay, he observes that the exiled writer's inherent condition of uprootedness and marginality induces a critical attitude not only toward his or her homeland, whose image is viewed from a distance, but also toward all established systems (religious, political, social, etc.). Referring to his personal battles with censorship, he alleges that even the democratic system is not beyond reproach. In democracy, where the obstacles impeding creative production are less clearly specified than in dictatorship, artists often find themselves on extremely unstable ground as they are forced to grapple with the unknown. Censorship, as it exists within a democracy, is difficult to evade and oppose, for it manifests itself in subtle, furtive, and insidious ways. "Whether explicit or subtle," Gómez-Arcos asserts, "the act of censorship is produced and reproduced day after day in totalitarianism as well as in democracy. In the former, a work considered subversive is prohibited by decree; in the later it is silenced by unspoken agreement. Censorship changes its mask, but not its undertaking." He underlines the importance of continually questioning the dominant order, whether democratic or totalitarian—"Who among artists, would dare deny that rebellion has more creative power than conformity"—and he warns against passively accepting a democratic *status quo*. It is his contention that democratic systems, despite their indebtedness to the concept of liberty, frequently produce a type of "castrated freedom," an "intellectual comfort" that diminishes creativity and promotes artistic stagnation: "The creative power of the rebellious is much more profound, more destablizing, because it has an ideological charge that the simple aesthetic is unaware of or ignores."

Gómez-Arcos's view of censorship is consonant with that of Michael Holquist, who emphasizes the notion that complete freedom of expression is an illusion and an impossibility: "To be for or against censorship as such is to assume a freedom no one has. Censorship *is*. One can only discriminate among its more and less repressive effects."[35] In a manner that parallels Foucault's conception of transgression as a play of limits, Holquist perceives censorship as a "dynamic" and "multi-directional" process in which there is a continuous dialectical exchange between oppression and rebellion. Censors, he observes, are "locked into a *negotiation*, an exchange with the works they seek to abridge."[36] Censorship is never without contestation, and paradoxically, its very existence is contingent upon the presence of an oppositional discourse.[37] Thus, censorship and rebellion, like taboo and transgression, coexist in a never-ending dialogue, a dialectic of reciprocity in which they are perpetually forced to rely upon each other for affirmation of being.

For Holquist, one finds at the core of censorship a "monolinguistic terror of indeterminacy."[38] Censorship is driven by an inherent desire to stabilize meaning and avoid ambiguity. It, therefore, comes as no surprise that the following criterion appeared in the Spanish censorship norms of 1964, which were instituted under Fraga and applied to both theater and cinema: "The distinction between the characters' conduct and what they represent must remain sufficiently clear for the spectators."[39] Censorship stimulates in those writers who are willing to rebel a series of contestatory strategies and artistic transgressions designed to frustrate the desire for a fixed and determinate meaning. In dodging the inquisitorial gaze of the censors, many writers, such as Gómez-Arcos, have learned to write "between the lines," to create palimpsestic works of art in which one level of meaning is readily apparent while another remains suppressed. This is what Holquist calls the "ineluctably dual structure of the censored text."[40] Readers and spectators who contemplate censored works of art consequently have learned to *read* between the lines, to navigate this play of interlinearity in silent complicity with the author. Holquist notes, "One of the ironies that define censorship as a paradox is that it predictably creates sophisticated audiences. The reader of a text known to be censored cannot be naïve, if only because the act of interdiction renders a text parabolic. . . . The patent aspect of a censored text is only part of a totality that readers must fill in with their interpretations of what was excluded."[41]

While censorship endeavors to anchor each signifier to a fixed and immutable signified, Gómez-Arcos's theater frequently frustrates this endeavor through the employment of allegory. His allegorical discourse of *doubles entendres* establishes a gap between what is visible and what is invisible, creating an indeterminate zone of "slippage" (to use Holquist's term) that is beyond the grasp of the censors. At times, as we shall see in plays such as *Diálogos de la herejía*, this slippage of meaning is invoked through the creation of visual *tableaux*, which function as a kind of ironic subtext in their rapport with the spoken dialogue.

As Gómez-Arcos embarks on an artistic journey from censored artist living in dictatorial Spain to bilingual exile writer residing in democratic France, his gradual employment of the French language comes to allegorize his quest for freedom of expression. Here, the employment of French constitutes more than a simple linguistic substitution; it signifies a liberation and a rebellion with regard to his Spanish past and the censorship he experienced within a totalitarian system. In France, his writing is invested with a new attitude of openness as he catapults his literary personages into exilic realms situated far beyond the reaches of oppression. While Gómez-Arcos does manage in exile to evade the scrutiny of the Spanish censors, his desire to break away from the past and the tyrannies of Spanish fascism is, at least in literary terms, never entirely fulfilled. As we shall also see, the many voices of his exilic imagination appear to speak to the very impossibility of leaving behind his homeland in that to do so would imply a complete denial of cultural identity and historical memory. His exilic allegories appear to be locked in a dual aspiration: to renounce all ties to the past and, at the same time, remember and resuscitate the tragic history of authoritarian Spain.

In the chapters that follow, I shall follow Gómez-Arcos on his artistic voyage from Spain to France and back in order to reveal the allegorical strategies that emerge in his plays in his ongoing struggle against oppression.

2

A Poetics of Expanse and Enclosure: The Allegorical Way of Seeing

It is no longer the myths which need to be unmasked (the doxa now takes care of that), it is the sign itself which must be shaken; the problem is not to reveal the (latent) meaning of an utterance, of a trait, of a narrative, but to fissure the very representation of meaning, is not to change or purify the symbols, but to challenge the symbolic itself.

—*Roland Barthes*, Image Music Text

F<small>OR</small> Gómez-Arcos, the stage is an allegorical battleground where abstract concepts—political, religious, erotic, linguistic—engage in combat under the guise of a diverse series of concrete personifications and embodiments. During the post–Civil War years, Spanish theater-goers witnessed a copious outpouring of allegorical drama as many playwrights (those of the "realist generation," such as Antonio Buero Vallejo and Alfonso Sastre) found in this type of theater a mask or camouflage for their critiques of the oppressive doctrines of the Franco regime. With Franco's death in 1975, which was followed by the dissolution of official censorship and the transition to democracy in Spain, the predominant tendency among these playwrights and those of succeeding generations was to abandon the use of allegory in favor of more direct forms of expression. The allegorical nature of Gómez-Arcos's theater is unquestionably a crucial thread that links his work to that of other politically committed playwrights of his post–Civil War generation. However, unlike the majority of his Spanish contemporaries, and during the past three decades of living and writing in exile far from the political-historical-geographic-linguistic borders of Spain and what was Spanish fascism, he has curiously continued to explore allegory's potential as an artistic device.[1] How does one begin to account for Gómez-Arcos's apparent fascination with the allegorical way of seeing? A glance beyond the horizon of Spanish theater history to a broader map of contemporary literary-artistic practices reveals a striking coincidence between his employment of allegory and postmodernism's so-called "unmistakably allegorical impulse"—a tendency that, in 1980, Craig Owens identified as one of the prominent features of postmodern art.[2]

In recent decades, it has become increasingly apparent that critical views of allegory gradually have been shifting away from an attitude of indifference, and even scorn, to a renewed interest and reevaluation of what, since the advent of romanticism, has been widely regarded as an inferior mode of artistic representation.[3] The cause, and perhaps also the effect, of this revisionist stance is the prominent resurgence of allegorical expression among various branches of postmodern culture. Correspondingly, recent discussions of postmodernism point to the works of performance artist Laurie Anderson, photographer Sherrie Levine, installation artist Robert Longo, painter Robert Rauschenberg, and novelist Thomas Pynchon as among the most exemplary manifestations of this contemporary reemergence of the allegorical mode.[4] In his treatment of allegory, largely influenced by the work of Walter Benjamin and Jacques Derrida, Owens launches an attack against modern aesthetics' subordination of allegory to symbol and underscores the presence of allegorical representation in contemporary, and even modernist, art. He observes that, "despite its suppression by modern theory—or perhaps because of it—allegory has never completely disappeared from our culture. Quite the contrary: it has renewed its (ancient) alliance with popular art forms, where its appeal continues undiminished."[5]

The allegorical mode of representation is an analogizing device, a discourse of *doubles entendres*, which engenders a concrete image/transcription of a larger transcendental picture of chimeras, passions, powers, and desires. The presence of this dual structure is the essential defining element of the allegorical work of art; it is disclosed to the spectator/reader either implicitly or explicitly and sustained throughout the entire spatio-temporal extension of the work. It is, therefore, possible to contemplate an allegorical piece as though its entire constitution were one expansive metaphor.[6] In allegory, Owens explains, "one text is *read through* another, however fragmentary, intermittent, or chaotic their relationship may be; the paradigm for the allegorical work is thus the palimpsest."[7] Allegorical texts are inherently critical and self-referential, and Owens accordingly emphasizes the allegorist's role as interpreter: one who appropriates imagery from within a specific cultural context and lends new meaning to these images by reinscribing them and transforming them into "something other (*allos* = other + *agoreuei* = to speak)."[8]

Similarly, in his deconstructive consideration of allegory, Paul de Man accounts for this process of (meta)textual duplication when he notes that allegory forges its discourse within the temporal gap separating signifier and signified (sign and referent).[9] The material allegorical signifier infinitely defers to its corresponding immaterial signified, forever canceling the possibility that they will ever collide. Allegories thus portray the pursuit of an elusive disembodied text whose true image, situated at a previous moment in time, will never be captured or revealed but will instead remain a phantasmagoric abstraction. Deborah L. Madsen thus envisions the basic allegorical configuration of signifier in search of signified as a hermeneutic quest for knowledge:

> Allegory does presuppose a radically fallen world in which language has become an equivocal medium that expresses the opaque nature of signs as they appear to a degenerated spiritual understanding. So through its language, allegory attempts to establish interpretative principles which make possible the comprehension of realities that cannot be apprehended literally.[10]

In his seminal treatise on German baroque (tragic) drama, first published in 1928, Benjamin acknowledges allegory's religious underpinnings, observing the process by which it conveys a dialectical relationship between the realm of the sacred and that of the profane: allegorical expression insinuates the presence of a sacred (transcendental) text, which is systematically doubled and supplemented by a profane (material) text. According to this dialectic, the allegorist typically projects a mournful vision, a melancholic gaze upon the world as he or she discloses the empty void that exists between the eternal and the ephemeral: "To be named—even if the name-giver is godlike and saintly—perhaps always brings with it a presentiment of mourning. But how much more so not to be named, only to be read, to be read uncertainly by the allegorist, and to have become highly significant thanks only to him."[11]

Nowhere is this attitude of mourning more apparent than in what Benjamin calls the allegorical "cult of the ruin." Originally derived from the baroque opposition to classicism, the image of the ruin emerges as a direct corollary to allegory's endeavor to dramatize the passage of (sacred) history as it is transformed by nature into a decaying emblem: "Whereas in the symbol destruction is idealized and the transfigured face of nature is fleetingly revealed in the light of redemption, in allegory the observer is confronted with the *facies hippocratica* of history as a petrified, primordial landscape."[12] Benjamin's comments on the German baroque are equally applicable within the domain of the Spanish baroque. His dialectical notions are discernible, for example, in Diego Velázquez's pictorial allegories, which render celestial myth as pedestrian reality: *La disputa de Palas y Aragne* (also known as *Las hilanderas*) and *La fragua de Vulcano* are prime examples of this tendency.[13] Gómez-Arcos's work, as we shall see, is also derivative of this tradition.

Placed within the scope of the allegorical gaze, monuments to a heroic past, as well as sacred institutions intended to withstand the passage of time, collapse into relics of mortal demise. "Allegory," affirms Benjamin, "thereby declares itself to be beyond beauty. Allegories are, in the realm of thought, what ruins are in the realm of things."[14] Indeed, the very action of transforming a sacred figure into a concrete image and placing it within an artistic frame, such as the theater, is a desacralizing gesture, a bringing-down-to-earth of the divine. On the one hand, the allegorical process imparts a devaluative gesture of demystification as the ineffable celestial signified dissolves into an accumulation of earthly fragments. However, situated on the other side of this dialectic is the inclination toward exaltation and redemption, for as Benjamin also points out, allegory often attempts to seize hold of that which is transient and rescue it for eternity.[15] The identity of the material signifier hinges upon the fact that it is in essence pointing to something else—to a signified that is located on a "higher" plane. By virtue of this association, the realm of the profane is converted into a place where any regard for detail becomes virtually inconsequential and immaterial. A glow of transcendental radiance envelopes the terrestrial world, suggesting the possibility that through allegory profane objects can, in effect, transcend the limits of apotheosis.[16] The allegorical perspective, consequently, embraces a double-sided transformative process; it is endowed with the ability to secularize that which is considered sacred and also, to sanctify the profane.[17]

Within this dialectical scheme, Benjamin locates an implicit confrontation between sacred (spoken) script and profane (written) script: "For sacred script always takes the form of certain complexes of words which ultimately constitute, or aspire to become, one single and inalterable complex. So it is that alphabetical script, as a combination of atoms of writing, is the farthest removed from the script of sacred complexes."[18] The transcendental spoken word engages in a ceaseless endeavor to maintain an authoritative hold over the ephemeral written text. However, at the same time, the contestatory nature of the allegorical dialectic unmasks the semiotic chasm separating profane signifier and sacred signified; it endows the allegorist with the potential to undermine the authority of this dictatorial hold, to free writing from its subordination to the sovereignty of the divine *Logos:* "The division between signifying written and intoxicating spoken language opens up a gulf in the solid massif of verbal meaning and forces the gaze into the depths of language."[19] As a result, allegory can be understood to be a highly deconstructive tropological construct, which invokes an interrogation of the nature of representation and discloses the attempts by hegemonic cultural discourses to govern the way that an image is presented and received. Viewed in this manner, the Benjaminian conception of allegory anticipates the deconstructive "thrust" that Owens aligns with postmodernism:

> Decentered, allegorical, schizophrenic . . . —however we choose to diagnose its symptoms, postmodernism is usually treated, by its protagonists and antagonists alike, as a crisis of cultural authority, specifically of the authority vested in Western European culture and its institutions. . . . Not only does the postmodernist work claim no such authority, it also actively seeks to undermine all such claims; hence, its generally deconstructive thrust.[20]

Herein lies the main reason for postmodern art's affinity with the allegorical. The potentially subversive structure of allegory, as conceived by Benjamin, echoes postmodernism's concern with exposing the authoritative nature—the politics—of representation. Postmodern art, such as that of Gómez-Arcos, sequesters allegory's capacity to problematize the dialectical relationships between signifier and signified, the sacred and the profane, speech and writing, and—by metaphoric extension—author and reader, playwright and spectator, text and performance. The postmodernist allegory spotlights the workings of monolithic, totalizing cultural discourses—*les grands récits*, as Jean-François Lyotard would have it—that masquerade beneath an ethereal façade of sanctity, and it implicates the audience in this operation; it jars the spectators into recognizing the way in which they are habitually manipulated by the images that these discourses project.[21] As Owens notes:

> It is precisely at the legislative frontier between what can be represented and what cannot that the postmodernist operation is being staged—not in order to transcend representation, but in order to expose that system of power that authorizes certain representations while blocking, prohibiting or invalidating others.[22]

Likewise, for Gómez-Arcos, allegory is not merely a transparent formulaic technique of Manichaean oppositions; rather, his theater confiscates and cultivates allegory's potential as an illuminative and critical procedure.[23] The divine foundations of religion, totalizing systems of government, the censorship of artistic (and other forms of) expression, a network of sexual taboos and restrictions—Gómez-Arcos's postmodernist allegories expose the structure of these institutions which, throughout history, have stood as monuments to an established order. It is through allegory that he casts his own mournful gaze, toppling their sacred pillars and transforming them into crumbling ruins.

The quintessential Gómez-Arcosian hero or heroine is a zealous individualist, an iconoclast who engages in a fervent battle against oppressive systems of order as part of an endless quest for an anarchistic sort of truth. Here, the notion of "anarchy" has been stripped of any negative connotations so that it signifies the absolute freedom of the individual. Gómez-Arcos remarks, "Anarchy is for me, as always, the classic concept of total freedom, of the nonexistence of power, of the nonexistence of the system, of the individual living according to his or her own rules in a society of individuals who live according to their own rules."[24] In their unyielding defiance of sociocultural supremacy, his postmodernist allegories do not propose any sort of fixed ideological substitute, for to do so would imply the tyrannical triumph of one system of oppression over another. Stated another way, these allegories inhabit a space that is neither left nor right, nor above nor below oppression. Instead, in the spirit of postmodernism, they function as decentering machines, which through verbal and visual imagery, aim directly at the semiotic core of oppression in order to implode the structure of authoritative meaning from within; hence, their allegorical attitude of melancholia can be traced to the mournful loss of an ontological center. (Brian McHale aptly comments that "the revival of allegory in postmodernist writing can also be related to postmodernism's ontological poetics.")[25] In the absence of a fixed ontology—of an established discourse that would firmly specify the limits of the Real, of History, of Meaning, etc.— these postmodernist allegories display an essential attitude of indeterminacy. As Benjamin puts it, in allegory, "Any person, any object, any relationship can mean absolutely anything else."[26]

In Gómez-Arcos's theatrical universe, this ontological destabilization gives way to a subversion of the fundamental, Platonically derived dualisms that have served as the basic structuring principals of Western European cultures.[27] These include sanctity/profanity, taboo/transgression, male/female, censorship/freedom of expression, purity/defilement, good/evil, and order/disorder. In the blinding light of allegorization, the frontiers separating these diametrically opposed notions become obscured and entangled, thereby invoking a metaphoric rejection of binary thought—a rejection that is commonly attributed to the postmodern condition.[28] What emerges in the aftermath of this cultural denial and deconstruction is an ambiguous portrait of one of the essential and most cherished ingredients of any culture, and any allegory: the idea of *the sacred*. Gómez-Arcos's allegories interrogate the limits of this concept by redefining the relationship between sanctity and profanity. This reduction of difference between the sacred and the profane is a metaphorically charged gesture invoking a postmodern crisis of cultural authority.

Subverting the Sacred

Anthropologists, such as Mary Douglas, have revealed that most modern (Western) cultures tend to establish a clear barrier of separation and semantic distinction between the notions of sanctity and profanity. It was not, however, until the advent of Christianity that these two notions were placed at opposite poles in the belief that holy beings, objects, and places were to be shielded from contact with any form of contamination or impurity. For example, in certain "primitive" societies of the past and present, biological refuse—menstrual blood, sperm, excrement, a decaying corpse, etc.—was and is believed to be enveloped in a mystical, powerful aura, inspiring the same sort of terror and awe that is commonly attributed to divine objects.[29] This primordial notion of the sacred, embracing both the pure and the impure, is the key to Gómez-Arcos's allegorical interrogations of cultural authority. In his theater, these two concepts are not always situated at opposite poles; but rather, quite often, they are ambiguously intermingled in a definitive act of transgression: objects traditionally held as sacred are defiled and stained, while objects of repulsion and disgust are elevated to a sacred plane.

In light of Douglas's scheme, the comportment of Gómez-Arcos's personages and their attitudes concerning impurity, purity, and sacredness can be construed as allegorical indicators of their views of the established sociocultural order. In his plays, there are characters who exhibit an anarchistic attitude that mirrors the non-Western conception of sanctity. The *Peregrino* ("Pilgrim") of *Diálogos de la herejía* (Dialogues of heresy), for example, is characterized as a lascivious mystic, and Casandra of *Queridos míos, es preciso contaros ciertas cosas* (My dear friends, it's time we get certain things straight) is cloaked in rags and filth, while at the same time, she appears to posses divine, Christ-like powers. The nebulous identities of these characters are a reflection of their corresponding marginal rapport with the homogeneous sector of society. They are heterogeneous outcasts: placeless and indefinable, regarded by many as vulnerable, dangerous entities, and therefore, subject to persecution and censorship.[30] In contrast, there are also characters, such as the Duchess in *Queridos míos* and Pura in *Los gatos* (The cats), who advocate *from above* the perpetuation of a divine discourse of expiation and thus ostensibly personify the advanced Judeo-Christian conception of sanctity. However, as I shall demonstrate in subsequent chapters, the revelatory capacity of postmodernist allegory works *from below* to disclose for the spectator the hidden truth: that beneath the sacred façade that these characters project lies a contaminated, grotesque underside.

The Gómez-Arcosian cosmos, therefore, is not a black and white domain of binary oppositions; on the contrary, it is portrayed as an amorphous realm of oxymoronic combinations and hybrid beings who navigate the interstices of the societal grid.[31] In contrast with the advanced Judeo-Christian notion of sanctity, Gómez-Arcos's sacred territory is a place of fallen idols, a ruinous landscape that embraces a seemingly incongruous inventory of profane elements, such as eroticism, violence, disease, bodily secretions, and even communism; hence, in his allegories, he recuperates the primordial notion of the sacred as an ambivalent melange of the pure and the impure. He then reinscribes this notion within the context of a postmodernist critique of cultural authority, identity, and representation. In his theater, this desacralization of divine order is part of a large allegorical interplay, which operates within a variety of domains and ultimately (at least, in a metaphoric sense) places cultural order precariously on the verge of collapse.[32]

ALLEGORIES OF THE BODY

Frequently, this allegorical process is displaced to the erotic-biological landscape of the human body. Gómez-Arcos's erotic imagery suggests an iconoclastic traversal of boundaries pertaining to sexual activity, gender, political systems, and by extension, the text itself. His literary personages interrogate all limits regarding sexual comportment, creating an infinite spectrum of possibilities and situations. As in the work of Federico García Lorca, this diverse gallery of erotic imagery is drawn upon continually as a metaphor for all aspects of individual freedom, creativity, and self-expression. Sexual behavior in its varied guises and configurations is unceasingly challenged by the ubiquitous powers of sacred authority, which attempt to limit its existence to a minimal degree of expression: i.e., heterosexual intercourse carried out exclusively for the purpose of reproduction within the confines of marriage and the bedroom. (This definition also corresponds to the restricted sexual economy that was authorized by the dominant discourse of Spanish fascism and that is traditionally sanctioned by the Catholic Church.) Within this sexual economy, corporeal expressions that dare to venture beyond this minimal degree of eroticism (such as sex for the purpose of pleasure) represent excessive forms of expenditure, which evade fixed and determinate categories.[33] The "perpetrators" of these supposed transgressions consequently achieve an ambiguous, marginal status that situates them on the fringes of the sociocultural order.

Gómez-Arcos's allegories of the body are semiotizing machines that generate a multileveled discourse on eroticism. In such plays as *Adorado Alberto* (Adored Alberto) and *Pré-papa*, the body is a concrete signifier, whose various sexual manifestations and hybrids plot an allegorical discourse on gender identification and differentiation (biological and psychological). The protagonists of these plays are characterized as sexual hybrids who seem to elude any sort of fixed categorization. The situation depicted in *Pré-papa*, in which a man is able to become pregnant, epitomizes this ambivalence of gender. Additionally, as revealed in *Los gatos*, in which the young Inés becomes pregnant out of wedlock, the body is an allegorical transcription of society. Inés's transgressive erotic activity signifies a violation of all societal prohibitions. Finally, the body also serves as a site for the inscription of a metatextual commentary on censorship and the violation of discourse. An example of this situation is depicted in *Diálogos de la herejía*, where Tristeza de Arcos, a noblewoman who claims to be pregnant with the son of God, is accused of propagating "heretical dialogues."

In "The Roof: Essay in Systematic Reading," first published in *Tel Quel* in 1967, Philippe Sollers employs the term *écriture corporelle* in reference to this transgressive form of writing in which bodily violence is employed as a metaphor for discursive violence.[34] He perceives this metaphoric correspondence to be an essential feature of modern literature—part of a European (mainly French) artistic tradition that began with Sade and was later taken up by Lautréamont, the surrealists, Antonin Artaud, Bataille, Jean Genet, and others. Referring to Bataille's "inner experience" of eroticism, Sollers clarifies his view: "An inner experience—let us understand: an experience of corporal writing (and it could be shown how, from *Juliette* to the *Chants de Maldoror*, to *The Theater and its Double* and *L'Histoire de l'oeil*, all of modern literature is haunted by this real dimension, so much so that the body has become the fundamental referent for its violations of discourse."[35]

In "The Pornographic Imagination," also published in 1967, Susan Sontag discusses the artistic value of sexually transgressive discourse. For Sontag, the network of taboos and restrictions placed upon the "pornographic imagination" (i.e., censorship) are an outward manifestation of society's deep, underlying fears regarding the "uses of knowledge" and the degree to which all knowledge may be considered dangerous. Sontag, like Sollers, points to Sade, as the original source of this bodily writing.[36] However, as Juan Goytisolo notes, centuries prior to Sade, Spanish theater anticipates the appearance of this metaphoric, and essentially allegorical, dimension of erotic discourse. Goytisolo detects a Sadian precedent in *La Celestina* (1499), where Fernando de Rojas's employment of erotic imagery subtly parallels his discursive transgressions, as well as his position as a societal outcast with respect to the Spain of his contemporaries. With Rojas, Goytisolo observes, "we witness a rebellion of the sign 'body' against the dominant ideologies and their all-embracing rational constructions. Against an absurd, asphyxiating, and tyrannical social pyramid, which tears humans to pieces with its inexorable mechanisms, Rojas, as did Sade three centuries later, claims primacy for the erotic impulse along with its blind, inexorable fury."[37]

Gómez-Arcos's employment of bodily writing, like his bilingualism, situates him at an artistic intersection between French and Spanish traditions. He presents this transgressive thematic material as an incongruous blend of subversive violence and intense lyricism. While his overall candor—which, logically, grows in exile, following his departure from Spain—is an affirmation of the independence and individual freedom garnered by his dramatic characters, it is, furthermore, a display of irreverent defiance on the part of the writer with regard to a full range of cultural taboos. It also can be interpreted as an indication of his desire to give free rein to the imagination in the creation of the literary text by refusing to be inhibited by the limits of censorship. The metaphoric transgressions of Gómez-Arcos's allegorical domains, and the hyperbolic portrayal of his characters are tendencies that situate his theater within the European-Spanish traditions of the absurd, the carnivalesque, the *esperpento*, the grotesque, and the surreal—epitomized in Spain by the work of painters Francisco de Goya and Salvador Dalí, writers Ramón María del Valle-Inclán and Fernando Arrabal, and filmmakers Luis Buñuel and Pedro Almodóvar.

The foregoing general arguments will help us to appreciate the crucial issues and artistic strategies that emerge throughout the trajectory of Gómez-Arcos's theater.

I

Spectacles of Sacrifice

3
Diálogos de la herejía
(1962 / 1980)

Sa connivence avec Dieu est si étroit, si poussée que, par là même,
elle a besoin d'être habitée par le Diable. Ou cohabitée.... Elle
ressent obscurément que son équilibre de femme ne peut se réaliser
que dans un cataclysme de prière et de péché.[1]
—Agustín Gómez-Arcos, *Scène de chasse (furtive)*

In *Diálogos de la herejía* (Dialogues of heresy) and in *Los gatos* (The cats), Gómez-Arcos depicts the theme of inquisitorial authoritarian order as a sacrificial process, a divine discourse of expiation that continually attempts to expand the gap between the sacred and the profane. Through allegory he is able to expose the hidden realities behind this process, thus revealing a dark underside where the powers of good and evil are indeterminately intermingled. The spectator is summoned to this clandestine world, where one can easily lose one's footing, and is implicitly asked to question all previously established notions of the truth.

Set amid the sacrificial flames of the Spanish Inquisition, *Diálogos de la herejía* is a historical drama that portrays the turmoil and hysteria that rock a sixteenth-century Extremaduran village when its inhabitants are seduced by a bizarre outbreak of Illuminism (in this case, feigned mysticism), embodied in the characterizations of a lustful religious pilgrim and two devoutly sensuous nuns. While Gómez-Arcos casts this allegory within the context of sixteenth-century Spain, he also demonstrates that this process of expiation is one that traverses historical boundaries, and he thereby frustrates any attempt on the part of the spectator to distinguish between the past and the present.

Gómez-Arcos was still quite new to the Madrid theater scene when, in 1962, he won his first Lope de Vega National Prize for this play. However, what began as an impressive triumph, rapidly dissolved into an deluge of controversy and scandal. The prize was declared null and void in a gesture of censorship that denied the play a *mise en scène* at any of the state-supported "official" theaters. Two years later, in 1964, a censored version of *Diálogos de la herejía* finally premiered at Madrid's Teatro Reina Victoria under the direction of José María Morera, with the celebrated actors Gemma Cuervo and Julián Mateos in the leading roles. Also that year, the censored text was published in *Primer Acto* along with a series of articles addressing the play's audacious subject matter and its rather polemical and tumultuous reception.[2] A general commentary included in the program notes subtly alludes to the problems of censorship that enveloped the production of this play:

> This is a spectacle conceived and produced with love; and we should note with all fairness that what will be seen on stage tonight is the result of a common endeavor. We would not point this out if, during the entire period of preparation, there had not been so many difficulties that impeded its realization. All of those who are have participated in this production have endured innumerable sacrifices of every type, all the more burdensome when their responsibilities were greater.

In the conflicting reviews that appeared in the daily press following the première, several critics refer to the mixed reaction of audience members. Only the young actress Alicia Hermida, who, by all accounts was especially adept at interpreting the role of Ursulina, seems to have come away unscathed by harsh criticism. When, during the curtain calls, the playwright himself appeared on stage with the director and cast, he was confronted with a combination of enthusiastic applause and shouts from hecklers. Enrique Llovet of the daily *ABC* noted that during the curtain call, "The author saluted the audience among intense clapping and 'bravos,' which were mixed with less but ample protests and shouts of 'Get out!'" Alfredo Marquerie of *El Pueblo* offered the following testimony: "Alicia Hermida, largely ovationed in silence, was in the end the object of special preference on the part of spectators while the author and the director bid them a greeting among strong applause and violent foot stomping."

In his own commentary included in the playbill, Gómez-Arcos openly states his critical intentions with regard to *Diálogos de la herejía*: "It is, naturally, a critical work, critical of individuals more than of systems. Its basic plot is rigorously historic, as is its philosophical basis."[3] Reading "between the lines," one could argue here that Gómez-Arcos is, in fact, stating the exact opposite of his true intentions. In a strategy designed to evade censorship, he appears to foreground the historical dimension of his play, contextualizing it as a work of art that reflects a series of events pertaining to a particular group of individuals during a specific moment in time. However, a sophisticated spectator, accustomed to navigating the play of interlinearity inherent in censored, and allegorical, works of art would be able to see that, in reality, these temporal and spatial boundaries are continually questioned throughout the duration of the play. In a review appearing in *Madrid*, critic Elías Gómez Picazo replies to Gómez-Arcos's program notes with a reproach that serves to demonstrate the type of disapproval and condemnation that *Diálogos de la herejía* incited:

> The critique, whether it be of individuals or of systems, is nowhere to be seen. . . . It is not enough to link together a series of blasphemies in order that, through the disagreeable impact produced in one's ears, the author be considered valiant or that the work be considered important. Nor is this achieved by mixing with these blasphemies a rape, an Inquisitional trial and an auto-da-fé, in addition to any other cliché that contributes to completing the confusing and, for so many reasons, naive (?) religious melodrama that bears the title *Diálogos de la herejía*.

In contrast with Gómez Picazo's seemingly naïve disapprobation, Marquerie offers a more positive impression of the production, noting that Gómez-Arcos's play demands the presence of a knowledgeable spectator:

> With *Diálogos de la herejía* it seems that he has confirmed his condition as an important author for the lofty and ambitious effort that drives this work. . . . It incites interest and is emotionally moving. It has "spunk."
>
> *Diálogos de la herejía* brings to the stage a trial of *alumbrismo* or Illuminism initiated by the Holy Office, a case of collective feminine hysteria that ended with the bonfire. The theme is risqué, harsh, disagreeable. Nothing is dodged or spared, no matter how intense it may be, for the eyes and ears of the spectators. The play is only suitable for a prepared audience.

So controversial was the reception of *Diálogos de la herejía*, that the editors of *Primer Acto* invited Gómez-Arcos and Morera to write their own rebuttals which were included alongside the published version of the play. Their responses, nevertheless, barely begin to address the reasons why this play apparently touched a very sensitive chord among Spanish spectators. Gómez-Arcos's "Autodefensa" ("Self-defense") centers on the question of "influences" that critics have attributed to him (Federico García Lorca, Ramón María del Valle-Inclán, Antonio Buero Vallejo). Morera's "Reflexiones de un director después de un estreno polémico") ("Reflections of a director after a polemical première") focuses primarily on the problems of character development and the creation of a historical setting: "For me, the possible critique of a system, and even of a specific historical situation, demands an intellectual approach to the problem. The setting was pure decoration. It is possible that this suggestion was too attractive for the spectator, despite the fact that I have tried as little as possible to slip into a documentary-type treatment . . ." It is perhaps somewhat ironic that, despite this flurry of debate and discussion, *Diálogos de la herejía* has yet to be staged in uncensored form, and one can only speculate as to what the reception might be like if it were to be restaged today. In 1980, at the encouragement of the distinguished actress/director Nuria Espert, Gómez-Arcos returned to the original text of his play and redrafted a new uncensored version. The analysis that follows is based on my reading of this more recent, and as yet, unpublished, text.

The unbalanced reception of *Diálogos de la herejía* is an indicator of the deep divisions in opinion that remained engraved in the Spanish political landscape throughout the post–Civil War years (and that continue to persist even today). Yet this display of fluctuating opinion with regard to this play also can be seen as a confirmation of allegory's potential to demystify and decenter meaning. Walter Benjamin's observation that in allegory "any person, any object, any relationship can mean absolutely anything else" is especially applicable to this situation.[4] As a camouflage for a critique of cultural supremacy and totalitarian discourse, allegory draws its strength from the visual and verbal impact of indeterminate double-sided imagery. Hence, the allegorical mode is always endowed with an essential attitude of ambiguity, exploitable for a broad spectrum of political motives and inferences. It presents the spectator with the often irreconcilable task of locating a precise meaning—a situation that can be especially frustrating for the theater critic writing for the daily paper or for the censors.

Of the many allegorical forms that flourished during the post–Civil War period, historical dramas in particular garnered a formidable degree of prominence on the Spanish stage. Martha T. Halsey summarizes:

During the final years of the Franco era and the critical period of transition from dictatorship to democracy, disaffected Spanish playwrights have turned with increasing frequency to the past to dramatize images of the nation at crucial times that present important parallels with their own time. Their dramas thus reflect Hegelian and Marxist theories according to which history represents an ongoing process that culminates in the spectators' own present.[5]

Among the various factors that motivated the widespread appearance of this genre, José Monleón underscores the singular influence of Bertolt Brecht, whose epic theater had already demonstrated the power of reverting to the past in order to encourage the spectator's critical, distanced contemplation of the present. An additional factor (which Monleón prefers to de-emphasize) was censorship: the historical drama frequently employs the past as a strategic camouflage for an ironic portrayal (and protest) of current sociopolitical conditions.[6] Monleón includes Gómez-Arcos's *Diálogos de la herejía* as part of the following lengthy roster of exemplary postwar historical dramas: Buero Vallejo's *Un soñador para un pueblo*, *Las meninas*, *El concierto de San Ovidio*, and *El sueño de la razón*; José Martín Recuerda's *Las arrecogías del beaterio de Santa María Egipcíaca*; Claudio de la Torre's *El cerco*; Alfonso Sastre's *Guillermo Tell tiene los ojos tristes*; José María Rodríguez Méndez's *Flor de otoño: Una historia del barrio chino*; Antonio Gala's *Noviembre y un poco de yerba*, Ana Diosdado's *Los comuneros*; and Carlos Muñiz's *La tragicomedia del Serenísimo Príncipe Don Carlos*.[7]

In his deconstructive consideration of allegory (which interrogates the romantic presumption of a hierarchical subordination of allegory to symbol), Paul de Man focuses upon the role of time as one of the key elements in any allegorical configuration. According to de Man, allegory's two constitutive texts remain on separate temporal planes, destined never to collide as the allegorical signifier infinitely defers meaning to its corresponding signified, which is located at an anterior moment in time: "Whereas the symbol postulates the possibility of an identity or identification, allegory designates primarily a distance in relation to its own origin, and renouncing the nostalgia and the desire to coincide, it establishes its language in the void of this temporal difference."[8] De Man's assertions acquire a special sort of relevance when viewed within the context of historical drama, a theatrical genre that, by definition, plays upon the temporal relationships inherent in allegory. Historical dramas characteristically partake of the polysemous nature of allegorical representation by drawing a series of parallels between two (or more) temporal planes. Francisco Ruiz Ramón accordingly emphasizes the historical drama's capacity to express the simultaneous presence of two texts that, although distanced by time, engage in an ongoing dialectical confrontation: "The past and present are reflected mutually, like two juxtaposed mirrors in movement, whose dynamic contents are deciphered by utilizing their reciprocal codes."[9] In this oscillating dance of reciprocity, there is no semblance of interpretative authority, no primacy of one temporal plane over the other; but rather, the dialogue between past and present establishes a zone of *différance*, as Jacques Derrida would have it, a chiasmus of ambivalence that renders impossible any semblance of closure with regard to time and meaning.

In *Diálogos de la herejía*, allegory—with its implicit indeterminacy and overtly critical stance—functions as a theatrical strategy in the deconstruction and demystification of authoritative sociocultural structures and of the hierarchical (Platonically derived) oppositions and signifying processes that throughout (Spanish) history have empowered and upheld these structures. As the plot unfolds, a temporal dialogue is gradually evoked between sixteenth-century Spain (i.e., the reign of Philip II) and Spain's postwar state of affairs during the ruthless domination of the Franco regime. The historical setting of the play represents a time when, in a manner reminiscent of fascist Spain, an absolute monarchy and the Catholic Church had become intricately intertwined in the formation of a combined political-religious institution: the Inquisition. The primary aim of the Holy Office of the Inquisition (*el Santo Oficio*) was the purification of the Spanish state, achieved through the rigorous scrutiny and censorship of thoughts, words, and actions. Hence, in *Diálogos de la herejía*, Gómez-Arcos appropriates images from the annals of history that, in light of their ostensible parallels with Spain's recent past, would be widely recognizable to the twentieth-century spectator. Through the use of ambiguity, however, he defamiliarizes the spectator's perception of these images, subverting their meanings and endowing them with new significance.[10]

The polysemous title of *Diálogos de la herejía* invokes at least four possibilities for interpretation. First, the word *diálogos* represents a historical reference to the time of the Spanish Renaissance, in which *dialogues*, colloquia, and other dialectical arts pertaining to the tradition of Plato were common forms of expression. Second, the concept of heretical *dialogues* refers to the supposed acts of heresy that are committed by the protagonists of the play. Third, the title invites a metatextual interpretation with regard to the actual linguistic subversions of religious metaphors that are constructed by the author in composing *dialogues* for his characters. Fourth, in light of the exterior circumstances surrounding the performance and publication of this historical drama, the title can be construed as an extratextual reference to the heretical discourse, or *dialogues of heresy*, which the censoring authorities of the Spanish government accused Gómez-Arcos of perpetuating.

By the sixteenth century, the Iberian peninsula had evolved into a heterogeneous population composed of Jews, Christians, Muslims, Protestants and *erasmistas*, along with an infinite variety of ethnic-racial-religious hybrids and cultural ambiguities (i.e., *mozárabes*, *moriscos*, *conversos*, etc.). Spain lacked a uniform set of religious beliefs and rituals, and cultural differences were not always readily distinguishable. Heretics suspected of deviating from the doctrines of Catholic theology were regarded by the Inquisition as impure pollutants, dangerous threats to the order of the Spanish state. Consequently, they were considered prime targets for ritual sacrifice, often witnessed as a public spectacle in which the victim was burned at the stake (fire, being an extremely effective metaphor and method of purification). During the Counter Reformation, Protestants/Lutherans and *erasmistas* were also singled out as potential victims for the bonfires of the Holy Office. In addition, two other spiritual movements that flourished during the sixteenth century, mysticism and *alumbrismo* were continually scrutinized for their questionable interpretations of Catholic theology.

As Marcel Bataillon notes in his study of Erasmus and Spain (1966), *alumbrismo* (also known as *iluminismo*) manifested itself as an excessive display of spirituality, an anarchistic variation of mysticism in which the *iluminado* was somehow predisposed to divine revelations and to communication and unification with the Holy Spirit.[11] The *alumbrados* claimed to be orthodox Catholics; yet at the same time, they introduced a variety of revolutionary practices and beliefs. While the so-called *alumbrados recogidos* (meaning "collected" or "withdrawn") obeyed a strict code of asceticism in order to facilitate the purification of their divine passions and desires, the *alumbrados dejados* ("careless," "lax"), in contrast, professed a kind of "moral radicalism," which emphasized the importance of giving one's self to God; that is, letting one's soul be completely possessed by the love of God: "'leave one's self to the love of God,' since this love 'ordains the person in such a way that he or she can neither sin mortally nor venially.'"[12] The implications of this notion of impeccability caused alarm among Inquisitional authorities, and the *alumbrados dejados* became particularly renowned for their unrestrained public displays of ecstasy. Their erotic transgressions seemed to intermingle sensuality and mysticism, and quite often, their religious interests evolved into a mere pretext for sexual promiscuity.[13] Gregorio Marañón comments: "All that sublimated eroticism of the mystics, that sometimes in its expression brushes up against the limits of direct sensuality; in the *alumbrados*, above all in those of this period, degenerates and is converted into cynicism and carnal wantonness."[14]

In allegorical terms, the *alumbrados dejados* embodied an ambiguous mélange of taboo and transgression, a blending of religion and eroticism that coincides with Derrida's interpretation and interrogation of the word *pharmakon*, a term that connotes both "remedy" and "poison": "If the *pharmakon* is 'ambivalent,'" he tells us, "it is because it constitutes the medium in which opposites are opposed, the movement and play that links them among themselves, reverses them or makes one side cross over into the other (soul/body, good/evil, inside/outside, memory/forgetfulness, speech/writing, etc.)."[15] For Derrida, the *pharmakon*—along with its related terms *pharmakeus* (sorcerer/magician/poisoner) and *pharmakos* (scapegoat)—is an ambiguous intersection, a locus and play of *différance*, which simultaneously reinforces and subverts the hierarchical oppositions designated by the Platonic way of seeing. The historical circumstances surrounding *iluminismo* and the *alumbrados dejados* thus provided Gómez-Arcos with an apt scenario for the deconstruction of sacred institutions: in this case, an exploration and interrogation of the relationship between mysticism and eroticism and the sometimes hazy line of differentiation that runs between them.[16]

Almost inevitably, the widespread, scandalous fame achieved by these dubious, indeterminate entities sparked the appearance of a vast parade of tricksters, charlatans, and other manifestations of false Illuminism, who viewed this spiritual movement as a window of opportunity to take advantage of the repressed passions of innocent nuns in cloistered monasteries, as well as lonely, vulnerable women whose husbands had departed for the newly colonized American territories of the Spanish Empire. Marañón cites the existence of a so-called *Peregrino Raro* who took advantage of a Prioress named Doña Teresa and the young, desirable nuns of her convent. He also recalls a famous and legendary episode of *alumbrismo* which occurred in Llerena (Extremadura) between 1574 and 1578, the village that inspired the story portrayed *Diálogos de la herejía*:[17]

> In this city of Extremadura, almost emptied of its best sons who ran off to the Americas in search of gold and of glory, and inhabited in large part by people of alluvion, *Moriscos*, *conversos*, and Jews, there emerged an epidemic of *alumbrismo* which reached a great number of women, already crazed as a result of various unlearned clergymen. The unhappy women would go with fanatical fervor from the ecstasy of mystic quietism to that which is directly sexual. The austere country life of the Extremadura was converted into an outrageous bacchanal.[18]

Eventually, the flames of *iluminismo* in Llerena were suppressed by another type of blaze—that of the Inquisition.

The main action of *Diálogos de la herejía* centers around a large feudal estate, located within a small Extremaduran village. The proprietress of this estate, Doña Tristeza de Arcos, is an educated, wealthy noblewoman, enduring a lonely existence with her two ladies in waiting (*La Dueña* and *La Dama*). Each day, Tristeza attempts to console her anguish in the solace of prayer, but she finds to her dismay that religion does not satisfy the profound sensation of emptiness that is her greatest torment: "Who can release the solitude from these walls? Dueña, I am slowly dying. Do you not see? From my house to the convent, from the convent to my house . . . Nobody *en route*, the street deserted, nothing can happen. Each day the same veil covering my face . . . that is withering away."[19] Later, it is revealed that Tristeza's marriage to a wealthy nobleman was never actually consummated because immediately following their wedding ceremony, the court ordered his departure for the Americas. Soon after, he was named Viceroy of a far-off land, where he married a young Indian princess. The Church has since annulled Tristeza's marriage, but for reasons of honor and dignity, she, unlike her former husband, cannot remarry. She is, therefore, left alone as the heir to his estate with only the company of her embroidery and her loyal servants. The managers of the property, generically referred to as *La Capataza* and *El Capataz* (one of the few remaining men—"old and decrepit," according to the stage directions) also reside on the grounds of the estate with their adolescent daughter, Ursulina.

During part one of the play, the vulnerable inhabitants of this community desperately crave the arrival of somebody (a remedy) with the capacity to render order from their emotional, physical, and spiritual havoc. The opening stage directions describe the setting as a village nearly depleted of men, most of whom have either gone off to war or have departed for the new Spanish American colonies:

> *A village in Extremaduran lands, towards the south, near the boarder. Nearing the end of the sixteenth century.*
> A village emptied of men, enrolled in the troops of His Majesty, or embarked on the colonization of the American Indies. The women have taken charge of the masculine chores, the field, the vineyard, the pasture, the hunt, they dress half man half woman, they behave similarly. Nevertheless, their resignation is only apparent: a longing for men and a desire for maternity gnaws at their insides.[20]

With this preliminary scenic description, Gómez-Arcos presents a situation of chaos that potentially encourages the obliteration of traditional family structures and institutions, as well as the violation of kinship taboos. The absence of the masculine sex from this community also has led to a demolition of conventional signs of gender differentiation, as signified by the women's dress (half male, half female). These women have thus been forced to take on a sort of hybrid, hermaphroditic role within this society, performing both masculine and feminine duties. Despite their apparent ambiguity of gender, on an emotional level (and in a manner reminiscent of many of García Lorca's feminine characters) they find themselves in constant confrontation with a surmounting maternal instinct and the intense urge to express themselves erotically, yet the Catholic religion and the honor code by which they live inhibit their possibility of satisfying these sexual yearnings. As Mujer 1ª ("Woman #1") declares: "My house is filled with men whom I do not see, of shadows of men, who grope at my flesh without touching me."[21] Held captive by their sexual desires, and the taboos prohibiting them, they intently await the arrival of news regarding their sons and husbands: whether they are dead or alive and when they are expected to return.

In an act of desperation, Mujer 3ª ("Woman #3"), an older woman and the voice of both wisdom and skepticism throughout the play, has requested the inscription of her son's name on a cross beside the tomb of her deceased daughter-in-law. She has not received any definitive information regarding his whereabouts, and she is convinced that in declaring him dead, she will be able to restore a semblance order to her daily life. Her commentaries regarding her son and the troops she has sighted along the nearby Portuguese border accentuate the correspondence between the situation portrayed in this village and the analogous circumstances of the Spanish Civil War, in which many husbands and sons went off to battle and numerous women were left behind:

> My years are wise. Almost ten, already, since my son went off to wage war against the Indians, to bring those savages the Christian word . . . Far off, on the plain, when the sun begins to rise, I see the troops go by on their way to the border. Men, horses, and carts. And lances that shine in the sunlight like lightening from a storm. Among the soldiers, I have been able to discern boys of no more than fourteen years of age, dragging themselves along beneath the weight of their armor.[22]

Most of the villagers hold the belief that sacred beings—saints, mystics, and *alumbrados*—possess special visionary powers, wondrously enabling them to conjure information about the missing men, and perhaps even incite their return. However, as Mujer 2ª declares, their village is not located within close proximity of the royal court, where most of these saintly entities tend to congregate; nor is it situated along any of the common routes of sacred pilgrimage. In the isolation of Extremadura, these women not only find themselves out of touch with the masculine sex; they also find themselves beyond the geographic reaches of the spiritual bond of Christianity. Consequently, the power of ritual has begun to lose its rigid hold upon their lives, and their village has become immersed in a chaotic crisis of distinctions, or what René Girard terms "a sacrificial crisis": a situation in which the mechanisms of sacrificial rites are absent.[23] A community enveloped in sacrificial crisis is the equivalent of a cultural order plagued by an anarchistic epidemic of ambiguity, which negates all perceivable differences between good and evil, virtue and sin, purity and defilement. Individuals are stripped of their distinguishing features: the boundaries of gender differentiation, the limits designated by kinship systems, and even linguistic structures become confused and blurred. As a result, metaphoric systems of signification begin to deteriorate, societal institutions lose their force and credibility, and sociocultural order is placed on the verge of collapse through the contagion of reciprocal violence. According to this perspective, only the exclusionary mechanisms of sacrificial ritual can render order from this ambiguous upheaval.[24]

The scenario presented in *Diálogos de la herejía* is that of a community cloaked in cultural ambivalence, in which the boundaries of cultural dualisms, such as mysticism/eroticism, sanctity/profanity, taboo/transgression, and male/female, have become obscured and intermingled. The circumstances of the Spanish Civil War entailed a parallel crisis of distinctions between good and evil, whereby blood relations within a single community were pitted against one another as enemies caught up in a generative cycle of reciprocal violence. During this period, the limits of kinship were figuratively and literally transgressed: families were split in their respective alliances, brothers murdered brothers, fathers murdered sons. In the end, multiple lives were sacrificed in the name of a "sacred" *caudillo* until a Fascist system of order was finally erected.[25]

Once this situation of crisis is established during the initial scenes of the play, the sexually enticing *Peregrino* ("Pilgrim") and his faithful cohort *Madre Asunta* (Mother Asunta) make their entrance. They are characterized as two marauding birds of prey, motivated by greed and masquerading as *alumbrados*. Asunta is already known to the villagers as a sacred entity who often frequents their land to visit the cloisters of the renowned *Sor María de los Ángeles* (Sister Mary of the Angles). According to rumor, Sor María, an enigmatic being—a grave-digging nun—who resides in the nearby convent, is able to enter into a divine, trancelike state, placing her in direct communication with God.[26] Some call her an *iluminada*, while others, such as

Mujer 3ª, insist that she is merely a worthless witch. Together, Asunta and Sor María are responsible for having brought about the "miracle" of Ursulina's birth when the *Capataza* was expected to miscarry.

The following stage directions herald the arrival of Asunta and the *Peregrino*. This is one of many elaborate textual descriptions that occur throughout the dramatic text, creating a series of powerful visual *tableaux*. Gradually, these written didascalia forge an ironic narrative that at once reinforces and subverts the dramatic action and dialogue of the (hypothetical) *mise en scène*. Significantly, the most intensely subversive moments of the play are not so much dependent upon the power of verbal language (the spoken word); but instead, they are intricately tied to the visual implications of stage directions such as these. Not surprisingly, these ironic commentaries are conspicuously absent from the censored (published) version of the play:[27]

> *Madre Asunta and the* Peregrino, *false nun and false cripple, advance beneath the sun. As with all marginal characters of the period (typical products of two opposing poles: glory and misery), a confusing mixture of vice and virtue will form the only mask upon their faces, so that they themselves do not know when they are lying and when they are telling the truth. Since the moment will arrive in which the instinct to survive will fail them, if one had to attribute a moral code to them it would be that of a river run wild; in this aspect, their similarity with certain characters of the present day should be evident.*[28]

Gómez-Arcos appropriately characterizes Asunta and the *Peregrino* as visionaries (of apocryphal visions), marginal outsiders, strangers from beyond the limits of the community, ambiguous entities from the land of transgression who bear a resemblance to "certain" twentieth-century counterparts. Their image is an indeterminate confluence of beneficent and maleficent violence, in which the distinctions between good and evil ("vice and virtue") are not readily apparent. They simultaneously personify both the remedy and the poison that the villagers have been anticipating. Consequently, when the time arises for the restoration of order, these *alumbrados* will make exemplary *pharmakoi*.[29]

As the godmother of Ursulina, Asunta has been invited, with her coconspirator, to pay a visit to the home of the *Capataces*. The villagers greet these mysterious strangers with confidence and awe and are eager to incorporate them into their community. Blinded by their desperation, the women of the village are only able to perceive the benevolent, saintly side of the *alumbrados'* imprecise aura of *doubles entendres*, and they do not even slightly question their dubious authenticity. Mujer 3[a] predictably accuses the visitors of charlatanism, but she is promptly dismissed as a senile old woman. Virtually all the other women are extremely eager for the opportunity to meet with the *Peregrino* who, with the help of Asunta, stages daily spectacles of erotico-mystical trances and divine revelations. He tells his cohort, "My pilgrimage has a mission: to accompany those who are lonely, to give warmth to the lonely souls."[30] Each day, the women of the village gather at the door of the *Capataces'* house in the hope that the Pilgrim will be able satiate their irrepressible yearnings: the desire to ascertain information regarding the future homecoming of their men, and the urge to fulfill an indescribable emptiness whose source they cannot identify with words. Asunta, who is also eager for the *Peregrino* to satisfy her own sexual cravings, evaluates the profitable implications of this scenario:

> Now you have seen them, Peregrino. A new type of female. The village and the region is full of them, the entire country, I dare say. Land of misery, land of absence. Result? Patently clear. Women alone and grief-stricken, with the men absent. Unbeatable Olympus for the gods. The purpose of the King our Lord and of human avarice, the colonizing mission of our holy faith and of a longing for adventure, I say . . . they have pardoned neither son nor husband, neither young man nor old; not counting my godfather, of course—he has been gelded. Straw mattresses, and beds of grand lineage, burning with fever . . . insatiated . . . In this place . . . of la Mancha the kindness of your words is needed. You and your visions will give them comfort and relief . . . I say. Lean upon me.[31]

The theme of colonialism, which is briefly evoked in Asunta's speech, is a common motif recurring throughout Gómez-Arcos's literary trajectory. It appears once again in *Pré-papa* (the play and novel) and in *Interview de Mrs. Muerta Smith por sus fantasmas* as an allegorical quest to impose and establish a system of belief. With Asunta playing the role of pimp and the *Peregrino* that of her gigolo (also, a scenario that resurfaces in *Interview de Mrs. Muerta Smith*), he acquires a series of sacred properties that endow him with the ability to exert power, both sexual and religious, over the women he receives in his chambers.

In establishing the relationship between eroticism and mysticism, Gómez-Arcos constructs a series of powerful visual *tableaux* that present the audience with overlapping images from these two systems. While, on the one hand, the villagers who witness the *Peregrino*'s spectacles are able to perceive only one side of this allegorical system of dual meaning, the spectator, on the other hand, is confronted with a double-sided flood of overlapping visual images that (sacrilegiously) traverse the limits of Platonically grounded divisions and semantic groupings: signs typically embracing sexual connotations intermingle with signs traditionally associated with religion. Eroticism and mysticism oscillate in an unstable ambivalence, and in accordance with Benjamin's view of the allegorical process, allegory exercises its power to secularize that which is considered sacred and, correspondingly, to elevate profane objects to a sacred plane.[32]

This semiotic form of transgression, or "metonymic violence"—as Roland Barthes would have it—surfaces repeatedly in Gómez-Arcos's literature, enabling him to portray, simultaneously, both the subversion of religious taboos and the subversion of traditional linguistic structures.[33] In the *dialogues* sustained between the Pilgrim and Asunta, the aromas of the Church are blended with those of the brothel, and religious discourse becomes continuous with sexual discourse. Asunta attempts to seduce the Pilgrim on repeated occasions. She addresses him as "santurrón mío," ("my big saint") a term of endearment which blends, linguistically, her terrestrial affection and his celestial saintliness. When she invites him to "penetrate" her in the same manner that he has penetrated the souls of other women, he declines her propositions, declaring, "You smell of incense, something which does not repulse me, but you wreak of the brothel, and that degrades me. The agreement we made was clear: you are here in my service; not for your own benefit."[34] Following this reproach, the Pilgrim commands Asunta to bring him a glass of water, but she would rather continue to serve him wine from a sacred chalice (she seems to be in a constant state of intoxication, herself). She tells him, "Do not drink wine, you prick. I know of a wine that will calm your thirst. A thick, red, sleepy wine, but alive. It's name is Tristeza, Doña Tristeza de Arcos, a noblewoman of old and illustrious birth."[35] In a later seduction scene between the inebriated nun and the Pilgrim, she discovers his scourge, an instrument of flagellation which, as he explains, he regularly keeps on hand as a kind of tool of his trade: "Attributes of my profession. Less spectacular, but wilder . . . than a crown of thorns."[36] Within the semantic domain of mysticism, the *Perigrino*'s scourge functions as an instrument of religious sacrifice and flagellation; but when an erotic context is transposed upon this visual image, the scourge is converted into a sadomasochistic whip, an instrument of erotic sacrifice.

In Gómez-Arcos's theater, these semantically dissonant constructions overflow from the realm of the spoken word, into the context of nonverbal, visual imagery. The following scene, which takes place at Sor María's convent, exemplifies this nonverbal form of transgression. Once again, the sixteenth century serves as a pretext for the creation of an analogy between past and present events. In this visual *tableau*, the *alumbrados* engage in an erotico-mystical bacchanal resembling a psychedelic orgy of the 1960s, in which the Illuminati— Sor María, the *Peregrino*, and Asunta—double as drug-using hippies. The following stage directions evoke this visual effect of ambiguity:

Darkness.

In the convent cell of Sor María de los Ángeles, which will be reminiscent of a large cage surrounded with lattice work, three characters etched into this scene who may resemble three birds of ill omen: the Illuminated nun, Madre Asunta and the Illuminated Pilgrim. The nun appears to levitate in Sulpician ecstasy, the alumbrado's trance is more carnal, sweat and shakes related to the image of a drug addict of several centuries later. Naturally, the entire scene will have a certain mystical tonality, lent by the text, which will be falsely inscribed against the sensuality, the libido and, why not, the profound desperation of the characters. Madre Asunta oversees the Peregrino's trance, she wipes the sweat from his brow, she withdraws the chalice from his mouth.[37]

The ironic tone of this textual description invokes the importance of leaving open to the spectator the possibility of visualizing the presence of two (or more) simultaneous representations. The twentieth century is superimposed upon the past in a sort of theatrical palimpsest, so that one text is perceived through the other.[38]

In *Diálogos de la herejía*, the *dialogue* between allegory's two constitutive texts is both temporal and spatial, and the allegorical process can be seen at work along two coordinating axes: vertical (paradigmatic) and horizontal (syntagmatic). Viewed in this manner, Gómez-Arcos's historical drama exemplifies Craig Owens's definition of allegory as a representational mode concerned "with the projection— either spatial or temporal or both—of structure as sequence."[39] As Figure 1 illustrates, ambiguity in this play is established across both time and space.

In the preceding descriptions of the villagers and the *alumbrados*, allegory can be perceived as spanning a vertical axis, whereby the dual images of allegorical double talk—mysticism/eroticism, good/ evil, male/female, etc.—are linked spatially and synchronically. At the same time, the horizontal axis is never completely absent from this picture. At certain key dramatic moments, it is brought into the foreground, emphasizing the presence of a temporal, diachronic relationship between layers of imagery and establishing an ambiguous gap of *différance* in the historical overlap of the sixteenth and

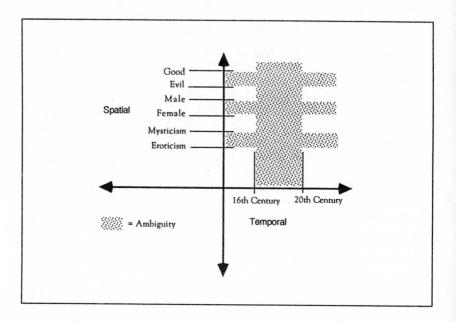

twentieth centuries. At the end of part one, the news of the *Peregrino*'s powers finally reaches Doña Tristeza, who decides to pay him a visit at the monastery. He is extremely nervous about his encounter with the *hidalga*, for he knows that she is an upper-class, educated women and fears that she will be clever enough to recognize the charlatan that he really is. Before her arrival, another erotico-mystical *tableau* is staged (this time, with a kiss from Sor María) as the *Peregrino* dramatically attempts to conjure his powers of seduction:

> Powers of light, powers of shadow, be my faithful friends, illuminate me! (*He crosses his arms. Opening her own arms, the illuminated nun draws near to him, she presses the palms of her hands against those of the* Peregrino, *and she seals his mouth with a kiss that is like a breath of air; then she pulls away from him and returns to her ecstasy.*) Let my mouth pronounce the exact word, the anticipated word, let my hand initiate the desired gesture. She is a beautiful woman. I want to comfort her.[40]

During her conference with the Pilgrim, Tristeza explains that she has become the victim of an unfortunate set of circumstances: "A wife without a husband, married without child . . . condemned! How else to describe it?[41] A sixteenth-century rendition of a modern-day feminist (to whom Gómez-Arcos has cunningly bequeathed his own surname), she expresses her resentment that the patriarchal rules of conduct mapped out by society prohibit her from taking charge of her own destiny.[42] As the embodiment of freedom and anarchy, she is determined to rebel against the established system, and she pleads with the *Peregrino* to help her replenish the empty space within her womb. She is convinced that conceiving a child with the *alumbrado* will invoke a repetition of the miracle of the Immaculate Conception. (In Girardian terms, the birth of a new savior would also induce a reprieve from the sacrificial crisis and a restoration of order.) As the *Peregrino* initiates his seduction, Tristeza remarks that she can already sense the sacred fire of the Holy Spirit entering her body: "Wail, howl like a gale, flail my flesh, hardened by lack of faith, overcome my resistance, tear me to pieces . . . !"[43] At this point, Asunta (with wine jug in hand) appears on stage, lingering in the shadows, and gradually, the other women join her—all of them voyeurs who bear witness to the sacred event: "*The Illuminated nun covers the sacred coitus with a liturgical cloth. The violent gusts of the gale are heard, the lubricious moan of the women, the ethylic laughter of Madre Asunta. . . . The women drag themselves along in the shadows of dawn.*"[44] The Immaculate Conception is thus transformed into a torrid seduction scene, and Gómez-Arcos seems to imply that Mary of Nazareth, likewise, may have been the victim of similar debauchery. Following this saintly seduction, rumor quickly spreads throughout the village that the noblewoman is pregnant with the son of God. Asunta is enraged and envious, telling Tristeza, "I would like to seize that miracle and cradle it in my womb! Steal it from you!"[45] In a move that eventually proves to be her own undoing, Asunta communicates the news to Mosén Blas, the chief clergyman of the village, who pronounces Tristeza "hysterical" and refuses to recognize the "miracle" of her pregnancy.

In part two, the *Peregrino* makes additional lecherous advances toward the young, virginal Ursulina. He informs her that he holds the power of the Holy Spirit, enabling him to convert her into a saint in just the same way that he has brought about the transformation of Tristeza. "Your greatness frightens me and it bring me happiness," she ambivalently declares, as she yields to his tempting words, but at the last moment, she flees his grasp. Traumatized, she whips him with his scourge, hysterically screaming, "It's the devil! Confession! Confession!"[46] The neighbors declare Ursulina a heretic for having mistreated their prized saint, and they implore the *Peregrino* to "pay them a visit," too. (When Tristeza hears the latest murmurings re-

garding this occurrence, she, too, becomes somewhat jealous: "A miracle like the one that is growing inside me every day cannot occur
often among mortals . . . and even less in the same place," she declares.)[47] Ursulina continues with her incessant ranting and ravings,
Mujer 3ᵃ points an accusatory finger at the Pilgrim and Asunta, and
eventually, a Knight of the Holy Office (*Caballero del Santo Oficio*)
and an Inquisitor (*Inquisidor*) are called in to extinguish the chaos;
their main concern: to establish whether an incident of heresy has
actually occurred, or whether all this mayhem merely can be attributed to a phenomenon of "collective feminine hysteria" that has
evolved from the women's anguish-ridden situation.[48]

The *alumbrados*, along with Tristeza, are subsequently summoned
to an Inquisitional hearing, whereupon they are accused of blasphemy and "illicit trafficking with the term 'sanctity.'" A metaliterary
discussion of dialogues and verbal discourse transpires, in which
Gómez-Arcos places into question the notion of the sacred. The
Knight of the Holy Office accuses the *Peregrino* of pretending to deliver
the Divine Word of God, while Tristeza proudly announces, "Together,
this saint and I have sustained spiritual *dialogues* that narrow-
minded people categorize as heresy. A stupid word" (emphasis
added).[49] Heresy is thus defined in terms of discursive violence, and
in this manner, Gómez-Arcos establishes a clear correspondence between censorship—which is itself a sacrifice of the text—and the
sacrificial blaze of the Inquisition.

While the *alumbrados* are condemned to be burned alive for their
heresies, Tristeza's life is momentarily spared because of her pregnancy. Still, she remains adamant in her defiance of the authoritative
Word of the Inquisition, and she believes that if eventually she is
placed upon the stake as a sacrificial victim, angels will be sent down
from heaven to extinguish the flames. In her words, "The law of
sacrifice . . . the law of man. I am willing to endure it."[50]

In the final scene, which takes place in the Inquisitor's chambers
at the ecclesiastic palace, the play reaches a dramatic paroxysm
through the use of nonverbal imagery and Brechtian alienation. The
Inquisitor appears on stage and prays before an eerie life-size crucifix.
He is dressed in a monk's habit with a large hood that obscures his
face from the spectator. Meanwhile, the pandemonium of a large
crowd is heard gathering outside (offstage). Cries from the villagers
are heard—"Depraved!", "Heretics!", "Burn them!"—as they bask in
the catharsis of sacrificial ritual. Asunta and the *Peregrino*'s
screams—"I deny it! Have pity! Confession!"—are heard as the bonfire devours their mortal flesh. After five weeks of confinement to a
cloister, Tristeza has been summoned to a meeting with the Inquisitor

who forces her to observe the spectacle through an open window. (The audience presumably can see the flames through this window.) In her final speech, Tristeza expresses her conviction that her "religion"—an anarchistic antifaith that questions and has the courage to disobey—is the "true" faith, and that one day, it will prevail over the Inquisitor's religion—an oppressive discourse of exclusion and purification, sustained through blind adherence to the expiatory mechanisms of sacrifice. The supposedly immortal child that she carries within her womb is a metaphor for her confidence in the future triumph of her aspirations:

> (*Pausing.*) I believe in life. You cannot pray to life, you hold it in your womb, you feed it with your own entrails, you defend it. The Inquisitor imposes a sterile faith, and demands that we pray to it . . . because he only lives in order to confer death. He has accused me of conceit and arrogance. Unjustly. It is easier for the conscience to define the enemy as rebel than to reflect upon her rebellion; the conscience is lazy. Mine is not, and I will give him proof of that . . . in that I beseech him to accept as proof of my humility: inspired by this Son of mine, who is alive, I will pray for the soul of the Inquisitor, not for that of the heretic. (*She exits definitively.*)[51]

After Tristeza's exit, the Inquisitor remains on stage. Then, in a shocking gesture designed to jar the spectator's sense of equilibrium, his hood falls to his shoulders, and it is revealed that his face is exactly identical to that of the *Peregrino* (both roles are played by the same actor). Gómez-Arcos indicates in his stage directions (omitted from the performed/published version) that this disturbing revelation should be carried out with absolute simplicity: "like a coin that has two identical faces."[52]

In the "game" of the sacrificial process, sociocultural order (the Inquisition) is supposed to have triumphed over the anarchy and chaos of the *alumbrados*, yet Gómez-Arcos, who plays by different rules, subverts this process of signification with his bizarre final revelation. His text thus represents an iconoclastic interrogation of sociocultural order, a celebration of the "sacrificial crisis"—in the sense that such a crisis breeds ambiguity, and consequently, anarchy and freedom. It is no longer possible for the spectator to distinguish between the Inquisitor and the *Peregrino*; their two faces of good and evil have become blurred, forming a hazy image of double exposure. Order has not won the game; ambiguity has triumphed in the final round, and the Extremaduran village appears to have become even more deeply immersed in a crisis of distinctions than ever before. The Inquisitor/*Peregrino* raises his head to the life-size Christ figure and makes his final accusations: "How much pain, how much blood is yet to cost us your pain and your blood? How much death will cost us your death? . . . If my tongue were free . . . I would blame you as an assassin. Someone will do it . . . someday."[53] In this deconstructive dialogue that fuses past and present centuries, history is allegorized as a cycle of eternal return, an endless quest for freedom of expression, yet somebody has finally garnered the freedom to accuse Christ of murder for the sacrificial blood that has been shed in his name. That "somebody" is Gómez-Arcos.

4

Los gatos
(1965 / 1992)

Pour le faire exister, une seule façon: l'inventer.
Inventer Dieu est une obligation, pénible, dure, qui nous demande
des sacrifices quotidiens innombrables dont le résultat final sera
splendide: avoir les mains pleines du vide de Son Existence....
Disons donc que l'invention de Dieu, indépendamment de son op-
portunité, est un besoin logique né du chaos de la foi, comme l'in-
vention du franquisme a été un besoin logique né du chaos de la
liberté (certains appelent le franquisme fascisme, sans se rendre
compte que le fascisme est un élan universel et le franquisme un
usufruit opportuniste).[1]
—Agustín Gómez-Arcos, *Maria Republica*

In the final scenes of *Diálogos de la herejía* (Dialogues of heresy),
sacrifice is played out as a collective spectacle of death designed to
restore order to a community immersed in chaos and corruption.
The frightful dénouement, however, does not bring closure to this
scene of confusion, for rather than purify the supposedly defiled domain that is depicted in this play, the performance of sacrificial ritual
yields unexpected results: a collapse of difference and distinctions
that is exemplified in the perplexing image of the *Peregrino*/Inquisitor.
Los gatos (The cats) continues Gómez-Arcos's exploration of sacrifice,
eroticism, and religious fanaticism. With this play, he takes up the
theme of sacrifice as a rite of purification and purgation, a preventa-
tive mechanism designed to channel and satiate unavoidable violent
desires and aspirations, but this time, he recontextualizes this theme
within a more modern bourgeois setting. The end result is a powerful,
chilling piece of theater, a sacrificial spectacle steeped in passion,
violence, and death, which straddles the balustrade between the emotional intensity of a Lorcan tragedy and the grotesque hyperbolism
and dark humor of Valle-Inclán's *esperpentos*.

In September 1965, a censored production of Gómez-Arcos's play, directed by Juan de Prat-Gay, premiered at Madrid's Teatro Marquina, and while the reviews were not altogether favorable, the play's reception was somewhat less controversial than that of *Diálogos de la herejía*. In some instances, this first production of *Los gatos* (starring Cándida Losada, Luchy Soto, and Alicia Hermida) even incited laudatory words from some of the more conservative critics. For example, in a review published in the daily *ABC*, Enrique Llovet declared, "Gómez-Arcos's adventure deserves respect. *Los gatos* is the work of a true writer. Nobody has ever substantiated the claim that the mission of literature is, in our modern times, a sugarcoated mission."

In November 1992, nearly thirty years after its original première, the dramatic force of this allegorical piece seemed as potent and as relevant as ever when one of Spain's most prominent young directors, Carme Portaceli, revived and restaged this post–Civil War allegory for a new generation of theatergoers. The acclaimed actors Héctor Alterio of Argentina and Paco Casares of Spain were cast in the leading roles, with a set conceived by the celebrated Catalan designers Isidre Prunés and Montse Amenós. The two-week run at the María Guerrero during Madrid's Festival de Otoño was so successful that the Ministry of Culture agreed to fund the production's national tour of Spain, and in June 1993, Gómez-Arcos accompanied the cast and crew to Buenos Aires, where he witnessed the play's Latin American première.[2] For the most part, the reviews throughout Spain and Argentina were extremely laudatory. Enrique Centeno of *Diario 16* wrote:

> Go and see one of the crudest and truest testimonies of what a committed theater could be and never has been; go and see how a good dramatic structure does not impede the poetic literary style; go and see an excellent inheritance from Valle-Inclán, a theater of scenic richness paired with that of Genet and superior to Arrabal's "panic"; go and see how cruelty becomes a defense for religious taboos; see, finally, how a good *mise en scène*—talent galore of Carmen Portaceli and of the designers—demonstrates, still one more time, that we do harbor exceptional actors.[3]

Predictably, there were some critics—particularly those associated with the religious right—who responded to the production with an attitude of denial, thereby exhibiting the type of rejection of historical memory of which Gómez-Arcos so often speaks. Alberto de la Hera's review, which appeared in the ultraconservative *Ya*, is indicative of this refusal to confront the relationship between Gómez-Arcos's "esperpentic" visions of reality and reality itself: "*Los gatos* possesses an outrageous plot, not the product of a historic reality, but of a sick

Héctor Alterio as Pura and Paco Casares as Ángela in *Los gatos.* **Teatro María Guerrero, Madrid, 1992. Photo: Courtesy of Ana Jelín, Producciones Teatrales Contemporánas, S.L.**

fantasy. The contexts, the exploits, the form of intolerance, the crimes, cannot be situated in the moment in which they are supposed to take place."

In her program notes, Portaceli observes a similarity between the image of Spain portrayed in Gómez-Arcos's play and the cinema of Luis García Berlanga, whose work is most often associated with the Spain of the 1950s and 1960s.[4] Although *Los gatos* was not originally meant to be a historical drama, by situating her *mise en scène* during this period (thirty years earlier) Portaceli in effect converted Gómez-Arcos's play into a work of art that, upon first glance, may seem to be a kind of artifact or remnant from the past. Nevertheless, upon closer inspection, it becomes exceedingly apparent that this play does not necessarily represent a historical document and that many of the attitudes that manifest themselves in this work are still very much a part of the fabric of Spanish culture even at the end of the twentieth century. Portaceli comments:

In 1976, there was a radical change in our country and perhaps as a result of the enormous desire to grab the train of reason and democracy, everybody forgot the past in a matter of seconds: as if nothing had ever happened. But we are, after all, our own history and years later, when we are already living a different way and the euphoria has calmed, we look back to learn and understand where we come from and the reason for some manifestations that are still present. . . .

An *esperpentic* world seen thirty years later (then, such a world would not have been able to be seen, it could not be seen), a world structured according to the style of comedy, but of a comedy that freezes our laughter because it is converted into a tale of terror (like our history) . . .

In this two-part tragicomedy—or, "esperpento burgués," as he calls it—Gómez-Arcos foregrounds the oxymoronic dynamics of sacrificial ritual so as to reveal the inner workings of oppressive authority. Sacrifice, as René Girard points out, can be perceived as the bedrock of sociocultural order, manifesting itself in both modern and ancient cultures as an expiatory procedure designed to channel and satiate unavoidable violent desires and aspirations. However, the underlying essence of this process is paradoxical and seemingly hypocritical, for sacrifice is also a form of transgression exercised within the context of taboo, a "coincidence of the permitted and the prohibited."[5] Gómez-Arcos's play casts an accusatory spotlight upon the inherently paradoxical nature of sacrifice in order to expose the grotesque entrails of authoritative institutions (concretely depicted here as the Catholic Church) that shroud themselves in sanctity. In this manner, *Los gatos* leads the spectator into a dark, hidden realm of transgression, where violence lurks behind a sacred façade of taboo.

In his treatise on eroticism (1962), Georges Bataille poses the somewhat disconcerting assumption that we are all potential transgressors in that the aspiration toward violence—toward a rupture of tranquil, civilized order—is an innate desire imbedded in the human persona.[6] In light of Bataille's perceptions, our cultural history can be construed as a perpetual series of "no's": of denials, restrictions, and constraints whereby society struggles to map out and superimpose upon its inherent inclinations toward anarchy and disorder an orderly and authoritative grid that would dominate and silence these primordial impulses. While this natural passion for violence often culminates in death, it also reveals itself through the experience of eroticism. The violence of eroticism plunges all semblance of existence and individual autonomy into a state of flux and suspension whereby life itself appears perilously close to slipping away.

"Underlying eroticism," declares Bataille, "is the feeling of something bursting, of the violence accompanying an explosion."[7] *Los gatos* is subtly evocative of Bataille's conception of eroticism in that Gómez-Arcos's text suggests that human nature takes on new significance when contemplated from the perspective of violence and that violence—in this case, a sacrificial brand of violence—is the thread that ambiguously intertwines death with sensuality. According to Bataille, both death and eroticism represent violent transgressive forces that attempt to sever any semblance of order. Both traverse barriers and push existence to its limit: death irrevocably defies life; eroticism simulates and approximates this defiance—as exemplified by the French term *petite mort*. Eroticism is, therefore, the expression of an instinctive longing to shatter all sense of being, to saturate life with as much violence as it can possibly withstand without completely destroying it.

In *Los gatos*, Gómez-Arcos allegorizes this relationship between eroticism and death, and collapses the distinctions between these two concepts. Death and eroticism come to represent parallel gestures, movements in a common direction signifying a transition from order to anarchy and from difference to ambiguity. Both imply a violent sacrifice of what Bataille calls "discontinuous" existence, in which one living entity is merged with another person or thing.[8] This abrupt fusion, or "continuity," occurring on a physical, emotional, or religious plane marks a fatal union, which yields a death (literal or figurative) of the individual, a dissolution of the discontinuous self, and a surrender of difference. In this play, even the sensations conjured by the image of a putrefying dead body—a simultaneous rush of anguish and fear, desire and pleasure—appear to coincide with the emotions that spring forth during the inner transgressive experience of eroticism: "In the parallels perceived by the human mind between putrefaction and the various aspects of sexual activity the reelings of revulsion which set us against both end by mingling."[9]

Eroticism offers a viable threshold on continuity through which one may escape the solitude and isolation suffered at the expense of individual separateness. Similarly, sacrifice invokes a parallel sensation of continuity through the collective experience of ritual death. The sacred ceremonies of sacrificial rituals unite their participants through the emotional contagion of violence. Those who witness the spectacle of a victim's continuity are able to experience vicariously a sensation of full and limitless being. Through identification and catharsis they are able to bask in the continuity of existence that the victim has achieved through death.[10]

The theatricality, and with it, the cathartic function of sacrificial ritual—which approximates certain notions of the theater proposed by such historically distant figures as Aristotle and Antonin Artaud—can be ascribed to what Richard Schechner calls "an ancient, persistent, and robust therapeutic tradition of performance."[11] In effect, Girard includes theater among a roster of cultural institutions that derive from the sacrificial process, and in a statement that conjures visions of the *alumbrados* in *Diálogos de la herejía*, Stephen Greenblatt observes, "Indeed, there is no more theatrical event in the Renaissance than a public execution."[12] Both sacrificial ritual and the theater event induce collective experiences of violence, performances defined by the presence and participation of the spectator. Both strive to achieve an outcome that is a function of a certain measure (plus or minus) of identification between spectator and victim, or between spectator and actor.[13] In this nexus between drama and sacrifice, theatrical violence induces a violation of individual autonomy (psychological, as well as physical).[14] The theater event, consequently, can be viewed as a form of transgression: a sacrificial ritual whose violence destroys the barriers—the boundaries of discontinuity—that separate spectators, actors, director, and author; it merges its participants in a collective fusion of continuity.

While many of Gómez-Arcos's plays reflect this violent, transgressive dimension of the theater event, *Los gatos*, in particular, can be singled out as a dramatic work that presents a significant inquiry into the possibilities derived from the conception of the theater as a harrowing, assaulting experience. Indeed, in his 1965 review of the play, José Monleón noted that during the performance, he was able to detect a substantial degree of uneasiness among audience members:

"There are also moments in which a certain auditory avidity on the part of the audience, a general restlessness, convinces us with regard to the play to the extent that this supposes a rupture of the habitually cool house-stage relationship."[15] *Los gatos* is a theater piece that attempts to engage the spectator in an exploration of a dark, hidden realm of transgression—of erotic passion and violence—that lies at the core of human existence.

The action of Gómez-Arcos's tragicomedy is played out against a backdrop of sexual repression and religious obsession. The setting for this tragicomedy is the living room, or parlor, of an old provincial home inhabited by two unwed sisters in their fifties. For the new production, Portaceli incorporated an intriguing and fitting transvestic twist into her *mise en scène* by casting two male actors, Héctor Alterio and Paco Casares, in the principal female roles. In this manner, she was able to underscore the notion of patriarchal authority that is curiously incarnated in the images of these two women. As Javier Villán of *El Mundo* observes, "The sexual repression reaches such a demolishing and transformative level that it creates a series of sexually amorphous, indefinable beings. Confused materializations, a mixture of male and female."[16]

The outrageous proportions of this grotesque painting of *la España negra* ("Black Spain") create a caricature of life in a small Andalusian village. At the same time, it is an allegorical version of a much larger picture that extends beyond Spanish borders. While the dramatic text does not explicitly specify the historical period in which the play is situated, Gómez-Arcos's scenic descriptions do contain a few temporal references, such as the presence of an electric lamp, which suggest a twentieth-century setting. The stage directions at the beginning of part one describe an oppressive atmosphere of decadence and decline whose tenebrous, somber tones are reminiscent of a Spanish artistic tradition marked by Francisco de Goya and José Gutiérrez Solana. The living room decor is composed of a dark, musty assortment of religious kitsch in the midst of decay:

> *The parlor of an old, provincial home, frozen in time: dark paintings done by friends of the family or relatives, of flowers and recent ancestry, of cats entangled in balls of yarn, paintings framed in cloth, embroiderings, sketches yellowing with age, old flowers, realist virgins, an array of cherubim and saints draped in embroidered or hand-painted robes, enclosed in bell jars and glass cases, with that singular, stilled gesture, as if caught in the dead air of the cases, dark furniture, just as fiercely Spanish as uncomfortable, musty velvets, old doilies, dark curtains, ostentatiously dark, nineteenth-century luxury at its moment of decay, antique smells, old parlor plants in plaster and earthen pots....*[17]

Within the enclosed space of this parlor, Gómez-Arcos presents the story of Pura and Angela, two women whose obsessive attitude with regard to eroticism and religion situates them within a Spanish literary tradition of sexually repressed females, such as those created by Benito Pérez Galdós, Leopoldo Alas ["Clarín"], and Federico García Lorca. Both are virgins, as their names imply, although Pura is by far the more prudish of the two. Her most distinguishing feature is her ultrapious disposition: she spends her days cloistered like a nun, sitting in her rocking chair with her back to the window (that is, to the outside world), maintaining her composure through her contemplative readings of the religious meditations of her spiritual adviser Padre Carrión ("Father Carrión"). At one point, she declares that marriage never held any importance for her and that she feels sufficiently fulfilled by her unification with God. Her first communion served as the sacramental substitute for a wedding; in her words, "there is a big difference between receiving God and receiving a man."[18] Angela, who is characterized by her intense fascination with all forms of transgression, expresses more of an interest in the subject of men and marriage. When, on one occasion, she suggests that she even may have gone so far as to have kissed a man, Pura is both horrified and scandalized. Like a dictator who derives great pleasure from the tyrannical rule of the inhabitants of her regime, Angela delights in the sense of power she garners from the heavy-handed discipline of her cats, whom she is punishing for having committed a supposedly abominable crime.

While superficially Pura and Angela project a sanctimonious façade of purity and restraint, nevertheless, they are capable of performing a most extreme, violent act of transgression: a sacrificial murder of surreal proportions that will propel them into the realm of continuity, fulfill their erotic yearnings, and banish violence from their consciousness (as well as from their living room). Their religious beliefs have become so twisted and exaggerated, and their ideas about sexual comportment have become so contorted and misconstrued that they have lost all sense of differentiation between right and wrong (a condition of sacrificial crisis). Moreover, their blind obedience and adherence to sociocultural taboos ironically has had, and will have, the effect of converting them into transgressors. In Pura's words, "Sometimes, the border between good and evil is minimal. A subtlety."[19]

On the day of the 1965 première, an enhanced version of Gómez-Arcos's program notes appeared in *ABC*, explaining his own conception of these grotesque depictions and setting up a series of parallels between his play and the (anti)aesthetic of systematic deformation of Valle-Inclán's *esperpentos:*

> I am especially fascinated by individuals who, immersed in a social, political, or religious system, adjust their beliefs or their personal anecdotes to their own points of view, evading reality or converting it into an *esperpento.*
>
> Such are the characters in *Los gatos.* Pura and Angela live their lives in a bourgeois manner, they move and speak like others, yet they are irremediably situated with their backs to reality. The have taken their religious beliefs, their obsessions, their frustrations, and their sense of justice to the limit. Having lost all social equilibrium of coexistence and moderation, of good and evil, these "pious souls" are converted into ferocious beings, that even snatch from God His faculty of judgment and punishment. Julien Green wrote: "There is nothing as ferocious as those pious souls who decide to take justice into their own hands instead of leaving it to God." I am unable to find a better definition for my own characters.[20]

As in the case of Valle-Inclán's *esperpentic* dramas, the imagery of *Los gatos* naturally conforms to several interrelated interpretative alternatives. On the one hand, Gómez-Arcos's *esperpento burgués* is a distorted illusion, a hyperbolic (in)version of a world that is grounded in sociohistorical reality but appears as though it were deformed and reflected by the renowned concave mirrors of Valle-Inclán's *Luces de bohemia.* On the other hand, one may perceive this imagery as a faithful representation of a world whose "real" dimensions have been rendered disproportionate by the presence of an oppressive hierarchical system—i.e., a fascist regime, such as that of Franco—which was already in place prior to the moment of artistic representation. According to this second alternative, it becomes the task of the playwright simply "to tell it like it is."[21]

Curiously, in his review of the 1965 *mise en scène*, Juan Emilio Aragonés finds fault in what he interprets as Gómez-Arcos's inadequate sense of dramatic proportion: "That in Agustín Gómez-Arcos Spain has a new author was already confirmed with his first première *Diálogos de la herejía,* staged in Madrid in 1964. That in the construction of his scenic plots he almost completely lacks a quality as essential for a playwright as a 'sense of balance,' was also evidenced in that drama and he has reiterated this lack most notably in his second staged play: *Los gatos.*"[22] Ironically, what Aragonés critiques as a negative feature of the play (or of both plays) is apparently the aesthetic effect of disequilibrium that Gómez-Arcos intended to achieve. With this grotesque portrayal of bourgeois society (in effect, a theatrical form of *tremendismo*), the question that the spectator is implicitly asked to ponder is not whether this is an appropriate theatrical device; but rather, whether the agent of distortion is the playwright/ artist or, indeed, the system itself.

The hyperbolic characterizations of Pura and Angela create a turbulent intermingling of continuity and discontinuity, transgression and taboo—a situation that is mirrored in the design of the scenic space. For the 1965 production, set designer Víctor María Cortezo emphasized the ecclesiastical atmosphere of the living room through the addition of a vaulted ceiling containing a set of large stained-glass windows.[23] Lighting technicians projected an eerie sort of glow through these windows, bathing the stage in an ominous aura of sanctity. For the second *cuadro* of part one, which takes place specifically during the period of *Semana Santa*, Gómez-Arcos's written text calls for the presence of a distinctly purple hue that would cast a mood of spirituality upon the stage, optically creating an illusion of ethereality: "The dense silence and aromas blur all the angles of the objects there. As if by magic, there has not remained one color that might possibly suggest another time of year: it is, for certain, Holy Week, and any other impression is out of the question. Also, in places where there were none, purplish table scarves and violet figures of the Nazarene of natural proportions seem to have appeared. Purplish Sacred Heart figures, pierced with silver blades. . . ."[24] In this original production, the images of the saints, Virgins, and Nazarenes were represented not as miniature figurines, such as those that one might customarily find in a traditional Spanish living room, but as looming life-sized or larger-than-life figures, reminiscent of Spanish cathedrals and Holy Week processions. At the edge of the stage, off to one side, Cortezo positioned a gigantic hooded penitent (a *Padre Nazareno*) who seemed to hover and lean toward the audience. For the 1992 *mise en scène*, Amenós and Prunés positioned a giant image of the Virgin at the entrance to the living room. Each character made his or her entrance on stage by emerging from beneath the Virgin's skirts. Together, these scenic elements, incorporated into both the new and old productions, worked to reinforce the idea that in *Los gatos* profane acts of transgression are carried out within the sacred frame of a church, or churchlike space.[25] Figure 2 depicts a hypothetical rendering of the sisters' parlor as designed by Cortezo for the original production.

In his stage directions, Gómez-Arcos describes the presence of an adjoining room, "the cats' room," distinguished by a door containing special holes for the feeding and observation of the cats.[26] The door marks a boundary between the living room (the realm of taboo) and the cats' room (the realm of transgression). In the 1965 *mise en scène*,

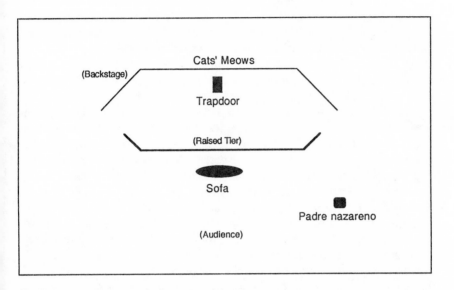

Prat-Gay and Cortezo further emphasized presence of these two realms through the use of a raised tier or platform which designated a kind threshold on the (under)world of the cats. The invisible world situated beyond the door is thus a psychic interior region, while the realm of the living room, as signified by an old-fashioned sofa, is an exterior world of appearances and quotidian mundaneness. In other words, if the cats represent eroticism, then the door represents a kind of chastity belt.

For the 1992 production, Portaceli and the design team of Amenós-Prunés, no longer constrained by the limits of censorship, added a more overtly concrete political dimension to Gómez-Arcos's allegory. Along the perimeter of the stage, they installed a backdrop of red-yellow-red stripes, thereby creating the impression of an enormous Spanish flag, which literally and figuratively enveloped the living room within a sociohistorical context. Also, as Centeno notes in his review of the play, the set contained a sideboard, on top of which was placed a portrait of Franco.

While the cats play a key role in this spectacle, they never actually reveal themselves to the spectator as a physical entity, for they are portrayed by a harrowing sound rather than a material form, a noise rather than words. In the 1965 production, the cats' meows were represented through the use of a recorded soundtrack, which was often amplified to a level that exceeded any realistic proportions. Whenever the meows were heard, the *Padre nazareno* would simultaneously veer out toward the audience. This nonphysical/nonverbal feline imagery denotes a significant point of correspondence between Gómez-Arcos's play and the theater experience as envisioned by Artaud, who proposes a subordination of the spoken word to the nonverbal aspects of the *mise en scène*. The Artaudian performance endeavors to express spiritual states through a language of "animated hieroglyphs"; through poses, gestures, noises, sudden cries, forms, and shapes, which express attitudes and sensations that words are incapable of capturing.[27] The howls of the cats, which resemble metonymically the erotic moans and orgasmic cries of a human being, are in effect an acoustical manifestation of the sisters' displaced sexual urges, a resounding representation of transgression, eroticism, and violence. These resonating sounds, at once horrific and erotic, emanate from behind the door (backstage) and penetrate the entire theatrical space. Coinciding with the Artaudian conception of the theater as an assaulting sacrificial spectacle, the presence of the cats inspires an intense rupture of the margins of theatrical representation, as well as a jarring violation of the boundaries separating actor and spectator.[28] The disharmony of these unnerving sounds shatters the silence and placidity that in a more traditional (realist/naturalist) setting would typically characterize the space occupied by the audience. The meows are, therefore, an instrument of sacrifice in that they have the power to violate and dissolve the discontinuous nature of the individual spectators, to engage them in a collective ritual of sacrifice and inspire in them the essential emotions associated with transgression: desire, fear, excitement, and anguish.[29]

At times, the boundaries between the two worlds depicted on stage—the realm of the cats and the realm of the sisters—also seem to dissolve and overlap. The juxtaposition of these two worlds reaches a point of extreme dramatic tension during a scene in which Pura presents a catechism lesson to Loli, the voluptuous nine year old and daughter of Manuela (the sisters' domestic servant). This episode is composed of two scenes occurring simultaneously. The spatial positioning of the characters, as designated by the written text, facilitates the spectator's perception with regard to this simultaneity of events. Angela stands near the cats' door (within the raised area of the stage) and torments the animals with the pungent odor that exudes from a package of fish scraps. Several days have passed since the cats' last feeding, and their incessant howling proportionally rises with the crescendo of Angela's emotional frenzy. This depiction of "continuity," occurring upstage, contrasts with the scene of taboo and discontinuity, occurring downstage, in which Pura and Loli (situated on or near the sofa) recite in a monotonous trancelike tone the questions and answers of the Catholic catechism:

> *Angela.* (*Thrilled.*) They have all climbed up. They're scratching at the floor beneath the door. They know their dinner is here. They're purring like kittens. I'd like you to see them, Pura.
>
> *Pura.* "Concerning the Sixth Commandment, I ask you: Who keeps it eternally?"
>
> *Loli.* "He who is pure in thought, word, and deed."
>
> *Pura.* Purity . . . Never forget that human glory, that stage of grace, that supreme pride . . .
>
> *Loli.* Yes, Miss.
>
> *Angela.* (*Picking up the scraps from off the floor.*) I'm going to push the food through the grating for them, to see what they do.
>
> *Pura.* "Is he who tries to cast off evil thoughts a sinner?"
>
> *Loli.* "No, Miss, rather he is deserving, since in that way he leads himself from temptation."
>
> *Pura.* Remember the Our Father: And lead us not into temptation.
>
> *Angela.* (*Giggling excitedly.*) They're confused. Do you hear them meowing?[30]

Angela, meanwhile, imposes her dictatorial strategies upon her oppressed feline proletariat. She curtails their uprising by tempting her captive animals with false hopes, and she tortures them physically and psychologically by depriving them of their basic needs. In a prophetic gesture of cannibalistic (and, almost incestuous) sacrifice, the cats eventually satisfy their hunger by devouring the smallest and weakest of their own; hence, two texts—one sacred, the other profane—collide within the theatrical space. On one side of the living room, Gómez-Arcos depicts taboo: order, religion, chastity, continence; on the other side, transgression: anarchy, hunger, torture, cannibalism.

This convergence of taboo and transgression gives way to a fusion of death and eroticism. When Angela witnesses the sacrificial violence that is taking place on the other side of the door, her crescendo of excitement mirrors the emotional pleasure associated with sexual ecstasy. While Pura's longing for sexual plenitude is not as explicitly evident as that of her sister, it is not entirely absent from this scene. Pura, as it would seem, has merely displaced her primordial cravings for violence to the other side of the room; she has psychically exiled

Héctor Alterio as Pura and Laura Jou as Loli in *Los gatos*. Teatro María Guerrero, Madrid, 1992. Photo: Courtesy of Ana Jelín, Producciones Teatrales Contemporánas, S.L.

her interior desire for continuity to a hidden realm where death and eroticism reign.

In the world of *Los gatos*, eroticism is thus portrayed as a potent force that Pura and Angela attempt to battle and suppress. So powerful is the erotic impulse that it invades all aspects of tranquil domestic life. This situation is epitomized in a scene in which Doña Rosa, a neighbor, joins the sisters for afternoon tea. Doña Rosa, whose husband has "disappeared" because she refused to consummate their marriage, displays the same type of aversion to sensual pleasure as does Pura. When Angela asks if she should "plug in" the electric lamp in order to brighten the atmosphere of the parlor, Doña Rosa shrieks with disgust and covers her ears. She takes extreme offense to Angela's use of the verb *enchufar* ("to plug in"), a word that is saturated with sexually connotative *doubles entendres*. During the same scene, Manuela offers Doña Rosa a dish of pastries with a spoon and fork, triggering the following dialogue:

Doña Rosa. No!

Manuela. Madam doesn't wish to have any?

Doña Rosa. I want pastries. I still like sweets. Moreover, I bought them. But I don't want to have the fork touching the spoon. Neither together nor mixed, if it's all the same to you.

Pura. It's always all the same to Manuela, Rosa. If you don't want to eat your pastry with a fork and spoon, you may eat it with the spoon only, or with your fingers, if you wish, and let that be the end of it

Doña Rosa. But this way of throwing everything together! In my home, everything is separated: some things in one drawer, and other things in another. And when we want more light, there are switches . . . none of this screwing in more bulbs. It's the way of the world, one big jumble. It must be sexual.

Pura. Well, hear her! Now she's going to tell us that forks, spoons, and light bulbs are to blame for the way the world is.

Doña Rosa. They are symbols, Pura.[31]

Eroticism, as it would seem, pervades the mundane realm of electrical sockets, light bulbs, and even the drawers where silverware is kept. In this absurd conversation, the allegorical intersection of intolerance and unbridled freedom emerges once again, and what one might offhandedly take for comic is in reality dead serious. In Bataille's terms, Doña Rosa disapproves of all manifestations of continuity; she wants everything—men, women, and even all types of silverware—to be stored in separate, orderly compartments. Her objection to electrical plugs and outlets, and to the mixing of two different genres/genders of silverware is a figurative expression of her personal aversion to sex—that is, to the consumption of sweets.

At other moments in the drama, Pura and Angela disclose fragmentary information regarding the activities of their only brother, Carlos, an artist who once lived in a coastal village and was known for his paintings of seascapes. Both his bohemian lifestyle and his proximity to the ocean are qualities that underscore his characterization as the personification of freedom. The sisters also mention that Carlos's wife abandoned him, presumably for another man, leaving him to raise his young daughter, Inés, on his own. Several years have passed and Carlos has recently died, leaving Inés (now eighteen years old) to live with her aunts.

Additionally, Pura and Angela allude to the presence of a third sister, Paloma (whose name also connotes freedom). Their nostalgic recollections reveal that Paloma, like Carlos, is no longer living and that she was the former owner of the cats who are now in Angela's custody. In a description that recalls the poetic imagery of García

Lorca's *La casa de Bernarda Alba*, the sisters refer to Paloma's sexually promiscuous behavior, remembering how she loved to venture out onto the balcony to chat with her suitors. The memory of Paloma, summoned like a ghost from the past at strategic moments throughout the play, serves as an *outlet* for the unrealized aspirations of her two sisters, whose exaggerated sense of piety and whose ignorant sense of their own human need for freedom of (sexual) expression have inhibited them from fulfilling their deepest hopes and desires. Angela reminisces, "I come downstairs here, and I look all around at everything, thing by thing, and it all makes me think what my life could have been . . ."[32]

Soon after Inés's arrival near the end of part one, Angela develops an almost pathological inability to distinguish between her niece and Paloma. In Inés, who is blond, as was Paloma, Angela perceives the resuscitated image of her dead sister. Like the *Peregrino* and the Inquisitor in *Diálogos de la herejía*, their faces seem to alternate, forming a hazy double image.[33] Angela repeatedly substitutes their names interchangeably, mistakenly referring to Inés as "Paloma," as though Paloma were still alive. Angela's confusion between her sister and her niece—which parallels the ambiguous intersections of taboo and transgression, eroticism and death—functions as an element of dramatic prophesy, casting a shadow of imminent doom upon the characterization of the young Inés.

When Inés inquires about the circumstances surrounding the death of Paloma, both *señoritas* vaguely insinuate that it is the cats who are somehow responsible. Once again, Gómez-Arcos presents a juxtaposition of two textual images, each offering a different perspective of the same incident, each allegorically deferring to the same referent. Pura's version exemplifies discipline and reserve. In her view, Paloma died of the blood poisoning that resulted from a simple scratch: "One day they scratched her. Cats have claws . . . (*Toward Angela*) . . . like men. The scratch became infected, and she died of septicemia. There was nothing anyone could do."[34] In contrast, Angela's version is a harrowing tale of transgression in which the cats ("those criminals") intentionally murdered Paloma by poisoning her with their hatred and their venom-saturated claws:

They put poison on their claws to infect her blood. A poison known as hatred, because they despised her. Men would come to visit her, and then Paloma would forget about them. She would sit at this window and talk with some of them, and listen to their stories and their little poems. She would be over there, and I here. We would laugh at each other. You know?, the cats would become restless, jealous. They would come up to her and purr around her legs—I know now what those shameless things were after—but Paloma paid no attention to them. I didn't either. First one came, then another, and another, and then they all came. And we didn't even notice, as if they didn't even exist. That is why they wanted revenge: they felt displaced.[35]

Angela's recollection of the murder is saturated with ambiguous syntax and suggestive imagery. It opens the way to a complex network of double meaning and foregrounds the allegorical value of the invisible presence of the cats. The cats, who have long occupied a place in literary history as a metaphor for sexuality and the embodiment of feminine genitalia (Bataille's own *Histoire de l'œil* is but one example), are the incarnation of a violent chimerical desire. They are an allegorical rendering of the innate aspiration toward Bataille's "continuity," the inner longing for violence that underlies the sisters' (especially Pura's) calm, placid façade of restraint. Pura and Angela's savage animal instincts and inner longings have thus manifested themselves in the concrete form of a feline. As a result, the cats are at once a remedy and a poison: they are a *re*placement for the sisters' erotic fulfillment and a *dis*placement of their repressed sexual energy, anguish, and frustration. Because they—this multibodied force of erotic desire—felt "displaced," they took revenge in the form of a violent crime, a sacrifice designed to yield continuity of being. In this manner, Gómez-Arcos seems to invert the process of the Bataillean "death wish." Here, the continuity achieved through death becomes a substitute for the continuity realized through the experience of eroticism, instead of vice versa. Paloma's blood poisoning signifies a defilement of her body and thus functions as a metaphor for her lost virginity, the result of a violent passion. At the same time, it is a sacrificial remedy through which violent urges may be channeled and expelled. In the program notes from the 1965 performance, Gómez-Arcos comments, "The cats are a reality and a symbol. They have physical presence on the stage and at the same time they serve to underline the psychic disequilibrium of the characters, the climactic moments of the drama. They are cats and they are chimeras. The instrument of crime and the arm of justice."

Throughout her commentary, Angela employs a third-person-plural pronoun (*ellos* = "they/them") whose antecedent is never clearly specified and, therefore, evades any precise interpretation. She refers, for example, to *their* purring sounds and to the manner in which *they* ("those shameless things") would shamelessly gather and purr around Paloma's legs. In effect, the spectator may wonder, "Who is this *they*?" "The men?" "The cats?" Angela's commentary seems to vacillate between each of these interpretative possibilities. Her double-sided syntactical constructions convey an implicit hesitation, a zone of slippage, whereby the allegorical referent infinitely escapes concretization. The employment of *they* carries a translucent poetic value which transcends the limits of language, of concrete signifiers and signifieds, and opens a window onto a world without linguistic barriers. Angela's ambiguity of expression is thus a form of linguistic continuity, in which signifiers are stripped of their corresponding signifieds and fused on a continuous plane of multiple meaning that eschews precision and, in what was an added advantage in 1965, eludes the wrath of the censors; hence, poetic language emerges as a form of transgression. As Bataille notes, "Poetry leads to the same place as all forms of eroticism—to the blending and fusion of separate objects. It leads us to eternity, it leads us to death, and through death to continuity."[36]

During the Holy Week episode, Pura and Angela go off to church to attend Padre Carrión's mass, leaving their niece at home with the cats. Like Paloma before her, Inés has developed a strong affinity for the animals. While the sisters are away, Inés receives a visit from her secret suitor, Fernando, a young sailor from her village with whom she has maintained a written correspondence. During their clandestine meeting, which occurs beneath the watchful eyes of Manuela and the cats, they declare their mutual love, and Inés reveals that she is pregnant with their child. Fernando, who, like Carlos, is the romantic incarnation of freedom, is due to set sail, but before his departure, he vows that he will write to Inés each day, and marry her upon his return. Following his visit, the music of a Holy Week procession is heard in the distance, and as the curtain falls, a *saeta*, whose foreboding verses subtly evoke the story of Paloma, rises above the rhythm of the drums. As it seems, Paloma, also, was once pregnant, and her tragic past is once again intertwined with Inés's inevitable destiny:

> Where are you going, White Dove,
> this hour of the night?
> I am off to look for my child,
> They're burying him tonight.
> (*The cats' meowing sets the stage a'tremble*)[37]

From the moment Fernando crosses the threshold and *penetrates* the sacred space of the living room, Pura and Angela's immaculately tidy domain appears transformed. As the stage directions indicate at the beginning of part two, "*The Holy Week decorations have disappeared. In the light and color there is a ray of hope, as if some new—*

or strange—motives unrelated to the two sisters had brought to the house an atmosphere of tolerance. Through the window, out in the narrow street, a tree or two has grown greener; its vigorous appearance, perhaps with ephemeral splendor, seems to penetrate the parlor so that it has a different air."[38] Signs of life and of crisis begin to spring forth. What was once—at least, on the surface—a pristine, virginal sanctuary of authoritarian order, has been violated and sullied by Fernando's masculine presence. (This juxtaposition of Fernando's masculinity with Pura and Angela's femininity was all the more ironically apparent in Portaceli's 1992 *mise en scène*. By casting two male actors in the roles of Pura and Angela, she placed the sisters' gender into question from the beginning, thereby accentuating the crisis of distinctions that emerges from their ambiguous characterizations as sexually repressed virgins/domineering masters of the household.) An uncanny feeling of disorder *impregnates* the air, and a combination of hope and anxiety accompanies the news that Inés is with child. Will the creation of a new life bring an end to the vicious circle of sacrifice, or will it merely serve to perpetuate the system as it stands by adding more fuel to the fire?

Inés receives a blue envelope in each day's mail, arousing suspicion that she may have a love interest. The sisters' excessive concern with Inés's (lost) virginity takes the allegorical form of a ridiculous preoccupation with the trivial issue of whether Fernando has purchased a package containing twenty-five blue envelopes or fifty. The ordinary envelopes are thus transformed into an extraordinarily absurd obsession, a portentous sign that will potentially forecast the date of Fernando's return:

> *Angela*. He must have bought a whole box. (*Pura doesn't reply.*) Yes, I bet that is just what he did: he went to a store and bought a whole box. What I would like to know is was it a box of twenty-five or fifty.
>
> *Pura*. (*A little vexed.*) You'll find out soon enough, in just a few days. If the twenty-sixth letter comes in a different envelope, I'll tell you: "Angela, it was a box of twenty-five."
>
> *Angela*. (*Accusing her for her tone.*) And I'll say: "Thank you very much." I think about things like that, even if they do seem silly to you. Everyone has his own way of measuring love or absence. It might be useful to us for finding out how soon he is coming, or if he is not coming for a while yet.[39]

In a later scene, Inés finally confesses to her aunts the news of her pregnancy, insisting that she has not sinned. Pura and Angela are, predictably, appalled by this revelation but at the same time, Inés's

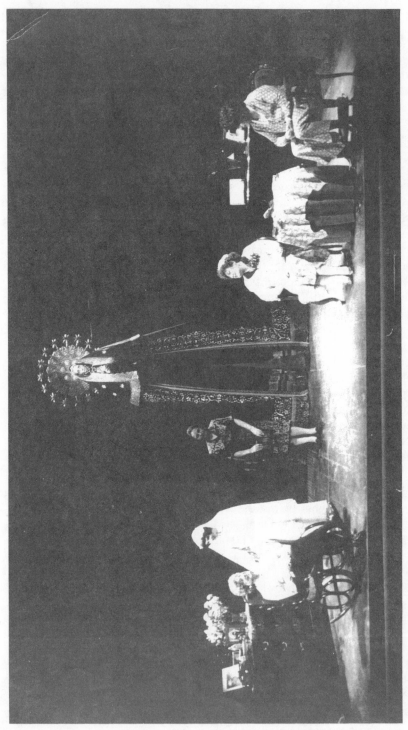

Los gatos. Teatro María Guerrero, Madrid, 1992. Photo: Courtesy of Ana Jelín, Producciones Teatrales Contemporánas, S.L.

confession incites a great deal of curiosity on the part of the virgin sisters. Angela, especially, wishes to hear all the minute details regarding the conception of Inés's child. She would like to sample vicariously a taste of the violence and sexual pleasure that Inés has experienced. Ironically, it is Pura, rather than Inés, who does most of the talking. Both sisters seem to savor the opportunity to discuss sex, in the hope that words will provide them with a semblance of erotic pleasure, of continuity, and of life in general:

Angela. Go on! Where did it happen? I want to hear everything! What did it feel like?

Pura. It felt hot, didn't it? A choking heat . . . that gave you life.

Angela. Hot . . . hot . . . More! You tell it, Pura.

Pura. And . . . the feeling of discovering the mysteries of life.

Inés. Aunt, for God's . . .

Angela. What mysteries? What mysteries?

Pura. Filth, dirt, pleasure, sin, transgression, everything people call the mysteries of life.[40]

For Pura and Angela, the only way to restore tranquil order to their household is through the performance of a sacrificial ritual. They punish Inés for her erotic transgressions and expel violence from their living room by battering her to death with their canes, thereby invoking a repetition of the death of Paloma. Virtue and sin thus converge within the walls of their sacred churchlike space. Once Inés is dead, they dispose of her body by throwing it to the cats. (Seventeen days have passed since their last feeding and the only way to continue their torment is to incite their hopes and desires with some food.) The cats devour Inés's body, and the sensations conjured by the image of the mutilated corpse—a simultaneous rush of anguish and fear, desire and pleasure—coincide with the emotions associated with eroticism. Death in this case has replaced eroticism, and order once again has been restored to this sacred realm. The cats delight in their banquet of human flesh and await their next victim.

In the final scene, Angela ambiguously declares, "It can be for Loli . . . in a couple of years. I don't need to rush to finish it."[41] The message is unsettling and disturbing, for it is unclear whether she is referring to the sweater that she is knitting or to the fact that Loli may indeed become the next sacrificial victim. As in *Diálogos de la herejía*, in this tragic cycle of sacrifice, the frontier between right and wrong is never clearly established and the line separating the saintly from the sinful effortlessly seems to dissolve away. Buenos Aires theater critic Gerardo Fernández indicates in his review of the 1992 production that Alterio and Casares removed their wigs following this final sacrificial episode in a peculiar gesture that heightened this lack of distinctions: " . . . once the sacrificial act is finished, the actors take off their wigs for a few minutes and the creatures appear to vacillate between grotesque and pathetic, more naked and vulnerable than if they weren't covered in rags from head to toe."[42] Through a theatrical process of identification, displacement, and catharsis, Pura and Angela are able to revel cathartically in the continuity that they have achieved through the violent horror of their niece's death. In witnessing the spectacle of the victim's continuity, they able to experience vicariously a sensation of full and limitless being.

The members of the audience also bear witness to this spectacle. As participants in this collective ritual of sacrifice, they too are able to experience a parallel sensation of plenitude, and they are, therefore, left to ponder the disturbing question of whether the characterizations of Pura and Angela merely represent a case of piety and intolerance taken to impossible extremes or if, instead, the sisters' actions are entirely plausible. Los gatos is thus a play in which individuals—Pura, Angela, and perhaps, even the spectator—are projected beyond themselves. It uncovers the nexus between death and sensuality, exposing the spectator to a limitless, interior domain of violent excess, which lies buried at the core of sacred authoritarian order, and at the core of human experience, itself.

II
Allegory and the Absurd

5

Mil y un mesías
(1966)

J'avais l'impression d'être en présence du négatif d'une photo déjà vue. L'angoisse m'a serré la poitrine. N'y aurait-il jamais de véritable changement dans ma vie? Pourquoi devrait-on retrouver partout la copie maladroite d'un éternel original? Ou l'original presque effacé d'une série de copies distribuées sans discrimination à doite et à gauche? Etait-ce une maladie de famille, de la ville, du pays tout entier? A toutes ces questions, jamais je n'ai trouvé de réponse. Mais depuis que je suis tout petit, j'ai conçu la soupçon que le pays, la vie étaient oeuvre d'un photocopieur qui ne tombe jamais en panne.[1]

—*Agustín Gómez-Arcos*, L'agneau carnivore

B Y 1966, the decisive year in which Gómez-Arcos begin his exilic journeys, his theater had already evolved into an art form that was firmly grounded in an anti-Aristotelian aesthetic. Seeds of Brechtian-style alienation had taken root in *Diálogos de la herejía* (Dialogues of heresy), and his predilection for depicting the grotesque underside of reality—in the manner of Luis Buñuel, Ramón del Valle-Inclán, Benito Pérez Galdós, and others—had become readily apparent in *Los gatos* (The cats). During the months preceding his definitive departure from Spain, as he contemplated the possibility of abandoning his homeland in search of artistic freedom, Gómez-Arcos completed two thematically and stylistically similar plays, *Mil y un mesías* (One thousand and one Messiahs) and *Queridos míos, es preciso contaros ciertas cosas* (My dear friends, it's time we get certain things straight). In constructing these theater pieces, he brings the themes of censorship and exile to the fore and appropriates the conventions of still another anticlassical theatrical mode, that of the European theater of the absurd. By adapting these conventions to his dramaturgy, he is able to elaborate his critique of oppression while offsetting

99

the constraints of his situation as a playwright swimming against the tide of artistic censorship.

In these works, the cyclical battle between dialectically opposed notions that is so characteristic of Gómez-Arcos's earlier theater pieces is stripped down to its very essence. It is played out within a minimalist setting in a style reminiscent of the eminently allegorical Spanish baroque *autos sacramentales*, the mystery plays that were originally performed as part of the Corpus Christi festivals in praise of the Eucharist. Gómez-Arcos comments, "In reality, *Queridos míos* is practically an *auto sacramental*. It works in the same manner because it is a philosophical proposal about the imposition of silence and the right to speak out."[2] Like the *autos sacramentales*, *Mil y un mesías* and *Queridos míos* employ the sacred (pre-)text of the Bible as a primary point of departure. In his postmodern variation of these metaphysical mystery plays, however, Gómez-Arcos replaces what was once a religious and often propagandistic intent with a contrarily parodic and sacrilegious undercurrent in order to reveal the absurd underside of the sacred.[3] (A similar type of parodic appropriation of the *auto sacramental* genre also can be found in the theater of Francisco Nieva.)[4] Embedded in the allegorical layers of *Mil y un mesías* is a parodic take on the subject of Messianism, while *Queridos míos* offers an ironic reprise of the story of Jesus Christ. By undermining the representation of traditional religious (Catholic) concepts and consecrated exemplary archetypes, Gómez-Arcos carries out a demystification of this baroque allegorical genre, deriving from it a thematic reversal: an absurd *anti-auto sacramental*.

In 1961, Martin Esslin introduced the term *theater of the absurd* in reference to a set of shared artistic tendencies that he perceived as exemplifying a modern dramatic aesthetic which has stylistic counterparts in other twentieth-century art forms.[5] (Esslin was drawing upon the notion of "absurdity" as employed by Albert Camus in *The Myth of Sisyphus* [1942]). The absurdist temperament, appearing under varying guises in the work of playwrights, such as Samuel Beckett, Jean Genet, Eugène Ionesco, and Harold Pinter, is an aesthetic medium through which these and other dramatists are able to translate to the stage the metaphysical anguish, senselessness, and disharmony that characterize the modern human condition. Stylistically, this attitude of absurdity is expressed as a decisive rupture with all dramatic devices that commonly endeavor to create a rational (i.e., Aristotelian, naturalistic) depiction of reality.[6] Esslin identifies several recurrent tendencies in this theater (or "anti-theater," as Ionesco would have it) that contribute to this rupture with rationalism; notably, a devalued role of spoken language, a diminished importance of the written dramatic text, an abandonment of psychological character development, an irrational dreamlike depiction of time and space, a correspondence between subject matter and form, a rejection of the traditional notion of *plot* (i.e., as a sequence of events with beginning and end), and the employment of allegory and archetypal imagery.

Essentially, the prevailing attitude among critics—including Esslin, Arnold P. Hinchliffe, and Ionesco himself—has been to interpret absurdist allegory as a theatrical device that portrays the abstract metaphysical or psychological dimensions of the human experience. According to this perspective, the theater of the absurd generally is viewed as an apolitical genre of autonomous modernist creations, divorced from any specific reference to the concrete sociohistorical realities of the modern (or, postmodern) world and, as such, commonly regarded as the absolute contrary of the *pièces à thèse* of Brechtian epic theater. Indeed, during the 1950s, the supposedly "uncommitted" nature of absurdist theater roused an ongoing debate between Kenneth Tynan and Ionesco which was played out on the pages of the London *Observer*. Tynan criticized Ionesco's "anti-realist" strategies, while Ionesco defended the merits of absurdist theater, proclaiming his art to be potentially superior to ideology.[7] When confronted with the allegorical images of the absurdist aesthetic, the initial reaction of many spectators and critics, in fact, was to limit interpretation to a level of universally recognizable values and abstract notions. Esslin cites the reception of *Waiting for Godot* as an example: when staged for intellectually sophisticated audiences in Great Britain and the United States, the play was branded with apolitical connotations.[8]

With successive performances and varied audiences, however, it became increasingly apparent that such a play, which translates spiritual and psychological states of being into abstract scenic poetry, could be interpreted as representing multiple planes of reality, from the most abstract to the most concrete. Hence, Warsaw spectators in 1956 viewed *Waiting for Godot* as an allegorical version of their own yearning for freedom from Russian rule.[9] In effect, within the restrictive walls of oppressive governmental structures, the theater of the absurd often emerges as a committed, politically-conscious genre. History has shown that when faced with the artistic confines of an oppressive governmental system and a desire to portray an uncensored vision/version of reality, many twentieth-century playwrights around the globe—such as those living in Francoist Spain, communist eastern Europe, and in the numerous military dictatorships of Latin America—have turned to the theater of the absurd as a common form of dramatic expression. (Czech dramatist Vaclav Havel and Argentinean dramatist Griselda Gambaro are but two examples of this phenomenon.) Over time, they have come to recognize absurdist allegory as a powerful artistic device that enables them to construct a subtly ironic portrayal of concrete sociopolitical conditions without ostensibly referring to politics *per se*. For these playwrights, the theater of the absurd represents a compelling contestatory medium through which they are able to express a critique of cultural imperialism, while at the same time it serves as an effective stylistic tool for frustrating the restrictive gaze of censorship.[10]

Likewise, for Gómez-Arcos, as for many dramatists of post–Civil War Spain, such as Fernando Arrabal, Ángel García Pintado, Jerónimo López Mozo, and Luis Matilla, the theater of the absurd is like a double-edged sword that carries a dual function as a device for confronting the spectator with psychic realities, as well as parallel social realities.[11] *Mil y un mesías* and *Queridos míos* are works that epitomize the way in which these and other playwrights have recast the conventions of the theater of the absurd within a politically committed context in order to depict the hyperbolic absurdity of existence within the limits of a dictatorial system. In this manner, the theater of the absurd itself comes to be an allegory of oppression, an allegory that self-referentially questions and underscores a representational process whereby concrete signifiers are hierarchically subjugated to the tyrannical rule of immaterial signifieds.

In each of these plays, the concept of order is farcically embodied in the esperpentic figure of the governor of a mythical realm. His disproportionate image is strongly reminiscent of another icon of absurd authority, Alfred Jarry's "Père Ubu." While the informed spectator of 1966 presumably would have been exceedingly capable of deciphering the allegorical coding of Gómez-Arcos's plays (i.e., that behind the governor's absurd mask lie the faces of Francisco Franco, Adolph Hitler, Benito Mussolini, etc.), the typically unsophisticated censor of 1966, in theory, may not have been so perceptive. Thus, contrary to the widespread vision of the absurd as an uncommitted, apolitical theatrical mode, Gómez-Arcos's absurdist allegorizing functions as a strategic camouflage allowing him—and his characters—to perform an irreverent critique of political oppression, while simultaneously eluding, or attempting to elude, the censoring authorities of Spanish fascism. (Here, I must emphasize the fact that this was merely an "attempt" on the part of Gómez-Arcos, because, in practice, both of these plays were banned from the stage. However, for a brief moment, it appeared as though he had eluded the censors' gaze when *Queridos míos* won the Lope de Vega Prize.) His appropriation of the absurd engenders a type of "writing between the lines," as described by Michael Holquist, in which "relations between censors and victims appear dynamic and multidirectional."[12] While the censor, in essence, seeks to fixate meaning and suppress ambiguity, Gómez-Arcos's absurdist texts create an indeterminacy that challenges this authoritative endeavor. In their attempt to alienate the censor, ironically, these texts encourage a certain level of complicity between the playwright and the informed spectator. In generating the meaning of the *mise en scène*, it becomes the role of the spectator—be it the year 1966 or 2000, etc.—to choose whether to remain on the absurd mythic level of allegory or to *read between the lines* and contextualize this allegory within the parameters of historical circumstance.[13]

With *Mil y un mesías*, a two-part farce, Gómez-Arcos elaborates a subtle and ironic critique of history that resists specificity with regard to time and place. In this *anti-auto sacramental*, he portrays the timeless notion of the Messiah as an absurd projection of false hopes and desires that are never fulfilled. In so doing, he conveys a portrait of history in which transgression alternates with taboo and freedom with oppression as part of an infinitely endless cycle. From the very first page of the dramatic text of this play, a correspondence between subject matter and form begins to crystallize. The configuration of the scenic space, as specified in the opening didascalia, functions as a metaphoric representation of the Nietzschean notion of eternal return, whereby certain universal characteristics appear forever engraved in the souls of all human beings and in the framework of their societies.[14] In its strategic endeavor to camouflage any sort of precise meaning, *Mil y un mesías* invokes ambivalence through a dissolution of temporality and spatiality. Here, Gómez-Arcos reconfigures the *mise en scène* as an allegorical empty space, an amorphous cyclorama that signifies at once a mythic sort of "every place" and a "no place." The opening stage directions read as follows:

Action: Today, in a nation, city, or village that perhaps does not really exist, but that partakes of the essential characteristics of our world and our civilization. Of course, each director will be able to dress the characters according to the customs and style of whatever period seems appropriate. For example, the Governor could constantly appear in eighteenth-century garb.

Scenery: A large cyclorama, upon which can be projected the appropriate motivations. The greatest possible absence of elements of attrezzo.... [15]

The ruler of this allegorical realm is an Ubuësque personification of plenipotentiary authority, known simply as *el Gobernador* ("the

Governor"). With few exceptions, such as the perpetual presence on stage of his thronelike armchair and the suggestion regarding the possible eighteenth-century style of his dress, this empty space contains a notable lack of determinate signs. Gómez-Arcos indicates that this minimalist cyclorama should possess some of the basic characteristics of "our world and our civilization," but he is not at all clear as to what these characteristics should be. Consequently, the referential nature of scenic elements is completely left open to interpretation by the director and, eventually, the spectator. In effect, the significance of these elements as signs (whatever they may be) is grounded in the fact that they are portrayed as insignificant.

The temporal incongruity evoked by Gómez-Arcos's juxtaposition of "today" and the "eighteenth century" further underscores his endeavor to escape determinacy and avoid localization. As Anne Ubersfeld observes, the configuration of an empty space alters the role of the spectator insofar as it obliges him or her to perceive the scenic universe as an autonomous artifact: "The theatrical space becomes the space of signs, the semiotic space *par excellence;* in the empty space, each sign has a value of its own and each sign speaks; instead of speaking only of a referential universe, it compels the spectator to lend meaning to it to *resemantisize* it."[16] Within an empty space, such as that of *Mil y un mesías*, each sign invokes a meaning that potentially transcends any sort of mimetic reference to a specific reality. It is, therefore, an extremely appropriate setting for the employment of allegory in that it cultivates ambiguity, potentially wavering (in the spectator's eyes) between the sacred signified and the material signifier, along with the apolitical and the political, atemporality and temporality, abstract myth and concrete reality, etc. Paradoxically, and unlike the case of *Los gatos*, the mythic, in this case, corresponds to the visible, while the concrete level of history corresponds to the invisible supplementary level of meaning. The concrete sociohistorical setting infinitely escapes the spectator's view. The empty space is, thus, an indeterminate zone of *différance*, a *tierra de nadie*, rather than a *terra firma*, that allegorically emancipates the *mise en scène* from the authoritative claims of History and the Real. Consequently, the spectator who wishes to contextualize this allegory within the parameters of a concrete (historical) setting must supply the absent meaning by reading between the lines.

The cyclorama that is the scenic space can itself be interpreted as a sign of enclosure—both spatial and psychic—within an eternally oppressive process. The cycloramic architecture of the *mise en scène* appears to envelop the characters of the play within a closed cycle— a situation that calls to mind a series of metaphoric parallels, such as the internal space of psychological repression and the exterior arena of political oppression. Rather than close itself off from the realm of the audience, the cyclorama opens onto the spectators, enclosing them within this space, and collapsing the distinctions between the scenic space (that is, the space occupied by the actors) and the spectator's space.

A key player in this process is the character known as *el Intelectual* ("the Intellectual"), a type of interlocutory go-between who establishes a line of explicit communication with the spectators while also taking part in the dramatic action on stage. Gómez-Arcos's employment of this type of self-conscious dramatic personage, a direct descendant of the chorus of classical Greek theater and the *gracioso* of the Spanish *comedia*, also represents a significant point of correspondence with Brechtian epic theater. (In the theater of twentieth-century Spain, one finds other examples of this device in Antonio Buero Vallejo's *Las meninas* and *El tragaluz*). By addressing the audience directly (*ad spectatores*), the Intellectual ruptures the imaginary screen, or "fourth wall," of theatrical illusion that separates the scenic space from the spectator's space. He ostensibly foregrounds and frames the action on stage. While initially, his direct commentaries to the audience have the effect of alienating or distancing them, the final effect is one that draws them into the fictional world of theatrical representation. His presence bridges the gap between the spectator's realm and the Governor's realm and mediates the allegorical relationship between concrete reality and abstract myth. In effect, the Intellectual modifies the architecture of the theatrical space, implicitly inviting the spectators to relinquish their roles as passive observers so that they may traverse the threshold of illusion and venture into the Governor's mythical realm.[17] In this manner, what was once, for them, a distant "every place" or "no place" is transformed into their "own place." The spectators are, at once, enveloped within the cyclorama and imprisoned within the Governor's system of order, transporting with them their own set of internalized concrete realities. From this interior perspective, they are more inclined to assume an active role within this fictional realm, to superimpose allegorically these concrete realities upon the empty space, or to uncover those realities which are already palimpsestically imbedded in its structure. It is, thus, the task of the spectator to render form from this spatio-temporal formlessness, but it is also a task that is relentlessly thwarted.

The Intellectual's characterization as an allegorical signifier is ostensibly ambiguous. Initially, he appears to be one of the rebellious opponents of the Governor's system: he is the editor of a "very combative and very cheap" magazine, designed to be read by a select minority. However, his subsequent commentaries indicate that, as a matter of convenience, he has decided to accommodate himself within the dominant system: "comfortably settled in the living room of my home with a whisky in hand, . . . it's already another story. . . . Within my house I want tranquillity. (*Confidentially*) I like elegant and perfumed women, and banquets, and public tributes, and colloquia . . . just like you do."[18] Consequently, the Intellectual, who has expectations of someday obtaining a high governmental post, not only collapses the border between the world on stage and the world of the spectator, but also problematizes the distinctions between the order code (portrayed by those signifiers who seek to uphold authority), and the disorder code (embodied by those who work against it).

Like the Intellectual, the other characters in this empty space are identified by generic names that underline their function as allegorical archetypes. The Governor is an emblem of order and absolute power (the "System") who, in terms of allegorical structures, represents the established sacred signified. At one point it is even noted that his name, like that of his father, is Adán ("Adam"), the so-called "father of humanity." Whenever he senses that the pillars of his system may be weakening (and this is usually the case), he calls upon his three Inventors to inject it with new vitality. Inventors 1 and 2 have already formulated many of the fundamental components of the system, such as respect, sacrifice, God, and prayer. According to Inventor 1, prayer helps the citizens of the Governor's realm to forget about foreign influences and their substandard quality of life and settle into an anesthetized state of obedient calm: "It guarantees eight hours of sleep. On Sundays and holidays in which there isn't a trip planned, ten hours of sleep. You get up in time for an aperitif and the midday religious services. It's marvelous. You get to see all your friends there."[19] Inventor 2, in turn, has invented heroes, geniuses, and saints—whose images will be reproduced and immortalized as statues, figurines, and stamps. In this manner, the people of this mythical domain presumably will learn to recognize and imitate these manifestations of sacred order. Inventor 1 has also invented the human conscience, but the Governor rejects this idea for fear that it could be detrimental to his system of blind obedience (especially when it comes to committing atrocities).

In contrast with the first two inventors, Inventor 3 is the dissenter of the trio, an allegorical rendering of transgression, who interrogates the prevailing system (or, sacred text) and consequently infuriates the Governor. At one point, he announces that he, too, has designed an innovative concept, which he calls "investigation." It consists of a disregard for hypocritical appearances and a (hermeneutic) search for truth, a questioning of the prevailing system of order. Since it does not produce any material earnings and it cannot be used as an instrument of oppression, however, the Governor rejects this notion. While the other two inventors are rewarded for their discoveries with extravagant salaries, fancy foreign cars, and luxury apartments, Inventor 3 is sentenced to a meager diet of bread and water, and eventually is imprisoned for his crimes of treason.

The feminine archetypes that inhabit this allegorical realm include Caridad (*Charity*) Jiménez, who from the beginning is placed in a foolish light, when she informs the audience, "At my house they call me Cary, with a "y."[20] She is a member of the *haute bourgeoisie*, who, after passing through a rebellious stage during her youth, eventually marries the Intellectual and assimilates to the dominant system: "Now I'm a conservative Catholic and I have a marvelous mink coat. I feel so protected! In heaven and on earth! . . ."[21] The characterizations of the *Señora* and of Jubilia, whose name refers to the jubilant triumph of the system, are dialectically opposed to that of Teresa la Roja, whose name refers to her left-wing (*red*) politics. Both Teresa and an anonymous woman, know as *"la Pobre"* (the Pauper) occupy marginal positions with respect to the Governor's realm. However, while Teresa maintains a rebellious attitude, the Pauper is literally and figuratively subordinated to the control of the system. She is the *Señora*'s obedient servant and her scapegoat, and she is often depicted kneeling or sitting on the floor beside her mistress, receiving a sparse diet of leftover scraps and crumbs.

As part one begins, the Governor appears on stage, seated in his thronelike armchair. When he claps his hands, the other characters (or allegorical signifiers) immediately obey his command and take their places atop a set of daises, with their faces in plain view of the audience. They are divided into two groups, distinguished by the masks they wear at determined moments. The members of one group (including Inventor 3, Teresa la Roja, and the Pauper) wear masks of joy, while the members of other group (composed of Inventors 1 and 2, Jubilia, and the *Señora*) wear masks of sadness. After the Intellectual makes his entrance, he explains to the spectators that they (that is, the people on stage as well as the audience) have all gathered to bid farewell to Lucio, a societal outcast who is about to depart from this mythical land, on the road to exile: "(*Very nice, very public relations*) Ladies and gentlemen, we have gathered here today to bid farewell. Lucio is leaving. Lucio is about to abandon us. Our dear Lucio, innate rebel, hope and desperation of society, product of a civilization on the rise and in crisis, is leaving us today . . . possibly forever. A sorrow. A joy. Behold the faces of our people! Joy and sorrow!"[22]

The masks that the characters wear have the effect of fragmenting their heads from the rest of their bodies, as well as establishing and emphasizing their fixed emotional states. With their clearly defined facial expressions, they potentially discourage the audience from speculating with respect to any variance of emotion.[23] However, embedded in the Intellectual's nonsensical double-talk is a bizarre paradox that surfaces when he warns the audience to beware in interpreting these facial expressions. Since the invention of hypocrisy, he explains, "sorrow and joy are no longer sorrow and joy." In this topsy-turvy *esperpentic* world, appearances can be deceiving, and the truth is often masked by a misleading disguise.

In addition, the Intellectual points to Lucio and describes his position as he is about to cross the border into exile: "In front of him, us; to his back, the border. In his own words, imprisonment and freedom."[24] Here, on an allegorical plane, Gómez-Arcos paints a figurative depiction of Michel Foucault's conception of the "limit" as the unstable boundary that runs between taboo and transgression. In *Mil y un mesías*, the border is the limit that runs between a territory imprisoned by order (*nosotros / la cárcel*) and a forbidden land of exile and freedom (*la frontera / la libertad*). Lucio stands in contemplation of this limit, in the region of anguish and pleasure that lies between taboo and transgression. Once he crosses the boundary into exile, he becomes the embodiment of transgression unleashed. He is transformed into a solitary, ambiguous being, no longer restrained by ideological grid-lines, an individual who has had the courage to rebel against the system. He comments, "A lone individual does not fear the truth, because the truth lies in thought, and a lone individual thinks without fear. (*To the others*) That is why, you are all afraid of the lone individual, because he is willing to risk his life for an idea, for a question of faith."[25] For him, thinking represents a form of transgression in that it is a continual interrogation of the limit. It is the search for the truth that lies behind false pretenses. By interrogating this limit, Lucio is able to defy the world of order and reason, and cross the threshold into a universe of excess, free of denial. His speech invokes a contrast between the oppressive, claustrophobic air of his homeland, and the fresh air of freedom on the other side of the border. Enclosure is compared to expanse: "One can go off with one's own body and thoughts, one's gasps from suffocation, one's insane desire to breathe a different air—that marvelous air of the border—, one can go off with one's rebellions that are known here as leprosy, cancer, dreams, courage . . ."[26] He also predicts that one day he will return, thus suggesting the notion of an endless spiral. His prophecy is evocative of the Messianic return of Jesus Christ: "Brothers and sisters, I will return accompanied by my truth that is now humbled. A truth that will be powerful. It will be dressed in gold. I will make it of the Jewish race . . . , clever, gentle, reasonable. I will become God! Why not . . . another god? And my truth will be invited to all the cocktails, it will receive all the public tributes, it will be the most venerated saint and the most highly paid prostitute. . ."[27]

Were this a strictly codified scholastic allegory, Lucio's exile would conceivably represent joy for the people of the order code and sadness for the people of the disorder code. Here, however, in this postmodernist allegory, the emblems of order wear hypocritical masks of sadness as they rejoice over Lucio's departure, and the dissidents, who presumably do not want to see him leave, wear hypocritical grins of joy. In other words, the allegorical signifiers do not obey the authority of the sacred text; instead, they undermine it. Their roles paradoxically have been exchanged. At this early moment in the play, the spectator, of course, would not yet be completely aware of this reversal of identities; however, the Intellectual's opening commentary, which recalls the strategies of Brechtian alienation, is designed to condition the spectator's gaze and defamiliarize his or her perceptions and judgments with regard to the metaphors that are projected on stage. As the Benjaminian precept states, in allegory, "Any person, any object, any relationship can mean absolutely anything else"; hence, Lucio, who's name signifies lucidity and truth may not be so lucid and truthful after all.[28]

As the stage becomes imbued with hypocrisy, the transcendental text that governs the allegorical archetypes is placed into question; meaning begins to slide, and the sacred ground of the Governor's realm begins to quiver and shift. He senses that an unnamable danger ("a certain *no sé qué*") is brewing within the proletariat sector of his domain. It threatens to bring down the walls of his carefully constructed house, and he is in desperate need of some new universal concepts to reinforce the established order. Gómez-Arcos forges the Governor's absurd discourse through a parodic appropriation of the allegorical rhetoric that typically characterizes the speeches of political leaders: "A slight uneasiness, a small boil—unspecified—in the divine order of my command, is beginning to emerge in the form of that detestable thing that you invented (*Points to Inventor 3*): rebellion. . . . In my nightmares there is a building that is suddenly collapsing, the result of a flaw in its foundation. And it gets to me inside. It's dreadful. The building looks like my house."[29]

At the end of part one, there is a slight pause in the main line of action. The Intellectual takes the stage, and assuming the demeanor of a music hall announcer, informs the spectators that the author is concerned that they may be growing tired, and has, therefore, decided to offer them an entertaining interlude. The Intellectual then introduces a short metatheatrical *entremés* entitled "El té de las señoras" ("The Ladies' Tea") which, as he enigmatically proclaims, "Has nothing and everything to do with this story."[30] Despite the apparent contradictions in his absurd prologue, the Intellectual's paradoxical statement calls attention to the tea scene; it invites the spectator—almost dares the spectator—to search for a semblance of relevance beneath the façade of absurd incoherence. During this dramatic interlude, Teresa, Jubilia, and the other women indulge in not only tea; but also, sherry, whisky, cigarettes, caviar, and small talk. At intermittent moments, they stop what they are doing and break into song, presenting a total of three musical numbers. Each of these songs is a cleverly devised miniature allegory, in which a subtle critique of oppressive order is shrouded in a seemingly innocent, childlike discourse apropos of nursery rhymes and animal fables. Each song also is accompanied by a short aphorism, which in the case of the following example, is recited by the Pauper:

Señora, Teresa, Jubilia. (Singing)	A dove flew away from its nest
Pauper. (With the chorus)	Pabú, Pabú, pabú, pabú.
Señora, Teresa, Jubilia. (Singing)	A delightful dove shapely. God, what a horror, did not return to the nest
Pauper. (With the chorus)	Pabú, Pabú, pabú, pabú.

(*Speaking*) Moral: behold the ease with which the pure bird loses her honesty.[31]

The moral of the story helps to render meaning from the absurd lyrics that precede it. Behind this Lewiscarrollian linguistic nonsense lies an unexpected denunciatory attitude. The image of the pure dove who flees the nest and loses its purity (i.e., its virginity) is a strategic, yet subtle, allusion to the hypocrisy of the Governor's realm, with the dove representing the sacred system whose integrity is in decline.

While the women take tea, Teresa la Roja makes several allusions to war and rebellion. With her commentaries, Gómez-Arcos employs the allegorical strategy of accumulation—an excessive piling up of signifiers—in order to camouflage his critical discourse and evade semantic exclusivity.[32] Teresa obscures the boundaries of past, present, and future by listing an absurd and all-inclusive inventory of the wars that she has waged: "All of them! That of thirty years, that of one hundred years, that of three years, that of fourteen, that of fifteen, that of sixteen, and the one that only lasted six days, because of I-don't-know-who's illness, I-don't-remember where."[33] Jubilia correspondingly replies that if Teresa has waged all the wars, then she, in turn, has waged all the postwars. As a result of this monotonous listing of battle upon battle, time becomes eradicated within this ambiguous space, and Teresa and Jubilia, as well as the other characters in the play, are converted into self-conscious allegorical images that, at once, *offer* and *defer* a precise meaning. Teresa represents not just one *specific* rebel; she is the embodiment of *all* rebels throughout the circular cyclorama of history. Likewise, Jubilia is the embodiment of *all* prevailing orders—including, but not limited to that of post–Civil War Spain.

A parallel instance of this strategy occurs during the tea episode when Caridad voices her future plan to give birth to three sons. (She is now married to the Intellectual following an initial love affair with Lucio):

My sons will be normal. Like their father. Like me. None will be a diplomat, none will join the military, none will be a playboy, none will be a priest, none will be gay, none a special envoy, none a dancer, none clever, none a philanthropist, none a dreamer. My sons will be as God wills them to be. Each will have his business, his office, his telephone, his wife, his car, his house in the suburbs, his lover. His bar where he is a regular, his Saturday blowouts, his Sundays and his days of obligation. . . .[34]

Caridad's children will, supposedly, incarnate her hope for a continuous repetition of the oppressive *status quo*. She, like the other citizens, maintains the expectation that Lucio will one day return to their realm as the personification of a new, radical order, and she predicts that when he does, her sons will obey her command to assassinate him.

Later, Caridad's resolution backfires when her three sons appear on stage as a trio of beatniks with electric guitars. Beneath the glow of a bright spotlight, they sing an antiwar rhapsody that recalls the iconoclastic attitudes of the 1960s—indeed, they seem to be an absurd parody of the Beatles. More significantly, the beatniks are signifiers of true anarchy that seek to overthrow the established structures of oppression and representation. Their refusal to conform to the norms of bourgeois society is also a refusal to acknowledge the presence of any previously written text (i.e., the preconceived ideas that their mother has laid out for them, as well as the cyclorama of history).[35] They do not embody a new ideological system; rather, they are an indeterminate antisystem. As cultural icons of the 1960s and as the first and only concrete reference to the era in which *Mil y un mesías* was written, the beatniks also represent a sudden and ironic clash with the previously established atemporality of the play. Consequently, they serve as a subtle reminder of the analogy that exists between the realm of the Governor and the realm of the spectator. Although Caridad's scheme may have yielded calamitous results (at least, according to her point of view) in that her sons do not coincide with her concept of normalcy, her forecast with regard to Lucio's return proves to be rather accurate.

In part two, the Governor gathers his people together in a propagandistic atmosphere of grandeur and applause. Standing before them, he delivers a political speech that is clogged with rhetoric: "*He will speak in what he considers to be an exquisite tone, lace handkerchief and snuff, eighteenth-century-type inflection, a little parlor speech, in such a way that the vulgarities that he pronounces will be all the more evident.*"[36] He announces that he and his inventors are finally ready to unveil a new breakthrough, which he will offer as a Christmas present to his people. It is designed to lift all hopes and spirits and reinforce the pillars of his decaying order. The new invention is the concept of Messianism. He declares (in what seems an ironic reference to *Waiting for Godot:*): "The Messiah is something that you wait, wait, and wait for . . . and it never comes. But someday it will come. Isn't that nice?"[37] Finally, amid several "ooh's" and "aah's," Lucio appears on stage as the incarnation of the new savior in a parodic rendition of the Second Coming. (Godot has ironically materialized.) The people rejoice, and the Governor decides to take a long-awaited *siesta.* He is extremely delighted with this situation because, having satisfied the hopes of his countrymen, he can finally catch up on his sleep and take a reprieve from his official duties. He relinquishes full charge of his realm to Lucio, advising him to take advantage of the people as much as possible. The Messiah is thus portrayed as an absurd human invention in a devaluative gesture that secularizes and renders provisional an eternal idea. Benjamin points out that the story of the life of Christ already supports "the movement from history to nature which is the basis of allegory," for in it, one can perceive a tension between mortality and immortality, immanence and transcendence.[38] Gómez-Arcos, nevertheless, has taken this process of degradation one step further by representing the Messiah as an instrument of political oppression and subordination.

Having been exposed to alternative ideologies during his exile to a foreign land, Lucio has imported a new order, and with it, he assumes the Governor's role as supreme representative of dictatorial authority: "Damn those established orders! Now we're in a new order, mine!"[39] On the occasion of Lucio's first speech to his people, the stage is decorated with flags and wreaths heralding his arrival. At strategic moments—whenever the Intellectual gives the signal—an audio soundtrack imbues the theater with the reverberating sounds of applause and cheers. The Intellectual's metatheatrical signaling establishes a certain complicity between him and the audience, jarring them into a *prise de conscience* with respect to the irony of the situation depicted on stage: that is, that the enthusiasm for Lucio is a mere spectacle, a fictional fabrication designed to create an illusion of grandiose pomp and circumstance. The rhetorical style of his speech is, in effect, just as absurd as the discourse of the Governor: "I beg of you to work with me in this common endeavor to save the nation, blá, blá, blá, blá, to invent progress. . . ."[40] There is even a point during the speech at which Lucio stops talking, but continues to gesticulate and "lip sinc," while the soundtrack replaces his words with a continuous series of *"blá, blá, blá, blá blá's."*[41] The substitution of his words with these nonsensical sounds is a gesture that betrays the signifying function of Lucio's authoritative discourse: his absolute *Logos*. It devalues and undermines the role of his spoken language, foregrounding the notion that, despite a façade of justice and revolution, his political structure—which resembles communism—has failed to exert an authoritative hold. It is merely another variation on the theme of oppressive order, and it is, therefore, expeditiously rejected by the proletariat.

Both Lucio and Inventor 3 are incarcerated for their crimes against the Governor's system, and eventually, they encounter each other as cell mates. The stage is inundated with grillwork, signifying their imprisonment. When their ideologies are juxtaposed, it is revealed that Inventor 3, rather that Lucio, is the true image of anarchy and disorder. In contrast, Lucio, the Messianic personification of hope, has offered nothing new to the people. As Inventor 3 explains:

> You began by sowing seeds of hope. But you have done nothing but continue the eternal game of classes, of religions, of politics. You have not invented anything new. "Wait for me! I will return! What stupidity. You liked the beautiful heroic image of yourself crying, "Wait for me!" And

the faces of the others were your mirror. Nevertheless, you're just a lousy criminal like so many others.[42]

In the final scene, the Intellectual discloses the news that Lucio, their Messiah, will be assassinated by firing squad in a "ritual of death" for his crimes against the state. Inventor 3, however, will be permitted to live (though imprisoned within the walls of the system). His life is spared since taboo (the Governor) cannot continue to exist without the presence of transgression. Additionally, Inventor 3 is given the honor of firing the first shot against Lucio. The firing squad, composed of the remaining cast members, completes the process in a scene that calls to mind the sacrifice of the original Messiah, Jesus Christ. By annihilating the savior of this allegorical realm, a gesture which "expulses God from the stage,"[43] the citizens—or material signifiers—carry out an analogous destruction of allegory's sacred text. They defy the sovereignty of the system that Lucio has attempted to impose upon their lives, and in so doing, they correspondingly mitigate the power that the abstract holds over the concrete. On the level of allegory, Lucio does not represent just one Messiah; he is the incarnation of all Messiahs—one thousand and one Messiahs, as the title would have it. Coinciding with the Benjaminian conception of the ruin, sacred history—the story of the Messiah—collapses upon the allegorical landscape in a process that incessantly duplicates itself. As Benjamin states, "Everything about history that, from the very beginning, has been untimely, sorrowful, unsuccessful, is expressed in a face—or rather in a death's head."[44] What was once part of a heavenly realm—the saintly, the heroic—becomes part of a stockpile of fragments within the cosmos of the profane.

Lucio's death does not yield a sense of closure; on the contrary, it simply paves the way for a succession of new Messiahs and new systems of oppression. For in this space, history is portrayed as a never-ending cycle of eternal return: an absurd cyclorama of repetition, which functions as a metaphor for the claustrophobic experience of enclosure within an oppressive system. Indeed, upon entering this empty space, any spectator may suddenly recognize it as his or her own.

6

Queridos míos, es preciso contaros
ciertas cosas (1966 / 1994)

Cette longue confession, s'étalant sur l'histoire de l'espèce, est faite
de bribes de mémoire, de cris de Cassandre, de témoinages de vic-
times, qui, toutes, signent du nom de Prométhée, ravisseur du feu
de la vie, escroc pour ses semblables mais vaincu lui-méme. Les
dieux, dictateurs tranquilles du massacre, n'y apparaissent pas,
bien qu'ils soient impitoyablement jugés par tant de détresse et
d'oubli, par le gaspillage constant d'un royaume de lumière. Et
par les ténèbres finales, ce gouffre où le monde s'est enfoncé après
le catastrophe.[1]

—Agustín Gómez-Arcos, Pré-papa ou Roman de fées

QUERIDOS *míos, es preciso contaros ciertas cosas* (My dear friends,
it's time we get certain things straight) represents Gómez-Arcos's
final theatrical endeavor before his definitive flight into exile. The title
is a reference to the utopian quest for the truth that underpins this
play, in which each character attempts to offer his or her own version
of reality or history. *Queridos míos* demonstrates how, throughout
the centuries, regardless of time or place, the dominant order has
been consistently prone to serving up a contrived version of the truth
as a means of empowering and disguising its own totalizing discourse. With this play, Gómez-Arcos continues the process initiated
with *Mil y un mesías* (One thousand and one Messiahs), in which he
recasts the conventions of the theater of the absurd within a political
and ideological context. His absurdist allegorizing functions as an
analogizing device, which engages in a simultaneous deconstruction
of both abstract systems of semiotic oppression and concrete systems
of political oppression—or, for that matter, religious, sexual, or linguistic oppression.

In the case of *Queridos míos*, these theatrical strategies were put
to the test in a most ironic series of events. In 1966, Gómez-Arcos
garnered yet another Lope de Vega Prize for this absurdist drama. It

was an honor that represented a somewhat unexpected occurrence, for during this period, government-sponsored prizes such as this one were not regularly accorded to theatrical works that were critical of the Franco regime.[2] *Queridos míos* is saturated with anti-Fascist undertones, yet curiously it seemed, at least at first, to have evaded the wrath of the censors. However, the censoring authorities engineered a rather insidious plan in order to impede the play from being staged at one of Madrid's "official" state-run theaters. They declared the first prize *desierto* ("void") and thereby made Gómez-Arcos a *de facto* "second place" winner, a condition that entailed forfeiture of the government-subventioned production that customarily would have accompanied the award. Having already witnessed four years earlier the annulment of his first Lope de Vega for *Diálogos de la herejía*, he decided to convert the winnings from his second prize into a window of opportunity that would lead both literally and figuratively to his "flight" into exile. He used the prize money to purchase a plane ticket to London, and *Queridos míos* thus became his ticket out of Spain.[3]

Nearly thirty years later, on the evening of 7 December 1994, in what seemed an almost miraculous occurrence, Gómez-Arcos finally witnessed the long overdue première of *Queridos míos* at the Teatro María Guerrero (Centro Dramático Nacional). Carme Portaceli, who had already staged *Interview de Mrs. Muerta Smith por sus fantasmas* and *Los gatos*, was responsible for the direction of this production, which ran until 22 February 1994. The première was attended by several prominent figures from the Spanish theater world, such as Antonio Buero Vallejo, Francisco Nieva, and Moisés Pérez Coterillo.[4] Also in attendance were several well-known representatives of the then dominant (albeit, gravely injured) socialist party (PSOE). Their presence was a testament to the political significance of this long-awaited event, for the staging of this play, in effect, represented a form of vindication for Gómez-Arcos and his rebellion against fascism and censorship. Enrique Centeno of *Diario 16* describes the impossibility of staging Gómez-Arcos's works in 1966 and laments the limitations of the Spanish stage under Franco, which prevented spectators from seeing this play during the period in which it was written:

> Impossible to think that Gómez-Arcos might have imagined in 1966 that he would be able to stage this play, even though he may have won the Lope de Vega Prize. The censorship of the then young Fraga Iribarne was capable, from his Ministry of Information and Tourism, of prohibiting things that were much less offensive. The commentary is necessary because once more it demonstrates that lost time is irreparable, and that the condemnation of progress witnessed on our stage, headed up by the

above-cited personage and other equally sinister characters, incites as much rage today as it did during the period of repression.[5]

The 1994 production of *Queridos míos* featured a first-rate cast that included award-winning actress Rosa Novell as the Duchess, along with Manuel de Blas, Antonio Duque, and Alicia Hermida. These latter three had appeared in earlier productions of Gómez-Arcos's plays. The set design and costumes were conceived by the talented team of Montse Amenós and Isidre Prunés, the same designers who had worked on *Interview de Mrs. Muerta Smith* and *Los gatos. Queridos míos* was well-received by spectators and critics. Javier Villán of *El Mundo* declared, "It is a mixture of humor and drama, of innocence, of astonishment."[6] A few critics, nevertheless, complained about what they perceived to be a somewhat excessive rhetorical discourse imbedded the dialogue. Centeno notes, "Although excessively prolix, Gómez-Arcos's prose is extremely beautiful, seething with reflections that he spits forth—inexhaustibly, undoubtedly more so than the audience, upon whom it begins to take its toll—, but furthermore, as I have already pointed out, he takes a chance on a very risky, new—at least, back then—dramatic construction that in this production has been achieved with great care."[7]

In this play, as in *Mil y un mesías*, the configuration of the scenic space metaphorically invokes the notion of eternal return while evading specificity of time and place. But, whereas in his earlier piece, the scenic space rebels against semiotic determinacy through the use of an empty space, with *Queridos míos*, Gómez-Arcos presents an alternative solution to the challenge posed by the dominant discourse of censorship—a discourse that is grounded in the idea of univocal signification. Gómez-Arcos calls for the construction of an allegorical theatrical realm whose concrete spatiotemporal dimensions are infinitely and instantaneously alterable and indeterminate. The scenic space is thus conceived as a perpetually oscillating zone of deferral: "*The set is a special circuit which may either be or be converted into anything; palace, prison, public square, street, the countryside, or any of the five divisions of the world, or any nation, city, or home whatsoever.*"[8] A total of thirteen scenes are performed within this convertible setting in one full sweep, without interruption.[9] As the plot progresses, the scenic space seamlessly transforms itself into several historical contexts, transgressing the limits of linear or rational chronology (i.e., a seventeenth-century Spanish colony, the nineteenth century, the Middle Ages, 1966, Nazi Germany, etc.).

The characters appear indifferent to these successive transfigurations and reconfigurations. They emerge and reemerge, scene after scene, within the different periods and places as reincarnations (and *pre*incarnations) of their former selves with only occasional self-conscious reference to the (meta)theatricality of this situation (such as when the Barker remarks, "Now it's the antechamber. Last night it was the garage. Next it might be the throne room. Do you understand?").[10] Gómez-Arcos's stage directions suggest that the scenery be kept to a minimum within this dreamlike domain. As an alternative to an elaborate set design, the surrounding historical contexts are signified primarily through the presence of music and through the use of meticulously detailed costumes: "*The characters will appear meticulously dressed, carefully bejeweled, styled, and coifed, in such a way that their mere presence indicates beyond a shadow of a doubt the chronological era which they are living at each moment of their presence on the stage.*"[11]

Portaceli's *mise en scène* was largely faithful to the text. The actors were dressed in elaborate and ornamental (seemingly baroque) costumes that appeared to intermingle styles from the past and present day. The scenery was kept to a minimum. During the first half of the play, a curtain containing red and yellow horizontal stripes, reminiscent of the Spanish flag, could be seen along the back perimeter of the stage as a subtle indicator that appeared to envelop the action within the context of Spain's history. (A similar element of design was used in the 1992 production of *Los gatos*.) However, in her program notes, Portaceli comments on the sense of universality and ubiquity that she perceives in Gómez-Arcos's plot: "Always, in every century, throughout history, in all countries and cultures, there has been an ideology identified with a ruling social class whose members have considered power to be something that corresponds to them by birthright. To manipulate according to their own whims, laws, concepts, discourses, with the impunity typical of those who believe that they are entitled to something without having to earn it."

In *Queridos míos*, the semiotic function of concrete scenic signifiers is propelled into a state of flux and perpetual instability—as in the ongoing alternation invoked in *Diálogos de la herejía* between sixteenth- and twentieth-century Spain. In this absurdist allegory, there is a successive, almost obsessive, accumulation of time periods and locations, a seemingly arbitrary and indeterminate piling up of one signifier on top of another. This strategy of accumulation is, for Benjamin as it is for Owens, one of the principle tendencies of the "allegorical impulse."[12] Here, it functions as paratactic device enabling the allegory to *underline* and at the same time to *evade* specificity of time and place. While each particular scenic context (i.e., Nazi Germany, Francoist Spain) carries for the spectator its own meaningful relevance, when all is said and done, these sites lack permanence; they point to transient moments in time that are tied to concrete circumstance. What is perhaps of greater consequence for the spectator, then, are the additional implications of this strategy of accumulation: that the actions witnessed on stage have occurred, are occurring, and will occur within all contexts—scenic and otherwise. Through successive layerings, metamorphoses, and modifications, the collection of spatiotemporal indicators are emptied of their individual significance as signifiers of the particular. The transformative setting, as a result, points to an ambiguous "everywhere" signifying the combination of past, present, and future. It underscores the gap that characteristically exists in allegory between the eternal and the ephemeral by attempting to rescue for eternity that which is transient and by simultaneously revealing both the particular and the universal. Consequently, the specificity of the setting begins to take on a diminished importance, for although the concrete locations and historical periods continually vary from scene to scene, the story to which they incessantly refer stubbornly seems to resist change. In this manner, Gómez-Arcos's dynamic scenic space invokes a sensation of timelessness, of a never-ending "process" and a "closed cycle" (to translate the playwright's words) in which history seems forever condemned to repeat itself.[13]

To create the illusion of a seemingly automatic scenic metamorphosis, Gómez-Arcos proposes the employment of a set of anonymous "servants" or "retinue" (*criados y comparsas*) who seem to surge out of nowhere at specified moments. While their presence is never visibly acknowledged by the actors/characters on stage, they remain, however, within conspicuous view of the spectator.

> *Servants and retinue, at designated moments, will make available to the players the little equipment that these need to act out their roles, as if the equipment appeared out of nowhere the very instant at which it is mentioned. This will give the impression of an action that is parallel to and independent of the text, yet serving the text. The players will neither see nor speak directly to the servants on stage, in spite of the fact that the servants' bearing ought to be, at all times, natural and realistic.*[14]

Instead of employing traditional stagehands who furtively do their work between scenes or in the wings, Gómez-Arcos seems to turn the *mise en scène* inside out and transgress its limits by bringing these behind-the-scenes workers into plain view of the audience and converting them into signifiers within the scenic space. His employment of overt stagehands (which, in practice, was not used by Portaceli) parallels a similar dramatic device found in the Japanese Nōh theater. As the stage directions imply, their actions and gestures impart a parallel nonverbal subtext in relation to the primary action on stage, thereby delineating yet another dimension of this multilayered allegory. In addition, they inject the *mise en scène* with an aura of fantasy and absurd illusion in that when a character mentions aloud a certain object that is to serve as a prop (such as a cocktail glass) the stagehand, immediately on cue, causes the object to materialize. In this manner, verbal signifiers are instantly transformed into their corresponding concrete representations just as quickly as they are enunciated.

The first scene is situated on the public plaza of a seventeenth-century Spanish colony, where the supreme figures of sociocultural authority emerge as a collection of absurd incarnations that includes the Governor, the Governor's Wife, the Captain, and a pompous Duchess. The play commences with the arrival of a sideshow tumbrel that immediately infuses the stage with an air of the carnivalesque. Portaceli's *mise en scène* contained several additions that underscored this Felliniësque atmosphere. The set contained a long catwalk that spanned the entire length of the space occupied by the audience and divided this space in half. The actors made their stage entrances by traversing this catwalk. In this manner, the catwalk served as a point of rupture with the famous "fourth-wall" of naturalist theater, intermingling dramatic characters and audience within the same space and enabling the spectators to establish physical and psychological linkages with the characters (as a function of their proximity) that would not have been possible in a more conventional *mise en scène*. During the opening scene (as well as the final scene), organ music was piped through the theater—the type of music that one would associate with carnivals and festivals. The frontal curtain (in reality a large, somewhat dilapidated and dingy-looking mirror, also reminiscent of carnivalesque celebrations) remained in a lowered position, and the action was played out on the catwalk and in the area of the forestage. The spectators were able to see themselves and others reflected in this mirror (perhaps an ironic reference to Valle-Inclán's *esperpentos*), and as they stared at the characters along the catwalk, their gaze was also forced beyond these fictional beings to the eyes of the other spectators. All of these strategies of immersion, implemented by Portaceli, Amenós, and Prunés, had the effect of infusing the theater with a circuslike atmosphere, drawing the spectators attention to the spectacularity and theatricality of what they were witnessing and making them a part of this realm of fabricated façades and contrived appearances where the truth is continually placed into question.

The tumbrel, according to Gómez-Arcos's text, is pushed toward stage center. It is accompanied by a raucous barker (*el Feriante*) with Casandra, his main attraction, in tow. Their physical demeanor, as well as their verbal discourse, suggest the presence within the theatrical space of a set of hierarchical boundaries delineating the high and the low, the exalted and the base. They are newcomers to this realm, and they are clad in a slovenly sort of garb that clashes with the more aristocratic, ostentatious attire of the Governor and his counterparts. The Barker, a rather coarse, unrefined individual, expresses himself in a crude, pedestrian manner, while the Duchess employs a more lofty, contrived sort of discourse. The lower regions, occupied by the Barker and Casandra, signify the domain of the carnivalesque, a ritual suspension of the sacred order which later on will serve to deconstruct the established hierarchical boundaries.[15]

In his opening speech, the Barker, addressing the audience as well as the characters on stage, urges passersby to witness the forecasts and divinations of Casandra, a psychic visionary who knows all and who always speaks the truth.[16] His speech serves as an invocation and an invitation to the audience to play a role within the fictional realm of the spectacle.

> (*Shouting*) Ladies and gentlemen, saints and sinners, sons of Spain and the Spanish Indies, Christians, in a word, here you have Cassandra's cart. Cassandra, the sibyl, reader of hands and cards, reader of the heart, teller of fortunes and foreteller of fate, of tempest and plague, of gold and coppers . . . because not everybody was born to possess gold. Come near! Step right up! For a few pennies I shall open up the innermost being of this wise creature; I shall lift the clouds from her thoughts and make her word brighten your future. . . .[17]

Also imbedded in the Barker's discourse is a warning to the spectator to proceed with caution when venturing into this mythical realm and to be attentive to certain asymmetries and inequities that may inherently exist in the established sociocultural hierarchy: "The difficult thing is to recognize Injustice, to know what are its various camouflages, under what masks of order or disorder, peace or revolution, it disguises itself. That is why, my dear friends, it's time we get certain things straight. . . ."[18] His employment of the Spanish "personal/accusative 'a'" with the word *injustice* ("a la injusticia") calls attention to his presence within an allegorical realm where personification functions as a principal rhetorical strategy. Within this theatrical space, several versions of the truth will be placed on display for all to behold. Injustice, for example, may assume several disguises. The task put forth for the spectator, therefore, is that of a hermeneutic quest for the truth, a search for the elusive transcendental signified that may never be fully disclosed as it lurks behind an infinite assortment of masks and veils.

As the Barker continues his speech, he recounts the first of several allegorical parables that are intercalated within the wider allegorical frame of the play. These brief tales are evocative, in an absurd way, of the biblical parables of Christ. With the help of the those on stage who function as his chorus, the Barker offers a dramatic rendition of the story of Fray Jacinto, the presumed hero and benefactor of this realm. During an earlier period in history of severe drought, hunger, plague, and hardship, Fray Jacinto invoked his mystical powers and prayed for rain. A destructive deluge followed, which endured fifteen days and nights and obliterated ninety percent of the civil population. While the flood—a parodic reference to the original biblical *diluvium*—was extremely detrimental to the proletariat sector of society, the Duchess and her cohorts view it as having remedied all previous burdens of excess population. According to her "official" (and absurd) version of the truth, their (sacred) domain has never again been plagued by hunger: "We produce just the amount that we eat. Of course, unfortunately, we are unable to carry on any export trade. But since it is the will of God, we are resigned to this."[19] Nevertheless, from the point of view of the spectator, the statue erected in honor of Fray Jacinto, signified on stage through the projection of his immense silhouette, comes hazily into focus as an emblematic expression of the ambivalent sacred, a testament to a duplicitous system of masquerade whereby what appears to be a remedy (for the Duchess) is also a poison (for the proletariat). The monument to Fray Jacinto is thus an allegorical portrayal of Derrida's ambivalent *pharmakon* ("remedy/poison"), as well as the equally ambivalent *pharmakeus* ("sorcerer/magician/poisoner"), a place where opposites converge "(soul/body, good/evil, inside/outside, memory/forgetfulness, speech/writing, etc.)."[20]

Casandra's powers of incantation also define her role within this allegorical scheme as that of a *pharmakeus*. She signifies the ambiguous intersection of the sacred and the profane, a locus and play of *différance*, which simultaneously reinforces and subverts the hierarchical oppositions that are designated by the Platonic way of seeing; that is, the cultural dichotomies that are intrinsic to the Governor's hegemonic order. Through the art of divination, as the Barker infers, Casandra will play a revelatory role in this scheme, disclosing "certain things" that lie beneath the exterior façade of the Governor's realm. As the Barker puts it, "That is why I have brought you Cassandra, the sibyl. So you won't make such mistakes. For less than you would give a beggar, she will tell you which is the best herb for curing your rheumatism, with which snakeskin you will conquer your loved one, with which organ of which deadly animal you will ward off Injustice!"[21] However, it is unclear whether the sacred words of this unkempt sorceress will serve as remedies or poisons. Her name, derived from classical mythology, is an allegorical allusion to prophesy and revelation, but here, the allusion is likewise an ominous and ambiguous one. The Cassandra of ancient myth, having resisted Apollo's love, witnessed as punishment a systematic rejection of her truths when he extinguished the prophetic abilities that he had once bestowed upon her. Cassandra's rejection—in effect, the censorship of her words—eventually culminated in her sacrifice (decapitation) at the request of Clythemnestra.

Like the *alumbrados* of *Diálogos de la herejía* (Dialogues of heresy), Casandra and the Barker are outsiders who have arrived from a strange, unknown land situated beyond the limits of the Governor's territory. They are bearers of new, foreign ideas and "poisons" (communism, for instance), and their arrival threatens to open windows of change into the minds and souls of the people of this realm. The Duchess describes Casandra to her friends, who are repelled by her ambiguous image:

> *Duchess.* A sort of palmist, or witch, or student, or Jewess, or Negress, or devotee of contradiction . . .
>
> *All.* God, how horrible!
>
> *Duchess.* . . . who travels the paths of the kingdom, roams the city streets, wanders through cafés, night clubs, racetracks, football fields, calling black white and white black . . .
>
> *All.* God, how horrible!
>
> *Duchess.* . . . hacking to bits the meager mind of the people with language unbefitting to our civilization: souls like swamps, hearts like swamps, swampy minds . . .
>
> *All.* God, how horrible!
>
> *Duchess.* Horrible, my love.[22]

Despite her nonsensical tone, the Duchess' commentary represents an authoritative discourse based on exclusion and purification. In an absurdly ironic way, it subtly reverberates with the familiar sounds of fascism, the Inquisition, Nazism, and other oppressive orders that were (and are) sustained by the mechanisms of sacrifice. Casandra is the simultaneous embodiment of all marginalized, exiled, and disenfranchised "Others"—witches, Jews, blacks, students, homosexuals, woman—whose voices have questioned and challenged the

Mònica Glaenzel as Casandra and Juan José Otegui as El Gobernador in *Queridos míos, es preciso contaros ciertas cosas*. Teatro María Guerrero, Madrid, 1994. Photo: Chicho. Courtesy of the Archive of *El Público*.

dominant hierarchy at one time or another ("calling black white and white black"). As a proselyte of the word *no*, she is the definitive image of the transgressor who refuses to conform to the system. Like a censored writer, condemned for his or her artistic creations, her words are regarded as her most volatile weapon. She is a person who "tells it like it is": she claims to speak the truth and does not seek to camouflage reality behind a protective shroud of hypocritical sanctity.

The Duchess, however, describes Casandra's heart, mind, and soul as being murky and muddled. Her perceptions concur with Mary Douglas's observations regarding the metaphoric status ascribed to displaced, "formless" entities: the amorphous, undifferentiated beings and substances that tend to navigate and accumulate—like dirt and waste matter—in the marginal, interstitial zones of society.[23] Casandra's spiritual powers assign her this type of ambiguous status in relation to the internal societal grid. She is a placeless, anomalous enigma, a sort of witch who, like the *Peregrino* in *Diálogos de la herejía*, appears to be in a transitional state between mortality and immortality, possessing both human and godly characteristics. For Douglas, witchcraft is an "anti-social psychic power" commonly attributed to persons located within the nonstructure. Witches and their alleged powers represent "inarticulate" forces that probe the margins and limits of societal systems. They are the "social equivalents of beetles and spiders who live in the cracks of the walls and wainscoting. They attract the fears and dislikes which other ambiguities and contradictions attract in other thought structures, and the kind of powers attributed to them symbolise their ambiguous inarticulate status."[24] In order to maintain their plenipotentiary stature and preserve the authority and integrity of the system, the official, "articulate" powers of society habitually attempt to suppress the anomalous and mysterious powers of witches by demanding that their ambiguity be reduced and that they conform to the patterns inscribed by sociocultural boundaries.

In *Queridos míos*, the Duchess, the Governor, and the other articulate powers treat Casandra as though she were cloaked in filth and pestilence (indeed, as though she were an insect), and they regard her as a dirty stain they will attempt to remove from their pristine world. Their behavior can be understood as an extreme representation of the Christian conception of the sacred, expressed as an ongoing endeavor to expel all manifestations of defilement and profanity—often, through rites of purification—from the immaculate realm of their deity. As an emblem of contrived purity and taboo, the Duchess believes that her god will eventually rid the world of polluted beings and ideas. Whenever she wishes to express herself in vulgar terms, she does so in English (i.e., "son-of-bitch") so as to distance herself from any impurity that might emanate from the mere utterance of such an expression. In her view, sanctity is a hygienic, sterile order, a clean house swept free of dirt and contamination.

Whether Casandra's powers are genuine or fraudulent is unclear, but she, nevertheless, is regarded by the social hegemony as a supernatural being in both the literal and the metaphoric sense. As a chiromancer, she is perceived as the embodiment of danger, power, defilement, and transgression. She represents a hazard to the sacred order and a powerful threat of change. Her ambiguity of being provokes terror among the Duchess and her cohorts in that it signifies the presence of an uncontrollable force that cannot be comprehended rationally nor categorically absorbed by the system. The Duchess equates Casandra's formlessness and her apparent "disorder" with the notion of injustice: "Injustice! Their mouths are filled with the word 'injustice,' as if stuffed with potatoes. And how does one recognize injustice? My dear friends, it's time we clarify certain things. Injustice, like a lie, has only one face: disorder. All the rest is confusion, Confusionism."[25] The Duchess' definition of injustice is an expression of her authoritative endeavors to reinforce the internal grid of the Governor's realm and to delineate with unambiguous clarity the boundaries of order and disorder, sanctity and profanity, truth and falsehood. Her quest for the truth is exemplified in her constant search for blue eyes: "Blue is the color of God's eyes, and God's alone. It's my secret. It's my quest."[26]

The concept of blue eyes, a recurrent motif in much of Gómez-Arcos's literature, carries special significance as a metaphor for the truth. He explains:

> I'm from a land of generally dark people with dark eyes, and so for me, blue eyes have always held the meaning of the contrary. Perhaps like a doubling: the Other, the possibility that the Other, although he or she may be similar to you, is always different because he or she has other features. All of this is naturally metaphoric but at least in my novels, in all that I have written, blue eyes communicate a translation of the truth that is contrary to or at least different from that of everyday life.[27]

The Duchess appears unaware that the blue eyes that she so avidly desires represent an alternative sort of truth, unlike that which is commonly accepted, and unlike that which has been fabricated by the established order. Casandra, emblem of disorder, paradoxically professes to speak the truth, and to *be* the truth: "No, no, no, no, no! . . . I am not a lie! . . . I am humanity's truth!"[28] Curiously, as is later revealed, she also has blue eyes; thus, her "confusing" image seems to suggest the presence of that "other" truth of which Gómez-Arcos speaks. The Barker confirms this point of view when he declares, in reference to Casandra: "The truth is deaf, and blind, and mute. And hunchbacked, and crippled, and leprous, and thalidomidic, and . . ."[29]

Casandra looks into the Duchess' eyes and foresees a future of sin, death, and misery, but this is not the sort of truth that the Duchess was hoping to hear. The Governor decides that Casandra must be silenced in order to suppress the power of her contaminated words. He calls for her arrest, and she is promptly quarantined within the silent walls of his prison. There, she will be held captive and her words censored, but she will not be executed, for as the Duchess explains to the audience, a dead voice is also a hero's voice. In her view, Casandra's image is far from that of a hero: "My dear friends, it's time we clarify certain subtleties. . . . For dead voices, silence does not exist. Neither physical nor spiritual. That is why it is dangerous to kill a voice, even when it is the voice of an agitator. The great rulers of History have comprehended this."[30] Her explanation reveals the inner workings of her own totalizing discourse, which sustains itself through sacrificial mechanisms, such as censorship. However, censorship is part of a dynamic process of negotiation and give and take. Just as taboo cannot exist without the presence of transgression, censorship paradoxically cannot exist if there is nothing to silence; thus, Casandra, though mute, will be sentenced to live.

For the second scene, the setting is transformed without interruption into a cocktail party. The year is 1966, and the music of a portable phonograph is heard in the background. The characters, clad in typical sixties fashions, carry cocktail glasses and smoke cigarettes. The Duchess accordingly removes her seventeenth-century accouterments and hands them off to a "servant," revealing her modern dress underneath. At this point, Leticia, a friend of the Duchess, recounts the absurd story of her recent encounter with a human cadaver while engaged in humanitarian work at a Red Cross hospital. On this occasion, the coroner kindly invited her to participate in the autopsy of a dead soldier, whose decomposing body emitted a pestilent odor. Fascinated with the idea, Leticia accepted his invitation and assisted in the operation—but only after having been served tea (specified as a mixture of Ceylon and jasmine) and biscuits by the chauffeur of her Rolls-Royce. As a result of the autopsy, she and the coroner were able to verify that the soldier had perished in the Vietnam War. He was found with a strip of barbed wire wrapped around his head, resembling a crown of thorns, and his eyes were noticeably blue.

Leticia's narrative performance juxtaposes two incongruent semantic contexts, exaggerating the distinctions between the pure and the impure. Her characterization as a *beau monde* socialite—her chauffeur-driven Rolls-Royce, her distinctive tea and biscuits, her fashionable dress, her exceedingly polite discourse, and even the cocktail she tinkles in her hand—clashes with the image of the putrefying cadaver. In addition, her performance sets up several metonymic linkages between the dead body and Casandra. The decaying corpse, like Casandra, is a manifestation of formlessness. It is an object in the midst of transition and decomposition, still possessing some semblance of identity—that of a once-living person—yet, eventually, it will reach a state of complete unrecognizability as an indistinguishable lump of dust. Leticia and the Duchess are at once intrigued and disturbed by the image of the corpse. Their behavior can be interpreted as an expression of their willingness to place themselves within close proximity of a taboo in order to feel the excitement of being near the limit—but only while under the protection of a surgical mask and gloves. Like Casandra, the dead soldier is for them an object of repulsion, but also of fascination—especially since the soldier possessed blue eyes.

In scene three (still the year 1966) the Captain, who is serving as prison guard, enters with Casandra. The Duchess and her friends immediately flee her presence as though trying to avoid contamination. They then call upon Casandra to communicate her revelations, which she recounts in the form of an allegorical parable entitled the "Historia del pan" ("Story of bread").[31] At this point, her incantations, composed of shifting focalizations and syntactical spirals, take on a poetic, trancelike performative quality reminiscent of the work of Samuel Beckett:

> Corrupted saints, truth abused, here I am born and here I die, here like beggars' bread, here I grow weak and fall, here I open my veins, here I shout and my words have no echo, the closed room, dark room here I summon my men and my men are castrated men, here my castrated children are born, race of solitude, here I have no song, here I have no bread. . . .[32]

In this allegorical vision, the miracle of birth is represented as the miracle of bread. A man engenders his own precious offspring: he cultivates his soil, he sows the seeds which are spawned from his own mouth, he sweats blood and tears, and he watches as his fields sprout wheat. Eventually, the wheat is transformed into bread, but when the man attempts to ingest the fruit of his labors, the bread betrays and rejects his own father: "If you do not bring money, I cannot be your son, nor your sustenance, nor your peace."[33] No longer a mere means of subsistence, the bread has been converted into an object of material desire, a commodity with a price tag. Unable to pay for the bread, the man expresses his lament with tears. He then decides to seize his weapons and wage a bloody war of revenge: "and he picked up the knife, and he picked up the rifle, and he picked up the sickle, and the stone, and his nails, and rage, and the memory of Christ, and hate, and blood, and the open chest wound, and the guts spilling, and the dry tongue . . ."[34] The war eventually leads to the man's demise. Casandra continues, "They performed the autopsy on him yesterday. On his forehead he wore a strip of barbed wire, his crown of thorns. An elegant lady said: The havoc of war."[35] Leticia suddenly cries out that this was the same man whom she saw the previous day at the hospital. In effect, she was the elegant woman who witnessed the autopsy.

Casandra's "Story of Bread" suddenly converges both spatially and temporally with Leticia's story of the soldier with blue eyes as it is revealed that both allegorical depictions correspond to the same man. The stories of the soldier and the man invoke an allegorical repetition of the life of Christ, foregrounding his role as primordial outcast and sacrificial victim. In the end, he wears a crown of thorns/barbed wire, crucified when his own people/progeny turn against him. Just as Christ was betrayed by his own disciple Judas Iscariot in the name of material pursuits, likewise the man's children are motivated by capitalistic endeavors in the betrayal of their father. In a curious way, the man who inspired such feelings of repulsion in Leticia and the Duchess has been endowed with a series of divine attributes. He also has the blue eyes of God that the Duchess so devoutly pursues, and like a celestial Creator, he has engendered his own children/wheat. In effect, Leticia and Casandra have offered two sides of the same story, and at the intersection of their opposing perspectives, there emerges an oxymoronic depiction of God and/or Jesus Christ as a betrayed and desecrated deity: a divine figure of transgression whose crucified/putrefied cadaver is all that remains.

Furthermore, in a powerfully metaphoric gesture, Gómez-Arcos implicates the story of Christ with that of civil war—the Vietnam War of the dead soldier of 1966, the Spanish Civil War of thirty years earlier, the war in the former Yugoslavian territories, and so on. The final struggle between father and son/bread alludes allegorically to the patricidal/fratricidal/infanticidal circumstances that this type of war characteristically suggests. In this scenario of sacrificial crisis, cultural distinctions become blurred, and men and women, indeed, may find themselves pitted against their own "flesh and blood." In the aftermath of this crisis, when order is finally restored through sacrifice, the vanquished remain without bread—impoverished, betrayed or dead—while the vanquishers are left to reap a harvest of material spoils, disguising their unsightly activities behind a deceptive veil of purity.

The Governor proposes his own allegory for this hypocritical game of deception. For him, a nation is like an apple: "When it must be shown to curious neighbors, its skin must be polished; it must be shined up and placed in a showcase, in order to make it appear splendrous. If it is good on the inside, all the better. And if it is wormy, it's best to disguise the fact with exterior brilliance. That is the way to sell apples."[36] Similarly, during the period following the Spanish Civil War, Franco and his Nationalist breadwinners were able to fortify and sanctify their official story by appropriating the divine discourse of the Catholic Church and concealing their truths behind its sacred façade. In an ironic move, Casandra's allegory implicates God with the vanquished (i.e., the Republicans), rather than with the vanquishers, thereby invoking not only a rejection of the dictatorial order, but a radical reversal of its hierarchical structure.

In proclaiming the death, defilement, and dethronement of God, Casandra conveys an nihilistic absence (in the Nietzschean sense) of an authoritative center, a metaphoric interrogation of cultural supremacy, which is also, ironically, a portrayal of her own timeless and ill-fated destiny. Indeed, the stories of Christ and civil war are not the only texts that are signified here. The allegories of the soldier and the man are also allusions to the story of Casandra herself. Like Christ (not to mention her mythical namesake), she is a prophetess accused of blasphemy. Her words of truth are dismissed and disavowed, yet she possesses the supposedly blue eyes of a deity. Even her rags and tatters recall the garments worn by Christ prior to his celestial ascension.

Casandra's supernatural powers enable her to communicate with a world beyond the limits of the Governor's system and beyond the limits of Western metaphysics. In this allegorical realm that eludes temporal specificity, her revelations offer both an alternative "unofficial" view of history, as well as a portentous view of the future. The "truths" that she reveals do not endorse the Governor's fabricated, unsullied image of sanctity, and as a result, they only incite scorn from him and his followers. As the Captain drags Casandra away, the Governor's Wife discloses the portentous news that she has already requested that the firing squad wall be whitewashed to remove some of the stains that were left behind from the last war: "remember?— the one that went on here while we were in Biarritz. Blood stains that finally, after all that time went by, looked like stains from something else . . . , I don't know, from shame."[37] The whitewashed firing squad wall is a metaphor for the contrived purity and fabricated truths that the Governor's system has perpetuated in order to conceal a gruesome reality. It is also a primary locus of sacrifice, and accordingly, the Governor's Wife also announces her absurd plan to throw a party and serve martinis, while they all gather to contemplate the sacrificial spectacle of Casandra's execution.

Still, the Governor is convinced that he can change Casandra's truths by changing her appearance, and he sets out to prove to the Duchess that "clothes make the man"—a negation of the traditional proverbial expression "clothes *don't* make the man."[38] At the end of scene three, a gong sounds as a prelude to the "show" that is about to begin. In the scene that follows, the Captain enters once again, followed by Casandra, but this time, her exterior appearance is remarkably different. In contrast with the filthy tatters that she wore in previous scenes, she now appears elegantly coifed, adorned, and bejeweled in the latest fashions. Casandra's captors are filled with praise and admiration as they contemplate the new "look" that the Governor has bestowed upon her. In effect, she now appears as their own mirror image. She moves to center stage and, addressing both the offstage and onstage audiences, she performs another spectacle of prophesy, reciting an allegorical parable entitled the "Historia del Vino" ("Story of Wine"). The onstage audience applauds her performance, for it appears that they are focusing on her appearance rather than on her words. Even the Governor is convinced that he has proven his point: that clothes do, in fact, define the person who wears them. However, the "Story of Wine" is another allegorical meditation on the circumstances of civil war. In essence, it is the same tragic tale as the "Story of Bread." The offstage audience occupies the privileged position of being able to perceive the irony that is posed by this situation. The signifiers may differ in appearance (i.e., Bread/Wine, Casandra in tatters/Casandra in elegant attire), but the signified continually resists change.

Later on, in scene eight, the female characters gather for tea on the terrace of the Governor's castle. In Portaceli's *mise en scène*, the dark humor of this scene incited enormous laughter from the audience. As the women chatted, they snacked on *pipas* (sunflower seeds and the like) and spewed the shells all over the stage in a hilarious parody of a typical Spanish custom. The time is described as "*one of those boring Sunday afternoons common to every day and age*,"[39] and the women are correspondingly dressed in an "anachronistic" and incongruous array of styles. The Governor's Wife is in medieval dress, the Grandmother is in modern-day attire, and Leticia is clad in early twentieth-century clothing. They have climbed to the top of the highest turret (the Grandmother had to be hoisted up with a crane) to enjoy a panoramic view of Casandra's execution, but to their dismay, the spectacle has been canceled. The Governor, it seems, has decided that such an event would not be convenient at this time because, as his wife announces, he is presently on a tour through the Orient, known as "the Crusades," in search of the Holy Grail.[40] All the woman are extremely disappointed about the cancellation. Leticia has spent the entire afternoon putting on makeup for the occasion, and the Governor's Wife has a terrible migraine. She was up at the crack of dawn to inspect the firing squad wall herself, and it seems that the man in charge of cleaning it has left two curious stains: one in the shape of a chalice and the other in the shape of a thorn. Both thorn and chalice (the wine receptacle used during the Catholic rite

Eva García as Leticia and Gloria Muñoz as La Esposa del Gobernador in
Queridos míos, es preciso contaros ciertas cosas. **Teatro María Guerrero,**
Madrid, 1994. Photo: Chicho. Courtesy of the Archive of ***El Público.***

of communion) are emblematic references to the sacrifice of Christ. The stains, in this manner, strengthen the allegorical ties between the image of Casandra, the dead soldier, and Christ.

Just as Judas betrayed Christ, the Barker has betrayed Casandra by buying his own freedom. He no longer has the power to censor her words and thoughts, and so he has accepted a payoff to do the Governor's dirty work (i.e., clean the firing squad wall). Eventually, the Governor calls upon him to negotiate a deal with Casandra: the Governor will grant her freedom in exchange for her silence. When Casandra rejects his proposal of censorship, the Barker suggests exile as a final solution:

> Exiles are like roosters with their beaks cut off. When their crowing finally does reach our ears, from such a distance away, their voices are erstwhile voices, with erstwhile things to say. They are out of date. Out of tune. And although they could pick at old wounds a little, there is still an answer to that: foreign press and foreign publications are censored. Exile is silence.[41]

In the 1994 production, these lines seemed to take on special significance as they echoed throughout the theater. When heard from the
perspective of the 1990s they carry an almost prophetic, ironic value
as they appear to reflect Gómez-Arcos's own fears with regard to his
exile and his return to his homeland.

The Governor agrees to opt for Casandra's deportation. She will be
expelled to a place beyond the borders of his domain. In his view,
exile will serve as a preferable solution to an execution—where the
echo of single gunshot holds the dangerous potential of inciting a
war. Exquisitely outfitted in regal finery (cloak, crown, and scepter),
the Governor confronts Casandra face to face, self-consciously under-
lining their roles as allegorical signifiers: "I have dressed up as king
to see if you understand once and for all who I am and who you
are. . . . You and I are two opposing forces. Order and disorder. Better
said, disorder and order."[42] Casandra states her plea for a better
world: "A world of mouths that do not cry for bread, because they
are filled with bread. Mouths that sing."[43] The Captain, once a faithful
partisan of the dominant system, suddenly finds himself captivated
and inspired by the words of his captive: "And I, what should I do
when the enemy has no weapons, only words?"[44] Casandra's truth-
seeing eyes and truth-bearing words have penetrated ("contaminated," in the Governor's opinion) the Captain's mind and soul. He
has realized that Casandra not only *speaks* the truth; she is the embodiment of truth. "Cassandra," the Captain observes, "is something
else. She is truth."[45]

If Casandra is truth, then the hatred and censorship that challenge
her words and thoughts represent a rejection of the truth. The Governor's presumptuous decision to silence the voice of a prophetess implies a denial of her premonitory visions and, therefore, a complete
rejection of the future, as well as the historical past. In order to
perpetuate his system, he recognizes the need to remove the past and
future from her hands so that he may fabricate his own "false" truths.
He and his cohorts are hypocrites, more concerned with appearances
and falsely contrived purity than the veritable, underlying truth. Casandra is a sacred being in the original sense of the word: she is the
ugly, unadulterated truth. Like Gómez-Arcos, she is the soon-to-be-
exiled writer who dares to challenge the official story.

At his request, the Captain is granted permission to escort Casandra to the border region of the Governor's realm, to a narrow strip
of land known as the "tierra de nadie" ("no-man's-land"). Just beyond
the reaches of the Governor's system, they stand in an allegorical
empty space, at the limit separating taboo and transgression, freedom
and interdiction. During this sequence, in Portaceli's *mise en scène*,

the entire theatrical space was filled with smoke, and a mysterious, Eastern-sounding music was piped through the theater.

The no-man's-land is an in-between sort of place, neither here nor there, resembling the primordial void that existed prior to the establishment of sociocultural systems. The Captain observes, "The world must have looked something like this on the first day, when the first sun rose, and there was the first dawn, before it was parceled out into properties. Before borderlines were set up. . . ."[46] In this empty zone of *différance*, they are at last able to speak freely and openly, without fear of censorship. Before bidding farewell to his prisoner, the Captain candidly reveals the (com)passion and hope that she has inspired in him: "Don't ever die! I need for you to live! Every day, when my war ends, before I go to bed, I'll think about you. I shall think: 'She is alive. I am, too.' Permit me that hope."[47] For Casandra, however, the distinctions between life and death do not apply. She is an immortal being: timeless, ageless, eternal, and imperishable.

In effect, in scene eleven, the never-ending cycle of violence continues as Casandra, having returned from her exile, portrays a Jewish girl, raped and brutalized by the Governor and his coconspirators, who have assumed the roles of Nazi officials. Casandra's metatheatrical reincarnation further accentuates her characterization as the allegorical embodiment of marginality and disenfranchisement, while the Nazis epitomize the discourse of exclusion and ablution that constitutes the Governor's system. On stage, in plain view of the audience, the men discuss their obligation to the fatherland. At the same time, it is inferred that behind the scenes, each of them is taking his turn in the sacrificial violation of Casandra (with the exception of the Captain, who offers her his sympathy and love). History again appears infinitely unalterable as this time, the civil war/holocaust/betrayal of Christ is allegorically staged on the battlefield of Casandra's body.

In the penultimate scene, Casandra appears alone on stage and delivers a soliloquy that summarizes her situation. She is the decaying cadaver with the crown of thorns, the blue-eyed deity forsaken by her children who have gone astray, and her speech is a direct appeal to the audience to aid her in the recovery of her lost offspring:

(*To the audience*) My dear friends, it's time we get certain things straight. I have no parents. I have no companions. I have no beliefs. Nor glorious destiny. Nor system to back me. Nor enemies to show me respect. Nor silence to fill with speeches. I have nothing. I was born so that error, untruth, falsity, and injustice may live. They are the offspring of my flesh, favored sons, through whom I have given birth to war, the descendants of Cain, a false peace. And I seek them. Tortured by my thorns. I seek them, because they came out of me and strayed from me. . . .[48]

Her desperate pleas are an expression of her desire to start anew, to weave a new, alternative narrative of history that—unlike the "Story of Bread," the "Story of Wine," and the story of Christ—would bring closure to the established system of sacrificial violence. By implicating the spectator in her appeal, she subtly underscores the parallels that exist between the Governor's allegorical realm and the world beyond the limits of the stage.

In the final scene, the Governor, his Wife, and the Duchess—glasses of scotch in hand, signifiers of their bourgeois status—lament the unexpected return of Casandra, who, according to the Duchess, is now twice as mattedly dressed and raggedly combed. They can no longer tolerate Casandra's ceaseless cries for her children. This time, in order to silence her, the Governor decides to have her tongue surgically extracted. The censorship of Casandra is performed as a surgical rite of purification in a cold, clinical atmosphere that is saturated with elements of Brechtian alienation. The Barker (as usual, performing the dirty work) plays the role of surgeon, dressed in a white robe. Leticia, in the role of nurse, obeys the doctor's orders, handing him the surgical instruments with the robotic movements of a mechanical doll. In this manner, the story of her humanitarian work at the hospital is *re*-presented, and the image of the dead soldier is superimposed upon the image of Casandra who lies on the operating table. The Governor announces that precautions must be taken because Casandra's fetid breath is full of germs and may endanger their health. "Her voice is not only a sound," he declares, "It is sickness, besides."[49] The ruthless stoicism maintained by the Governor and his loyal subjects and the manner in which they appear to distance themselves emotionally from the disturbing surgery that is taking place on stage clashes with the piercing human scream that Casandra unleashes as her final expression of truth. The Barker/Surgeon summarizes the results of his medical exploits: "(*Professional tone.*) It was very simple. A clean incision. The nerves perfectly severed. Infection center; in vulgar terms, the tongue. The dream of the just lies asleep in the garbage pail. The dream of Beelzebub, that is. Rose water to wash the blood off my hands!"[50] As the play concludes, the Governor issues an official announcement to the press that the problem that once threatened to topple their system has been resolved, and the woman who had been searching for her children since the beginning of time is now in the midst of a convalescence that requires only silence and solitude. The spectator, however, is left with a more brazen image of reality: the revelation that the truth (that is, Casandra's tongue) has been tossed into the trash can.

The Barker assumes his original stance, as in the opening scene, shouting, "Ladies and gentlemen, saints and sinners, citizens of the world . . ."[51] This time, he offers to sell Casandra's story in leaflet form. The Captain leaves the audience alone with only Casandra's body remaining on stage and asks them to judge the situation for themselves. As the curtain falls, it would appear, at first glance, that there is no closure in this allegory of censorship. The story of Casandra seems forever enslaved by the singular presence of History, forever governed by the sacred authority of the Governor's system, and condemned to repeat itself *ad infinitum*. However, the notion of closure, as it applies here, is inherently paradoxical. Although it may seem contradictory, it is possible to perceive closure in what is, in reality, an endlessly repetitive cycle. As Derrida comments (in reference to Artaud), "Closure is the circular limit within which the repetition of difference infinitely repeats itself. That is to say, closure is its *playing* space."[52] Confronted with the infinitely transformative, elusive, and absurd playing space of *Queridos míos*, the spectator is able to witness the possibility of change (i.e., closure) in the ambivalent void of *différance* that allegory intrinsically engenders. The allegorical signified may continue to exert its authority over the signifier, and the oppressive political system may continue to impose a discourse of censorship and exclusion upon its citizens, but within the limits of these neverending parallel cycles there is, indelibly present, a discourse that will challenge and contest, that will resist subordination in the dynamic of representation. Indeed, *Queridos míos* is not only an allegory of censorship; it is also an allegory of freedom of expression which systematically frustrates and circumvents any attempts on the part of sacred authority to establish a finite level of meaning. The *breadth* of deferral is thus a *breath* of hope: that Casandra eventually may succeed in altering the cycle.

Indeed, there is a coda to this story that further emphasizes this semblance of hope: thirteen years after completing *Queridos míos*, Gómez-Arcos did, in fact, find a certain degree of allegorical vindication for Casandra's censorship (and for his own) when, in 1979, he appropriated her immortal words and gave them new life in his postexilic novel *Pré-papa ou Roman de fées* (Pré-papa or A fairy novel). In this futuristic fairy tale of fairy tales (derived from Gómez-Arcos's eponymous theater piece), a direct transcription and translation of Casandra's "Historia de pan" resurfaces in the form of a lost Spanish manuscript. At the half-way point in this meta-allegorical novel,

Mary, the wife of the pregnant John, recounts the "Histoire du Pendu" ("Story of the Hanged Man"), an oral memoir that has been passed down to her by her grandmother. A strong sense of obligation compels Mary to tell this story—to recreate, remember, and pass it on to her children and to her husband so that history will not repeat itself.

The "Story of the Hanged Man" is the parabolic tale of a *conteur*, a journalist/writer who wrote a book about the battle between order and anarchy that would serve as written testimony to the atrocities he had once witnessed. As Mary puts it, "The fact is that he had the nostalgia of the man of the past and he wanted to paint a portrait for the man of tomorrow."[53] The writer was a marginalized societal outcast, a rebel, an anarchist, and a romantic who exiled himself to the *esplanade*, a no-man's-land between the past (represented as the *ville troglodyte*) and the science fictive *Cité Future*, a city that was constructed during the *après-guerre* period of a devastating nuclear battle. As a starving artist, the writer began selling installments from his book, which became so famous, that eventually (like the Bible) it was known simply as the *Livre* ("the Book"). Others began to flock to the esplanade, opening boutiques and selling remnants from prewar, "ancient" civilizations. Over time, this zone of freedom and formlessness evolved into a haven for artists and intellectuals aspiring to live beyond the reaches of the dominant system and the aseptic purity of the *Cité Future*. Mary remarks, "Others organized meeting places, opened cafés, bistros, shops and taverns. There emerged after a time a social life parallel to that sanctioned by the *Cité Future*, marginal, not at all aseptic, and very lively."[54] The all-powerful *Centre* (the hub of power of the *Cité Future)* wanted to annihilate this community of freethinkers, but each time it attempted to do so, the residents would take to the street in protest.

The *Livre* is thus a book about the writer's quest for freedom. One day, Power (*le Pouvoir*) intervened, incarcerating the writer and condemning him to death. During the night, gallows were erected on the esplanade, and there he was publicly hanged. All who witnessed his sacrificial execution were horrified by the nightmarish sight of his swollen, purplish tongue which dangled from his gaping mouth. From then on, the street was known as the *esplanade du Pendu* ("Esplanade of the Hanged Man"). Mary continues, "People live there according to their own rules, more or less adapted to the present world and caught between two flames: the past which they ignore and the future which they reject. Oh no, not like outlaws : they do respect the law, but, rather as individuals who are not inclined to blind obedience. Free people . . ."[55] The book was also publicly burned—"*Un autodafé*"—in a bonfire recalling the book-burning rituals that centuries earlier had been carried out by the Inquisition. Still, there were some copies of the book that were spared and hidden from the *Centre*. Mary's grandmother has bequeathed to her one of these copies, which she guards under lock and key in the cellar.

The Story of the Hanged Man is a fairy tale which, like *Queridos míos*, does not appear to have a happy ending. It is the story of a censored exiled writer, executed for his crimes of heresy, his tongue (like Casandra's) symbolically mangled. One night, intrigued by the story, John ventures down into the cellar and finds his wife's sacred book. He opens it and reads the hanged writer's account, which evidently has been pieced together by an editor/translator. (In the Cervantine tradition, Gómez-Arcos employs the idea of a text compiled by a translator, thus placing the parable of the hanged man even one step deeper within the parergonal structure of allegorical fairy tales.) The tale of the *Pendu* reads like a cry of vengeance against past injustices, yet John also wonders if, perhaps, the book also might be a prophetic warning ("avertissement sibyllin") of things to come. He begins to read:

> Santos corrompidos, verdades ultrajadas, aquí nazco y aquí muero,
> *Saints corrompus, vérités outragées, je nais ici, je meurs ici, ici je*
>
> aquí como el mendrugo, aquí desfallezco, aquí me abro las venas,
> *mange le pain dur, ici je défaille, je m'ouvre ici les veines, ici je cri*
>
> aquí grito y mis palabras no tienen eco, cuarto cerrado, cuarto
> *et mon cri est sans écho, chambre close, chambre obscure, j'appelle*
>
> oscuro, aquí llamo a mis hombres y mis hombres están castrados,
> *ici mes hommes et mes hommes sont châtrés, race de solitude, ici*
>
> raza de soledad, aquí no tengo canción, aquí no tengo pan.
> *je n'ai pas de chanson, je n'ai pas de pan. . . .*[56]

The *Livre* is an allegorical pastiche composed of two texts running concurrently. Casandra's prophetic "Historia de pan" appears as an appropriated intertext, rescued from its censored past and reprinted with French subtitles that were supposedly supplied by the editor. At the bottom of the final page, John finds a editor's footnote explaining that the book was written by a shy, unknown writer with the initials A. G. A. (that is, "Agustín Gómez-Arcos"). The editor has decided to reproduce the text in the original Spanish language in the hope that someday, somebody with a "stateless" status ("une voix apatride") will have the power to transmit it to others.[57] With this self-referential footnote, Gómez-Arcos, in a manner that recalls Velázquez's *Las meninas*, implicates himself in the text of the novel, portraying himself in the act of writing/creating—and in the act of being censored. The dual image of the bilingual text invokes simultaneously Gómez-Arcos's own pre-exilic (Spanish) past and his post-exilic (French) present. It is a twice-told tale that ostensibly proclaims his status as a bilingual writer. The pre-exilic Gómez-Arcos is the mirror image of this *Pendu* (and of Casandra), hanged and rendered mute, his tongue mutilated by the forces of order. The post-exilic Gómez-Arcos is the "stateless" communicator invoked in the footnote. His bilingualism has accorded him the *extraterritoriality*—to use George Steiner's term—that is necessary to transmit the story.[58]

The *Livre* is thus an allegory that can be read as the key to all Gómez-Arcos's literature. In one sense, it is the story of and by a writer/Creator who, like Casandra, endeavors to speak the truth yet feels betrayed by his own people. In another sense, it represents a contestatory cry of freedom of expression, which seems to be telling us "certain things" about Casandra, the *Pendu*, and Gómez-Arcos himself: that they have finally stepped beyond the limits of the established Power, beyond the limits of censorship, and beyond the limits of the never-ending cycle of the Governor's system, to a place where their voices will continue to live on into eternity. The chapters that follow with examine these exilic voices and spaces.

III
The Language of Exile

7

Adorado Alberto
(1968 / 1969)

Ah, les bouquets de fleurs de la baronne! . . . Ineffables comme elle-même. Elle mélangeait les orchidées aux fleurs des champs, les roses aux chrysanthèmes, les marguerites aux mimosas. On avait l'impression d'un croisement contre nature, d'un arrangement déli-vrant quelque message sibyllin, établissant une fois pour toutes la confusion des genres et des espèces. Fausse impression, car il s'agis-sait plutôt d'un art: l'art de la ambiguïté. Une savante touche de vert entre un jaune et un mauve tempérait l'antagonisme larvé des formes et des couleurs, et chaque fleur, si éclatant, si individuiste fût-elle, se fondait dans un tout harmonieux, un ensemble de tons qui semblait peint. Son clef-d'œuvre achevé, la baronne souriait et son sourire reproduisait l'étrangeté de cette ambivalence florale.[1]
—Agustín Gómez-Arcos, La femme d'emprunt

Gómez-Arcos's initial years of residence in Paris represent an interval of transition with regard to his overall career as a writer. It is a period of both continuity and rupture, in which grim memories merge with new beginnings. The themes that defined his earlier plays—politics, religion, eroticism, and language—continue to inhabit his exilic writing, and the allegorical discourse of transgression that pervaded his pre-exilic drama remains the dominant mode of expression. At the same time, his departure from Spain logically induces a series of thematic and stylistic transformations that eventually will carry over into his work as a novelist. In exile, a new attitude of openness begins to animate his writing, invading it with fresh air from beyond the Spanish border. The language of his plays, while still prone to ab-surdism, is injected with candor, authenticity, and sometimes even a dose of optimism. No longer encumbered nor conditioned by the overbearing presence of Francoist censorship, his theatrical discourse acquires a more radically defiant, audacious tone as he seems to savor with passion and fury every newly garnered increment of freedom of expression. During this period, exile emerges as both principal theme and process of artistic creation.

Gómez-Arcos's Parisian beginnings can be traced to his work at the Café-Théâtre de l'Odéon, where in February 1969, French spectators witnessed the dual première of *Et si on aboyait?* (And if one were to bark?) / *Adorado Alberto* (Adored Alberto) and *Pré-papa / Prepapá.* Together, these one-act absurdist pieces (written in 1968 and 1969, respectively) share an inseparable history and exemplify his creative output during this transitional period. Both were originally conceived in Spanish and subsequently translated into French by Rachel Salik.[2] They were then staged in French under Gómez-Arcos's direction at the Odéon, where their extremely successful run of seventy-one performances, beginning in February 1969, led to the subsequent publication of *Pré-papa* in the bimonthly journal *L'Avant Scène Théâtre*.[3] The events surrounding this Parisian debut constitute a significant moment in Gómez-Arcos's artistic evolution, for it was on this occasion that he began to comprehend fully the creative implications of his exile and his freedom from the linguistic prison house of censorship. He offers the following recollections regarding the initial staging of *Et si on aboyait* and *Pré-papa:*

> We began to rehearse the plays—because I was responsible for the staging and the direction—and when the show was finished, I asked the director of the café-theater, "Well, now when will the censors be here?" Do you understand? I was waiting for somebody to come from some official institution in order to find out if what we had prepared could be presented or not, and then he said to me, "Well, you are crazy. That sort of thing doesn't exist here." That was the *déclic.* . . . I realized that I could write without fear and that was a marvelous thing. For the first time, I was in direct contact with the impunity of things and that seemed marvelous to me.[4]

In November 1972, Gómez-Arcos accepted an invitation to present these plays at the University of Paris-Sorbonne on the occasion of the Jornadas Internacionales Universitarias sobre el Teatro Español Contemporáneo, a conference organized by Ángel Berenguer and the Centre d'Études Ibériques around the theme of what was then known as the "new" Spanish theater. The week-long gathering—chronicled by Moisés Pérez Coterillo, Vicente Romero, and Ricard Salvat in the January 1973 issue of *Primer Acto*—featured a series of lectures, discussion sessions, and evening performances, all of which were eagerly attended by a large assemblage of students, critics, and dramatists.[5] Gómez-Arcos participated with playwrights Fernando Arrabal, Manuel Azaña, Josep Maria Benet i Jornet, Francisco Nieva, Alfredo

Crespo, José Martín Elizondo, José Guevara, and Miguel Romero Esteo in a roundtable discussion devoted to the difficult task of defining the new Spanish theater in relation to that of the previous "realist" generation[6] The evening drama series at the *Jornadas* was inaugurated with the presentation in French of *Et si on aboyait?* and *Pré-papa*, this time directed by Gómez-Arcos's long-time friend and collaborator Antonio Duque.[7] For the playwright, the meeting at the Sorbonne represented not only an occasion to showcase his work before a group of French spectators; but it also afforded him a rare opportunity to reacquaint himself with and, perhaps, even reawaken the interest of a group of Spanish critics and playwrights who were largely unaware of his activities in France. Pérez Coterillo describes the meeting as an occasion of rediscovery:

> The events in Paris offered us the opportunity to rediscover an unjustly lost author and no less unjustly erased from the fragile memory of the Spanish theater of recent years. Years, on the other hand, in which he has guarded the strictest silence, until now, in which he returns, having mastered a whole process of acclimatization, to present himself publicly before French society, with a theater that is very different from that which he had written up until now.[8]

Both *Et si on aboyait?* and *Pré-papa* were met with enthusiastic applause. Romero underlines the dignity with which they were presented despite a very small and inadequate theatrical space, and Pérez Coterillo characterizes Duque's production as "a *mise en scène* filled with rigor and meaning."[9] Following the experience at the Sorbonne, the plays enjoyed still another successful run at the Odéon in 1973, again under Duque's direction.

As Gómez-Arcos's work evolves in exile, his gradual employment of the French language comes to allegorize his quest for freedom of expression, for it signifies much more than a mere linguistic shift; it implies a liberation and a rebellion with regard to the past, a discursive disengagement from the artistic constraints that are attributed to his Spanish past and to his existence within a totalitarian system. This emancipatory process begins with the staging in French of *Et si on aboyait* and *Pré-papa*, and reaches a decisive climax with the publication in 1975 of his first novel written directly in French *L'agneau carnivore* (The Carnivorous Lamb, winner of the Prix Hermès). In France and in French, his fictional characters are able to express what was inexpressible and forbidden in Francoist Spain. Curiously, however, the liberation that Gómez-Arcos found through exile also compelled him to confront a new series of artistic dilemmas, derived from his status as a dramatist writing and staging plays for an audience whose linguistic, cultural, and historical footings were often quite different from his own. His deep-seated consciousness with regard to these circumstances surfaces as a recurrent motif in his countless personal declarations and interviews published both during and after this early period of residence in France. For example, Pérez Coterillo relates that, at the Sorbonne in 1972, Gómez-Arcos publicly and provocatively voiced a desire to sever his ties with all that he had done previously in the theater, announcing that with *Et si on aboyait?*, he had reached the end of the line in dealing with Iberian themes. According to this schema, *Pré-papa* would represent the first work in a new thematic cycle. Pérez Coterillo elaborates:

> Agustín Gómez Arcos affirmed the day of his presentation in the Salle Liard that six years after his flight from Spain, he found himself like a traveler who had lost his luggage and his fortune, and that, consequently, he had to start over again, from zero, the difficult route to communicating with a society that receives him as a strange and foreign intruder. A. Gómez Arcos confessed that he was no longer at all interested in Spanish themes and that he had decidedly and premeditatedly forgotten his past in order to look for new and universal concerns, foreign to what he likes to call the "provincialism" of Spanish theater of recent generations.[10]

Ostensibly, the rejection of provincialism referred to here is an indictment of the theater of bourgeois tastes and sensibilities *à la* Jacinto Benavente, an ideologically evasive theater that had dominated the Spanish stage for decades. However, Gómez-Arcos's new theatrical aspirations also may be understood as a rupture with the ideologically committed alternatives posed by Spanish "realists" of the 1950s and 1960s, for even these playwrights were known to recur (albeit in an ironic sense) to *sainetismo* and *costumbrismo* in critiquing the realities of Spanish fascism. Viewed in this manner, Gómez-Arcos's universalist stance represents a rejection of any theater of insular thematic scope that limits itself to the portrayal of a very specific (that is, Spanish) sociohistorical reality. Although he recognizes the sincerity of the playwright's statements, Pérez Coterillo is, nevertheless, skeptical with regard to Gómez-Arcos's search for a theater that pretends to maintain its validity for all people in all places. Speaking from the point of view of a Spanish spectator, Pérez Coterillo observes in his reviews of *Et si on aboyait?* and *Pré-papa* that both the former as well as the latter piece are quintessentially Spanish in their respective thematic orientations (although this condition is most overtly apparent in *Et si on aboyait?*).[11] Following these observations, he goes on to note that, "One . . . cannot stop believing that theater takes root in culture, in history and in the sociopolitical situation in which it exists and that it is that terrain which guarantees the validity of its intention and of its language," and that, "for a man, especially for an artist, it becomes impossible to erase the trace of what was his and still pertains to him."[12]

Pérez Coterillo's reflections on the impossibility of erasing one's cultural identity convey a prophetic kind of accuracy, as we shall see, with regard to Gómez-Arcos's work in exile. However, the playwright's condemnation of thematic provincialism *does* acquire legitimacy when considered from the pragmatic angle of spectatorship. In exile, Gómez-Arcos's seemingly utopian quest for a theater that would transcend geographic, cultural, and linguistic borders is more than mere aesthetic idealism; it is a necessity resulting from his awareness that if his plays are to be staged in France, it is imperative that they have meaningful implications for spectators living beyond the narrow spatiotemporal horizons of post–Civil War Spain.[13] In exile, he no longer needs to concern himself with allegory's potential as a camouflage for his critical views of the Franco regime. Instead, he is able to seize hold of allegory's potential to deconstruct and demystify, sacralize and secularize. He is able to deal more candidly with a set of eternal ideological issues that transcend the limits of what is plainly real and visible. His exilic drama is filled with both subtle and literal references to Spanish culture (as Pérez Coterillo is quick to observe), but these allusions to the particular never relinquish their allegorical capacity to signify a larger, more expansive sphere of reference. When asked about the creative implications of his exile, Gómez-Arcos responds by pointing to the emergence of a new attitude in his theater, which tends to orient itself toward a more "universal spectator":

For me, it was a difficult test but at the same time it was very healthy, for it made me realize that when you write in your own language in your own country—such as Spain, which was very isolated from the exterior world, very closed up upon itself—in reality, you are not addressing a universal spectator (or reader), you are exclusively addressing a spectator from your own country, a spectator who is too close, too confused with your own relations, etc. So, the first thing that exile makes apparent is the absence of that type of spectator. That type of spectator no longer exists; so you have to address another, a spectator who doesn't have your past, who doesn't have your recollections, who doesn't have your memory; in effect, who doesn't have your history, and although we all pertain to a common culture, it is undoubtedly true that things change when you address a type of spectator who is unfamiliar with your everyday culture. As a result, you have to begin to renounce a whole series of things.[14]

In an attempt to address a more international range of spectators, Gómez-Arcos finds himself confronted with a growing aspiration to leave behind a vast reservoir of culture and history before venturing into foreign waters. While he does find emancipation from the oppressive gaze of the Spanish censors, his desire to divorce himself from the past and from the historical reality of Spain is, at least, in literary terms, never entirely fulfilled. Paradoxically, the many voices of his exilic imagination seem to speak to the very impossibility of leaving behind a stockpile of cultural and historical baggage, for to do so would imply a complete renunciation of identity and historical memory. As a result, Gómez-Arcos's exilic allegories appear to vacillate as though immersed in an ambivalent love-hate relationship between a desire to renounce all claims to the past—to a specific (Spanish) history—and, conversely, a desire to recuperate, resuscitate, and remember at all costs a Spanish historical reality. His exilic drama—and later, his narrative fiction—bears indelible scars from his Spanish past that never seem to heal completely. The grotesque phantoms of oppression, censorship, and religious fanaticism continue to haunt and pursue his fictional characters even as far along as 1993, where, in his thirteenth novel *La femme d'emprunt* (The woman of artifice), a Spaniard moves to Paris as part of a quest for individual self-expression through transsexuality. (The plot of this novel bears significant traces of both *Adorado Alberto* and *Pré-papa*.) Indeed, five years after the meeting at the Sorbonne, in a 1977 interview published in *L'Humanité Dimanche*, Gómez-Arcos made the following declaration in reference to his deeply embedded Spanish temperament:

> I don't agree with the traditional ideas on the subject of the "roots" that a man would lose upon changing place. It is, in my opinion, a folkloric and superficial image. I think that a human being always carries what is inside of him. Wherever I shall find myself, wherever I may go, I will be myself. That is to say, profoundly Spanish. My Spanish roots are not buried deep in one place or another from where they cannot be extracted. They travel with me.[15]

His words seem to echo those of Pérez-Coterillo, as well as those of Michael Seidel, who observes in *Exile and the Narrative Imagination*, that "the exilic mind, no matter where it projects, no matter how unknown its art, emanates from familiar or local territory. Imaginative powers begin at the boundaries of accumulated experience."[16] For Seidel, who treats exile as both theme and process of literary representation, allegory is an inherent characteristic of the exilic imagination. "An exile," he declares, "is someone who inhabits one place and remembers or projects the reality of another."[17] Both allegory and exilic literature are governed by double-sided values and an artistic yearning to represent a kind of otherness. "Exile serves narrative as an initiating and supplementing action, and it also serves, as Dante pointed out, as a figure for allegory itself."[18] In a similar manner, Gómez-Arcos and his characters often carry with them on their exilic journeys their memories of Spain and oppressive orders. Their constant evocations of the past are overlaid upon the present and even the future. In a sense, Gómez-Arcos's exilic writings have remained in a state of flux and suspension, in that no-man's-land of *Queridos míos, es preciso contaros ciertas cosas* (My dear friends, it's time we get certain things straight); an ambiguous cultural *carrefour* situated between past and present, and between two worlds, two cultures, two histories, and two linguistic codes: one Spanish, the other French.

In *Adorado Alberto* and *Pré-papa*, allegory maintains its function as a deconstructive procedure, a contestatory mode that foregrounds the contemporary problematic of representation. In a move that is perhaps indicative of Gómez-Arcos's newfound artistic freedom, the human body emerges in these works as a prominent site of allegorical transference. In these bodily allegories, the grid-lines of differentiated, discontinuous existence are often blurred with regard to the representation of gender. The protagonists of these plays—Alberto, a cross-dressing homosexual, and John, a pregnant father-to-be—are characterized as sexual hybrids who elude any sort of fixed categorization. Underlying their ambiguous characterizations is an implicit rejection of any sort of mimetic relationship between sex and gender. Instead, Gómez-Arcos presents gender as a culturally and psychologically constructed notion whose existence is never predicated upon its relationship to biology. A similar attitude can be found in the writings of feminists, such as Judith Butler, who notes that, "When the constructed status of gender is theorized as radically independent of sex, gender itself becomes a free floating artifice, with the consequence that *man* and *masculine* might just as easily signify a female body as a male one, and *woman* and *feminine* a male body as easily as a female one."[19] Gómez-Arcos's underlying discourse on sex and gender foregoes any claims to a binary logic of male/female or masculine/ feminine. In his view, whatever differentiation may exist between male and female is an ephemeral occurrence, which evolved in nature out of a reproductive necessity, but which could just as easily return to a primordial state of nondifference: "the sexes separated because of a biological or reproductive necessity, but nowhere is it written that the sexes might not join together once again in a single individual if the necessity for the perpetuation of life were to dictate it in that manner.[20] His literary treatment of gender issues coincides with—and even anticipates—Hélène Cixous's view of bisexuality as an innate predisposed condition in all human beings. Unlike the Freudian concept of inherent bisexuality, which Cixous situates within "the false theater of phallocentric representationalism," she proposes an "other bisexuality," one that remains in a perpetual state of flux and transition.[21] Cixous's other bisexuality moves beyond so-called phallogocentric conceptions of gender, which are typically grounded in a Platonic logic of binary oppositions. It "doesn't annul differences but stirs them up, pursues them, increases their number."[22]

Gómez-Arcos's parallel abandonment of a patriarchal system of signification implies a transgression of social norms and a renouncement of cultural imperatives that are easily attributable, though not limited, to the construction of sacred, homogeneous order in fascist Spain. The nebulous sexual and gender identities of Alberto, John, and other Gómez-Arcosian characters are manifestations of their marginal rapport with the dominant sociocultural order.[23] They are societal outcasts: placeless, anomalous, and indeterminate entities, regarded by many as vulnerable and dangerous, and therefore subject to persecution, censorship, and exile. Their sexual and generic ambivalence characterizes them as transgressors. Furthermore, by eluding the traditional categorizations of male and female, their bodies become allegorical expressions of the individual freedom that Gómez-Arcos and his literary characters so often seek.

Adorado Alberto is subtitled "Esperpento en un acto" (*"Esperpento* in one act"); thus, as in the case of Gómez-Arcos's earlier works, it continues to participate in the traditions of the Valleïnclanesque, the grotesque, and the absurd. It is a play that is particularly evocative of the absurdist theater of Genet in that, with this piece, Gómez-Arcos embarks upon an exploration of the indeterminate nature of reality, illusion, and identity. He uses this exploration as a point of departure for an audacious interrogation of sovereign institutions.

The adored Alberto is a cross-dressing cabaret performer from Spain who has been living in exile in France. The opening scene of the play is situated in Paris, where Alberto has found freedom in both his art and his life. The rest of the play focuses on the events surrounding Alberto's vacation in Spain. Upon returning to his homeland for the first time in six years, he finds himself at the center of a tug-of-war between his dead mother (Mamá), his mother's sister (doña Julia), and Julia's godchildren (Romualda and José-Mari)—all of whom engage in a battle of wills with regard to Alberto's destiny.

It is this conflict of interests that serves as the principal source of dramatic intrigue in the development of the plot.

Gómez-Arcos, whose own exilic journey bears an obvious resemblance to that of his protagonist, portrays Alberto's homeland as a dark, backward place, devoid of cultural sophistication, a country held captive by the intolerance of the Church and the oppressive hands of an unnamed dictatorial regime whose presence is subtly intimated. This portrayal sharply contrasts with the depiction of France (i.e., Paris) as a more cosmopolitan setting, a place where tolerance and freedom of expression have become highly coveted values. The historical setting for *Adorado Alberto* is not directly specified, but the play does contain obvious allusions to the popular culture of the 1960s and the postwar generation. At one point, for example, Romualda and Alberto refer to the sexual allure of two icons of the European cinema of this period, Romy Schneider and Marlon Brando. Romualda announces that she prefers to be known as "Romy," and Alberto confesses that like Romualda, he too has dreamt of kissing Marlon Brando. These cinematic allusions are also conceivably part of Gómez-Arcos's endeavor to address a more international and cosmopolitan range of spectators.

Throughout the play, Alberto's gender identity is continually placed into question. He is characterized as an aesthete who goes to great lengths to cultivate his feminine side. He appears on stage as a sexual hybrid, an hermaphroditic being who perpetually eludes classification as male or female: he has breasts (he takes hormones), yet he also has a penis; he wears perfume and makeup, yet he also wears a fake mustache. By fashioning his own discourse on gender and sexuality, he effectively situates himself beyond the reaches of the fascist discourse of homogeneity that is subtly referenced in the play.

In the opening scene, the spectator is confronted with a metatheatrical situation that offers a glimpse into Alberto's life in France. He is seen in a Parisian cabaret, performing the role of a female striptease artist. Here, as is typical in Gómez-Arcos's theater, the *didascalia* are essential to the establishment of allegory and irony:

> *As the curtain rises, Alberto performs his transvestite number in a cabaret in Paris: a strip tease in which he only undresses his hands. He acts as though he were singing some song with a double meaning (force of habit), but he doesn't sing: he recites a poem, accompanied by a picaresque, vulgar tune. Naturally, the poem and the music are two absolutely distinct things, not meant to go together.*[24]

The stage directions invoke a series ambivalent gestures that metaphorically reference Alberto's transgendered performance: he does a striptease, *but* he only bares his hands; he acts as though he were singing a song, *but* he recites a poem; the poem is lyrical, *but* the music is vulgar. The spectator is invited to supplement this list of ambivalent gestures with the analogous perception that Alberto appears to be a woman, *but* he is also a man. In the same way that Alberto is already in the habit of singing songs invested with double meaning, so his transvestism is also invested with double-sided values. He appropriates and intermingles the codes of dress and comportment that are traditionally defined as either masculine or feminine. This ironic system of doubling coveys the underlying message that the person appearing on stage (i.e., a man, a woman, or a man dressed as a woman) is not necessarily what s/he seems, and that what one may take for reality, indeed may be an illusion.

Alberto's cross-dressing is a gesture that destabilizes binary conceptions of gender and sexuality. Furthermore, by positioning Alberto's transvestism within the context of a cabaret performance, Gómez-Arcos is able to underscore the notion of gender as a culturally *engendered* construct.[25] Alberto's gender remains in a perpetual state of flux. It is depicted as that unstable "free floating artifice" of which Butler speaks, and its definition is infinitely variable according to Alberto's own creative endeavors. While, at first glance, he seems to be playing a role, his actions suggest that his stage *persona* may, ironically, approximate a more authentic representation of his true identity than the spectator may have originally anticipated. His appearance at the beginning of the cabaret scene is described as "*Blond or brunette, made up, glamorous, displaying all his apparent feminine charms.*"[26] At first, his feminine side appears to be part of an illusory process of artistic invention. However, immediately following his performance, Alberto is depicted in his dressing room, caught in the act of creating still another role: "*The music ceases. Alberto bows. Immediately afterwards he is in his dressing room, taking off the wig, the eyelashes, the nails, etc., and putting on trousers, a false mustache, a scarf ... 'dressing up as a man,' just as we will see him in subsequent scenes.*"[27] In undoing the illusion of femininity, Alberto does not, as the spectator might anticipate, uncover an authentic male self; rather, he is merely dressing up as a man; he is creating a sexual identity. His fake mustache (emblem of masculinity) is an important part of this illusion, for it is no more authentic than the wig that Alberto wears when he appears in drag. His fabrication of a male role is thus an alienating, defamiliarizing gesture that undermines the spectator's ability to lay an authoritative claim to his true identity by situating his masculine and feminine role-playing beneath the same illusory light. Authenticity is confused with artifice, male with female, and theater with life in a situation that suggests that the female stripper who appears at the beginning of the cabaret performance may not have been a role at all. In effect, it is implied that Alberto's "real" performance may be his male *persona*. This masculine role functions as a kind of metatheatrical mask that Alberto will don throughout the rest of the play when he returns to Spain. His exile to France represents not only a search for artistic freedom, but an ontological quest for his authentic self.

During the cabaret scene, Alberto recites the following poem, which, as he later reveals, was composed by his mother and enclosed in one of her letters to him:

1   For example, your hands.
       Do you know yet what they are searching for?
       If you leave them astray
       they will be humiliated, searching for
5   a God that does not exist.
       Or they will cut the flower .
       Or they will strike the child.
       Or they will pull without fear
       the trigger
       —without fear and without pity.
       And if for that they exist
       your hands
       cut them off, and throw them away.
       Because it is better that they be left
       in the mouth of a dog
       or in the trash
       than be your daily
       assassin, my assassin,
       without constructing life,
20   constructing death.

21   Or if you love them so
       your hands,
23   give them reason to live,
24   creation of chimeras,
       realization of dreams,
       houses, trees, people,
       love to achieve,
       simple and beautiful things
29   to do . . .
30   but don't give them gods
       nor death:
32   They are your hands.[28]

While the poem can be read in broad terms as an allegory of the relationship between oppression and freedom of expression, on a more concrete level, it conveys Mamá's words of advice to her son during the period of his exile. It is her way of telling him that his life is in his own hands and that he has the freedom to choose his own destiny. The first stanza portrays the hands (concretely, Alberto's hands) as an instrument of death (lines 1–20). They are fearless and merciless hands, endowed with the capacity to engender ruin and destruction: "Or they will cut the flower. / Or they will strike the child. / Or they will pull without fear / the trigger." The violent images of this first stanza are subtly reminiscent of the land of oppression and intolerance that Alberto has attempted to flee. This negative perspective is countered by the optimistic imagery of the second stanza (lines 21–32), in which the hands are depicted as a benevolent instrument of life, endowed with the capacity to carry out creative endeavors: "creation of chimeras, / realization of dreams / houses, trees, people, / love to achieve." The imagery of the second stanza is evocative of France, a place where Alberto is able to remove his "mask" and candidly engage in a search for his authentic self. Should he choose to live in Spain, his destiny will be governed by the sacred values of the Church and the regime. However, Mamá admonishes her son not to subject his destiny to the whims of a higher power, exemplified by the figure of God, whose existence is nihilistically denied (line 5). She would like Alberto to realize his dreams and create beautiful things, and she advises him to choose life (line 23) over death or God (lines 30–32). The underlying message of her poem is thus an admonition to Alberto that he not let himself—his hands, his body, his mind, his spirit—be dominated by a sacred authority and that he live without hindrance as a free individual. Mamá is warning him not to return to Spain, where his musical numbers have been prohibited. Hence, the creative endeavors that Alberto has been able to realize through his art are converted into a metaphor for the freedom that he has garnered in life.

Alberto's mother, who is positioned on stage during the entire play, completes the metatheatrical frame of this opening cabaret scene. She is a spectator who offers ecstatic praise for her son's performance: "Adored Alberto! What a fun number, that one about the girl from the provinces . . ."[29] Her brief exchange with Alberto in this opening scene marks the only point at which she engages in direct dialogue with another dramatic personage. Even on this occasion, however, the conversation appears absurdly disengaged and strangely anachronistic in that she does not refer to the poem that Alberto has just recited, but instead, to a musical number about a girl from the provinces. Additional spatiotemporal incongruencies can be detected in Mamá's mode of dress. In the opening stage directions, for example, she is "*sitting on a beautiful wicker chair, for the beach or garden, in a photographic pose, dressed with summer elegance in the style of fifteen years ago. Or perhaps ten. (Anyway, she must be dressed so that, as she changes adornments, she coincides with the style of the last ten or fifteen years.)*"[30] She remains motionless throughout most of the play, as though frozen in time, maintaining her photographic pose, and it is here that one can locate an explanation for her anachronistic exchange with Alberto: the character of Mamá is a theatrical rendition of a photograph (or series of photographs). During the course of the play, she depicts several freeze-frames from the past. She poses on her chaise longue while vacationing in Capri or Nice, she wears a black veil of mourning in a photo taken on the occasion of her husband's death, and she puffs on a cigarette in a portrait that displays her bohemian temperament. It is as though Mamá were a snapshot from the past, superimposed upon the present. With her image, Gómez-Arcos has created an allegorical effect that is comparable to that of photographic double exposure.

Doña Julia occasionally reconfigures Mamá's pose and adjusts her dress, thereby signifying a change in the photograph. Because Mamá is dead, her clothing is always ten or fifteen years behind the times. Despite her defunct state, nevertheless, she has managed to attain a certain degree of immortality.[31] Her photographic presence constitutes a curious traversal of the boundaries of space and time. She is both animate figure and inanimate object, at once absent and present. She exists on an ethereal plane as a memory or ghost from the past, and still she manages to intervene in the space occupied by the other characters who exist in the material world of the present. She presides over the present scene and sits in judgment of her family's actions. They, in turn, speak to her frozen image and stare right through her silent gaze. They often comment on the photos of Mamá, pausing to recall when and where each snapshot was taken. Her image serves as a kind of catalyst for resuscitating their memories of the past.

Mamá's position in the realm of the eternal afterlife endows her with the capacity to transcend the limits of life and death, past and present. It also accords her a divine sort of wisdom, which is most clearly revealed during the moments when she stirs from her fixed position in order to offer the audience her personal impressions of the events that are transpiring on stage. In this manner, Mamá, like the Intellectual in *Mil y un mesías* (One thousand and one Messiahs), establishes a bridge of communication between the fictional world represented on stage and the world inhabited by the audience. She is suspended in space and time, between reality and illusion. Her personal reflections, which are always candid and often amusingly sardonic, impart privileged information that is intended for the spectator's ears only. She is able to speak her mind without trepidation because the other characters are unable to hear her voice. Her commentaries, which stem from the vantage point of historical hindsight, offer the audience an alternative point of view, a critical perspective that clashes with doña Julia's version of reality and the truth.

Alberto's mother feels nothing but total adoration for her son, and unlike her sister, she does not wish to change him. Even in death, Mamá continues to offer Alberto the same unconditional love and devotion that she offered him during her lifetime. She explains, in a commentary that is only audible to the audience, "My adored Alberto. When someone would ask me why I loved you so much, I couldn't answer with a single word. I would be dumbfounded. It wasn't enough to say, 'I love him because he is my son.' (*She laughs a bit.*) The love of a mother is so easily understood . . . No. I loved you for something else. For you, Alberto. For you, yourself."[32] Mamá possesses the same artistic, creative spirit that so strongly manifests itself in her son. She vigorously supports Alberto's desire to express himself freely, without censorship, and she confronts the oppressive norms of society, the Church, and the regime with an air of defiance. She maintains an attitude of indifference with regard to the opinions of others—especially the disapproving comments of her sister Julia, a devout Catholic with ardent fascist inclinations.

While speaking to a "photograph" of Mamá, doña Julia is reminded of the outrage she once felt regarding the presumably scandalous portrait of her nephew that was commissioned by her sister when Alberto was still a very small child: "Portray his little nude body, with those ringlets, on that satin cushion. I suppose you're paying for it now."[33] Mamá's sympathetic endorsement of Alberto's ambivalent sexuality is an expression of her own rejection of patriarchal sociocultural norms, such as those imposed by Franco's fascist order.[34] Alberto's bodily transgressions are invested with powerful metaphoric implications that situate both mother and son on the fringes of the dominant system.

On the day of her death, Mamá offered Alberto the following final words of advice, which she recalls for the audience: "Don't ever come back, Alberto, do not come back. Not even to lay flowers upon my grave. Not even to say hello to me. Because if you return, you will fall into her hands. (*Small pause. Smiling:*) Did you know that Alberto has never said 'good-bye?' In realty he has never thought about my death. He has always thought about my life."[35] Again, as in her poem,

Mamá advises her son to remain in exile, but this time she couches her concerns in more prosaic terms. She is worried that if Alberto were to return to Spain, he would fall into the oppressive clutches of doña Julia; hence, Mamá's reference to the hands ("your hands") is imbued with double meaning. It indirectly reprises the image of the tyrannical hands of destruction, which emerged in Alberto's prior poetic recitation, and more concretely, it is a reference to doña Julia's hands of intolerance. Both sets of hands are allegorical images of the dictatorial system whose grasp Alberto has attempted to elude. Mamá fears that these hands will attempt to castrate her son's freedom, deny his true identity, and convert him into somebody who he is not.

Doña Julia, the embodiment of totalitarianism, is willing to go to the most absurd extremes to defend her faith, her traditional moral principles, and her patriarchal values. Her obsessions with external appearances, "el qué dirán" (social scuttlebutt), and an anachronistic honor code lead her to a life of hypocrisy and deception (attributes that establish a kind of parodic alliance between her character and Benito Pérez Galdos's doña Perfecta).[36] Doña Julia's hypocritical attitude is summarized in an emblematic gesture that she repeatedly performs, in which she seals her lips closed with the sacred sign of the cross. Like many of Gómez-Arcos's characters, she cloaks her transgressions in a virtuous façade of sanctity in order to perpetuate her own self-serving image of the truth. Somehow, she always finds a way to justify her sins, no matter how reproachable they may seem. "What matters is what matters," she declares. "I'll confess, later."[37] While her morally ambiguous characterization is somewhat reminiscent of Pura and Angela in *Los gatos* (The cats), doña Julia's behavior is, in fact, more foolish than evil, and more humorous than perverse. She perceives Alberto's controversial image and lifestyle as a dangerous threat to her family's reputation, and as a result, she becomes thoroughly consumed by her desire to defy her sister's dying wishes and bring an end to any questions that may exist regarding her nephew's ambivalent sexual identity. Mamá explains:

[M]y dear sister is so hypocritical, so fundamentally hypocritical, that she doesn't even realize it. I don't know if you have noticed, but she is trampling on all her beliefs, her moral principles, her God, in order to defend her social prejudices. And all because my son Alberto is . . . "that way," and performs as a transvestite in a cabaret in Paris. Ah, did I tell you that the day I conceived Alberto was a beautiful day in springtime, full of birds and flowers, and that his father was a man whom I never met? Well it's true. It's historic.[38]

As a first step toward achieving her goals, doña Julia makes sure that Alberto travels to Spain by train so as to avoid any risk that her friends might see him. (Her friends, she reveals, always travel by air). Next, acting upon the advice of her spiritual director, she attempts to conjure an absurdly incongruous marriage between her nephew and Romualda with the intention that such an alliance will confirm Alberto's heterosexuality for all the world to see. Her greatest aspiration is a wedding announcement that would read: "Doña Julia García is delighted to communicate to all her friends that her nephew Alberto was married yesterday . . ."[39] The circumstances of the marriage she so strongly desires are inconsequential to her—that is, until, to her great dismay, her devious machinations yield a series of surprising results.

One could conceivably define Alberto and Romualda's relationship as that of two cousins (Julia is both Alberto's aunt and Romualda's maternal guardian), but this is an essentially minor drawback compared with the more crucial defects that plague doña Julia's scheme, one of which pertains to the enigma of Romualda's physical demeanor. Oddly described as having her "brows together and heavily mustached" ("cejejunta y bigotuda"), Romualda appears to be just as sexually unclassifiable as Alberto. His mustache is false, but hers, ironically, is genuine. Despite doña Julia's excessive preoccupation with appearances, it seems that paradoxically, in the case of Romualda, she has decided to forgo her concerns with aesthetics and refrain from encouraging her goddaughter to improve even her most unbecoming features. Such "frivolities," she tells Romualda, would be dishonest: "I never permitted you to wear skirts, nor for you to shave your armpits, nor for you to tweeze the hairs from your mustache, so that Alberto, finally bored sick from such frivolity, would find in you the ideal woman, honest. My poor sister would let out a scream every time she set eyes on you, as if she had seen the devil. She said that you had become 'anti-aesthetic.'"[40] With her excess facial and body hair, her unfashionable dress, and her awkward leaps into the air, Romualda hardly conforms to the image of a polished young ingenue who would be likely to incite male desire. Even less plausible is the assumption that she could possibly inspire in Alberto a transformation to heterosexual male.

Doña Julia appears to be blind to these obstacles. She remains steadfast in her role as *Celestina* and even encourages the unlikely couple to engage in premarital sex in the hope that their unholy union will eventually lead to sacred matrimony. She describes her preparations for their sinful alliance: "Sheets of a pale, salmon color, of silk, that I imagined to be lascivious, exciting; on the balcony, five tropical plants, of a green color that makes one lose one's head, and something that I read about in my book of meditations, which was a sin, and which incites sin: oriental incense."[41] Following the couple's illicit encounter, doña Julia is extremely disappointed to learn that Alberto has remained indifferent to Romualda's sexual overtures, and that the only transformation that has taken place behind the closed doors of the bedroom pertains to Romualda's physical appearance. In an effort to help her look more like Romy Schneider, the actress she so idolizes, Alberto has given her beauty advice. Moreover, in keeping with the 1960s vogue, he has employed his sophisticated sense of fashion in order to convert her long skirt into a stylish "mini." Romualda explains, "Alberto, who has some marvelous hands, took some scissors, needle and thread and went to work." And *voilà!*[42] In contrast with the prior reference to Julia's hands of intolerance, here Gómez-Arcos re-appropriates the image of the hands as an instrument of artistic creation.

José-Mari's role in doña Julia's scheme is just as problematic as that of his sister. As children, José-Mari and Alberto enjoyed a rather unorthodox sort of friendship. For example, on the day of their first communion they each wanted to ingest one half of a single Host so as to strengthen their bond with each other—as opposed to their sacred covenant with God. (A similar image is repeated in *L'agneau carnivore*.) It is also implied that during their youth, they shared an intimate relationship as army buddies. Doña Julia, predictably, appears to overlook these details when she calls upon José-Mari to teach Alberto to behave more like "a man" by taking him to a football match. José-Mari obeys her request, but returns from the football stadium alone and discouraged. Doña Julia demands an explanation regarding his apparent mood of devastation:

José-Mari. There were a lot of people . . . more than there were seats. Pandemonium. That's the way everything happened.

Julia. (*Stunned, slowly making the sign of the cross as she speaks.*) I believe . . . I have to bless myself. (*Mamá begins to smile openly.*)

José-Mari. The fact is that the two of us did not fit in one seat . . . (*Justifying*) . . . although I bought two tickets . . . and Alberto sat down directly on my knees . . . He said that he was more comfortable. Doña Julia, I don't know if it was the heat . . . or the perfume he was wearing . . . which wasn't cologne, but rather, perfume . . . or that the fabric of his shirt was very fine and I was embracing him . . . so that he wouldn't fall off each time he would yell to a player "Beautiful shot, man!" . . . the fact is that everything of mine began to grow . . . to grow . . . and my trousers became small.[43]

The result of the men's adventurous outing is the exact contrary of what doña Julia had originally anticipated. The perfume that Alberto wears, the finely woven fabric of his shirt, and the way he sits on José-Mari's lap are features that, rather than affirm his manliness, serve to corroborate his feminine inclinations. Furthermore—and to doña Julia's utter disgust—José-Mari's experience at the football game has served to substantiate his own homosexual proclivities, as indicated by his apparent erotic arousal when Alberto sits on his lap. What was originally conceived as a scenario designed to encourage a routine sort of *macho* camaraderie—the kind that is customarily associated with sporting events—has evolved into an adventurous liaison containing sexual overtones. In the end, José-Mari informs doña Julia that Alberto has remained at the stadium in order to visit with the football players in the locker room.

Mamá finds great humor in doña Julia's foolish actions and continues to watch in amazement as her sister prepares to execute her next plan. Julia gives José-Mari one thousand pesetas, enough for two prostitutes (one for each of them), and demands that he take Alberto to what she happens to know is the only remaining bordello in the city, ironically situated at number five, The Love of God Street ("calle del Amor de Dios"). When José-Mari proposes that they economize and split one prostitute between the two of them in a kind of *ménage à trois*, she disapprovingly dismisses his proposal, reminding him that such a gesture bears a dangerous resemblance to the time they attempted a three-way communion with the sacred Host. The rendezvous at the whorehouse proves to be a disastrous undertaking that propels Alberto into a nervous frenzy. He is outraged and offended by José-Mari's proposal that they indulge in the services of "two harlots ("dos furcias") and informs doña Julia that her godson has remained at the bordello to enjoy the offerings of the two prostitutes on his own.

Mamá offers the audience her own critical view of her sister's failing attempts to coerce Alberto into a life of heterosexual husbandry: "Poor Julia. I feel so sorry for you. Do you know what love is? No. When, as a child, they spoke to you of the love of God, and you followed that route, you were completely wrong. And already you see what there is at number five, The Love of God Street: a whorehouse."[44] Divine reverence has dissolved into earthly passion on the street named after divine love. Indeed, the most virtuous manifestation of love that is disclosed in Gómez-Arcos's play is far removed from the celestial world, for it is revealed to be the unconditional love that exists between a mother (Mamá) and her son (Alberto). Mamá's adoration for Alberto (hence the Spanish title of the play) is love in its purest form. It is a love that is indifferent to appearances, for it began long before she ever saw her son for the first time. Mamá explains, "When I had my adored Alberto in my womb, and I would feel him grow day after day, my love did not have limits. I loved his father, who had helped me to engender him, and my little one who was growing moment by moment inside of me. But I could never speak of that love in my poetry."[45] Mamá's love for Alberto derives from a point in time and space that exists prior to the construction of gender. Her adoration for her son emanates from within the undifferentiated, primordial world of her sheltered womb and is completely oblivious to the oppressive limitations of the exterior world. Thoroughly untainted by the patriarchal way of seeing, Mamá's love is, consequently, a prohibited, censored form of love, suppressed by tyrannical hands. It has never shown its face in her verses, yet it continues to survive, albeit tacitly, on an immortal plane in the realm of the eternal afterlife.

Following his *ménage à trois* at the whorehouse, José-Mari finally returns home in a completely debilitated state, and he blames his godmother for the friction that has consequently surfaced between him and Alberto. Then, in a surprisingly climactic moment, he comes forward with a suggestion that is so inconceivable and so startling to his god-mother that it causes her to collapse on the floor: " . . . if you want to marry off Alberto," he announces, "marry him to me!"[46] Romualda, equally stunned by her brother's unforeseen revelation, lets out a shriek of hysteria. The unconventional proposal of a marriage between José-Mari and Alberto may not seem as unusual today as it did when Gómez-Arcos wrote his play in 1968, nevertheless, the metaphoric implications of such an unorthodox union are timeless. Their iconoclastic union encompasses a nonreproductive sexual economy based exclusively on principles of pleasure and supplemental excess—quite the contrary of the utilitarian view of sexual intercourse that is typically sanctioned by the Catholic Church.

José-Mari's unorthodox marriage proposal represents a turning point in the play, which sets into motion an absurd process of grotesque deformation whereby ambiguities multiply and distinctions collapse. The influence of the theater of Valle-Inclán is all the more discernible here as the two women progressively take on the qualities of domestic animals. They appear to relinquish all sense of civility, yielding to the power of their bestial urges. "This world is a bitch . . . . ," declares doña Julia as she drags herself along the floor, "This modern and corrupt world is a bitch. And I'm a bitch. And my dead sister is a bitch. . . ."[47] Her outcry of disgust (the equivalent of the colloquial English expression, "life is a bitch") is more than a mere figure of speech; her words also take on a literal value as she barks like a dog. (Hence, the reference of the French title *Et si on aboyait?* becomes clear.) Romualda, on the other hand, jealous and catlike, meows and scratches her brother on the face. The disintegration of sacred values, which doña Julia attributes to the advent of the modern world, is thus metaphorically inscribed upon their bodies in the form of an absurd metamorphosis.

Despite her apparent debacle, doña Julia still has one final recourse available to her in her insidious attempts to maintain a hold over Alberto's destiny. This time, she resorts to the faculties of her imagination in concocting an outlandish lie that betrays both her nephew and the memory of her dead sister. As Mamá listens in bewilderment, Julia tells Alberto that his mother, immediately prior to her death, asked her to see to it that he marry.

> *Julia.* . . . But your mother was even more of a saint. Extremely saintly. Moments before dying, after receiving communion . . .
>
> *Alberto.* (*He looks at her, unable to understand.*)
>
> *Julia.* . . . she took my hands between hers and she said to me: "Julia, my adored sister Julia, see to it that Alberto marry. (*Mamá is stricken with a coughing fit.*) What will become of him, without a good wife to care for him?"
>
> *Mamá.* Ay, if the dead could speak. (*Alberto has become sad, silent. He slowly sits down on the sofa.*) Adored Alberto, I didn't say it. I didn't say it!
>
> *Alberto.* (*Following a pause.*) Mamá received communion?
>
> *Mama.* No!
>
> *Julia.* Yes.
>
> *Alberto.* Auntie, have you ever lied?
>
> *Mamá.* Always!
>
> *Julia.* Never.
>
> *Alberto.*—So, Mamá received communion. (*Mamá begins to cry, desperately, without a sound.*) She died . . . having repented. Having repented for a life as beautiful as hers.[48]

Doña Julia's story completely contradicts Mamá's genuine dying wishes for Alberto: that he remain in exile and that he continue live as a free individual. Moreover, the supposition that Mamá ever asked God for forgiveness for her transgressions is a ridiculous fabrication that totally undermines her rebellious character. If doña Julia is the embodiment of the regime, continually seeking to hide the truth and place her definition of reality at the service of her own social and political goals, then Mamá represents a more authentic historical memory, forever striving to correct the falsely fabricated projection of reality that the dominant order has invented. Doña Julia takes out a handkerchief and wipes Mamá's eyes, leaving two black makeup smudges on her face. She then stretches Mamá's lips into the shape of a smile. Her gestures emphasize her deceitful endeavors to create her own rendition of the truth. Unfortunately, Mamá's cries and tears of frustration are in vain, for she and her son can no longer hear each other's voices.

In the play's surprising dénouement, Julia lets down her inhibitions and resolves to play her deceitful games by more modern rules: "We've been hit with the twentieth century, so, twentieth century it is."[49] She lights up a cigarette, offers one to "Romy" (who has since shaven her mustache) and encourages her goddaughter to commence a gradual seduction of Alberto. Both women fondle him affectionately with their tyrannical hands as they slowly remove his clothes. Doña Julia's language becomes increasingly candid and unrestrained: "Alberto . . . Now that you are about to get married, I should tell you a secret that is told to all fellows on the eve of their weeding, and that you will love: women also like to take it from behind."[50] Her brazen and rather lewd allusion to sodomy, hardly in keeping with her supposedly refined temperament, clashes abruptly with the repressed attitudes towards sexuality that she displayed earlier in the play. It is here that one can readily perceive the unconventional blend of lyricism and anarchism that is so characteristic of Gómez-Arcos's literature. Moreover, when Romy removes Alberto's shirt and exposes his breasts, doña Julia can no longer contain her bestial instincts. She is thoroughly overcome with erotic desire: "Don't you touch them, opportunist, lesbian! Albertito, marry me! Oh, what tits!"[51] It is not until José-Mari enters the room and takes part in the seduction that Alberto finally acquiesces to the caresses: "Alberto . . . (*The voice of José-Mari has sweetness, joy, surprise, a whole series of new emotions.*) Are you . . . a woman . . . with a prick? (*Alberto by now doesn't even know what he is, because little by little they have been converting him into a monster.*)"[52] José-Mari asks Alberto for his hand in marriage despite doña Julia's barks and Romualda's meows of disapproval. Alberto, on the other hand, is only willing to have José-Mari escort him back to Paris as his gigolo. The couple, in turn, agree to take Romualda along with them as their servant.[53] As the play concludes, Julia addresses the audience with her final observations:

This modern and corrupt world is a bitch. . . . And my spiritual director is a bastard. A bastard who said to me, "Doña Julia, my child, marry off your nephew Alberto. His life is a scandal." A bastard. And tomorrow morning I will go and tell that bastard: "Father, my nephew Alberto got married . . . to a twenty-five-year-old guy built like you wouldn't believe." And moral principles, bitches. Social prejudices, bitches. Religion, a bitch. And those three who have run off, three bitches . . . three bitches with four tits, three behinds, a cunt, two pricks and two pairs of balls.[54] I memorized it. Bitches, bitches, bitches, bitches. Bow, wow, wow, wow. (*She gets up.*) Anyway. It's better to put an end to memories.[55]

Doña Julia turns to Mamá and tears apart her sister's accouterments as though she were destroying a photograph. The image of Mamá, a vanishing memory, is imbued with infinite sorrow, for she is the historical consciousness that Gómez-Arcos so desires to recuperate. Nevertheless the end of this play, written in exile, is much more optimistic than Gómez-Arcos's earlier plays. Alberto may not know "what he is," but this is actually a victory rather than a tragedy. His ambivalence of gender has invested him—along with José-Mari and Romualda—with the freedom to invent new categories of being, to explore the possibilities of an existence without oppressive limitations and constraints. Doña Julia's endeavors to "regenerate" her nephew have been to no avail even though her desire to unite him with Romualda has been fulfilled in an ironic sort of way. Julia bids good night to the audience and announces that tomorrow she will confess to her sins.

Unlike Gómez-Arcos's pre-exilic works, *Adorado Alberto* offers the spectator an optimistic outlook with regard to the future. At the end of the play, a spark of hope surfaces from the darkness as exile manages to open the threshold to freedom, a threshold that is even further widened in his next play *Pré-papa*.

8

Pré-papa
(1969)

*Ma sublime décision: me placer en marge des us et coutumes, vivre
sans papiers d'identité, telle une Martienne.*[1]
—Agustín Gómez-Arcos, Bestiaire

In Gómez-Arcos's exilic literature, the themes of censorship and exile
combine with bilingualism to produce a sense of rupture with previously established paradigms. Both Alberto, the protagonist of *Adorado Alberto* (Adored Alberto) and John, the protagonist of *Pré-papa*,
share a common allegorical aspiration for transcendence. They long
to be liberated from the oppressive confines of existing structures of
signification. Gómez-Arcos catapults them into exilic realms where
they endeavor to shed the heavy burdens of the past and float freely
in search of a transcendental otherness. At times, the thematic
threads that comprise this fictional scenario—the desire to flee oppression and leap into freedom—appear to cross paths with Gómez-
Arcos's own *curriculum vitae* as an exiled writer. However, while
Alberto and John are granted the opportunity to live out the dream
of wiping clean their memories of the past, to fashion their own
individual identities without any regard for what may have existed *a
priori*, Gómez-Arcos, in his exilic writings, appears unable and unwilling to abandon completely his memories of the Spain that he has
left behind. His exilic discourse is underpinned by a persistent desire
to remember and recount. Indeed, even a world that is as strange
and different as the science fictive realm of *Pré-papa* is filled with
remnants and echoes of Francoist Spain.

These remnants are not merely nostalgic evocations of the past;
they emerge as part of a cathartic process through which Gómez-
Arcos is able to dispel the authoritative voices that continue to haunt
his present. Memory, in consequence, is converted into a form of

insurgency, an act of rebellion. As Michael Ugarte points out in *Shifting Ground*, the urge to bear witness, to recreate, to recall, and to give written testimony regarding past events—a past that has been left behind—is a frequent tendency among writers who have experienced exilic displacement.[2] In the work of the exilic writer, the past is continually juxtaposed with the present (or the future), the old culture with the new. Gómez-Arcos appears to be well aware of the risks inherent in the act of forgetting, for to erase the ghosts of his pre-exilic past would imply a complacent acceptance of the dictatorial order that attempted to suppress his memories.[3] The fictional realms of *Adorado Alberto* and *Pré-papa*, therefore, are converted into allegorical domains of resistance where Gómez-Arcos resuscitates the authoritative voices of his past, only to betray them in the present. Bilingualism, as I shall demonstrate in this chapter, is an essential element in this art of betrayal, and it emerges as both a thematic and structural element in Gómez-Arcos's exilic writing. Bilingualism signifies the convergence of temporal and spatial plains that is so crucial to the allegorical way of seeing.

Of all Gómez-Arcos's theater pieces, the term *bilingual* is perhaps most applicable to *Adorado Alberto* and *Pré-papa* in that together these plays comprise a linguistically complex scenario in which both Spanish and French play key roles. Although these works were originally written in Spanish, they have been staged only in French, and only the French version of *Pré-papa* has appeared in print.[4] It is for this reason that I shall refer to the French version in the analysis that follows. In 1979, Gómez-Arcos published an extended novelistic rendition of *Pré-papa*, titled *Pré-papa ou Roman de fées* (Pré-papa or a fairy novel), which he wrote directly in French. The novel contains many of the dialogues and speeches (e.g., Professeur Kedrova's lecture) that appeared in the original dramatic text.[5]

While the staging of *Et si on aboyait?* and *Pré-papa* under Gómez-Arcos's direction in 1969 does not represent his first artistic endeavor involving the French language (during the early part of the 1960s, he had already translated and adapted for the Spanish stage plays by Jean Giraudoux and René-Jean Clot),[6] the *mise en scène* of these two one-act plays and the subsequent publication of *Pré-papa* are, nevertheless, decisive events that mark the first stage in an emancipatory process whereby Gómez-Arcos is able to achieve artistic freedom through bilingualism. As a direct consequence of his exile and the censorship that he experienced in Spain, bilingualism is for him an act of pure rebellion that is intricately intertwined with the notion of freedom of expression. He refers to this situation in the essay titled "Censorship, Exile, Bilingualism: A Long Road to Freedom of Expression," which he presented at the Dia Art Foundation's Critical Fictions Symposium in May 1990:

> Bilingualism could be the metaphor for this inherent need for free expression in the act of writing. The acquisition of another language adds supplementary material to what one already had; it enriches it and distances it; it strips it of localism, of folklore; it transforms it into communicative material that is beyond linguistic barriers; it universalizes it. There will never be censorship strong enough to gag or castrate writers while they have the capacity to learn and, consequently, to possess this instrument of freedom which is a second, or a third language. Regimes of all types have shown that the monolinguistic prison is much more destructive for writers than the other prisons, the real ones.

For the bilingual writer living in exile, the transgression of linguistic borders is a daring feat that paradoxically yields both pleasure and danger. The new language is a virgin tool, unblemished and uncontaminated by connotations from the past. Like a painter who stands before a clean white canvas, the bilingual writer is faced with an extraordinary opportunity to start anew. Each brush stroke, and hence each word, holds the potential to take on unprecedented meanings that break with established paradigms and representations of reality. The creative implications of this situation are infinite, and the opportunity is undoubtedly cherished with delight, but the task of taking on a second language and making it one's own is also filled with tremendous risks and uncertainties. Gómez-Arcos describes this bilingual process as a perilous "jump into the void":

> This dangerous adventure of writing in a foreign language (a language that is very difficult to master and which forces you always to be a student, and, of course, to be guilty of all types of excesses, of assaults against others), this dangerous adventure, I repeat, is, in my understanding, the most exciting act of rebellion, the most enriching thing that a writer can do, forcing him or her to be twice as conscious and twice as responsible with regard to his or her voluntary freedom of expression.[7]

The writer who dares to take this plunge often finds him or herself deeply immersed in linguistic politics as language appears forever tied to the notion of cultural identity. Drawing upon his personal experiences, Gómez-Arcos describes in a second-person narrative how the bilingual exile is forced to dodge a flow of disdainful accusations emanating from both sides of the border. He or she is confronted with a succession of authoritative voices intent on maintaining the "integrity" of both the old language and the new. For Gómez-Arcos, to inhale and exploit the expressive power of a new language implies a two-fold act of aggression. It is an "invasion" of the new language and, at the same time, a "betrayal" of the language that has been abandoned:

> No longer natural: having not been learned from the cradle or from a childhood of expensive and foreign boarding schools, this new wealth that wasn't assigned to you is almost attained by your fingernails, struggling with a great many difficulties that mold character, those inherent in the language that you are learning, others in the very stock of the culture. In this way, this act of learning is transformed little by little into an authentic act of aggression, a war that must be won above all else, a war in which the enemies are not only in front of you, blindly defending the virtues of the language that you are invading, but also behind you, in all those (people and institutions) that, not content with having expelled you from your own language, vent their anger by accusing you of having betrayed it. As if you were committing adultery with a language that is not your own "legitimate language." To them, your act of liberty is illegal and, as a consequence, worthless. This freedom of expression becomes covert freedom, illegal freedom and its quality (literary or human) is left questioned by the mere act of expressing one's self outside the norm. It is a freedom beyond the law. A freedom that is outcast, or exiled.[8]

As Gómez-Arcos suggests, bilingualism has a direct influence upon a writer's rapport with a culture. It represents a liberating gesture that positions the exiled writer in a marginalized zone, a neither here nor there, so that he or she neither pertains thoroughly to the old culture nor to the new. In a 1971 essay titled "Extraterritorial," George Steiner offers a series of insights regarding the implications of literary bilingualism, and his observations are especially illuminating when viewed alongside the circumstances that encircle Gómez-Arcos's experience as a bilingual exile writer. Steiner perceives literary language as a reflection of a writer's rapport with the physical/geographical world. Consequently, the writer who has become "linguistically unhoused," who has chosen to express him or herself in a "strange" language that does not pertain to the territory of birth, brings a sense of displacement to his or her writing.[9] The bilingual exile is alienated with regard to the native country and likewise alienated with regard to the native language. Nevertheless, in exile, this writer projects upon the new country and new language a set of internalized codes that have been imported from the native country and native language. According to this perspective, the bilingual *exilé* never pertains completely to one country, nor to one language; rather, he or she belongs to an "extraterritorial" region of linguistic and cultural crossings.

Thus, if the words of the exile writer are located beyond the reaches of censorship and the boundaries of citizenship, then bilingualism only enhances their power of rebellion. It situates the writer in an indeterminate zone that is oblivious to the constraints of any particular code or system and enables the writer to forge his or her own nondifferentiated discourse. Steiner comments:

> A great writer driven from language to language by social upheaval and war is an apt symbol for the age of the refugee. No exile is more radical, no feat of adaptation and new life more demanding. It seems proper that those who create art in a civilization of quasi-barbarism which has made so many homeless, which has torn up tongues and peoples by the root, should themselves be poets unhoused and wanderers across language.[10]

Steiner observes that binary values inevitably characterize the life and work of the bilingual exile writer. This situation is even further complicated in the case of a multilingual writer, such as Vladimir Nabokov, whose multicultural/lingual situation is inseparable from the thematic motives that define his work. According to Steiner, the images of mirrors and incest that are common features of Nabokov's novels (such as *Ada*) are metaphorically linked to the linguistic infidelities and "constant meshing of languages" that also characterize his literature. Steiner perceives a similar correspondence between subject matter and form in the works of Oscar Wilde noting, in reference to Wilde's *Salomé*, that bilingualism can be construed as a linguistic expression of sexual duality and, thus, a metaphor for the expression of sexual freedom. In effect, as Steiner's analyses imply, bilingualism is analogous to bigenderism.

Correspondingly, in Gómez-Arcos's exilic allegories, bilingualism is more than merely a matter of pragmatics; rather, it is an underlying attitude that invests his writing with a sense of displacement, biculturalism, and, above all, freedom of expression. This bilingual attitude is manifested allegorically and thematically throughout the course of his exilic literature, affirmed and reaffirmed in the binary nature of his literary expression and in the cultural dichotomies that are constantly brought into the fore and systematically subverted. The dualisms of gender and sanctity that left a subtle imprint on his early pre-exilic plays take on even more conspicuous roles in his exilic works. In *Pré-papa*, the notions of exile and bilingualism—construed in the manner proposed by Steiner as a meshing of linguistic and cultural codes—emerge as dominant themes, allegorically duplicated in the traversals of kinship, gender, and sexual expression that surface throughout the play.[11] In addition, this bilingual attitude is reflected in the double-sided tension that emerges in *Pré-papa* between, on the one hand, the will to remember the errors of past history, and on the other, the desire to erase the past in a rebellious move toward freedom.

In his introduction to the French version of *Pré-papa*, published in the bimonthly *L'Avant-Scène* (1969), theater critic Raymond Gérome writes about his disenchantment with the Parisian café-théâtre scène, confessing that initially he was not particularly inclined toward the idea of spending an evening at the Café-Théâtre de l'Odéon, where Gómez-Arcos was presenting *Et si on aboyait* and *Pré-papa*. However, Gérome later admits that his initial impressions were highly misconceived:

> I was delighted with Gómez-Arcos's two plays. An authentic playwright, doubled as a true director; that—one knows, the proof abounds—is extremely rare. Gómez-Arcos brings us a coherent universe, a series of critical observations (often irresistible, sometimes troubling—I have in mind the end of *Pré-papa*—always sharp.)
>
> Gómez-Arcos is fierce, idealistic, and disrespectful. Marvelous combination at a time when one mixes all too willingly indifference, solemnity, bitterness, the "what-does-it-matter-as-long-as-there's-the-bomb" attitude, and materialistic obsessions.[12]

What is perhaps most striking about Gérome's enthusiastic praise for Gómez-Arcos's talents as both playwright and director is the curious blend of ferocity, idealism, and irreverence that he detects in these works. While the two short pieces that Gérome saw at the Odéon are part of an impassioned critical enterprise, at the same time, as he intimates, they offer the spectator an optimistic, hopeful, and even humorous vision of humanity. For the French critic, this was a welcome contrast to the mood of pessimism, existential anguish, and indifference that had infiltrated much of the French stage during the postwar decades of the 1950s and 60s.

Furthermore, Gérome confirms the presence of an idealistic element, which appears to have filtered into Gómez-Arcos's writing during this exilic period. Prior to his departure from Spain, Gómez-Arcos tended to conceive his works as closed cycles of violence and oppression, in which any semblance of faith in humanity would be promptly extinguished or exiled in an allegorical re-creation of the expiatory procedures that served to empower the Franco regime. Doña Tristeza de Arcos of *Diálogos de la herejía*; Inés of *Los gatos*; Lucio of *Mil y un mesías*; and Casandra of *Queridos míos, es preciso contaros ciertas cosas*—all central characters in his pre-exilic works—are personifications of hope who suffer tragic fates. *Adorado*

Alberto and *Pré-papa*, in contrast, are works that are pervaded by optimistic tones, expressing a sense of hope that was previously undetectable in Gómez-Arcos's theater.

In *Adorado Alberto*, as we have seen, the eponymous protagonist's allegorical voyage is situated on a geographic plane that is ostensibly an absurdist derivation of a particular historical reality: that is, Spain and France during the 1960s. *Pré-papa* is equally absurdist in character; however, unlike *Adorado Alberto*, it is situated in a science fictive realm, an allegorical space *par excellence*, whose rapport with reality may not be immediately obvious to the spectator. At first glance, the futuristic fantasy world of *Pré-papa* appears to contain only very few vestiges from Gómez-Arcos's homeland as well as his new exilic terrain. The setting seems strangely removed from any identifiable time or place, and it is this remoteness that potentially produces a series of temporal, spatial, and psychological gaps between spectator and scenic space. The theatrical strategies employed here are, thus, similar to those associated with Brechtian alienation. The spectators view the action from a critically distanced, defamiliarized perspective, which allows them to perceive with objective eyes the ironic rapport that is established between the futuristic world of the play and the social, historical, and political realities of our modern (or, postmodern) world—a perspective that is not unlike that of the exiled writer. The spectators, indeed, are exiled from the absurd world of *Pré-papa*, and rather than readily identify and empathize with the characters on stage, they are implicitly invited to assume a more impartial, dispassionate attitude with regard to the allegory they are witnessing. If this process of critical distancing is successfully accomplished, the audience will reach a heightened state of awareness, a *prise de conscience* in relation to what they are seeing. They will be able to recognize the process of allegorical transference that is at work in this play: that Gómez-Arcos has superimposed the themes of his preexilic existence within a dictatorial regime upon an allegorical plane located in a future century. In effect, the science fictive world of *Pré-papa* is a metaphor not only for Francoist Spain but also for any authoritative system.

The protagonists of *Pré-papa* are John and Mary Ferguson, a young couple whose names are evocative of the biblical "pretext" that underlies many of Gómez-Arcos's allegories. The spectator is provided with only schematic information about the Fergusons. John is twenty-five years old and Mary's age, it can be assumed, is close to that of her husband. They are newlyweds who have been married for only three months. Both are "foreigners"—a detail that is disclosed by the all-knowing Mademoiselle Adèle as a way of explaining the couple's supposedly radical behavior: "They are said to be married, but really, no one knows anything about them: they are foreigners."[13] The spectator is also led to believe that the Fergusons may be Americans, as intimated by their Anglo-sounding names and the fact that John was once a "boy-scout."[14] Their relationship appears to be a rather conventional one, and they have reached a point in their marriage in which they have begun to contemplate the possibility of engendering children. They are, in Mary's words, *"petits bourgeois. A petite* car, a *petit* television set and a *petit* cocktail in our *petit* apartment at the end of every month . . . eight *petit* guests . . ."[15]

The principal conflict, which is revealed during the opening moments of the play, involves the Fergusons's search for a diagnosis and cure for a mysterious malady that has suddenly besieged John. He has been experiencing fainting spells, nausea, and strange cravings; he has suddenly grown excessively pale; and he has been gaining weight at an exceedingly swift pace, despite the fact that he is on a diet. As the action progresses, the Fergusons's search takes on more profound ontological and epistemological dimensions as an allegorical quest for a way of life that will transcend all previously established limits.

Here, as is typical of Gómez-Arcos's theater, the allegorical way of seeing extends from plot and character development to the conception of scenic space. The scenic landscape functions as a concrete site upon which he is able to map out a series of confrontations between old and new; past, present, and future. The opening stage directions propose the construction of a tripartite space portraying three distinct domains, the limits of which are designated by the presence of three different pieces of furniture: *"The sofa of a doctor's office where John and Mary are found seated. A lecturer's desk behind which Professeur Kedrova prepares her text."*[16] Gómez-Arcos's description of the stage suggests a modest, uncomplicated employment of space and scenery—a situation that is perhaps in part due to the low-budget economics normally associated with café theater and the small, cavernous confines in which this type of theater was, and still is, frequently produced. All three domains are constantly in full view, and each piece of furniture functions as a metaphoric extension of the character(s) who occupy its corresponding domain. The sofa, for example, is evocative of the waiting process in which the Fergusons are engaged throughout the duration of the play. The audience bears witness to a continuous dialogue between John and Mary as they sit on this sofa in the waiting room of a doctor's office, nervously anticipating the test results that will unravel the mystery surrounding

John's enigmatic ailment. As Mary puts it, "The doctor is there so that we can give him the concrete facts. It's up to him to decide."[17]

While John and Mary await medical opinion, the characters occupying the two remaining domains present the Fergusons as well as the audience with their own observations regarding John's bizarre condition. Behind the desk sits an iconoclastic scientist known as Professeur Kedrova. At intermittent moments, she offers the audience segments of an ongoing lecture in which she touches upon a myriad of topics ranging from theology and colonization to the metaphysical implications of space travel.[18] Her desk is an emblem of her authoritative stance as the futuristic voice of science and technology. Alternating with the voices of the Fergusons and Professeur Kedrova is that of the ultrapious Mademoiselle Adèle, an old-world Catholic who happens to live next door to John and Mary. The *prie-Dieu* that defines her domain is an emblem of the religious authority that she claims to profess in the name of the Catholic Church.

In setting up these spatial designations, Gómez-Arcos is able to achieve an illusion of simultaneity of action among three non-contiguous allegorical realms. Three separate views of John's enigmatic condition converge within a single scenic space: the Fergusons's bourgeois-banal perspective, stemming from their present-day experiences; Mademoiselle Adèle's religious-traditional perspective, derived from the old-world values of the past; and the scientific-progressive perspective of Professeur Kedrova, offering an optimistic vision of the future.[19] In addition, it is possible to designate a fourth domain that is subtly insinuated: that of the invisible space occupied by the *Docteur*, whose enlightened medical perspective is so eagerly anticipated by John and Mary. The Doctor never actually makes an appearance on stage as he is extremely preoccupied with his behind-the-scenes battle for a cure for cancer. However, his medical opinions are transmitted through the presence of an *Infirmier* (Male Nurse), who acts as a go-between, navigating all scenic domains.[20]

As the play begins, the Nurse, playing the metatheatrical role of a waiter, enters with a tray of glasses, offering the Professor and then the Fergusons a cocktail and declaring, in a condescending tone of voice: "The consultation is scheduled for nine o'clock and it is but eleven o'clock. You can go ahead and have an apéritif. The Doctor is beginning to put on deodorant. Me, I need to go and wake up the cancer, since he's sleeping very late. Around forty-five minutes."[21] Thus, from the moment the curtain rises, the spectator is presented with an absurdly incongruous universe where a nurse serves cocktails to the patients in the waiting room and an anthropomorphic rendition of cancer is described as eating, sleeping, laughing, and even coming down with a cold. In the collision of past, present, and future perspectives, time appears to have lost all purpose and meaning. It is so illogically inconsistent that eleven o'clock in the morning precedes nine o'clock (unless, that is, Gómez-Arcos is pretending to mock those doctors who, typically, do not actually see their patients until long after the scheduled time of the appointment).

Nevertheless, beneath this portrait of absurdism and irrationality lie images of oppression and censorship, remnants of the dictatorial Spanish past that Gómez-Arcos has left behind. Most notably, these allusions to the past are embodied in the personage of Mademoiselle Adèle, a religious fanatic who prides herself on her singular ability to detect all sins, no matter where they may lurk. "If the Church had a police corps, I would be the Chief Inspector," she declares.[22] She engages in a kind of ecclesiastic espionage, periodically informing God by telephone of the scandalous embroilment of her neighbors John and Mary. When Adèle makes her entrance, she is carrying an enormous bag containing an unusual assortment of objects, which she will use to carry out her inquisitorial endeavors: a swatch of velvet, upon which she will kneel in prayer, a chalk board for jotting down any sins that she may happen to observe, special vitamins and a sandwich with which to "fortify" her prayers, and a telephone that will serve as her direct line of communication with God. She coughs as she politely introduces herself:

> Good-day. The atheists have let a gust of air seep into these parts. I've caught a cold. (*No one responds to her.*) I'm Mademoiselle Adèle. (*To the Fergusons.*) Married, but without children. Widowed, but without lovers. (*To all, with pride.*) I'm what the moralists call an exemplary individual, the product of a perfect and traditional society that, with the aid of God, no one will be able to ruin. At least, as long as I am living. (*To the Professor, with an innocent grin.*) I'm in very strong health. (*She goes toward the prie-Dieu, takes a nice new piece of velvet out of her sack, lays it out with care and then kneels. The nurse appears behind the confessional.*) Oh Mary conceived without sin.[23]

The Nurse, no longer playing the role of waiter, inhabits the role of priest as Adèle confesses the recently witnessed sins of others. Since she presumably lacks any transgressions of her own that would warrant confession (she is, after all, an "exemplary individual"), she is willing to bear the burden of the rest of the world's wrongdoings upon her own shoulders: "The whole world is but a sin. Above all, the young people. Where are we headed? Fortunately, I'm here—yes I am—to confess it all, commandment by commandment."[24]

The sins that Adèle chooses to confess span an oddly disproportionate scale of significance ranging from the Russians' venture to send a man to the moon, to the Fergusons's heated love-making. She lances a series of sanctimonious judgments in John and Mary's direction, accusing them of deviant behavior, sexual and otherwise. She is scandalized by their erotic activities and convinced that they are heretics who will burn in hell for their supposed sins of fornication: "Since they've been married, they haven't stopped committing atrocious sins against the sixth commandment. 'You will not fornicate, period.'"[25]

Adèle's limited view of the world, her bigotry, and her fanatical adherence to a rigid system of beliefs are characteristics that are juxtaposed with the attitude of tolerance and open-mindedness expressed by Professeur Kedrova. One of the focal points of the Professeur's lecture is the notion of space travel, an issue that incited widespread debate and international attention during the 1960s when the Soviet Union and the United States engaged in a competitive battle to send the first human beings into outer space. Professeur Kedrova expounds upon the metaphysical and theological implications of this exploration of unearthly realms, and her insights invoke a series of parallels between space travel, the nature of exile, and the allegorical way of seeing. She is deeply critical of all established systems of order and perceives the advent of space travel as an extraordinary opportunity for the human race to start anew with an unstructured, undifferentiated universe, untouched by the *grands récits* of preceding centuries: "Ladies and Gentlemen, we have opened up outer space. Life is about to begin for Man. From now on, time no longer exists. Only the conquest of the universe. A marvelous perspective."[26] This "marvelous perspective," which Professeur Kedrova attributes to the conquest of the universe, is analogous to the situation confronting the bilingual exile writer who embarks on the exciting, although uncertain, adventure of appropriating a new language and establishing a new residence. Space travel, thus, is comparable to that perilous "jump into the void" to which Gómez-Arcos refers in his description of the bilingual writer's exilic journeys into uncharted terrain.

However, the idea of traveling into space, of transgressing the frontiers of mundane reality with the objective of conquering and colonizing the universe, also invites a series of ontological questions with regard to the configuration and creation of the cosmos, the function of God as the authoritative center of that cosmos, and the relationship between human beings and their supposed Creator. For if modern scientific advances have furnished mortal humans with the ability to launch themselves into the heavens—a privileged space normally occupied exclusively by celestial beings—then how do these advances fit into a belief structure that acknowledges the presence of a sacred world? The realm of the sacred, as Professeur Kedrova would argue, has been replaced by the technological progress of secular domains: "Finally, Man, with the support of technology, has pierced the heavens. Those heavens, reserved throughout the centuries for God and his angels, are now our domain, a terrain open to a new life. Upon pronouncing the words *new life*, the question surges once again: is Man prepared to begin a voyage of which he only knows the point of departure?"[27]

Professeur Kedrova expresses a profound interest in the allegorical nature of religious thought, attributing the conception of heavenly beings to a metaphoric process of subjective invention, whereby human fears and desires are transferred from the earthly material world to an immortal celestial plane: "Let me explain: is there anything more metaphorical than the existence of God? . . . When something conjures fear for us, we invent a mystery around it, a metaphor."[28] The conception of God as metaphor, as the end product of an allegorical transference of fears and desires, places into question the traditionally accepted view of the realm of the divine as existing prior to the creation of the mortal world. According to Professeur Kedrova's perspective, God is not a supreme signified existing *a priori*; rather, the human being has been assigned the role of Creator. The sacred world is, consequently, a mirror image and signifier of human aspirations and apprehensions, and its conquest is no less accessible than any other mortal achievement.

Upon journeying into outer space, the human race, according to Professeur Kedrova, will be faced with another important question regarding the conquest of otherworldly realms: "Will he carry with him, for this fabulous mission, the same baggage that he carried with him on his previous discoveries?"[29] Her allusion to "baggage" is a metaphoric one, referring to the type of cultural baggage that one often associates with colonization, diaspora, and exile. In forging and mapping out new territories, a common tendency throughout history has been for colonists, exiles, and other displaced persons to impose the values of the old system upon the new, and the past system upon that of the future. (The Spanish conquest of America is an obvious example of this tendency.) Professeur Kedrova critiques the inhabitants of newly conquered domains, who, rather than seek out the innovative possibilities that the future may bring, remain constrained by the heavy burdens of history in the construction of their systems. They carry with them on their journeys a set of previously established ideas and values (religious, political, social, linguistic, economic, etc.), which they, in turn, project upon the newly discovered undifferentiated spaces. As a result, the "new" world often bears a paradoxical resemblance to the old world. It is nothing but a "museum" filled with artifacts from the past. The Professor elaborates:

> *Professor.* Let us summarize. What did Man carry with him on his previous discoveries? An immutable system. A system based on religion, homeland, family, power, economic interests, social and racial prejudices, and a ridiculous quantity of grammatical rules that are completely useless.
>
> *Adèle.* (*screaming.*) All that—it's outmoded now. The newspapers say so.
>
> *Professor.* (*furious.*) Shut up, you madwoman! (*She continues.*) Result? Hunger, war, sickness, incomprehension . . . Useless to proceed to a detailed analysis of colonial systems. We haven't enough time. It's sufficient to take for example any colonial empire. Those voyages dictated by avarice—Man did not undertake them for himself with the idea of purity or evolution. The pursuit of the future was not what he was interested in. He only wanted to establish the past. Burdened with crime and hopelessness.[30]

The Professor is concerned about the ability of the human race to transcend this vicious cycle of colonization, which only serves to perpetuate past errors. Her postcolonial attitude is indicative of her desire to see humans venture into outer space unencumbered by cultural *a prioris* in order to break with the past, traverse new horizons, and explore new structures of signification. She proposes that contemporary human beings who truly wish to express themselves freely travel into outer space, where they will find a completely unstructured universe, free of all systems, laws, and taboos. Consequently, her speech can be construed as a metaliterary commentary through which Gómez-Arcos is able to voice his concerns about the quest for freedom of expression through exile. In the paradigm proposed by Seidel in his description of the exilic imagination, exiled authors, while physically breaking their ties with their homeland and the past, often guard within themselves and within their literature a nostalgic view of their former world.[31] While they may believe that within the artistic space of their writing they are establishing a new exilic realm, free of restraint, their memories often anchor them to the older order. Moreover, many exile writers flee one oppressive system only to find themselves incorporated within another system that in reality is not as free as they may have originally anticipated. The result is comparable to the striking image that Gómez-Arcos presents in his novel *L'agneau carnivore* of two houses—a principal family residence in the city and a vacation home in the country—each of which is an identical mirror image of the other. He comments on this situation:

> Perhaps, unconsciously, what I was writing about when I spoke of those houses, one of which is the exact reflection of the other, is the idea of having abandoned one country in order to go to another that in a way— well, because we are still in the same system—was exactly the same. Perhaps it was the impossibility of escaping the system. The system is always the same. You can commit a whole series of acts of aggression against the system, but you always end up as a prisoner of the system; you always end up with an image of the system, with an image reflected in the mirror.[32]

In the preceding statement, Gómez-Arcos does not refer to any particular political or ideological system *per se*; rather he speaks of the continuous presence of a "System" in an abstract-allegorical sense. If indeed he were able to locate a pure, undifferentiated space, completely devoid of systems, then he will have found total freedom— and anarchy, in the positive sense in which he understands this term as a complete liberation from the shackles of oppression.[33] While for Gómez-Arcos, the absolute and unconditional evasion of the System is an unrealizable goal, for John it is an attainable aspiration, and John's own body serves as the point of departure for the fulfillment of this dream.

As the play progresses, John gradually reveals his peculiar symptoms to the Nurse. Adèle, in the meantime, confesses to God by telephone the bizarre activities of her neighbors: "She, she's working a little more each day, she's slimming down and she's drinking. No one understands anything about her. She wasn't like that before getting married. And he, he's growing paler. He already has dark circles around his eyes. He's getting fatter. Two contrary phenomena."[34] Adèle also mentions a gruesome episode in which John murdered his small dog with one swift blow to the head and then devoured the animal's brain. After running a variety of tests, the Doctor is finally able to determine the cause of John's bizarre metamorphosis. The Nurse makes the following announcement, informing him that he is pregnant: "(*he stops laughing and with a very social tone, he addresses John.*). *Mon petit chéri*, you are pregnant . . . pregnant. (*There is a silence.*) Totally pregnant. Three months."[35]

John's body has become a site of allegorical transference where the aspiration toward freedom of expression is inscribed. Anarchy reigns within his physiological system as his desire to have a child has materialized within his own body rather than that of his wife. John's pregnant bodily topography is thus an undifferentiated space where masculine and feminine codes converge, interrogating the borders of sexual difference. His sexually ambiguous body is a kind of bilingual text that expresses itself in the language of both man and woman. This meshing of cultural codes maps out, in Steiner's terms, an extra-territorial region of the flesh that is far removed from the authoritative grasp of the dominant system.

In the field of psychiatry, John Money and Anke A. Ehrhardt have observed a series of parallels between gender identity and native bilingualism. Whereas the bilingual child is confronted at an early age with two separate linguistic systems of communication, likewise, all children, whether male or female, are generally exposed to two gender systems, masculine and feminine. In responding to these dual stimuli, children are typically able to understand the discourse expressed by both systems. Nevertheless, there is always one mode of communication that tends to surface as the dominant system, one language or one gender with which the child ultimately chooses to identify and appropriate as his or her principal form of expression. According to Money and Ehrhardt, "When the models of gender identification and complementation have unambiguous boundaries, then a child is able to assimilate both schemas, the same way that a bilingual child assimilates two languages, the users of which are clearly demarcated and non-overlapping. The analogy with bilingualism is closer than it seems, if one considers those cases of the children of immigrants who learn to listen and to talk in the language of the new country, but only to listen in the language of the old country."[36]

John is bisexual in a physiological, rather than a psychological sense, and his hermaphroditic state undermines any possibility of his ever being able to express himself in an unambiguous manner. His hybrid sexuality implies not only a traversal of the cultural borders of gender identity; but it inspires a string of linguistic and semantic infidelities, inverting the conventionally accepted definitions of mother and father. The title of the play is the first indicator of this linguistic turmoil. The term *pré-papa* is a neologistic invention of Gómez-Arcos that derives from its feminine counterpart *pré-maman*, a designation frequently invoked in reference to French maternity fashions. Mary's severe reaction to her husband's state of expectancy is likewise indicative of the transgression of linguistic codes that John's bizarre condition implies: "John," she demands, "how could you do something like this to me? For three months, I've waited for you to make me a mother, and *voilà*, you've made me a father. You bastard!"[37] She envisions herself in a paternal role and her husband in a maternal role, a situation that is further accentuated when the

Nurse announces to John, "*Mon petit chéri*, you're going to be a mommy."[38]

As the dialogue continues between John and Mary, Mademoiselle Adèle and the Nurse (in the role of priest) begin to beat their chests with their fists in a kind of "savage and primitive" rhythm, while Professeur Kedrova takes out a yardstick and begins to measure John's body "*with a mixture of scientific curiosity and tenderness.*"[39] Mary, who is extremely concerned with the maintenance of honor and appearances, proposes a series of desperate measures though which she and John might avoid scandal and discretely resolve their dilemma. She suggests an abortion, only to be reminded by Adèle that the Church prohibits this possibility. Mary also suggests that she and John take refuge at a center for clinical research where they might receive payment for their services as scientific subjects, or that they retreat to a deserted island during the final trimester of John's pregnancy. All these suggestions are rejected by John, whose bilingual body is an allegorical signifier of the desire for freedom of expression. He assumes the roles of both mother and father and is determined to bring up his child on his own: "He is mine," he declares. "I am his mother."[40] Consequently, Mary, who has been deprived of her maternal role as well as her reproductive function, concludes that she has no other choice but to abandon her husband.[41] From a biblical standpoint, the impending birth of John's child represents an ironic critique of the primordial Nativity, a scene from which the Virgin Mary is this time notably absent.

In driving Mary away from John, Gómez-Arcos creates, on the one hand, a sarcastic caricature of the traditional phallocentric point of view which perceives a woman's role in society to be a function of her reproductive capacity. According to this view, Mary no longer has a real "role" to play in this absurd tale, so she is free to leave. On the other hand, Mary's decision to abandon John is evocative of Gómez-Arcos's personal declarations regarding sexual difference and his view that the distinction between male and female is an arbitrary and perhaps temporary situation which evolved out of a reproductive necessity:

> That is to say, I believe that humanity as a project is infinitely more important than the difference among individuals. The difference is an accident. In any case, it's completely scientific. The difference between the sexes occurred because the conditions made it necessarily so in order for life to continue, but the meaning of life is something else. The day in which life no longer needs the two sexes to perpetuate itself, the sexes

will become joined once again or there with be some other type of evolution, some other type of mutation.[42]

In the science fictive world of *Pré-papa*, that future day of which Gómez-Arcos speaks, in which two separate sexes are no longer needed for human life to perpetuate itself, has finally arrived. In this sense, Mary's presence on stage is redundant. Still, not only does John face rejection from his wife; his bilingual body also makes him an outcast who is forsaken by society and its institutions. The Nurse informs him that the world of medicine has turned its back on him. According to Mademoiselle Adèle, the Church, too, has closed its doors to him, although it will continue to monitor his activities from afar.

John, however, is not totally alone in his endeavor to express himself freely. Toward the end of this one-act play, the circumstances of his extraordinary, *insolite* condition appear to collide in time and space with the philosophical forecasts of Professeur Kedrova. The Professor, an exemplary dissident, describes the characteristics of the type of person whom she envisions as being most inclined to engage in a successful voyage through outer space with the objective of inhabiting this undifferentiated landscape: "A special kind of being, with a brain cleansed of all tradition, without memory and without a body open to evolution. A being pertaining to a new race or even one that creates it himself, outside the prison of our limits, of our prejudices."[43] Her vision of the future coincides perfectly with John's desire to traverse a set of deeply entrenched social, cultural, and linguistic boundaries by going through with his pregnancy and giving birth to his child. Recognizing this fortuitous coincidence, Professeur Kedrova presents John with a solution to his dilemma, offering to launch him into outer space, where he will be able to give birth in peace, without persecution and perpetuate a new race: "You and your descendants," she explains, "you will be the new race, the new life. Doesn't that seem marvelous to you?"[44] For John, her plan is like a fairy tale ("un conte de fée"). What Professeur Kedrova proposes, in effect, is an exilic journey to an ethereal plane where John and his child will be able to turn their backs to the past and float freely as signifiers liberated from the oppressive influence of previously existing signifieds. There, John and his future offspring will be able to start anew and express themselves in unprecedented ways. Realizing that he is already the incarnation of Professeur Kedrova's proposed new race, John agrees to place his destiny in her hands. His baby will be born in a totally unstructured universe, a place resembling the world in its primordial state, prior to the invention of censorship, intolerance, and restrictions. Before his departure, Professeur Kedrova insists that John adhere to only one promise—that he teach his child the exact opposite of what he has seen on earth.

The image of the child, understood as a metaphor for innocence, optimism, and hope, is a common motif in Gómez-Arcos's exilic literature, appearing with especially great frequency in his novels (e.g., *L'agneau carnivore*, *L'enfant miraculée*, *L'enfant pain*, *Bestiaire*, *L'aveuglon*, and, of course, *Pré-papa ou Roman de fées*). The child inside of John is the embodiment of his inner hope to free himself from the prison walls of the system, a metaphor for his longing for an innocent, untainted place where he can construct the future. John's unborn child is, correspondingly, a manifestation of Gómez-Arcos's desire to "write" his own utopian version of the future through the creation of a bilingual, exilic discourse. The bilingual exile writer's perspective is akin to that of a child discovering the world for the very first time, and the employment of a second language endows him or her with the power to bellow and shout all the words that were prohibited in the native language. The result is a sensation that Gómez-Arcos describes as "perpetual levitation," the feeling of having expressed the inexpressible, of having transgressed seemingly impossible limits. It is inferred that John, while suspended in outer space, will be able to achieve a similar sensation of perpetual levitation. Gómez-Arcos comments, "The day that the French language placed this possibility within my reach was without a doubt the most plentiful day of my life. That day, I understood that no one in my country, no institution, would ever have the right to silence me. . . . My deepest conviction is that . . . I would continue to be mute, silenced, if I were not bilingual."[45]

At the close of the play, Adèle, the Nurse, and Mary bark like dogs and bemoan the progress of the contemporary world. "This modern and corrupt world is a bitch," declares Adèle, echoing Julia's final pronouncements in *Adorado Alberto*.[46] John, as in the case of Alberto, will be given the chance to fulfill his dreams in an exilic, extraterritorial space. The optimism expressed in these plays sets up a significant point of contrast between Gómez-Arcos's work and that of his contemporaries of the Spanish "realist" generation, whose critical views of post–Civil War Spain most often expressed a lack of confidence in the future.

It is perhaps Gómez-Arcos's exile, coupled with his bilingual attitude, that sets him apart from this generation and aligns his exilic writing with the playwrights associated with the "new" Spanish theater. *Adorado Alberto and Pré-papa* are evocative of a specific moment of transition in Gómez-Arcos's life, and as such, one can perceive in them an underlying tension between an aspiration toward a rupture with the past and the anxiety of remembering history so as not to duplicate it. The structure that emerges in these works is no longer the oppressive endless cycle of eternal return of pre-exilic plays; rather, it is open-ended and infinitely optimistic. John promises to adhere to Professeur Kedrova's request that he turn his back on the past and agrees to be launched into outer space. As I shall demonstrate in the chapter that follows, the science fictive theme of space travel is taken up once again in *Interview de Mrs. Muerta Smith por sus fantasmas*, where images of displacement and diaspora cross paths with surrealism in the creation of a series of gargoylesque, hallucinatory visions.

IV
Sanctifying the Scatological and Debasing the Divine

9

Interview de Mrs. Muerta Smith por sus fantasmas
(1972 / 1991)

Y a-t-il rien de plus métaphorique que l'existence de Dieu?[1]
—Agustín Gómez-Arcos, Pré-papa ou Roman de fées

*I*NTERVIEW *de Mrs. Muerta Smith por sus fantasmas* (Mrs. Dead Smith's interview with her phantoms), written in 1972, is one of Gómez-Arcos's most brazenly irreverent theater pieces. It represents a culmination point in the evolution of his search for freedom of expression through allegory and the exilic imagination. It was, perhaps, a befitting gesture that this would be the play he used as a springboard for reestablishing his voice on the Spanish stage following his twenty-five year silence. *Interview de Mrs. Muerta Smith* premiered in February 1991 at Madrid's Sala Olimpia, the Centro Nacional de Nuevas Tendencias Escénicas, and on this occasion, Gómez-Arcos's theatrical voice appeared to be as powerful and compelling as ever.[2] The language of this play exhibits the same fiercely audacious tone that he later carried over into his work as a novelist. By the time he wrote this piece, he had clearly left behind the tendencies of the realist generation. In contrast, *Interview de Mrs. Muerta Smith* is a grotesque farce anchored in the traditions of the avant-garde (the surreal, the absurd, the *esperpento*), in which no sacred taboo is left untainted by the machinations of transgression. This firmly grounded attitude of dissent coincides with Gómez-Arcos's view of the theater as a contestatory art, able to raise consciousness regarding issues of cultural identity and representation by touching and trespassing upon all those regions, spaces, and places that are traditionally designated as prohibited domains. On the occasion of the première, in an interview with Juan Antonio Vizcaíno of *El País*, Gómez-Arcos made the following declaration expressing his displeasure with the long-standing vogue on the Spanish stage—already decades old—of a theater created for the sole purpose of entertainment: "I believe that I write with the intention of fixing the world by explaining it. Theater or literature conceived as entertainment is something that is horrifying and inconceivable to me."[3]

In general, critics were generous with their praise for the 1991 production of *Interview de Mrs. Muerta Smith*, which, like the other two recent productions of Gómez-Arcos's plays, was staged under the direction of Carme Portaceli with costumes and set designs by Isidre Prunés and Montse Amenós. Julieta Serrano (most recently recognized for her work in a series of Pedro Almodóvar films) played the role of Mrs. Muerta Smith and Manuel de Blas (who, three years later, would go on to play the Captain in *Queridos míos, es preciso contaros ciertas cosas*) appeared in the role of Boby, Mrs. Muerta Smith's dog. Regarding the première, Enrique Centeno of *Diario 16* wrote that the staging of this play was a "fair recuperation" and that Gómez-Arcos represents "the impossible essence of past decades."[4] Eduardo Haro Teclen of *El País* made the following observations:

> The dialogue, with Gallicisms and all, is free-flowing and sharp. . . . All of this drew attention at first, laughter later on—the play seems to be composed of two works joined together—and real enthusiasm from the audience at the Sala Olimpia. Not only for the actors and Gómez Arcos's text but also for Isidre Prunés and Montse Amenós's costumes and set design and for Carme Portaceli's good understanding and explanation of the play.[5]

In *Interview de Mrs. Muerta Smith*, the violent collision between religion and sacrilege, already present in his pre-exilic plays, acquires an even more potent odor as it becomes inundated by a deluge of bodily waste. This play epitomizes a process whereby the holy is intermingled with the scatological, and saintly icons of the Catholic Church—saints, God, even the pope—are grotesquely deformed, metaphorically inverted, and characterized in terms of their rapport with the lower regions of the body and the fluids discharged from these regions. The hyperbolic portrayal of these characters and the surreal depictions of the worlds in which they navigate are elements that situate Gómez-Arcos's literature within a long trajectory of grotesque realism, established in his native Spain by such artists as Fernando de Rojas, Miguel de Cervantes, Francisco de Quevedo, Francisco de Goya, Ramón del Valle-Inclán, Salvador Dalí, Francisco Nieva, and Luis Buñuel.[6]

According to Mary Douglas, the human body can be construed as an allegorical representation of any sociocultural system, whereby its margins and orifices—mouth, anus, vagina, etc.—signify the power-ful, vulnerable, and precarious areas of society.[7] A culture's fears with regard to these regions of power and danger are paralleled in its rapport with the human body. Mikhail Bakhtin poses a similar con-ception in his study of Rabelais (originally published in 1965) whereby the grotesque image of the body is interpreted as a metaphor for the transgression of societal and linguistic structures. His discussion of the carnivalesque and the grotesque—tendencies that are clearly manifest in Rojas's *La Celestina*, Goya's *pinturas negras*, Valle-Inclán's *esperpentos*, and the cinema of Buñuel (to mention only a few of the many Spanish precedents)—centers on the Renaissance conception of the body as cosmos; that is, the body perceived as a microcosmic image of society, the world, or the universe.[8] Consequently, grotesque realism can be interpreted as a form of literary/linguistic subversion that conveys a political meaning as well. Whereas the conception of the medieval cosmos is grounded in the hierarchical principles of Aristotelian order, the grotesque tradition, like the allegorical cult of the ruin, is informed by an anticlassical impulse: it carries out a metaphoric inversion/subversion of the hierarchical ordering prin-ciples of the Aristotelian cosmos by turning it inside-out and plotting a new bodily-cosmic topography. According to the grotesque per-spective, immaterial concepts from exalted levels of the classically designed cosmos (sacred ideas, abstract notions associated with the heavens) are, in a manner reminiscent of allegory's mournful gaze, reduced to a material level and represented in earthly terms. Heaven becomes hell, for example. When this degradation is trans-ferred to the context of the human body, the result is a grotesque "cartwheel" image, emphasizing the "lower bodily stratum" and the portrayal of the body in terms of its natural biological processes and excrescences: eating, drinking, sexual activity, and defecation. The grotesque body is thus an allegorical body, a "body in the act of becoming": it undergoes hyperbolization, transgresses its own limits, and is converted into an inverted double, in which apertures and protrusions of the lower bodily stratum, such as anus and phallus, play leading roles and at times, even come to lead independent lives.[9] For Bakhtin, this "material bodily principle" of debasement is the fundamental principle of grotesque realism.[10] In *Interview de Mrs. Muerta Smith por sus fantasmas*, it functions as an allegorical strat-egy, which metaphorically decenters the power and meaning of sa-cred structures through an implicit interrogation of the notion of representation.

With this play, Gómez-Arcos establishes his critique of cultural supremacy through a series of parodic gestures with respect to religious icons and rituals that, over the course of centuries, have become allegorically coded within the context of Catholic sanctity. During the course of this single act, he interrogates the meaning of these allegories by deconstructing and rewriting them within the context of a theatrical piece that is itself allegorically coded. In this play, allegory comes to play the roles of both form and content: not only is it the dominant mode of expression; but at times it is brought into the foreground and parodied through the creation of a meta-allegorical *mise en abyme*, a strategy that shifts the principal focus from the work of art itself to its margins; that is, to its representational frame.[11]

The scenic space of *Interview de Mrs. Muerta Smith* is a futuristic universe of surreal invention, guignolesque caricature, and dark humor, in which elements drawn from popular culture and science fiction intermingle with parodic evocations of religious ritual.[12] Accordingly, the opening stage directions describe this space as the "*Hibernation cabin of Mrs. Dead Smith's space vehicle. Impression of a temple dedicated to a special cult, unique in kind.*"[13] Javier Villán of *El Mundo* gives the following description of Portaceli's *mise en scène*, which substituted an old dilapidated car for the space ship:

> Upon a backdrop of barbed wire and bellicose signs, what stands out, in the foreground is a large American flag, with the patriotic realism of a Jasper Johns painting. And an old car, residue from an advanced and contrapuntal capitalism and the golden metallicness of Mrs. Muerta Smith. The latter, emptied of her vital organs, cannot cry.
>
> The direction has not skimped on violence nor on acidity in a work that may have echoes from the Artaudian universe of cruelty, abrupt, intentional and lyrical.[14]

In this dream world of phantoms, absurd logic, and nonsensical language, Mrs. Muerta Smith, a resuscitated cadaver, "a young old woman," traverses the barriers of space and time as part of her own allegorical and exilic quest for the ultimate sacred signified: God. She is accompanied by two faithful companions: Boby, her talking dog (a well-bred animal of refined speech and sophisticated tastes, who adores wearing her chinchilla coat) and "Doble Nick, blanco y negro," (Double Nick, black and white), her gigolo (whose only words—in English, no less—are "Thank you, baby"). As the play unfolds, Boby seamlessly inhabits the roles of a surgeon, a journalist, God (disguised as Catherine the Great), and Satan (disguised as Mao-Tse-Tung). However, his theatrical metamorphoses do not represent a succession of fixed and absolute transformations. On the contrary, as indicated by the written text, each of the dog's roles contains a vestige (or "ghosting") from one or more of his former personae.[15] For example,

Manuel de Blas as Boby and Julieta Serrano as Mrs. Muerta Smith in *Interview de Mrs. Muerta Smith por sus fantasmas*. Sala Olimpia, Madrid, 1991. Photo: Chicho. Courtesy of the Archive of *El Público*.

the text reads, "DOG-GOD" ("PERRO, *en Dios*"); "DOG-SATAN" ("PERRO, *en Satán*"); "DOG-SATAN-MAO" (*"El Perro-Satán-Mao"*); etc. This polymorphic process of characterization presents the actor (as well as the spectator) with an endless series of performative/interpretative possibilities for, in allegorical terms, Boby is a chameleonlike multilayered signifier whose concrete image is infinitely indeterminate. He is an ambiguous accumulation of sacred and profane elements; in sum: a-man-playing-a-dog-playing-a-journalist-playing-God-playing-Catherine the Great-playing-Satan-playing-Mao. A parallel system of palimpsestic accumulation occurs in the characterization of Doble Nick. He is portrayed by two actors who simultaneously depict a doublesided image of multicultural ambiguity (Aryan and African), thereby evoking an interrogation of the cultural dualism "black/white." Doble Nick is a literal representation of a man and his ethno-racial Other, frozen in a block of ice that is defrosted at opportune moments—that is, whenever he is called upon for his erotic services. His name, a linguistic pun on the vulgar expression "Noble Dick," is a parodic reference to his sexual prowess.

During the initial scenes of the play, the decomposing, yet garrulous, remains of Mrs. Muerta lie upon an operating table. As Boby performs his mistress' resuscitative surgery, they discuss her cause of death, attempting to agree upon an official explanation to be issued to the press. In this conversation, it is revealed that earlier, Mrs. Muerta had been speeding through the Utah desert in her red Cadillac—in a manner reminiscent of Cruella de Ville, chasing after the "hundred and one Dalmatians"—when suddenly, her mind began to wander and (in her words): "I tore my cunt off in the Utah desert when I ran into a cactus that wasn't foreseen in my itinerary. I was driving along, and my mind began to wander."[16] The comparison with Cruella de Ville, the Walt Disney character, enhances the cartoonlike quality of Gómez-Arcos's imagery. Like her two (three?, or more?) companions, Mrs. Muerta is a multilayered indeterminate signifier. She is characterized as a former American diplomat, who is also a whore and a saint ("Saint Perpetual American Whore"), and although she is dead, she often behaves, contrarily, as though she were immortal. In allegorical terms, she is a simultaneous embodiment of the sacred and the profane, the personification of a divine imperialistic ideal whose downfall and decadence have finally arrived. Gómez-Arcos associates this abstract concept of plenipotentiary authority with the image of the United States. He comments with regard to his play, "In reality, I think that the United States is a profoundly castrated country—not in the sexual sense; but rather, in the visceral sense, in an infinitely more complex and broad sense. Hence, I see the country as a bloody cadaver."[17]

The tropological correlation that Gómez-Arcos proposes in his personal declarations and in the play itself between bodily space and topographical space is echoed in Douglas's anthropological formulations and in Bakhtin's study of the Rabelaisian grotesque (and carnivalesque), whereby the body is perceived as a metaphoric image of any sociocultural system. The body's margins and orifices—such as Mrs. Muerta's vagina—thus signify the powerful, vulnerable, and precarious areas of society. The grotesque portrayal of Mrs. Muerta's body, grounded in this "material bodily principle" of debasement can be contemplated, therefore, as a metaphor for the transgression and inversion of societal structures. Mrs. Muerta, accordingly, is both a castrated woman and castrated sociocultural system, whose lower bodily stratum has been fatally ruptured as the result of a collision with a phallic cactus. In the allegorist's hands, her saintly monolithic image has collapsed into a profane heap of ruins, thereby evoking a metaphoric debasement of oppressive institutions. Her vaginal area, an allegorical zone of sociocultural vulnerability, is also a powerful

center of both erotic and reproductive activity. Consequently, her biological debilitation has hampered, at least momentarily, her ability
to engender any new authoritative systems.

The delicate surgery performed by Boby entails the complete ex-
traction of his mistress' viscera, and the substitution of her old clitoris
("Universally known") with a new model, made of plastic, and of
Japanese design. After completing the operation, Boby makes an official announcement concerning his monumental surgical exploits:

> Done. (*Announces with an official tone:*) Today, modern surgery advances
> in great steps. Mrs. Dead Smith, well-known American millionaire, politi-
> cal ambassador of the United States in almost every country of the world,
> has celebrated her ninety-fifth year of birth by substituting her old clitoris
> for a new and almost new-born one, made of plastic, a Japanese
> fabrication. . . .[18]

Boby then fills his mistress' hollowed/hallowed body with gold, the
substance most pleasing to her extravagant tastes, and gives her the
face of a Hollywood starlet so that she can look in the mirror each
morning and say, "Darling! You look marvelous today!" (Gómez-Arcos
satirically inserts popular expressions in English throughout his Spanish text.) Finally, he lifts the mortuary sheet and the new and improved Mrs. Muerta (likewise, a new and improved System) makes
her debut: "*this splendid golden woman without life, a statue, symbol,
mechanical and automaton, her left breast a scarlet red color.*"[19] To
her absolute horror, she discovers that even in death as in life her left
breast remains a deep red hue, indelibly tainted by the left-wing
ideology of her son. (She explains to the audience that her son, born
a Communist in the supposedly left-wing state of Utah, developed
while nursing an irresistible Oedipal affinity for his mother's left
breast.) Mrs. Muerta is thus characterized in terms of a body politic
that allegorizes the image of the United States, and in broader terms,
the entire cosmos. Her golden body, a map of allegorical double-talk
has been equipped with a new and improved (plastic, Japanese) lower
stratum, with which she is able to resume the secretion and propaga-
tion of her oppressive imperialist ideology. At the same time, however, one of her most cherished attributes, her breast, blatantly
displays evidence of sinful contamination by left-wing propaganda.
(Her breasts are themselves doubly coded: one left [-wing], one right
[-wing].)

As Mrs. Muerta recounts the story of her son's Communist legacy—
he now languishes in a Utah state prison—Boby sets a table that
resembles a church altar and prepares his mistress' sacred breakfast-

communion. At intermittent moments, he interrupts her dialogue with the audience in order to remind her that the sacred hosts are becoming cold, soon they will become indigestible, "her God" will be spoiled, etc. Finally, she is ready to eat:

> *Slowly she approaches the table-alter that the dog has prepared, a white liturgical cloth, a gold recipient for the sacred hosts, a golden chalice for the sacred wine. She herself, a priestess, consecrates the divine food. Interior prayer, exterior cold, and ceremony. Absence of music. Scathing light.*[20]

In performing her breakfast-communion, Mrs. Muerta plays the roles of both priest and communicant, receiving communion from herself. In this scene, as in subsequent episodes, her performance constitutes a parody of religious allegory. In the same way that allegory both secularizes and sanctifies, parody—according to Linda Hutcheon—is, in the postmodern sense, a doubly coded device that both inscribes and undermines. In Hutcheon's view, the postmodern practice of parodic reprise is fueled by an ironic and critical regard for history and the politics of representation.[21] "It de-doxifies our assumptions about our representation of the past. Postmodern parody is both deconstructively critical and constructively creative, paradoxically making us aware of both the limits and the power of representation—in any medium."[22] Here, the sacramental rite of communion, an allegorical sacrifice of the body of Christ, inscribed over the course of centuries within the allegorical framework of the Catholic Mass, represents a sacrosanct monument to the historical past, which is appropriated and placed within the context of a mundane breakfast ritual. This strategy of parodic reprise establishes a chain of metaphoric linkages between the Catholic Mass (a sacred text) and an ordinary daily meal (a profane text); for example: table = altar, tablecloth = liturgical cloth, bowl of breakfast cereal = ciborium with hosts, breakfast beverage = chalice of wine. The parody of the communion—its reconstruction and deconstruction within the context of breakfast—is, therefore, a secularizing gesture implying a semiotic transgression that mitigates the signifying power of religious ritual. In a reciprocal manner, however, Mrs. Muerta's communion also can be viewed as an appropriation of profane elements (table, breakfast cereal, etc.), which are then placed within the context of sacred ritual. In this manner, the allegorical dialectic can be perceived as exercising its sacralizing power. The spectator who contemplates Mrs. Muerta's allegorical performance occupies the privileged (distanced) position of being able to perceive an ambivalent oscillation of the two texts (breakfast and communion), an implicitly flickering image that in theory renders indistinguishable the limits of the sacred and the profane.

In addition, Mrs. Muerta's performance adds an overtly metatheatrical, meta-allegorical, and metarepresentational dimension to the play. The breakfast-communion is an allegory, framed within the allegorical theater piece, framed within the representational realm of the spectator, and so on. It is a subsystem of an infinitely larger semiotizing machine, of an allegorical *mise en abyme*, whose structure suggests an analogous internal (re)duplication of the representational structure that contains it, while naturally implicating the spectator in this process. This parergonal structure diverts the spectator's gaze away from the gestures themselves, to the exterior representational frames that embrace them; that is, to the metaphoric systems and hierarchical structures that govern the representational process. It is a structure that foregrounds for the spectator the arbitrariness of the sign (host = body of Christ, wine = blood of Christ, etc.), undermining the sovereign power of these religious signifiers and plunging the spectator's gaze into the semiotic abyss separating signifier and signified, ephemeral and eternal.

While Mrs. Muerta takes communion, Boby covers her with the chinchilla coat (so that she will not appear nude before the press) and announces that a reporter has already arrived for her interview. At this point, the dog undergoes a theatrical metamorphosis, whereby he is converted into a journalist. He dons a trench coat, takes out a pad, and explains to his spectators that Mrs. Muerta is about to embark upon the most fabulous cosmic mission ever to be carried out. (He is supposedly addressing a group of imaginary television spectators, whose identity is inevitably confused with that of the "real" theater spectators—a gesture which, moreover, implicates these "real" spectators in the dramatic action.) According to the dog-reporter, Mrs. Muerta's transparent gold space ship—constructed under the auspices of IBM (emblem of technological supremacy) with the sacrifice of several million human lives (from "third-world" countries)—will launch her into outer space, where she is scheduled for an interview with God. The new century will commence with a new colonization of the heavens:

> *Dog-Reporter, playing the role of reporter, taking out his note pad. . . .*
> The well-known all-powerful ambassador from the United States of America, . . . ambassador of Man (with a capital "M"), prepares herself physically and spiritually for an interview with God. The time has come for the human being, anxious about conquering new horizons, finally

to meet his or her Creator and to explain herself to Him. The earth can
no longer be repaired. Let us repair Heaven!

Mrs. Dead Smith, a simple woman of gold and chinchilla, takes her
breakfast, simple and frugal. Consecrated, vitamin enriched hosts.[23]

Mrs. Muerta's encounter with the dog-reporter is the first in a series
of three absurd interviews that she will have with her "phantoms."
When he inquires about her breakfast of consecrated hosts, she explains that, in her opinion, the single aspect of human civilization
most worthy of perpetuation in their conquest of a new realm is
Catholicism: "The United States of America, despite certain false appearances, are profoundly Catholic."[24] When he asks why the hosts
are "vitamin-fortified," she reveals that they are part of a brilliant
initiative launched by her own foundation, La Fundación Mrs. Muerta
Smith por la Extensión de los Valores Universales (The Mrs. Dead
Smith Foundation for the Extension of Universal Values), whose intent
is to demonstrate that Catholicism, despite certain false claims, can
be nutritious: "our chemists invented the vitamin enriched hosts. A
balanced composition of vitamins."[25] Nevertheless, there were some
problems at the beginning of this enterprising initiative; i.e., the vitamins so enhanced the Pope's sexual appetite that he began to take
part in clandestine love affairs with various officials from the Vatican,
as well as Communists, Arabs, and Jews: "A sort of enormous evan-
gelical ardor."[26] Fortunately, word of the Pope's sexual transgressions
never reached the news media. (There was a "cover-up" at the Vatican
in order to avoid the danger of scandal.) As a solution to the Pope's
problem, Mrs. Muerta's foundation decided to remove the specially
formulated "erection vitamin" from the vitamin-enriched hosts. Presently, the new formulation has inundated the American market, and
eventual worldwide sales are projected: "My compatriots are now less
horny, but more religious."[27] (The leftover hosts from the original
formula have been reserved for Doble Nick's use.)

During Mrs. Muerta's interview with the dog-reporter, Gómez-
Arcos carries out an irreverent allegorical subversion of the sacred
image of the Eucharist, epitomized by the semantically dissonant
term "consecrated and vitamin-fortified host." In referring to this
hallowed symbol, he employs a discourse normally reserved for
breakfast cereal advertisements (i.e., "vitamin-enriched," "fortified
with nutrients," etc.), once again intermingling the concepts of sanctity and profanity.[28] In addition, a farcical cause-and-effect linkage is
established between the hosts, the erotic adventures of a Pope, his
relationships with both Christians and non-Christians, and the sexual
excitement of a gigolo.

If the Catholic principle of transubstantiation is considered in conjunction with these semantically violent juxtapositions, then the implications of this transgressive imagery continue to multiply. Transubstantiation, essentially an allegorical process of semiosis, transforms the immaterial body of Christ into a series of material signifiers, or sacraments (bread, wine, the Eucharist, etc.).[29] During the Catholic Mass, these sacraments function as surrogates, which take the place of the primordial sacrificial victim. The ritual consumption of the Eucharist thus enables the mortal communicant to become one with, and to identify with, the immortal victim, and to benefit cathartically from this sacrificial process.[30] When the communicant ingests the Eucharist, he or she metaphorically "receives" the body of Christ, and Christ correspondingly "receives" the body of the communicant. This allegorical system of reciprocity invokes a simultaneous secularization and sacralization: it is a ritual transgression exercised within the context of taboo, which characteristically blurs the distinctions between the sacred (Christ) and the profane (the communicant). In *Interview de Mrs. Muerta Smith*, however, the image of the Eucharist appears tarnished through metonymic association with the breakfast cereal and sexual activity, a situation that problematizes and destabilizes, in a figurative sense, the entire sacrificial structure of the Mass. What was once a process of identification between worldly being and divine entity is transformed into a process of defamiliarization (in the Brechtian sense), thereby plunging the spectator's gaze into the semiotic abyss separating the profane signifier and the transcendental signified.

Mrs. Muerta eventually departs with Boby and Doble Nick on her whirlwind voyage to the heavens. As part of her allegorical quest to colonize and concretize the transcendental cosmos, her second interview will be an encounter with the ultimate sacred signified. As she journeys through outer space, she anxiously wonders about the form that God will take: "Dog, what will He be like? . . . Will He be a gust of wind? An amoeba? A screech of light? Will He be nothing?"[31] When they arrive at their destination, Boby steps outside the spaceship. Only his head is momentarily visible through an open hatchway as he undergoes another metamorphosis: this time, he is transformed into God. When the Dog-God finally makes his/her entrance, s/he is the anthropomorphic image of a woman, dressed in an immaculate white gown, resembling a portrait of Catherine the Great. She is accompanied by a white angel who plays the sitar; hence, the abstract notion of God materializes on stage as an ambiguous signifier: a man-playing-a-dog-playing-a-woman clad in a Catherine the Great costume. (The fact that God is a female—portrayed by a male dog—

only further problematizes her characterization.) At first, they exchange a series of commonplace pleasantries: Mrs. Muerta compliments God's dress (they seem to have similar tastes in wardrobe), and God insists that Mrs. Muerta call Her "Señora." She also apologizes to Mrs. Muerta for having interrupted her meal:

> *Dog-God.* It smells good . . .
>
> *Mrs. Dead Smith.* Naturally, Madam! It's you I'm eating.
>
> *Dog-God, lets out a scream.* Me? Cannibal! (*To the Angel.*) Get her. *The Angel barks, menacingly.*
>
> *Mrs. Dead Smith.* But, calm down, Madam. It's only in a metaphoric sense that I'm eating Madam.[32]

Once again, Gómez-Arcos undermines the divine authority of the Eucharist. God is offended when She learns that the metaphor employed to signify Her image is called a "host": "But I have a name! I do!"[33] Her reaction indicates a dissatisfaction with the idea that a seemingly arbitrary mixture composed of minuscule quantities of flour, water, and vitamins (all secular ingredients) could be used to signify Her divine Self, and She also suggests, in the sinful spirit of consumerism, that a price be charged for the receipt of communion. In Her opinion, if a monetary value were placed upon the hosts, more people would appreciate Her, and at the same time, She would be able to collect a small commission.

In the next part of their interview, God offers to tell Mrs. Muerta about Her life, but Mrs. Muerta replies that she is already familiar with the life of God for she has studied the catechism (a sacred text). God, nevertheless, insists on recounting the details of Her daily routine, which include rising at noon, skipping breakfast because She is concerned about Her weight, and taking a stroll around the cosmos:

> *Dog-God.* Then I go out for my walk. I call it my "zenithal walk": nice, isn't it?
>
> *Mrs. Dead Smith.* Charming!
>
> *Dog-God.* And I shit.
>
> *Mrs. Dead Smith.* Pardon me?
>
> *Dog-God.* I shit! Right and left, wherever I find a place that I like. It's a modest pleasure.[34]

In this conversation, the catechism is converted into a comical series of questions and answers regarding the activities of the lower bodily stratum, and God is characterized in terms of Bakhtin's material bodily principle. Her body is a grotesque scatological image, and

Manuel de Blas as Boby (dressed as Catherine the Great) and Julieta Serrano as Mrs. Muerta Smith in *Interview de Mrs. Muerta Smith por sus fantasmas.* **Sala Olimpia, Madrid, 1991. Photo: Chicho. Courtesy of the Archive of** *El Público.*

Her role as the holy Creator of the universe is secularized and debased, allegorized as series of mundane activities and mortal necessities from the realm of pedestrian reality: sleeping, eating, walking, and the discharge of biological waste. Indeed, the very act of concretizing the sacred figure of God and bringing Her eternal image down to earth is in itself a devaluative gesture of debasement.

The heavenly cosmos is also allegorized in terms of bodily secretions, portrayed as a defiled accumulation of solid excrement. According to God, the purgation of Her sacred bodily debris is the basis for the formation of the entire universe. God spends Her afternoons ridding Her body of solid waste, which eventually crystallizes in the form of galaxies, nebulas, etc. "Shitting cosmos" ("Cagando cosmos") is the graphic term She employs to describe this process: "And all this, while I'm on a diet. Imagine if I ate everything I felt like. For Christ's sake!"[35] Not surprisingly, Mrs. Muerta appears dazed at the revelation that, what she had always referred to as "Theology," is actually a lowly process of defecation. The scatological has been sanctified, elevated to a transcendental plane, and Mrs. Muerta becomes increasingly disquieted by the image of God that has materialized before her. God knows nothing of the illustrious Smith family of Utah, nor is she even slightly familiar with the Catholic Church.[36] God also remarks that She has absolutely no idea what Catholicism is, adding that it must be an invention of the people on Earth, a planet that She has never bothered to visit. Mrs. Muerta's God is, in effect, her own allegorical invention, a phantasmagoric projection of an idea, fabricated by her own imagination and her own dreams. Gómez-Arcos has thus inverted the process of divine creation as recounted in the Bible. In a statement that resonates with Nietzschean nihilism, he summarizes, "up until now, all that has been created is a God in the image and likeness of Man; not a man in the image and likeness of God."[37] The human being—and a dead one, at that—is portrayed as the true Creator, and not vice versa. In this manner, Gómez-Arcos, like Cervantes, employs his literary inventions as a vehicle for an implicit commentary on the creative process. Through desire and the imagination, don Quijote was able to transform grotesque entities and quotidian objects into outward projections of his interior Platonic ideals. Gómez-Arcos seems to invert this process of *quijotización*. Mrs. Muerta's fabricated phantom image of God, as based on her squire-dog, is not a projection of a classical ideal; rather, it is allegorized as a grotesque, excrement-stained entity: an *esperpentic* mirror image of herself (ironically, accompanied by a divine white angel).

When the God-dog removes a satin shoe, and repeatedly asks Her hostess to replenish it with vodka (rejecting the American "Coca-

Cola" that She is offered), Mrs. Muerta begins to suspect the possibility that another outside influence—namely, the (former) Soviet Union—may have been involved in the cultivation of God's sacred image. Her suspicions are further enhanced when she discovers that God also has a habit of impatiently stomping Her shoe on the table-altar in a gesture reminiscent of Nikita Kruschev. At this point, Mrs. Muerta discloses her proposal to buy, colonize, and subordinate the transcendental world to the constraints of her system. In delineating the irremediable problems on earth, she describes a situation that suggests not only the presence of war (or civil war); but also the presence of a postmodern crisis of cultural authority: "I don't know why the ideas on Earth have decomposed. And a putrid odor even emanates from the perfumes. Nevertheless, our olfactory sense has not atrophied. Uninhabitable. What was always logical, is now anachronic. Men turn against each other, tirelessly, as if the human species were an error. A lamentable error."[38]

Earth is in ruins. It has been inundated by corruption, the established system is in a state of decomposition, and ambiguity reigns. The United States, with Mrs. Muerta as ambassador, has therefore decided to take the initiative in occupying the heavens in an endeavor to establish a new cosmic order. Yet, to her disillusion, Mrs. Muerta learns that heaven is no longer for sale, because the Soviets have been the first to arrive and God has made a business deal with a group of left-wing atheists. It was they who provided Her with the vodka and the Catherine the Great costume as tokens of their appreciation. Mrs. Muerta, betrayed and disappointed, banishes God from her spaceship. (The sexual prowess of "Saint Perpetual American Whore" ironically has been outshined by that of Catherine the Great, whose erotic exploits were legendary.) Feeling deceived by her own phantoms, and her own mirror image, Mrs. Muerta laments, "I forced all other dreams out of my life so that only He would remain as the dream of my life. And He is only a phantom."[39] Nevertheless, she proclaims that it is still not time for her to awaken from her sleep. She, like don Quijote, would rather continue dreaming, and she refuses to return to earth empty-handed.

As an alternative to heaven, Mrs. Muerta decides to reverse the direction of her spaceship—and her ideology—and plunge downward into the infernal underworld in the hope that Satan will open his doors to her. The phantasmagoric image of God vanishes and Boby re-materializes, eager to help in the preparations for their new mission: a descent into the world of transgression. Boby provides his mistress with a red dress, drapes her in decadent jewels, and they begin their rituals of sin. The dog removes his clothes and Mrs.

Muerta lifts the sacred chalice used in the earlier communion scene, bathing her breasts with red wine: "Red left tit, grow, grow, grow, convert yourself into something redder and larger than the entire Universe, than all of creation! Overflow, poison, oh sacred symbol of revolution, spread like gangrene!"[40] Mrs. Muerta's red left breast is converted into a supreme metaphor of cosmic subversion. Boby defrosts Doble Nick and together, the three perform an erotic dance of sacrilege in which the sacred objects of the table-alter are this time appropriated and reinscribed as sexual icons. The chalice is transformed into a phallus and the host is stabbed with a dagger in an allegory of copulation:

> Mrs. Dead Smith begins her dance of sin, lewd, biblical, sacred chalice in her hands, phallic chalice that caresses the most intimate parts of her lifeless body.... Mrs. Dead Smith offers a dagger to Double Nick white, she takes a host, performs the Eucharistic gesture of elevation and Double Nick white thrusts the dagger through the host.[41]

Hell is portrayed as an absurd antithetical double of the previously depicted image of heaven, and it is here that Mrs. Muerta will encounter her third and final phantom. The great gates open, and the dog appears as the character of Satan, personification of evil, dressed in a black Catherine-the-Great-style dress and accompanied by a large fire-spitting black angel. At precise moments, Satan erupts with diabolic laughter, covering his face with a Venetian carnival mask resembling the face of Mao-Tse-Tung. Mrs. Muerta informs Satan that she is prepared to sell her soul at a very good price, but Satan is not interested. He is already attempting to construct a left-wing government because hell has been sold to the Chinese:

> I'm presently preoccupied with constructing socialism. My passion. A world without traditional sins. The possibility of surprise. Of completely original sins, perhaps. And again, the same old shit about Man in his heyday.[42]

The entire cosmos already has been conquered, and Mrs. Muerta, concrete signifier in search of transcendental signified, has failed in her attempt to gain a tyrannical hold over the immaterial world. Her desire to colonize the cosmos, and to superimpose upon it a new imperialistic order, has been "perpetually frustrated," "perpetually deferred."[43] One can only wonder if John of Pré-papa may have suffered a similar fate in his venture into outer space. Neither heaven nor hell is a sacred place—in the modern/Western sense. Instead, both the celestial world and the underworld have been sold as material commodities to left-wing governments whose systems appear to be just as absurdly contaminated as that of Mrs. Muerta herself. Even the "phantom" fabrications of her own imagination have deceived her, and in the end, she has no other choice but to return to her home planet empty-handed. The spaceship-temple touches down upon earth, the walls explode open, and an "apocalyptic rain" showers the stage with an accumulation of earthly fragments: pieces of forest, land, sea, mountains, human and animal limbs. Even the head of Mrs. Muerta's son, her sinful legacy, appears out of nowhere and bites her red left breast. Mrs. Muerta, as much a ruin as her terrestrial landscape, moves about like an automaton, portraying the sterile mechanization of a totalizing discourse that has failed to exert its authority. The stage is inundated with cataclysmic anarchy and Boby shoots himself with a pistol. Mrs. Muerta's final lament is that she is unable to emit tears of frustration for she is an empty body without viscera and without memory. Paradoxically, she cannot subject herself to the same fate as her dog because she is already dead, condemned to live in a perpetual state of decay as an eternal ruin, void of viscera and void of meaning, a sign without referent. In portraying Mrs. Muerta's frustrated endeavors, not only has Gómez-Arcos questioned the authoritative structure of representation; but he also has revealed the profane underside of divine monolithic structures of meaning. Mrs. Muerta, her spaceship, and her oppressive system have been plunged into ontological oblivion.

When Gómez-Arcos wrote *Interview de Mrs. Muerta Smith* in 1972, he was already living in exile. It was the period of the Cold War and a moment in history in which Spain had yet to witness the demise of Franco's totalitarian regime. At that time, he could only have prophetically dreamed that nearly twenty years later his play would finally première in Spain to an audience already living in democracy. Ironically, on the evening of the 1991 première, two additional allegorical spectacles were being staged, televised live from the contemporary earthly landscape: first, there were scenes from the fall of the Berlin Wall, a sacred emblem of authority and of the Cold War, crumbling into an allegorical stockpile of rubble; and second, there was a science fictive allegory of oppression, portrayed as a high-tech war between the United States and an Ubuësque Middle Eastern dictator. Today, when talk of a "new world order" has become a commonplace ingredient of contemporary international discourse, *Interview de Mrs. Muerta Smith* is a play whose allegorical rendition of the cosmos is as timely as ever.

Epilogue

Un monde où ton passage sera une promenade. Pas une conquête.
Pas un massacre. Pas une exploitation irrationnelle. Une
promenade.[1]

—*Agustín Gómez-Arcos*, Pré-Papa ou Roman de fées

In his voyage from Spain to France and back, and in his evolution from censored artist to bilingual *exilé*, Gómez-Arcos adapts his allegorical way of seeing to the constraints and freedoms that confront him. In his theater, as the preceding chapters have revealed, allegory is part of a discourse of transgression that at once sacralizes, secularizes, and thereby exposes the arbitrary and subjective nature of representation. It creates an indeterminate zone in which meaning vacillates and flickers before the spectator's eyes. It thereby mitigates the power of hegemonic sociocultural discourses, frustrating their ability to signify, to represent, and to maintain an authoritative hold.

During Gómez-Arcos's Spanish pre-exilic period, allegory serves as a camouflage for his critical and committed views. He draws upon this artistic strategy in the creation of the historical drama *Diálogos de la herejía* (Dialogues of heresy), in which the notion of sacrifice is exposed as a procedure that, contrary to popular conceptions, does not propagate order, but yields chaos and a crisis of distinctions. In *Los gatos* (The cats), the grotesque underside of the sacrificial process is once again disclosed and contextualized within a more contemporary setting. In *Mil y un mesías* (One thousand and one Messiahs) and *Queridos, míos, es preciso contaros ciertas cosas* (My dear friends, it's time we get certain things straight), he employs the conventions of the theater of the absurd in the creation of mythical and convertible empty spaces that oscillate as signifiers of everywhere and nowhere, the universal and the particular. In these early plays, he portrays history—that of Spain and Western culture in general—as an endless cycle, propelled forward by the violence inherent in the notions of expiation, censorship, banishment, and exile. These are the ghosts of oppression, derivative of his experience in Francoist Spain, that continue to haunt his exilic literature and follow him on his border crossings; they are the memories of the past that he is unable and unwilling to erase.

As an exiled writer living in France, allegory provides him with a vehicle through which he is able to extend the thematic scope of his theater to a broader, international audience while maintaining his critical perspective. It is during this latter period, in such plays as *Adorado Alberto* (Adored Alberto) and *Pré-papa*, that bilingualism emerges as both content and form, reinforcing the double-sided values that constitute the allegorical way of seeing. This is also the period in which his theater is injected with a refreshing kind of openness and candor, the consequence of his newly-garnered freedoms. *Interview de Mrs. Muerta Smith por sus fantasmas* (Mrs. Dead Smith's interview with her phantoms), a play that touches upon global themes and concerns, epitomizes the impassioned attitude of dissent that characterizes Gómez-Arcos's theater at its most highly evolved stage.

In 1975, the year of Franco's death, Gómez-Arcos wrote his second novel *Maria Republica* (published in 1983). The narrative centers on the life of a syphilitic nun and former Barcelona prostitute who plots to overthrow a convent/system by furtively incorporating herself within its walls and toppling the entire structure from the inside. The novel concludes with a poem invoking an image of a bird that wondrously rises like a phoenix from the ashes of a battlefield. The final verses read as follows:

> Up above, in the burnt air,
> an unwonted bird
> Sings
> An old song
> Forgotten
> But that little by little returns to their memory
> To all
> And that they recover.
> A single word.
> Republic
> Seems to reawaken in all their mouths,
> in all their recollections.
> Memory excites them,
> What joy
> —they think—
> to finally realize
> that we were crying over a cadaver
> that never existed,
> a cadaver that never ceased to be alive.
> Now, the anesthetized and the soldiers,

all the men finally awakened
begin to make plans,
to think about tomorrow.
For tomorrow
is also itself a living word.
Living.
Let them speak of life.
It's the most beautiful topic of conversation
That humanity could have.[2]

The bird, who sings a long-forgotten song, conjures images of the
vanquished Spanish Republic, which appears to awaken and rise like
a phoenix from the depths of history. However, from a present-day
perspective of democratic Spain, the bird becomes a prophetic metaphor for the rebirth of Gómez-Arcos's theater and his return to the
Spanish stage. Like the image of the Republic, it was never really
dead, but just temporarily absent from recent memory.

Although some may wish to deny the truth, Spain's present-day
democratic landscape is a place that still bears significant traces and
ruins of civil war and dictatorship. Spaniards are repeatedly forced
to confront this historical legacy as it continues to cast a subtle
shadow upon many aspects of their culture. It is perhaps for this
reason that Gómez-Arcos's plays are still capable of cultivating the
interest of contemporary audiences. The thousands of spectators,
young and old, who only recently were granted the opportunity to
discover and enjoy his theater stand as a reminder of the importance
of listening to a voice that were once silenced. It is very likely that
many of these spectators share with Gómez-Arcos an awareness that
the notion of intolerance, whether manifested in a dictatorial order
or a democratic society, is as valid a theme today as ever both within
Spain's borders and beyond.

*   *   *

This story would not be complete without the following sad note:
Agustín Gómez-Arcos died on 20 March 1998 in his beloved Paris.

Appendix A: Premières and Performances

Works are listed in alphabetical order. In listing the names of cast members, I have given the actors' names that I was able to find recorded in reviews and playbills. This list, therefore, does not account for possible changes and replacements that may have occurred during the course of a play's run. I have tried to be as precise as possible regarding dates, but in some cases, more specific information was unavailable.

ANA NON

Téléfilm: 1980s, France. Director: Jean Prat.

DIÁLOGOS DE LA HEREJÍA

Première: 23 May 1964, Teatro Reina Victoria, Madrid. Director: José María Morera; Scenery: Enrique Alarcón and Viuda de López y Muñoz; Figurines: Miguel Narros; with Gemma Cuervo as Doña Tristeza de Arcos, Julián Mateos as El Peregrino, María Luisa Ponte as Madre Asunta, Asunción Montijano as Mujer 1ª, Alicia Hermida as Ursulina, Terele Pávez as Mujer 2ª, José Antón as El Posadero, Pilar Bienert as Mujer 3ª, Julia Avalos/Luisa C. Torrens/Carmen Rubio/Amparo Alonso as Otras mujeres, María Isabel Pallarés as La Dueña, Carlos Criado as Mosén Blas, Antonio Gandía as El Inquisidor, Fernando Hilbeck as El Caballero, Concha Lluesma as Sor María de los Angeles, and María Luisa Arias as La Posadera.

DÎNER AVEC MR & MRS Q

Première (of French translation/adaptation of Cena con Mr. & Mrs. Q): 1972, Café-Théâtre Campagne, Paris.

Elecciones generales

Première: 3 April 1960, Primer Festival Nacional de Teatro Nuevo, Teatro del Colegio Mayor de Santa María de la Almudena, Madrid. Until 4 April 1960. Director: José Manuel Azpeitia; Scenery: Vicente Domínguez Urosa and Viuda de López y Muñoz; Produced with the Collaboration of the Ayuntamiento de Madrid, Diputación Provincial de Madrid, Dirección General de Bellas Artes, Comisaría de Extensión Cultural, Sociedad General de Autores de España, and the Sección Femenina de FET y de las JONS; with Carmen Luján as La Mujer, Josefina Martín as La Viuda, Miki Suárez as La Otra, Alberto Blasco as El Otro, Fernando Santos as El Alguacil, Conchita Leza as La Tortola, Felisa G. Barrientos as La Mendiga, Mariska Berki as La Hija, Enrique Júlvez as El Novio, Anastasio de Campoy as El Señor Alcalde, José Luis Lespe as El Diputado D. Sebastián, Alfredo Landa as Gimeno, Agustín Gómez-Arcos as El Sacristán, Andrés González as El Pariente, Yolanda Monreal as La Parienta, José Lónchez as El Archivero, and Elena Granda as La Madre del Poeta.

Et si on aboyait?

Première (of Rachel Salik's French translation/adaptation of *Adorado Alberto*): 13 February 1969, Café-Théâtre de l'Odéon, Paris. 71 performances. Director: Agustín Gómez-Arcos; Assistant Director: Antonio Duque; with Daniel Dhubert, Annie Savarin, Jacques Audoux, Sarah Chandler, and Rachel Salik.

November 1972, Sorbonne, Paris. Director: Antonio Duque; with Jeanne David as Maman, Pierre Nunci as Alberto, Marc François as José Marie, María Ferret as Romualda, Elisabeth Kaza as Tante Julia, and Daniel Dhubert as Le Christ domestique. 1973, Café-Théâtre de l'Odéon. Director: Antonio Duque.

Los gatos

Première: 24 September 1965, Teatro Marquina, Madrid. Director: Juan de Prat-Gay; Assistant Director: Antonio Duque; Scenery: Víctor María Cortezo and Viuda de López y Muñoz; with Cándida Losada as Pura, Luchy Soto as Ángela, Alicia Hermida as Inés, Josefina Lamas as Manuela, Teresa Hurtado as Loli, Carmen Luján as Doña Rosa, and Eduardo Montaner as Fernando.

Première (of new version): 15 November 1992, Teatro María Guerrero, Madrid. Until 21 November 1992. Director: Carme Portaceli; Scenery and Costume Design: Isidre Prunés and Montse Amenós; Produced by Producciones Teatrales Contemporáneas, S. L. in collaboration with the Ministerio de Cultura (Institute Nacional de las Artes Escénicas y de la Música); with Héctor Alterio as Pura, Paco Casares as Angela, Concha Leza as Manuela, Laura Jou as Loli, Ana Frau as Doña Rosa, Gabriela Flores as Inés, and Joaquim Solano as Fernando. National Tour of Spain (1992–93). June 1993, Buenos Aires.

INTERMEZZO (Translation/Adaptation of Jean Giraudoux's *Intermezzo*)

Première: 1963, Teatro María Guerrero, Madrid. Director: José Osuna.

INTERVIEW DE MRS MORTE SMITH PAR SES PHANTÔMES

Performances (of Rachel Salik's French translation/adaptation of *Interview de Mrs. Muerta Smith por sus fantasmas*): 1986–87, Toulouse (France); Charleroi (Belgium); and Théâtre Marie Stuart, Paris. Dramatic reading: Summer 1992, Théâtre Atalante, Paris.

INTERVIEW DE MRS. MUERTA SMITH POR SUS FANTASMAS

Première: 22 February 1991, Sala Olimpia, Madrid. 17 performances. Until 10 March 1991. Director: Carme Portaceli; Scenery and Costume Design: Isidre Prunés and Montse Amenós; Coproduction of the Centro Nacional de Nuevas Tendencias Escénicas and the Centro Drámatico Nacional (Instituto Nacional de las Artes Escénicas y de la Música / Ministerio de Cultura); with Julieta Serrano as Mrs. Muerta Smith, Manuel de Blas as Boby, Tomás Ordóñez as Doble Nick blanco, and Gordon T. McMillan as Doble Nick negro.

LA LOCA DE CHAILLOT (Translation/Adaptation of Jean Giraudoux's *La folle de Chaillot*)

Première: January 1962, Teatro María Guerrero, Madrid. Director: José Luis Alonso; Scenery: Víctor María Cortezo; with Amelia de la

Torre, Julieta Serrano, Agustín González, José Bódalo, Antonio Ferrandis, Olga Peiró, Adela Calderón y Rosario García Ortega.

September 1989, Teatro Alcázar, Madrid. Director: José Luis Alonso; Scenery: Víctor María Cortezo; Produced by Juanjo Seoane in colaboration with the Festival de Otoño de la Comunidad de Madrid and the Instituto Nacional de las Artes Escénicas y la Música / Ministerio de Cultura; with Silvia Marsó as Irma, Emiliano Redondo as El Presidente, Amparo Rivelles, Margot Cottens, Margarita García Ortega, Lili Murati, Carlos Lucena, and Roberto de la Peña.

Pré-papa

Première (of Rachel Salik's French translation/adaptation of *Prepapá*): 13 February 1969, Café-Théâtre de l'Odéon, Paris. 71 performances. Director: Agustín Gómez-Arcos; Assistant Director: Antonio Duque; with Daniel Dhubert as John Ferguson, Annie Savarin as Mary Ferguson, Jacques Audoux as l'Infirmier, Sarah Chandler as Professeur Kedrova, and Rachel Salik as Mademoiselle Adèle.

November 1972, Sorbonne, Paris. Director: Antonio Duque; with Daniel Dhubert as John Ferguson, Maria Ferret as Mary Ferguson, Jeanne David as Mademoiselle Adèle, Pierre Nunci as l'Infirmier, and Marc François as le Curé.

1973, Café-Théâtre de l'Odéon, Paris.

Queridos míos, es preciso contaros ciertas cosas

Dramatic reading performed by Agustín Gómez-Arcos: 1966, Madrid.

Première (of Norwegian translation): 1982, Oslo, Norway.

Première: 7 December 1994, Teatro María Guerrero, Madrid. Until 22 February 1995. Director: Carme Portaceli; Scenery and Costume Design: Isidre Prunés and Montse Amenós; Produced by the Centro Dramático Nacional (Instituto Nacional de las Artes Escénicas y la Música / Ministerio de Cultura); with Walter Vidarte as El Feriante, Rosa Novell as La Duquesa, Mònica Glaenzel as Casandra, Manuel de Blas as El Capitán, Antonio Duque as Amigo, Carlos Velasco as Invitado, Gloria Muñoz as La Esposa del Gobernador, Eva García as Leticia, Patricia Mendy as La Tobillera, Alicia Hermida as La Abuelita, Juan José Otegui as El Gobernador, and Iñaki Guevara and Pedro García de las Heras as Soldados.

LA REVELACIÓN (Translation/Adaptation of René-Jean Clot's La révélation)

Première: 1962, Teatro Goya, Madrid. Director: José Osuna.

LA VILLA DE LOS LADRONES (Adaptation of a Norwegian children's musical by Thorbjorn Egner).

Première: November 1963, Teatro María Guerrero, Madrid. Presented by the Títeres de la Sección Femenina. Director: Angel Fernández Montesinos; Scenery: Viuda de López Sevilla; Musical Director: Alberto Blancafort; with Lucio Romero, Lola Gálvez, Emiliano Redondo, Emilio Laguna, Manuel Andrés, Alicia Altabella, and Tina Sainz.

Appendix B: Agustín Gómez-Arcos in New York

Interview: 14 May 1990

S. G. F.: Let's begin with the question of exile. What has it meant for you with regard to the process of literary creation?

A. G.-A.: I believe that exile is one of the most difficult and definitive tests for a writer. For me, it was a difficult test but at the same time it was very healthy, for it made me realize that when you write in your own language in your own country—such as Spain, which was very isolated from the exterior world, very closed up upon itself—in reality, you are not addressing a universal spectator (or reader), you are exclusively addressing a spectator from your own country, a spectator who is too close, too confused with your own relations, etc. So, the first thing that exile makes apparent is the absence of that type of spectator. That type of spectator no longer exists; so you have to address another, a spectator who doesn't have your past, who doesn't have your recollections, who doesn't have your memory; in effect, who doesn't have your history, and although we all pertain to a common culture, it is undoubtedly true that things change when you address a type of spectator who is unfamiliar with your everyday culture. As a result, you have to begin to renounce a whole series of things.

And begin to focus on more universal themes?

Exactly. Renouncing what is local—everything that brings you closer to your original audience, the audience from your country—you realize that little by little you begin to accept a completely universal spectator who has nothing to do with the exclusive spectator who pertains to your country.

And the fact that you didn't have to worry about Spanish censorship, having liberated yourself from its scrutiny, has given you a special sense of freedom with regard to literary expression, has it not?

It's a complete freedom! I'm going to tell you an anecdote . . . In a café-theater in Paris, the director, who was a Spaniard, asked me to write some plays so that we could stage them so that I could have a kind of *entrée* en France (they were *Et si on aboyait?* and *Pré-Papa*). I wrote them, and Rachel Salik translated the texts.[1] We began to rehearse the plays—because I was responsible for the staging and the direction—and when the show was finished, I asked the director of the café-theater, "Well, now when will the censors be here?" Do you understand? I was waiting for somebody to come from some official institution in order to find out if what we had prepared could be presented or not, and then he said to me, "Well, you are crazy. That sort of thing doesn't exist here." That was the *déclic*.

You realized . . .

I realized that I could write without fear and that was a marvelous thing. For the first time, I was in direct contact with the impunity of things and that seemed marvelous to me.

I would like to ask you about the first Lope de Vega prize that you received in Spain for Diálogos de la herejía *(Dialogues of heresy). What were the circumstances surrounding your winning of that prize? What exactly happened with regard to the censorship of the play? They gave you the prize and then they annulled it?*

The jury for the prize was composed of a series of people that included José Tamayo, who was at that time the director of the Teatro Español, which was then a national theater. Today, it is still a national theater but it depends on the government of Madrid for support, and at that time it was directly dependent on the Ministry. And so, they gave me the prize, and since the play had a lot of censorship problems, they put pressure on Tamayo to retract his vote. He called me, we had lunch together, and he explained to me what was happening. He said, "Well, either I retract my vote or they will take the theater away from me. So, I have no choice but to retract my vote." And so, naturally, he retracted his vote and my prize was annulled—although they did give me the money. Still, by annulling the prize, they prevented the play from premiering in an official theater. Some years later, I had to do thousands of things for the censors and the text that you have read was cut.

You mean to say, the text that I read in Primer Acto *is not the definitive version?*

No, it went though a series of cuts. The text that you have read is the text that premiered. And years later, on one occasion, Nuria Espert asked me—when she was one of the directors of the Centro Dramático Nacional—for a play, *Dialogues of Heresy*, and I reworked the text and returned it more or less to the original version. So in my house, somewhere, I have a revised text which is the one that I consider to be the definitive version—not the one that was published in *Primer Acto*, which is a text that is fine, but later I did a more solid, more efficient job with that text.[2] And I think that if someday that text were to be staged, I would title the new play *Chronicle of a Heresy* (*Crónica de una herejía*).

And, regarding the censorship of Dialogues of Heresy—*did it have something to do with the erotic elements, the theme of Illuminism, the problem of the women and their sexual yearnings, and also the fact that in that play you establish a correspondence between the seventeenth century (the period of the Inquisition) and the twentieth century? Is that not it?*

Undoubtedly. For me the character of Doña Tristeza—and this is much more apparent in the new text—is a feminist character, *avant la lettre, comme on dit en français*, and what that means is that she is a women who does not submit to rules, who wants to change them, and who is capable of committing any type of subversive action in order to achieve her goals. She is a typical character of mine: the victim who goes against the norm and who wants to do battle in a different way. Tristeza de Arcos, engraved in her own epoch is like Maria Republica in our period. It's a bit like that.

I have always found that in your plays, it is possible to perceive in embryonic form, themes and characters that you later return to in your novels. It also seems to me that there are some plays in which the employment of allegory is so noticeable that they could be read as autos sacramentales. I am referring, for example, to My Dear Friends, It's Time We Get Certain Things Straight *(Queridos míos, es preciso contaros ciertas cosas) and to* One Thousand and One Messiahs *(Mil y un mesías).*

In reality, *My Dear Friends* is practically an *auto sacramental*. It works in the same manner because it is a philosophical proposal about the imposition of silence and the right to speak out.

Casandra is the new idea, the truth. The Duchess represents the bourgeoisie.

She is the system, the oppressive system.

Order.

Order. She is a system that is sometimes attractive because she is intelligent and even would be capable of entering into dialogue with a rebel. There are two characters who are true metaphors for the system. They are the Duchess and the Governor. The Governor demonstrates what order is. There is a moment in which he disguises himself as the king of total order, absolutely totalitarian, so that Casandra will understand who he is and who she is.

And she is the one with the blue eyes.

Yes.

Why is it that they are blue? Are they the eyes of truth, clairvoyant eyes?

You know, it's something that I do a lot. I don't know if you've noticed that in almost all my novels there is a character—for example, the youngest son of Ana Paücha, of *Ana No (Ana Non)*—has blue eyes. He was born with the miracle of blue eyes. I'm from a land of generally dark people with dark eyes, and so for me, blue eyes have always held the meaning of the contrary. Perhaps like a doubling: the Other, the possibility that the Other, although he or she may be similar to you, is always different because he or she has other features. All of this is naturally metaphoric but at least in my novels, in all that I have written, blue eyes communicate a translation of the truth that is contrary to or at least different from that of everyday life.

Like a quest, the truth to which one aspires.

Yes, it's a kind of aspiration. It is a physical detail that I have chosen, perhaps unconsciously, in practically all that I have written, as a metaphor for the possibility of another truth.

And in the end they cut out Casandra's tongue in a graphic image of censorship, to silence her.

Exactly, in reality it is what they are doing with me in Spain right now. They have cut out my tongue in Spain.

And they also cut out the tongue of a character in Mil y un mesías— *a maid.*

Yes.

So, we could say that it is an image that surfaces continually....

Yes, it surfaces several times. It also surfaces in *Dinner with Mr. and Mrs. Q (Dîner avec Mr and Mrs Q)*. There, the problem of the cut-out tongue also emerges.

And the castration scene at the end of L'enfant miraculée (The miracle child) *can also be inserted into that system of metaphors ...*

Yes, it is undeniable that for the character in *L'enfant miraculée*, castration intervenes as a form of revenge against the system. Castrate the powerful, castrate the power of the system. In that novel, it is some nobody that she finds, and she personifies in that man the entire system that has reduced her to the image of a scarecrow that she is, and only by castrating—when she commits that act of castration against the power of the system—is she able to smile for the first time. When he is finally . . .

In Mrs. Dead Smith's Interview with Her Phantoms (Interview de Muerta Smith por sus fantasmas), *there is a scene in which her body is fragmented; the dog performs a type of surgery on her in which he removes various parts of her body.*

There, a different kind of image surfaces because in reality, I think that the United States is a profoundly castrated country—not in the sexual sense; but rather, in the visceral sense, in an infinitely more complex and broad sense. Hence, I see the country as a bloody cadaver.

And that is Mrs. Muerta, in the most literal sense.

Voilà! The ex-ambassador of the United States, of power, etc. And when I come to New York and I see this city in complete bankruptcy, I have the impression that it is like the character of Mrs. Muerta Smith.

In complete decadence.

In complete decadence, in complete bankruptcy. Still, nevertheless, with a kind of power and even faith in herself that seems pitiful.

It seems to me that Mrs. Dead Smith's Interview *is a play that lends itself to a possible existentialist reading, in that she embarks on a quest for a place where she can continue her death—or her life, or whatever—and she travels as far as heaven and later as far as hell. Yet she never does find what she is searching for.*

She is conscious of the fact that the system, her system, the American system, is in complete bankruptcy. So, she embarks on a quest for a new place, a new space where she can recreate that system to see if it might finally work. And she realizes that all the spaces are already occupied.

The Russians have already arrived, Mao has already arrived.

She realizes that there really isn't any place left in the world, that there isn't any place left in the universe for that conquest of power, for that conquest of the truth, for that conquest of the unique system, etc. She realizes that every place is occupied everywhere.

While we are on the subject of the Soviet Union and the United States, I would like to ask you if the political changes that are presently taking place in Europe will have any effect upon the ideological underpinnings of your literary works. We are currently bearing witness to the fall of communism, and yet, the tension between the two political poles—right and left—is a conflict that emerges with great frequency in your works.

I am so profoundly anarchist that I do not think that type of thing could ever have an effect on what I write. In any case, we are at the beginning of something, and we still do not really know what it is. Something about which we receive information that is completely trafficked because what the West wants is not the fall of communism. What the people want is the fall of the Soviet Union and of all those countries that form those solid blocks, but it is a completely absurd thing. I mean to say that one should not forget that China still exists, that Vietnam still exists, that all of Asia . . . All of this is absolutely complicated because, furthermore, you never know what the newspapers are talking about. They talk about the right, about the left in those countries. It's completely absurd. They use a Western language to bury a series of phenomena that I don't think can be hidden with those languages.

So, what you are interested in exposing through your writing is the possibility of total anarchy. And, as indicated in your presentation the other day at the Dia Foundation, we need a state of revolution, of rebellion, in order to engender creativity.

Yes. That is what will generate creativity, what will generate change— if change is possible. In reality, I am more a man of the left that of the right, undoubtedly. That is easy to see, but I have never ascribed to any political party, ever. I have never voted, and it is evident that I defend one type of ideas and that I attack another type of ideas.

Fascism.

For example. I attack everything that is totalitarian. I defend all that is freedom and even all that is anarchy. Sometimes, at least, I use anarchy as a metaphor for total freedom. In reality, what I always defend is freedom of the individual.

You mean that you could very well attack Marxism in the same way that you attack fascism?

Undoubtedly. Yes, what happens is that I do not believe that Marxism is of sufficient age to have been contaminated by humanity. I believe that humanity is more contaminated by our system than by Marxism. In the end, Marxism was not even born a century ago while our Judeo-Christian civilization, etc., is so many centuries old. And you look at history a bit and you realize that the contamination is total and absolute. We carry it in our genes and that interests me much more than the other thing. I have never written about eastern European countries nor have I written about Marxism, about that type of country. Nor have I ever visited them, because it seems to me that it is impossible to do as the immense majority of writers do: go for a weekend, a week, a month, and return with a book in which they disclose their truths about such matters. I believe that the truth is something infinitely more complicated. I, who live within our system, still do not know what the truth is. I write searching for the truth, undoubtedly, but I still do not know what it is. That is why I've never complicated my life with these things. You know? The immense majority of writers who belonged to the left twenty years ago are presently with the right. Vargas Llosa, Semprún, and company—all of them have changed their stripes, which means that they always hold their fingers to the wind.

Then, let's say, your concerns lie on a more transcendental level?

Undoubtedly. I believe that before attempting to overthrow any other system we have to analyze profoundly our own and know that it is not a system that is worth perpetuating. The words used in certain contexts are never truthful. One speaks often of democracy, freedom—of freedom of expression, for example. Freedom of expression requires blood and sweat even in our democracies which are apparently infinitely free. And it takes a lot out of you! Why? There are places where they prohibit you, like in the Francoist Spain of which I have spoken. There are also places where they don't prohibit you, like France. They don't prohibit what you write. Simply, when you go a bit too far, for example, with *Bestiaire*. Silence. The result is silence. It is a form like any other of imposing censorship. I spoke about this in my lecture. It is the censorship imposed by democracy. Silence.

In a furtive way, but it exists.

Exactly. For example, when my French editors began proposing my books to the publishers in the United States, the response that the Americans almost always gave was that they found me to be an excellent writer, etc., but, unfortunately, "too lyrical and too anarchistic for the American public." That is something that I have always perceived as an act of censorship, an act of censorship more towards the audience that could have the opportunity to read me than towards me alone. When editors impede a certain audience from reading certain writers by prohibiting a book for nonliterary reasons, they are exercising an act of censorship.

Could it have been merely a question of personal taste on the part of the editor?

No, not even, because the proof is that *The Carnivorous Lamb* (*L'agneau carnivore*) works very well in the United States. So, there is an audience for me as well as for any other writer. There is always an audience for a writer.

So, your editors have tried to publish more of your works in the United States?

Practically all of them. For example, the two novels that have been published in England, *Ana No* and *A Bird Burned Alive* (*Un oiseau brulé vif*)—they have tried to publish them in the United States and not a single publisher has wanted to buy them. And *Ana No* was translated by a very well-known American writer by the name of John Becker.

And in Spain, what happened? A Bird Burned Alive was published in Spanish, but . . .

In Spain they reject. They reject my memory. Spain is a country that has wanted to change overnight and bury Francoism, bury it because, naturally, practically the same people continue to govern who were there under Franco.

Well, the mere fact that one man has died does not mean . . .

Exactly. It does not mean that the regime has died, at all. So, people like me—we have a memory of a specific period, we reproduce it constantly, and we are not welcome. They don't want to know from us. They prefer younger writers who have not lived through "that," who do not talk about "that." It's a phenomenon of occultation of history, of occultation of memory—which is a very current phenomenon. It happened in France for many years following the war with the people of the Resistance. They never spoke of "occupation" in France.

You have already told me the story about the production of Ana No, *the film made for television based on your novel. French national television proposed to Spanish national television the idea of collaborating on the production of the film.*

For example . . .

And Spanish television (TVE) rejected the proposal; they refused to participate in the production of Ana No.

And then, Spanish television wrote to French television. They considered the book to be "a threat to the reconciliation of Spaniards." I think that sentence sums it up: "A threat to the reconciliation of Spaniards." In that sentence one finds all the reasons why the Spanish publishers systematically reject what I have written.

*As you've already mentioned, you often represent in a metaphoric sense
a transgression of the hierarchical oppositions that constitute the basis
of Western culture; for example, order/anarchy. Could you comment
on this aspect of your work?*

Yes. It's not that I am personally subversive. Not at all. I don't believe
that I've ever broken a law. In fact, I like to say that whenever I cross
the street, I usually wait for the green light, etc. I'm a very ordered
person. I reality, I am a person of order in everyday life, with regard
to what is known as "civic order." Furthermore, I like being that way,
and it's not at all difficult for me to be that way. However, in my
characters, in my work in general, there is the system and there is
the individual. So, in order for the individual to function according
to my view of things, I've had to transform that individual into a
system, also. The system is one thing, and the individual is transformed into a system in order to oppose the original system, the real
system. All my characters are absolute individualists, but at the same
time, they are also a metaphor for what could be a whole series of
individuals organized in another type of system—in a system of complete freedom, as is anarchy in the good sense of the word. Anarchy
is a word that has become denaturalized since the beginning of time.
It's been converted into a horrible word, absolutely negative, because
it's become assimilated by disorder. In my view, it's not that way at
all. Anarchy is for me, as always, the classic concept of total freedom,
of the nonexistence of power, of the nonexistence of the system, of
the individual living according to his or her own rules in a society of
individuals who live according to their own rules.

Freedom . . .

Freedom. Not libertinage. Freedom. I believe that in my works this
is always the case. I try to find the protagonist a moral, ethical, or
philosophical justification, even for the individual who rebels against
the system. I transform that individual in personage, in somebody
who can be a metaphor not only for a single individual, but for a
whole series of individuals, and that "whole series of individuals"
even could become humanity itself. It's a little like the *Quijote*. In
Dostoyevsky, too, that problematic surfaces constantly.

In Maria Republica . . .

Maria Republica, that's it, undoubtedly. *Ana No*, that's it . . .

What I would call the "red women" of your literary works. There are "red women"...

Completely ...

...who defend the freedom of human beings, and others who are what we could call "yellow women." And then there are characters like Paula Martín, for example, of A Bird Burned Alive, *who is a mixture of the two.*

Yes, exactly. Paula is a hybrid, a product of a system that was based on a *petite bourgeoisie,* upon an almost *petite décadente bourgeoisie* and on the army, especially on the military; hence, Paula is the result, the hybrid.

Her bicolor eyes reflect her interior conflict.

Exactly. Sometimes people have interpreted her as a negative character, but for me she is not. I do not take pity on her, but at the same time I treat her with immense compassion. I look upon her with compassion, although I do not have the pity to reveal her—to *la mettre nue,* as one says in French—to such a point that in the final pages of the novel, she realizes that, logically, human beings are condemned to live with each other—she with "Red," "Red" with her—and that there is no other solution but to find a *modus vivendi* in order to continue living. Nevertheless, in the end, she attempts to burn the metaphors of rebellion: the bird named "freedom."

Yes, of course, the bird ...

Which also emerges in *Maria Republica.* There, it surfaced earlier as a metaphor for total freedom.

While we're on the subject of A Bird Burned Alive, *I would like to talk about the grotesque images that you create in that novel and in other works. The grotesque is a literary device that you employ with great frequency.*

It is a device that is a Spanish literary tradition, undoubtedly. It is a Spanish *esperpento.* The *esperpento* was born out of all that, out of a literary tradition that can be traced back to *La Celestina.*

Quevedo ...

Exactly. Before Quevedo, *La Celestina*. Spain is such an extreme country that it produces that type of thing. And, although the Spain of today wants to give the impression of a modern country, of a more or less balanced country, Spanish tradition, Spanish art, whether it be literature, painting, etc., gives the image of a country that doesn't have anything to do with the image that they try to sell these days. That is to say, the real image is Goya, the real image is Picasso, the real image is . . .

Dalí, Valle-Inclán . . .

Especially Valle-Inclán. It's Quevedo, it's Cervantes, obviously, it's the *Quijote*, it's *La Celestina*, it's Don Juan . . .

Well, I would venture to say that your works also fit into that tradition.

I think that they are related, yes, in effect.

That is to say, the employment of grotesque imagery serves as a point of departure for situating your work within a Spanish literary tradition, within a trajectory that is indisputably Spanish—rather than a French tradition.

It's true. In effect, for me, the French language and the fact that I publish in France has been useful for me as a way of domesticating the anarchistic tendencies of my writing. But it is indisputable that none of my books looks like French literature, none of my books has anything to do with French literature. They are certainly Hispanic, but . . . perhaps the French language and the fact that I work in French has afforded me the possibility of bringing order to all that disorder that is Spanish.

I also perceive in your literary trajectory an important relation between the theater and the novel. There is a sense of spectacularity, of theatricality in all your novels.

I believe that in all my novels there is a sense of spectacle. The fact that I was involved in and wrote theater for such a long time has certainly influenced and contributed to my novels, in the first place with regard to dialogue, because in the theater I learned what it is to carry on a dialogue. For example, almost all novelists systematically have a problem with dialogue. I do not have any. I know almost instinctively when a character needs to speak. When the characters carry on a dialogue in one of my novels, they always do it because it is strictly necessary for the composition of the novel, to develop one of the dimensions of the novel. Since I learned to do this in the theater, I've never had any problems with it.

Of course, it's an ability that comes naturally to you.

Yes, it comes naturally. In the theater I also learned to create characters. For me, the reader of the novel is systematically confused with the audience of the theater. Thus, when I write novels, I do not make a distinction between the theater audience and the reader of the novel. For me it is the same interlocutor, and so, what I like to do is take advantage of the two possibilities within the novel specifically . . . so that the reader can enter as in a spectacle.

So that he or she can participate . . .

So that he or she can participate, exactly.

It's a device that Cervantes also used.

Yes, undoubtedly. I think that Valle-Inclán used it a lot. The Russian writers knew how to use it a lot. I think that I do it in all my books. In *Maria Republica* it is very clear. In *Ana No* it is very clear: when they invite her for lunch and crown her as a pauper; when she tells herself a story in a public plaza, she is performing a spectacle, when she finds herself under the gaze of the circus people. In *Bestiaire*, there is that way that the triplets have of inventing roles for themselves.

It is a metaliterary technique; that is, a text that self-consciously contemplates the process of literary creation.

Undoubtedly. *The Man on His Knees* (*L'homme à genoux*) is a man who performs as well. He is a man who is carrying out a horrible performance as he drops to his knees in front of people. But, in order to get to that point, there was Señora Ramona who invented a personage for him, who told him how he should act. In all my books, there is a sense of spectacle.

Literature about literature, theater about theater . . . Also, it seems to me that you like to experiment with diverse literary techniques. For example, after reading The Carnivorous Lamb, *I began reading* Ana No, *and suddenly, I found myself confronted with a completely different narrative style. The technique employed in* Ana No *seems closer to that of the* nouveau roman: *the fragmented narrative, the leaps between past and present, the repetition of scenes—as seen through different perspectives—and even the repetition of phrases, such as the refrain about the almond bread. You also employ some of these narrative techniques in* (Furtive) Hunt Scene *(Scène de chasse [furtive]).*

Yes, I always subject my technique to the needs of the character, not to my own needs as a writer. For me, what counts is the character; hence, when I write a novel, I think about how that character is going to express him or herself, and what techniques are needed. This has nothing to do with the style. The style is always my own, but the techniques that I employ are exclusively those that are used by the character in order to express him or herself. In *Ana No*, everything moves more slowly, more repetitively because it is an old woman who is learning as though she were a child. She must learn a series of things, before things start to pick up and move more quickly.

I would also say that I think that Ana No *is a contemporary version of the picaresque novel.*

Yes it is.

In it one finds the hunger motif, she embarks upon a voyage throughout Spain and does an apprenticeship with several masters.

Yes, undoubtedly. Thus, for example, in *(Furtive) Hunt Scene*, the character of the police chief is so furtive, so slippery, that to express it I created the technique of seeing his death through a whole series of characters that have had some relation to him.

The same event, seen through different perspectives.

The same event seen through different characters, and each character sees it in a completely different manner. The technique that I employ in each novel is always dependent upon the central character of the novel. For example, in the latest novel, when you read it, you will realize that there is an oral technique. It's a boy who is blind, and so there aren't any visual images in the book. There are only images that come to him through his ears or through touch. The other senses, other than sight, are the ones that give him images of the city.[3]

So, the narrative technique is always a function of the needs of the character.

Exactly. It is never a function of myself. It is always a function of the character in absolutely all my books. In *The Bread Boy* (*L'enfant pain*), it is the gaze of the boy, that gaze that does not understand, that gaze of a little boy that is obliged because of the events to convert itself into an adult gaze without, however, being able to understand what it all means. In *The Carnivorous Lamb*, it is exactly the same— a technique in which the boy begins to discover the two worlds of power and chooses the system in which he wants to seek shelter: his parents' system or the system that his brother's love offers him.

You are also very interested in children as characters, aren't you?

Very much.

Why? Is there a particular reason?

I believe that a character is not complete if he or she is not developed from the point of childhood.

In order to show the development of his or her ideology ...

Exactly. So, I almost always develop my main characters from the point of childhood: it is the case of Maria Republica; it is the case of Paula Martín; it is the case of the police chief in *(Furtive) Hunt Scene*; it is the case of *The Bread Boy*; it is the case of *The Miracle Child*; it is the case of *Ana No*, when she tells herself the story of when she was a small girl; it is the case of *The Little Blind One* (*L'aveuglon*), who is a small boy; it is the case of *Bestiaire*. In *Bestiaire*, those children—or at least one of them—becomes that frightful monster that the mother gives birth to at the end of the novel. Already, with the triplets, I am in a way reproducing the childhood of that monster that the mother gives birth to—the monster of torture, of totalitarianism, of fascism, etc.

The monster functions as a kind of Messiah, but in the contrary, malevolent sense.

The contrary, yes, the Antichrist. In reality, in *Pré-papa*, the child that he carries in his womb is a metaphor for his own innocence, because I chose an absolutely innocent character—John Ferguson— who is another one of my visions of America. I also believe at the same time that innocence is American, more than European.

Oh, really?

I mean that there are more possibilities for innocence in America than in Europe.

Well, it is often said that everything is newer ...

Newer, and it is where there is more of a possibility for innocence. And when I tried to write about an innocent person, for me, John Ferguson was the innocent *par excellence.* I chose an American character that was at the same time capable of engendering innocence.

Yes, a baby.

Yes, an innocent.

In that work, Pré-Papa *(the play and the novel), your interest, or your concern, stands out with regard to gender issues—masculine and feminine.*

Yes, it is a concern of mine because I have always believed that the difference between the sexes is a transitory state. That is, at the beginning of life, each individual pertained to both sexes because it was absolutely necessary for the creation of life, to continue reproducing life. Later, the sexes separated because of a biological or reproductive necessity, but nowhere is it written that the sexes might not join together once again in a single individual if the necessity for the perpetuation of life were to dictate it in that manner.

It seems to me that this is another way in which you metaphorically effectuate a transgression of the established order or system.

Undoubtedly. It means putting everything into question. Always questioning everything.

With that work, did you also intend to make a commentary about feminism?

No, absolutely not.

Then, is it that you wanted to invoke a transgression of the established order, of the societal rules imposed throughout time?

Exactly. I am only interested in what is everlasting. The transitory does not interest me at all. Feminism, as well as political ideas and ideologies, are all ephemeral things. I am more interested in the capacity of the individual. I believe that the individual will someday have the possibility to create humanity. I believe that God does not exist, but that someday we will be capable, nevertheless, of inventing Him; I mean, of concretizing His existence. For that reason, I always demand that artists look beyond. For that reason I detest aestheticized, circumstantial art. It seems to me that it is important to do much more, that one has to go much further, and that somehow one has to create a utopia. I believe that it is something that underpins all of my works—that necessity for the individual to aim higher to arrive at something else.

And that is John Ferguson.

That is John Ferguson and in reality that is Mrs. Muerta Smith. That is to say in *Mrs. Dead Smith's Interview*, she realizes that she has started with a false invention, that up until now all that has been created is a God in the image and likeness of Man, not a man in the image and likeness of God. And then she finds out that God is somebody who is as absurd as she, because in reality it is her phantom.

It's an invention.

It's totally an invention.

And also, Denise, in the novel Bestiaire, *is trying to create, to invent . . .*

Of course, the creation of the monster.

It's her own creation, and her triplets are like three parts of a single being who together form a whole, a baby.

A whole, yes. That is why all three have the same name.

Of course, the three Dominiques.

That is why I chose one name that in French is *passe-partout*. That is why I invented that absolutely ambiguous but self-sufficient relationship that the three have in the novel.

And in that work, one also finds the leitmotif of gender ambiguity. There is the masculine Dominique, the feminine Dominique, and the

*third who is a kind of middle ground between the two sexual
tendencies.*

Yes, undoubtedly, because in reality I believe that is only a *bâtard* of
nature. That is to say, I believe that humanity as a project is infinitely
more important than the difference among individuals. The difference is an accident. In any case, it's completely scientific. The difference between the sexes occurred because the conditions made it
necessarily so in order for life to continue, but the meaning of life is
something else. The day in which life no longer needs the two sexes
to perpetuate itself, the sexes with become joined once again, or there
with be some other type of evolution, some other type of mutation.

*And during the female Dominique's monologue, she recalls an episode
that occurred in school; a conflict that occurred when she decided to
question what the teacher had taught the class, and she invented an
unconventional way of conjugating a verb ...*

Oh, yes. She is absolutely feminist. Because . . . they always teach us
to write, "I, you, he, she . . . ," and she decidedly writes, "I, you,
she, he . . ."

And she displays a clear consciousness of her feminism.

Absolutely conscious.

*So, behind the development of this character, there is indeed a type of
feminist discourse.*

Yes, undoubtedly, in reality it exists in all my novels. There are critics
that at times have taken me for a misogynist, but I am the complete
opposite. My literature is about victims. I always choose the victims
from among women because I believe that a woman has more capacity for rebellion—or at least she could have it—because she is more
of a victim than Man. Feminism is a *bâtard* that has been completely
led astray, but feminism was also a good thing. It was, undoubtedly,
an absolutely extraordinary rebellion. I convert women into heroines,
and that is absolutely feminist.

Of course. And Matilde and Clara in the novel The Carnivorous
Lamb *...*

That duality undergoes a transformation. That is, Clara manages to transform Matilde into a heroine by the simple fact of dressing like her and of doing what she should have done. In reality, that is always the case. Ana No is transformed into a heroine by choosing her own death. Maria Republica is a heroine. The duality Paula Martín/Red is another heroine, victims of a system. Sometimes they pertain to a positive sign, sometimes they pertain to a negative sign, but that is literary creation.

I would like to talk about the end of The Carnivorous Lamb, *where you have written the following:*

> Mother-me is named Matilde. Alive
> Father-Carlos is named my brother. Alive.
> Our maid's name is Clara. Alive. (Detail not to be overlooked: she leans
>   toward terrorism.)
> My brother's name is Antonio. Alive
>
> My name is Ignacio. Here. Triumphant. Alive.
> And delighted to have met you.[4]

In this fragment one finds a series of correlations between the two brothers and the parents, which you have been developing throughout the novel. Antonio corresponds to Carlos, his father; and Ignacio corresponds to Matilde, his mother. In effect, each represents a kind of doubling of the other. The brothers seem to be reincarnations of the parents. The story repeats itself, but in a slightly different way.

Yes, there are doublings, and at the same time, they represent a transgression of the notion of a married couple as understood by the dominant order. In reality, they are still a couple, but they are no longer within the dominant system.

It has been perpetuated, but in a different way.

In a different way.

And it seems to me that there, Clara intervenes to form a kind of triangle.

She intervenes enormously. She is the one who blesses their union, and for that very reason, she facilitates it. She facilitates that symbol of the union of a couple that is the result of another couple but that now is different, and for that reason, they perceive her as a kind of terrorist.

And also, in that novel, there are two houses: one in the country and one in the city. They are identical but at the same time opposite; that is, one is the mirror image of the other. Why have you portrayed them in this way?

Because of the difficulties involved in escaping the system. Perhaps, unconsciously, what I was writing about when I spoke of those houses, one of which is the exact reflection of the other, is the idea of having abandoned one country in order to go to another that in a way—well, because we are still in the same system—was exactly the same. Perhaps it was the impossibility of escaping the system. The system is always the same. You can commit a whole series of acts of aggression against the system, but you always end up as a prisoner of the system; you always end up with an image of the system, with an image reflected in the mirror.

The incestuous relationship between the two boys represents another act ...

Of total transgression. That is, incest is the thing that is most ...

Prohibited, most taboo ...

Love can be prohibited, and it can be taboo in certain circumstances, but incestuous love is a total transgression of the system.

Nevertheless, Matilde applauds her children's actions. She gives her approval ...

Because Matilde is an absolutely extraordinary character. She is a double character: there is the bourgeois woman who finds it difficult to put up with those acts of transgression, and then there is her *true* character. At a certain point, she talks to herself about when she was a child and about how, for example, when she would cut flowers, she would always wear gloves. That is to say, there was a kind of screen between reality and herself. The system in which she was living, the family, etc. had always devised a screen, a dividing line, between her own freedom, her own nature, her own personality, and what her behavior should have been. So, for the first time—that's why she speaks of a cataclysm and why she feels so profoundly fasci-

nated—the only two things that fascinate her is the relationship between her sons. She condemns it in a verbal manner, but at the same
time, it is her passion. That fascination, which looks like hatred,
in reality, is an absolutely profound love, a love for the illegal, for
the illicit.

*Yes, it seems to begin with hatred but little by little that hatred is
converted into love. It began with hatred when the baby, Ignacio,
opened his eyes and Matilde had to cancel her pilgrimage, her trip,
her plans ...*

Yes, she had to renounce that completely social story. But later, gradually, she begins to become a part of that distortion of the system that
her own children represent. And in reality, she observes them almost
with more passion, her passion transferred from her husband to
her sons.

And she lets her sons ...

She lets them be. And later there is the presence of death. The fact
that she sees death born in the persona of her husband is the discovery
of death in the other that leads her to do all those crazy things, all
those trips that she takes ...

And she writes those letters.

And in her letters, in reality, she never speaks of her husband. She
speaks of death, of how death is born in her husband, and how it
begins to grow, as if that discovery of death had more importance
than her husband, himself.

And the title, The Carnivorous Lamb ...

The carnivorous lamb for me is the precise metaphor for transgression. Lambs are herbivores. A lamb that is carnivorous is truly total
transgression.

*Could you name some other influences, some memorable readings that
have influenced your literary formation?*

I don't know.

You've mentioned some Russian writers.

Yes, I've always had a passion for the Russian writers, all of them: Dostoyevsky, Gogol above all, even Tolstoy, Gorki, and also, undoubtedly, Kafka. They are writers whom I've always loved. I think that one of the readings that most affected me was the reading of Kafka's *Metamorphosis*. I must have been seventeen years old, and perhaps I found something of myself, some of my own tendencies in that text. The truth is that in practically all my books there is a metamorphosis of the character which leads to rebellion.

And usually those characters are women.

Usually those characters are women, yes.

Well, how do you feel about the future of Spain? Does the theme of Spain continue to play a role among your literary concerns?

Look, in reality, people talk a lot about change. I think that all changes need a lot of time so that we can see them happen. So, naturally, a writer cannot see change the way the politicians or everyday people see them. For us, change, in the end, needs centuries to happen.

You've said in another interview that sometimes you feel French. Nevertheless, the impression that I have from reading your works is that you feel profoundly Spanish.

Yes, undoubtedly, there is a kind of—I wouldn't say a dual personality. There is a type of process that works in a special way because of the fact that I write in the French language. I think that with the French language I have found the tool to express myself, the tool that does not produce any type of restriction for me. It is a tool that is virgin for me. Since I learned the French language when I was already an adult, in reality it is a language that doesn't have prohibitions for me. *Il n'y a rien qui m'est interdit en langue française.* If I had learned it as a child, surely they would have taught me everything that was prohibited and that wasn't prohibited, what one should say and what one shouldn't say, how to say it and how not to say it. Since I learned it as an adult, none of that matters to me, and the process is one of freedom of expression.

Nevertheless, do you think that censorship, on the other hand, can function as an incentive for creativity? I'm thinking of other Spanish writers of the post–Civil War period who, in order to avoid censorship, searched for other creative and subtle means of expressing their critiques.

It's undeniable. I don't know if that's happened to everybody. But anyway, as far as I'm concerned, that is already a proof of the way censorship functions. When I speak of writing in freedom, I am referring to when you employ a language as an instrument that, for you, doesn't have anything suspect, that you don't have to make a deliberately conscious effort to convert it into a symbol, to convert it into a metaphor, etc. And for me that is the French language. I don't have to use any type of euphemism, and so I can write freely, express myself freely. And that is something that you cannot understand until you become bilingual. There are very few people who understand that.

Moreover, to view your own country from afar gives you a certain perspective ...

From afar. From afar and from near, the linguistic instrument of distance. Even, if like me, you are living half the time in your own country—which is what I do, live six months in Spain, six months in France, so I'm there in the middle of the everyday *jaleo*—but my linguistic instrument already gives me quite an important distance.

And so, are you writing another novel?

I've started another novel.

Where does it take place?

This time it takes place in Paris, where I try to offer a very personal reflection about justice.[5]

Thank you very much.

Notes

PREFACE

1. It's the moment. You should undertake this voyage with dignity, without fear. With the hope that I myself will not be as cruel to you as Life.

2. Moisés Pérez Coterillo, "Breve interrupción de una ausencia," introduction to *Interview de Mrs. Muerta Smith por sus fantasmas*, by Agustín Gómez-Arcos, Teatro 15. (Madrid: *El Público*/Centro de Documentation Teatral, 1991), 9–12.

3. In reference to the première of Gómez-Arcos's *Queridos míos, es preciso contaros ciertas cosas* in December 1994, theater critic Rosana Torres wrote in *El País*, "With the return to the present of this writer from Almería we witness one of the most curious literary phenomena of contemporary Spanish culture. His plays as well as his novels are practically unknown in Spain but, each time that we are made aware of even a minimal part of his creative work, readers, spectators and critics alike bow at his feet, despite the fact that he continues to be unknown by editors and producers." ("Gómez Arcos recibe grandes honores de dramaturgo con 30 años de retraso," *El País*, 7 December 1994.)

4. Agustín Gómez-Arcos, "Censorship, Exile, Bilingualism," in *Critical Fictions: The Politics of Imaginative Writing*, ed. Philomena Mariani, 220–22 (Seattle: Bay Press, 1991). Here, I quote from the original version of Gómez-Arcos's paper (see note 34 of chapter 1).

5. María Francisca Vilches de Frutos, "La temporada teatral española 1992–1993," *Anales de la Literatura Española Contemporánea* 20.3 (1995): 470

6. The date of composition is given in parentheses.

7. María Pilar Pérez-Stansfield, *Direcciones del teatro español de posguerra* (Madrid: José Porrúa Turanzas, 1983), 157, 310; José García Templado, *El teatro español actual* (Madrid: Anaya, 1992); Alberto Miralles, *Aproximación al teatro alternativo, Damos la palabra* 3 (Madrid: Asociación de Autores de Teatro, 1994), 16; Juan Emilio Aragonés, *Teatro español de posguerra*, Temas españoles 520 (Madrid: Publicaciones Españolas, 1971), 88; César Oliva, *El teatro desde 1936*, Historia de la literatura española actual 3 (Madrid: Alhambra, 1989), 222, 224, 226, 233, 322, 324–26, 350, 434, 445; Teresa Valdivieso, "El intertexto como principio configurativo en el teatro de Fernando Arrabal y Agustín Gómez-Arcos," in *Teatro español contemporáneo: Autores y tendencias*, ed. Alfonso de Toro and Wilfried Floeck 167–90 (Kassel: Reichenberger, 1995); Phyllis Zatlin, *Cross-Cultural Approaches to Theatre: The Spanish-French Connection* (Metuchen, N.J.: Scarecrow Press, 1994), 76, 77–80, 83, 112, 191, 212; idem, "The Return of the Prodigal: The Theatre of Gómez-Arcos," *Hispanic Journal* 16.1 (Spring 1995): 55–63; Elena Gascón-Vera, "Los reflejos del yo: narcisismo y androginia en Agustín Gómez Arcos," *Cuadernos de ALDEEU* 7.1 (April 1991): 31–52; and Ann Duncan, "Agustín Gómez-Arcos," in *Beyond the Nouveau Roman:*

Essays on the Contemporary French Novel, ed. Michael Tilby, 151–76 (New York: Berg, 1990).

8. George Wellwarth, *Spanish Underground Drama* (University Park and London: The Pennsylvania State University Press, 1972), published in Spanish as *Teatro español underground*, prologue by Alberto Miralles, Hoy es Siempre Todavía (Madrid: Villalar, 1978). Regarding the merits and limitations of Wellwarth's study, cf. César Oliva, *El teatro desde 1936*, Historia de la literatura española actual 3 (Madrid: Alhambra, 1989), 345–47.

9. Jesús Barrajón, *La poética de Francisco Nieva* (Ciudad Real: Diputación Provincial de Ciudad Real, 1987); Ángel Cabo, *José Martín Recuerda: Génesis y evolución de un autor dramático* (Granada: Diputación Provincial de Granada, 1993); Elda María Phillips, *Idea, signo y mito: El teatro de José Ruibal* (Madrid: Orígenes, 1984); Virtudes Serrano, *El teatro de Domingo Miras*, prologue by Francisco Ruiz Ramón (Murcia: Universidad de Murcia, 1991); Juan Tebar, *Fernando Fernán Gómez, escritor* (Madrid: Anjana, 1984); Zatlin, *Jaime Salom* (Boston: Twayne, 1982); Gwynne Edwards, *Dramatists in Perspective: Spanish Theatre in the Twentieth Century* (New York: St. Martin's Press, 1985); Martha Halsey and Phyllis Zatlin, *The Contemporary Spanish Theater: A Collection of Critical Essays* (Lanham/New York/London: University Press of America, 1988); Marion P. Holt, *The Contemporary Spanish Theater (1949–1972)* (Boston: Twayne, 1975); Oliva, *Disidentes de la generación realista (Introducción a la obra de Carlos Muñiz, Laura Olmo, Rodríguez Méndez and Martín Recuerda)* (Murcia: Departamento de Literatura Española, Universidad de Murcia, 1979); Toro and Floeck, eds., *Teatro español contemporáneo: Autores y tendencias* (Kassel: Reichenberger, 1995).

CHAPTER 1. FROM CENSORSHIP TO EXILE TO BILINGUALISM

1. Because my memories, who could erase them? Especially now that I have finally found the way to make use of them. Like bombs to annihilate you. . . . But I finally do understand. You do not want my memories. My memories are also your history. Filthy history. Fine. It may be too late but . . . the time I have left is precious time. The time to settle the score.

2. Unless otherwise noted, the biographical information included throughout this study is derived from my personal conversations with Mr. Gómez-Arcos.

3. Interview with Pierre Canavaggio, "Un homme de *Caractères:* Agustín Gomez-Arcos ce soir sur A2," *Panorama du Médecin*, 5 October 1990, 21.

4. Interview with Rosa Montero, "Agustín Gómez Arcos: El creyente de la palabra," *El País*, 6 October 1985, suplemento dominical, 7–8.

5. Alfredo Marquerie, "*Elecciones generales*, de Gómez-Arcos," *ABC*, 6 April 1960, 63.

6. Throughout this study, my employment of the term *mise en scène* is concurrent with the sense in which it is used by Patrice Pavis, to designate the dynamic intersection of text and performance (otherwise known as "T/P") (*Languages of the Stage* [New York: Performing Arts Journal Publications, 1982], 131–61).

7. Interview with Feldman.

8. On censorship in post–Civil War Spain, see Manuel L. Abellán, *Censura y creación literaria en España (1939–1976)*, Temas de Historia y Política Contemporánea 9 (Barcelona: Península, 1980); idem, "La censura teatral durante el franquismo," *Estreno* 15.2 (Fall 1989): 20–23; idem, *El exilio español de 1936*, 6 vols. (Madrid: Taurus, 1976–78); Patricia W. O'Connor, "Government Censorship in the

Contemporary Spanish Theatre," *Educational Theatre Journal* 18 (1966): 443–49; "Torquemada in the Theater: A Glance at Government Censorship," *Theatre Survey* 14.2 (1973): 33–45; César Oliva, *El teatro desde 1936*, Historia de la literatura española actual 3 (Madrid: Alhambra, 1989); Anthony Pasquariello, "Government Promotion, Honors and Awards: A Corollary to Franco Era Censorship in Theater," *Cuadernos de ALDEEU* 1 (January 1983): 67–81; Janet Pérez, "The Game of the Possible: Francoist Censorship and Techniques of Dissent," *Review of Contemporary Fiction* 4 (Fall 1984): 22–30; and George Wellwarth, *Spanish Underground Drama* (University Park and London: The Pennsylvania State University Press), 1972. The aforementioned critics offer detailed accounts of Francoist censorship codes and document specific attempts at resistance on the part of dramatists and other Spanish writers. Hilde Cramsie examines censorship in Francoist Spain with regard to playwrights Alfonso Sastre, Carlos Muñiz, and José Ruibal (*Teatro y censura en la España franquista. Sastre, Muñiz y Ruibal*, American University Studies, Series 2, Romance Languages and Literatures, vol. 9. [Peter Lang: New York, 1984]). See also the collection of articles, grouped under the subtitle "Antifranquismo . . . todavía," which appeared in the April-May 1980 issue of *Primer Acto* under the coordination of Alberto Miralles. This issue contains essays by Manuel P. Casaux, Antonio Gala, Manuel Martínez Mediero, Guillermo Heras, Gerardo Malla, Miralles, Francisco Umbral, and Angel Fernández devoted to the theme of censorship and Spanish theater under Franco. It also contains the transcript of a roundtable discussion centering on this theme, coordinated by Angel Facio with the participation of actress Alicia Hermida, who appeared in the 1964 production of *Diálogos de la herejía*, the 1965 production of *Los gatos*, and the 1994 production of *Queridos míos*.

9. Regarding this polemic, see, for example, Ricardo Domènech, "El teatro desde 1936," in *Historia de la literatura española*, vol. 4 (Madrid: Taurus, 1980); José García Templado, *El teatro español actual* (Madrid: Anaya, 1992); Oliva, *El teatro desde 1936*; Francisco Ruiz Ramón, *Historia del teatro español. Siglo XX* (Madrid: Cátedra, 1977); and Buero, Paso, and Sastre's articles published in *Primer Acto* and reprinted in Luciano García Lorenzo, ed., *Documentos sobre el teatro español contemporáneo* (Madrid: Sociedad General Española de Librería, 1980).

10. See chapter 6 of this study for more details regarding the unusual circumstances surrounding this Lope de Vega Prize.

11. Cf. the interview with Moisés Pérez Coterillo, "Agustín Gómez Arcos: 'El pensamiento es más arriesgado (y más cauto) que la noticia,'" *Turia de Madrid*, 9/6 December 1994, 27–29.

12. Marvin Carlson, *Theories of the Theatre: A Historical and Critical Survey, from the Greeks to the Present* (Ithaca: Cornell University Press, 1993), 471.

13. André Camp, "L'actualité théatrale," *L'Avant-Scène Théâtre* 434 (1969): 46.

14. Cf., for example, Ann Duncan, "Agustín Gómez-Arcos," in *Beyond the Nouveau Roman: Essays on the Contemporary French Novel*, ed. Michael Tilby (New York: Berg, 1990), 153.

15. Ibid., 151.

16. Interview with Feldman.

17. Cf. José Monleón, "Premio Nacional de Literatura Dramática," *Primer Acto* 256 (November-December 1994): 4–5. José María Rodríguez Méndez won the prize for *El pájaro solitario*. Gómez-Arcos was nominated for *Los gatos*. The other three finalists were Jaime Salom for *Más que una diosa*, Lauro Olmo for *La Benita*, and José Sanchis Sinisterra for *Los figurantes*.

18. Cf. Oliva, *El teatro desde 1936* and Abellán, *El exilio español de 1939*.

19. José Monleón, "Nuestra generación realista," *Primer Acto* 32 (March 1962): 1–3.

20. Oliva, *El teatro desde 1936*, 226.

21. Ibid., 224.

22. Juan Emilio Aragonés, *Teatro español de posguerra*, Temas españoles 520 (Madrid: Publicaciones Españolas, 1971), 88.

23. Cf. Pérez Coterillo, Vicente Romero, and Ricard Salvat, who describe the events at the Sorbonne in the January 1973 issue of *Primer Acto*. I discuss Gómez-Arcos's experience at the Sorbonne in further detail in part III.

24. Nieva, for example, was born in 1927 and lived in exile until the mid-1960s.

25. Oliva, *El teatro desde 1936*, 338.

26. "Yo, cuando escribo teatro, hago la guerra," *Diario 16*, 30 June 1985.

27. Interview with Feldman.

28. Michel Foucault, "A Preface to Transgression," in *Language, Counter-memory, Practice*, ed. Donald F. Bouchard, trans. Donald F. Bouchard and Sherry Simon (Ithaca: Cornell University Press, 1977), 37.

29. Interview with Feldman

30. Here, I am drawing upon René Girard's concept of sacrificial ritual. (*Violence and the Sacred*, trans. Patrick Gregory [Baltimore: Johns Hopkins University Press, 1977]).

31. Juan Goytisolo, "Presentación crítica," in *Obra inglesa de Blanco White* (Barcelona: Seix Barral, 1982), 6.

32. Michael Ugarte, *Shifting Ground: Spanish Civil War Exile Literature* (Durham, N.C.: Duke University Press, 1989), 9.

33. Paul Ilie, *Literature and Inner Exile: Authoritarian Spain 1939–75* (Baltimore: Johns Hopkins University Press, 1980).

34. The symposium was organized by Philomena Mariani as part of the Dia Art Foundation's "Discussions in Contemporary Culture" series. Gómez-Arcos shared the stage with fellow writers Hilton Als, Jamaica Kincaid, and Elena Poniatowska in a roundtable discussion devoted to the theme of "Systems of Oppression and the Struggle for a Culture." In addition to the previously mentioned names, the other participants included Ama Ata Aidoo, Homi K. Bhabha, Angela Carter, Michelle Cliff, Nawal El Saadawi, Jessica Hagedorn, bell hooks, Arturo Islas, Anton Shammas, Luisa Valenzuela, and Michele Wallace. Over the course of three days, these writers engaged in a series of lively discussions that touched upon contemporary issues of cultural identity, gender, politics, postcolonialism, and oppression. The collected proceedings, along with an additional set of essays solicited from writers who were not in attendance have been published in the volume *Critical Fictions: The Politics of Imaginative Writing*, ed. by Philomena Mariani (Seattle: Bay Press, 1991). Gómez-Arcos's essay, originally written in Spanish and translated into English by an anonymous translator, is included in this volume, but the text has been inexplicably altered. In order to remain faithful to the original version, I have drawn my citations of this essay from my own unaltered copy, which I was asked to read aloud at the symposium while serving as Mr. Gómez-Arcos's interpreter.

35. Michael Holquist, "Corrupt Originals: The Paradox of Censorship," *PMLA* 109.1 (January 1994): 16.

36. Ibid., 17.

37. Cf. also Sue Curry Jansen, *Censorship: The Knot that Binds Power and Knowledge* (Oxford: Oxford University Press, 1988).

38. Holquist, "Corrupt Originals," 21.

39. Cited by Oliva, *El teatro desde 1936*, 218.

40. Holquist, "Corrupt Originals," 14.

41. Ibid.

CHAPTER 2. A POETICS OF EXPANSE AND ENCLOSURE

1. There are, most certainly, other dramatists, such as Fernando Arrabal, Francisco Nieva, and Alfonso Vallejo, whose theater has maintained its allegorical temperament throughout the post-Franco period.

2. Craig Owens, "The Allegorical Impulse: Toward a Theory of Postmodernism: Part I" *October* 12 (1980): 68.

3. Romantic criticism typically juxtaposes allegory and symbol and tends to view the latter as a superior rhetorical mode. Goethe, for example, summarized his position on allegory with the following statement: "There is a great difference between a poet's seeking the particular from the general and his seeing the general in the particular. The former gives rise to allegory, where the particular serves only as an instance or example of the general; the latter, however, is the true nature of poetry: the expression of the particular without any thought of, or reference to, the general. Whoever grasps the particular in all its vitality also grasps the general, without being aware of it, or only becoming aware of it at a late stage" (cited by Walter Benjamin, *The Origin of German Tragic Drama*, trans. John Osborne [London: New Left Books, 1977], 161). Although he does not condemn the artistic value of allegory, C. S. Lewis, in his study of medieval allegory, establishes a similar contrast between allegory and symbol (*The Allegory of Love: A Study in Medieval Tradition*, [New York: Oxford University Press, 1972]). On allegory, see also Angus Fletcher, *Allegory: The Theory of a Symbolic Mode* (Ithaca: Cornell University Press, 1964); Edwin Honig, *Dark Conceit: The Making of Allegory* (Chicago: Northwestern University Press, 1960); Lynette Hunter, *Modern Allegory and Fantasy: Rhetorical Stances of Contemporary Writing* (New York: St. Martin's Press, 1989); and Carolynn Van Dyke, *The Fiction of Truth: Structures of Meaning in Narrative and Dramatic Allegory* (Ithaca: Cornell University Press, 1985).

4. For example, on Pynchon, cf. Deborah L. Madsen, *The Postmodernist Allegories of Thomas Pynchon* (Leicester: Leicester University Press, 1991); Brian McHale, *Postmodernist Fiction* (New York: Routledge, 1987); and Maureen Quilligan, *The Language of Allegory* (Ithaca: Cornell University Press, 1979). On Anderson, Levine, Longo, Rauschenberg, and Sherman, cf. Craig Owens, "The Allegorical Impulse: Toward a Theory of Postmodernism: Part I" and "Part II," *October* 13 (1980): 59–80. On Levine, cf. Gregory L. Ulmer, "The Object of Post-Criticism," in *The Anti-Aesthetic: Essays on Postmodern Culture*, ed. by Hal Foster, 83–100 (Seattle: Bay Press, 1983). On the allegorical strategies in contemporary painting and photography, cf. Joan Simon, "Double Takes," *Art in America* 8 (October 1980): 113–17. For general discussions of the relationship between allegory and postmodernism, cf. James Applewhite, "Postmodernist Allegory and the Denial of Nature," *Kenyon Review* 11.1 (Winter 1989): 1–17; Stephen Melville, "Notes on the Reemergence of Allegory, the Forgetting of Modernism, the Necessity of Rhetoric, and the Conditions of Publicity in Art and Criticism," *October* 19 (1981): 54–92; Mihai Spariosu, "Allegory, Hermeneutics, and Postmodernism," in *Exploring Postmodernism*, ed. Matei Calinescu and Douwe Fokkema (Amsterdam/Philadelphia: John Benjamins, 1987) and Paul Smith, "The Will to Allegory in Postmodernism," *Dalhousie Review* 62 (1982): 105–22.

5. Owens, "The Allegorical Impulse: Toward a Theory of Postmodernism: Part II," 72.

6. On the association between allegory and metaphor, Joel Fineman comments, "In Roman Jakobson's linguistic formula, . . . allegory would be the poetical projection of the metaphoric axis onto the metonymic, where metaphor is understood as the synchronic system of differences that constitutes the order of language (*langue*), and metonymy the diachronic principle of combination and connection by means of which structure is actualized in time in speech (*parole*)" ("The Structure of Allegorical Desire," *October* 12 [1980]: 50). Cf. also McHale, *Postmodernist Fiction*, 140–47.

7. Owens, "The Allegorical Impulse: Toward a Theory of Postmodernism: Part I," 68.

8. Ibid., 69.

9. Paul de Man, "The Rhetoric of Temporality," in *Blindness and Insight: Essays in the Rhetoric of Contemporary Criticism*, Theory and History of Literature, vol. 7 (Minneapolis: University of Minnesota Press, 1983), 207. On allegory's relationship to commentary and interpretation, see Northrop Frye, *Anatomy of Criticism* (Princeton: Princeton University Press, 1957) and Paul de Man, *Allegories of Reading* (New Haven: Yale University Press, 1979).

10. Madsen, *Postmodernist Allegories*, 4–5.

11. Benjamin, *German Tragic Drama*, 224–25.

12. Ibid., 166.

13. For more on the ruin, see Charles Rosen, "Walter Benjamin and His Ruins, *New York Review of Books*, 27 October 1977; 31–40, 17 November 1977, 30–38. On Velázquez, see José Ortega y Gasset, *Velázquez* (Madrid: Austral, 1970).

14. Benjamin, *German Tragic Drama*, 178.

15. Ibid., 223. Cf. Bainard Cowan, "Walter Benjamin's Theory of Allegory," *New German Critique* 22 (Winter 1981): 109–22 and Rainer Nägele, *Theater, Theory, Speculation: Walter Benjamin and the Scenes of Modernity* (Baltimore: Johns Hopkins University Press, 1991). Richard Wolin views the Benjaminian conception of allegory as an "aesthetic of redemption" (*Walter Benjamin: An Aesthetic of Redemption* [Berkeley: University of California Press, 1993]).

16. Ibid., 175.

17. The title of a recent allegorical installation by postmodern artist Robert Longo epitomizes the workings of this dialectic: *When heaven and hell change places* (Galerie Hans Mayer, Düsseldorf, November 1992-March 1993). A similar process is also at work in the *tableau* photography of Andres Serrano.

18. Benjamin, *German Tragic Drama*, 175.

19. Ibid., 201.

20. Craig Owens, "The Discourse of Others: Feminists and Postmodernism," in *The Anti-Aesthetic: Essays on Postmodern Culture*, ed. Hal Foster (Seattle: Bay Press, 1983), 57–58. Owens's treatment of allegory is grounded in the Derridian notion of the supplement: "If allegory is identified as a supplement, then it is also aligned with writing, insofar as writing is conceived as supplementary to speech. It is of course within the same philosophic tradition which subordinates writing to speech that allegory is subordinated to the symbol. It might be demonstrated, from another perspective, that the suppression of allegory is identical with the suppression of writing" (1: 84). Cf. also Ulmer, "The Object of Post-Criticism," on the relationship between allegory and deconstructive criticism.

21. There are parallels between this endeavor to drive the spectator toward a *prise de conscience* and the principles of Brechtian alienation.

22. Owens, "The Discourse of Others," 59. Cf. also Owens, "From Work to Frame, or, Is There Life After 'The Death of the Author'?" *Beyond Recognition: Representation, Power, and Culture*, 122–39.

23. Cf. Brian McHale on the postmodern subversion of Manichaean allegory (*Postmodernist Fiction* [New York: Routledge, 1987], 143–44).

24. Interview with Feldman.

25. McHale, *Postmodernist Fiction*, 141.

26. Benjamin, *German Tragic Drama*, 175.

27. McHale observes a similar tendency in the novels of Pynchon, where "the polar opposites are allowed to 'bleed' into one another" (144).

28. Owens notes, "The critique of binarism is sometimes dismissed as intellectual fashion; it is, however, an intellectual imperative, since the hierarchical opposition of marked and unmarked terms (the decisive/divisive presence/absence of the phallus) is the dominant form both of representing difference and justifying its subordination in our society. What we must learn, then, is how to conceive difference without opposition" ("The Discourse of Others," 62). Cf. also Jean François Lyotard, *The Postmodern Condition: A Report on Knowledge*, trans. Geoff Bennington and Brian Massumi (Minneapolis: University of Minnesota Press, 1984), 29.

29. Mary Douglas, *Purity and Danger: An Analysis of Concepts of Pollution and Taboo* (New York: Frederick A. Praeger, 1966). On this primordial conception of the sacred, see also Georges Bataille, *Erotism: Death and Sensuality*, trans. Mary Dalwood (San Francisco: City Lights Books, 1986); Roger Callois, *L'homme et le sacré*, 2d ed. (Paris: Gallimard, 1950); Mircea Eliade, *The Sacred and the Profane: The Nature of Religion*, trans. Willard R. Trask (New York: Harcourt Brace Jovanovich, 1987); and René Girard, *Violence and the Sacred*, trans. Patrick Gregory (Baltimore: Johns Hopkins University Press, 1977).

30. My employment of the terms *homogeneous* and *heterogeneous* is commensurate with that of Bataille in the discussion of modern political structures appearing in his essay "The Psychological Structure of Fascism," in *Visions of Excess, Selected Writings, 1927–1939*, ed. Allan Stoekl, trans. A. Stoekl, Carl R. Lovitt, and Donald M. Leslie, Jr., *Theory and History of Literature*, vol. 14 (Minneapolis: University of Minnesota Press, 1985). For Bataille, the homogeneous component of a Fascist state denotes the area of stability that lies within the limits of society's grid of taboos. Homogeneity corresponds to order; it is composed of the productive and pragmatic elements of society that maintain the gap separating taboo from transgression.

31. Rosalind E. Krauss discusses the metaphoric nature of gridlike forms, tracing their development throughout the history of Western art in "Grids," in *The Originality of the Avant-Garde and Other Modernist Myths* (Cambridge: MIT Press, 1985).

32. This ontological interrogation of the sacred signified closely parallels the questioning of "absolute Logos" that Derrida has traced to Antonin Artaud's theater of cruelty. Derrida comments, "The theater of cruelty expulses God from the stage. It does not put a new atheist discourse on stage, or give atheism a platform, or give over theatrical space to a philosophizing logic that would once more, to our greater lassitude, proclaim the death of God. The theatrical practice of cruelty, in its action and structure, inhabits or rather *produces* a nontheological space. The stage is theological for as long as it is dominated by speech, by a will to speech, by the layout of a primary logos which does not belong to the theatrical site and governs it from a distance" ("The Theater of Cruelty and the Closure of Representation," in *Writing and Difference*, ed. and trans. Alan Bass [Chicago: University of Chicago Press, 1978, 235]).

33. Cf. Georges Bataille, "*Erotism* and 'The Notion of Expenditure,'" in *Visions of Excess, Selected Writings, 1927–1939*, ed. Allan Stoekl, trans. A. Stoekl, Carl R. Lovitt,

and Donald M. Leslie, Jr., *Theory and History of Literature*, vol. 14 (Minneapolis: University of Minnesota Press, 1985).

34. Philippe Sollers, "The Roof: Essay in Systematic Reading," in *Writing and the Experience of Limits*, ed. David Hayman, trans. Philip Barnard, with David Hayman 103–34 (New York: Columbia University Press, 1983). In his 1963 essay, "The Metaphor of the Eye," Roland Barthes poses a parallel assumption in reference to Bataille's erotic novel *Histoire de l'oeil* (1928). The Barthes essay as well as the two subsequently mentioned pieces by Philippe Sollers and Susan Sontag are cited by Susan Suleiman in "Pornography, Transgression, and the Avant-Garde: Bataille's *Story of the Eye*," in *Subversive Intent: Gender, Politics, and the Avant-Garde* (Cambridge: Harvard University Press, 1990). Suleiman refers to these studies in her examination of transgressive textuality and the avant-garde, foregrounding the process by which poststructural theorists, such as Barthes, Derrida, and Sollers, have extended Bataille's notion of transgression to encompass their own notion of *écriture* (which is opposed to logocentrism): "For *écriture*, in the sense in which they used that term, is precisely that element of discursive practice which exceeds the traditional boundaries of meaning, of unity, of representation . . . " (76).

35. Sollers, "The Roof," 17.

36. Suleiman translates *écriture corporelle* as "bodily writing."

37. Goytisolo, *Disidencias* (Barcelona: Seix Barral, 1977), 28.

CHAPTER 3. *DIÁLOGOS DE LA HEREJÍA*

1. Her complicity with God is so close, so driven that, for that very reason, she needs to be inhabited by the Devil. Or cohabited. . . . She somberly resents that her equilibrium as a woman can only be realized in a cataclysm of prayer and sin.

2. The abovementioned issue of *Primer Acto* (No. 54, June 1964) contains an introduction to the play by José Monleón ("Los mitos embalsamados"); reviews by Ricardo Domènech (who wonders whether Gómez-Arcos, in fact, ever received the Lope de Vega Prize), reprinted reviews from the popular press by Elías Gómez, Enrique Llovet, and Alfredo Marquerie; Gómez-Arcos's "Autodefensa"; Gregorio Marañón's commentary on the historical background of the play; and critical "reflections" by director José María Morera. See also reviews by Juan Emilio Aragonés ("*Diálogos de la herejía* de Agustín Gómez-Arcos," in *Veinte años de teatro español (1960–1980)* (Boulder, Co.: Society of Spanish and Spanish-American Studies, 1987) and Juan Mollá ("*Diálogos de la herejía*," in *Teatro español e iberoamericano en Madrid 1962–1991*, ed. Luis T. González-del-Valle (Boulder, Co.: Society of Spanish and Spanish-American Studies, 1993).

3. Program Notes, *Diálogos de la herejía*, Teatro Reina Victoria (Madrid: May 1964).

4. Walter Benjamin, *The Origin of German Tragic Drama*, trans. John Osborne (London: New Left Books, 1977), 175.

5. Martha T. Halsey, "Introduction to the Historical Drama of Post–Civil-War Spain," *Estreno* 14.1 (Spring 1988): 11.

6. On historical drama, see also César Oliva, "Breve itinerario por el último drama histórico español," *Estreno* 14.1 (Spring 1988): 7–10 and Herbert Lindenberger, *Historical Drama: The Relation of Literature and Reality* (Chicago: University of Chicago Press, 1975).

7. José Monleón, "Historia y drama histórico durante la Dictadura," *Estreno* 14.1 (Spring 1988): 5–6. Monleón's list contains a small inaccuracy: Gala's *Noviembre y*

un poco de yerba is not a historical drama, and it is possible that Monleón had in mind, rather, *Las cítaras colgadas de los árboles* (a play that is thematically linked to *Diálogos de la herejía*).

8. Paul de Man, "The Rhetoric of Temporality," in *Blindness and Insight: Essays in the Rhetoric of Contemporary Criticism, Theory and History of Literature*, vol. 7 (Minneapolis: University of Minnesota Press, 1983), 207.

9. Francisco Ruiz Ramón, "Pasado/Presente en el drama histórico," *Estreno* 14.1 (Spring 1988): 22.

10. This process of defamiliarization closely parallels the strategies of Brechtian alienation. Cf. *Brecht on Theatre*.

11. Marcel Bataillon, *Erasmo y España*, trans. Antonio Alatorre (Mexico City: Fondo de Cultura Económica, 1966), 167.

12. *Edicto*, cited by Bataillon, *Erasmo y España*, 173.

13. The intersection between religious ecstasy and sexual ecstasy is a recurrent literary-artistic theme in many cultures. (Gianlorenzo Bernini's *Ecstasy of Saint Theresa* is typically cited as exemplifying this erotico-mystical form of rapture.) Georges Bataille notes that both mysticism and eroticism stem from a universal idea of sacrifice of the self, which occurs when one being is united with another (*Erotism: Death and Sensuality*, trans. Mary Dalwood [San Francisco: City Lights Books, 1986], 23). In mysticism, the human soul is spiritually fused with a divine entity, while in eroticism, a carnal-spiritual fusion takes place between human beings.

14. Gregorio Marañón, "Los alumbrados y el espíritu español," *Primer Acto* 54 (July 1964): 19. Marañon's article appears in the same issue of *Primer Acto* that contains the censored text of *Diálogos de la herejía*.

15. Jacques Derrida, "Plato's Pharmacy," in *Dissemination*, trans. Barbara Johnson (Chicago: University of Chicago Press, 1981), 127. Derrida's commentaries on the *pharmakon* refer to Plato's use of this term in the *Phaedrus*.

16. Gómez-Arcos handles similar thematic material in his novel *Maria Republica*, in which a microcosmic rendition of a larger totalitarian system materializes in the concrete form of a Spanish nunnery during the late 1950s. The narrative centers on the life of Maria Republica, a syphilitic prostitute from Barcelona, who plots to overthrow the convent system by incorporating herself inside its walls and toppling the entire structure from within. Her sudden career move at age thirty-five from pornography to theology is prompted by the appearance of a "sacred" law ("Loi de protection social," "la Loi sacrée") issued by the Francoist regime, ordering the closure of all houses of prostitution throughout Spain and calling for the "regeneration" of all prostitutes. Her name ("Republica"), her corresponding left-wing ideology (inherited from her parents, now dead), and her ambiguous/marginal status as a harlot/syphilitic nun are all distinguishing characteristics that tie her personage to a vast lineage of rebels and outcasts (many of them, women) found throughout Gómez-Arcos's literature.

17. The plot also bears a subtle resemblance to the legend of Urbain Grandier, a seventeenth-century French priest accused of diabolism, whose tale is recounted by Aldous Huxley in his historical novel *The Devils of Loudun* (London: Chatto and Windus, 1961). (See also Stephen Greenblatt, "Loudun and London," *Critical Inquiry* 12.2 [Winter 1986]: 326–46.) Huxley's narrative was the inspiration for John Whiting's play *The Devils* (New York: Hill and Wang, 1961) and Ken Russell's film *The Devils* (1971). The plot also slightly resembles Arthur Miller's *The Crucible*.

18. Maránon, "Los alumbrados," 21.

19. *DH*, 20. ¿Quién puede desahogar la soledad de estas paredes? Dueña, me muero lentamente, ¿no te das cuenta? De mi casa al convento, del convento a mi

casa . . . Nadie en el camino, calle desierta, nada puede suceder. Cada día el mismo velo cubriendo mi cara . . . que se marchita.

20. *DH*, 2. *Un pueblo en tierras extremeñas, hacia el sur, cerca de la frontera. Finalizando el siglo XVI. Pueblo vacío de hombres, enrolados en los tercios de Su Majestad, o partidos a la colonización de las Indias de América. Las mujeres se han hecho cargo de los trabajos masculinos, el campo, la viña, el pastoreo, la caza, se visten mitad hombre mitad mujer, se comportan parecidamente. Sin embargo, su resignación sólo es aparente: el ansia del hombre o el deseo de la maternidad las corroe por dentro.*

21. *DH*, 6. Mi casa está llena de hombres que no veo, de sombras de hombre, que me palpan las carnes sin tocarme.

22. *DH*, 8. Mis años saben. Casi diez, ya, que marchó mi hijo a guerrear con los indios, a llevar a esos salvajes la palabra del cristiano . . . A lo lejos, en la llanura, cuando el sol empieza a levantarse, veo pasar los tercios camino de la frontera. Hombres, caballos y carros. Y lanzas, que relucen al sol como los rayos de una tormenta. Entre los soldados he distinguido a muchachos de no más de catorce años, arrastrándose bajo el peso de las armaduras.

23. In *Violence and the Sacred* (1972, trans. Patrick Gregory [Baltimore: Johns Hopkins University Press, 1977]), René Girard posits the theory that all religions— and all cultural systems and institutions (both secular and religious)—are universally derived from a primordial sacrificial event. In this original scenario, the members of a hypothetical community effectuated a metaphoric displacement of their cultural hostilities and maladies by collectively channeling them to a single sacred being. In disposing of this sacred *pharmakos*, the community cathartically expelled its own internal violence and duress to a remote, nebulous region of transgression. According to Girard, this initial sacrificial episode has become indelibly internalized within all cultures as a type of seminal paradigm, destined to breed an infinite number of variations and repeat performances in the ubiquitous rituals of abstinence, depravation, penance, etc. Each year, for example, during the Holy Week processions of Spain, the barefoot *nazarenos* evoke Christ's *Camino de la Pasión*, which took place prior to his sacrificial crucifixion. The Catholic Mass itself is a reenactment of the sacrifice of the body of Christ. This fundamental structure, or "sacrificial process," functions as a universal preventive mechanism in the suppression, censorship, and purification of violent impulses and dissension within the boundaries of a given community.

24. Paradoxically, the idea of ritual sacrifice is itself ambiguous in that it is at once both sinful and saintly, benevolent and malevolent, a "coincidence of the permitted and the prohibited" (Girard, *Violence*, 196).

25. Moreover, Franco, it can be said, metaphorically embodied the original dualism of the sacred: he was diabolical, according to his enemies; angelical, according to his champions. His role as supreme head of the Church, the military, and the Spanish state infused his sacred aura with elements of violence and terror, and even his seemingly endless life span contributed to his characterization as an immortal being. *El Valle de los Caídos* ("The Valley of the Fallen"), where Franco is buried, is a monument to sacrifice, which further exemplifies the double-sided symbolism of his sacred image; above: an enormous holy cross, immortally positioned atop a mountain of celestial height; below: a mammoth-sized marble crypt—all of which were constructed by the blood and sacrifice of slave labor.

26. The fact that Sor María is a grave-digger—in addition to being an illuminated nun—implies that she is in direct contact with death, violence, and defilement, and thus enhances her characterization as a sacred being.

27. Some of the distinctions between the original version and the new version are not necessarily the result of censorship, but are lexical and structural changes that were implemented by Gómez-Arcos. For example, in the new version, he substituted the generic names "Capataza" and "Capataz" for "Posadera" and "Posadero" ("female and male innkeepers"), changed the setting from the seventeenth to the sixteenth century, and restructured the new version into two parts from what was originally a three-act play. Other differences between the two versions appear to be tied more directly to the presence/absence of censorship: in the new version, nudity is overtly specified in the stage directions, while in the censored version, it is only subtly implied. In the new version, the language generally, and not surprisingly, acquires a more coarse, vulgar, and unrestrained tone. Finally—and perhaps, most significantly—there is a dramatic difference between the two versions with regard to the ending of the play: the new text ends with a surprising dramatic twist that was completely omitted from the censored version.

28. *DH*, 13. *Madre Asunta y el Peregrino, falsa monja y falso tullido, avanzan bajo el sol. Como en todos los personajes marginados de la época (productos típicos de dos polos opuestos: gloria y miseria), el vicio y la virtud confundidos formarán la única máscara de sus rostros, de manera que ellos mismos no sepan cuándo dicen mentira y cuándo sienten verdad. Como llegará el momento en que el instinto de sobrevivir les fallará, si hay que adjudicarles una moral será la de río revuelto; en ese aspecto, su semejanza con ciertos personajes de hoy día deberá hacerse patente.*

29. Cf. Derrida ("Plato's Pharmacy") and Girard. The successful performance of a sacrificial ritual requires that the victim pertain in some way to both the community (*intra muros*) and to the realm of the sacred (*extra muros*). For this reason, the sacrificial victim is often chosen from among the marginal, interstitial categories of being that are found in the crevices and peripheries of society. Often, these ritual victims are foreigners, such as Asunta and the *Peregrino*, who newly arrive, are incorporated within the community for a temporary duration, and are subsequently expelled or murdered.

30. *DH*, 15. Mi peregrinaje tiene una misión: acompañar a los solitarios, dar calor a las almas solitarias.

31. *DH*, 14. Ya las has visto, Peregrino. Una nueva especie de féminas. El pueblo y la comarca están llenos de ellas, el país entero, me atrevería a decir. Tierra de miseria, tierra de ausencias. ¿Resultado? Patente. Mujeres solas y desconsoladas, con el hombre ausente. Inmejorable Olimpo para los dioses. Los designios del Rey nuestro señor y la avaricia humana, la misión colonizadora de nuestra santa fé y el ansia de aventuras, digo yo . . . no han perdonado hijo ni esposo, joven ni anciano; mi compadre no cuenta, está capado. Jergones, y lechos de alcurnia, quemados de fiebre . . . insaciada . . . En este lugar . . . de la Mancha se necesita la bondad de tus palabras. Tú, y tus visiones, les darán el consuelo y el alivio . . . digo yo. Apóyate en mí.

32. Benjamin, *German Tragic Drama*, 175.

33. In his consideration of Sade's texts, Barthes underscores the presence of "metonymic violence," a recurrent linguistic construction in which, within the same syntagm, Sade "juxtaposes heterogeneous fragments belonging to spheres of language that are ordinarily kept separate by socio-moral taboo" (*Sade/Fourier/Loyola*, trans. Richard Miller [Berkeley: University of California Press, 1989], 33–34).

34. *DH*, 25. Hueles a incienso, cosa que no me repugna, pero apestas a lupanar, y eso me degrada. El trato que hicimos fue claro: entraste a mi servicio, no a tu beneficio.

35. *DH*, 25–26. No bebas agua, pinchón. Yo sé de un vino que calmará tu sed. Un vino espeso, rojo y adormecido, pero vivo. Se llama Tristeza, Doña Tristeza de Arcos, hidalga de vieja cuna.

36. *DH*, 48. Atributos de mi oficio. Menos espectacular, pero más . . . morboso que una corona de espinas.

37. *DH*, 24. *Oscuro. En la celda conventual de Sor María de los Ángeles, que recordará a una gran jaula de celosías, tres personajes de aguafuerte que podrían asimilarse a tres pájaros de mal agüero: la monja iluminada, Madre Asunta y el Peregrino alumbrado. La monja parece levitar en un éxtasis sulpiciano, el trance del alumbrado es más carnal, sudores y estremecimientos emparentados a la imagen de un drogadicto de varios siglos más tarde. Naturalmente, toda esta escena tendrá una cierta tonalidad mística, dada por el texto, que se inscribirá en falso contra la sensualidad, la libido y, por qué no, la desesperación profunda de los personajes. Madre Asunta cuida el trance del Peregrino, le enjuga el sudor de la frente, le retira el cáliz de la boca.*

38. Craig Owens, "The Allegorical Impulse: Toward a Theory of Postmodernism: Part I," *October* 12 (1980): 69.

39. Ibid., 72. Joel Fineman describes this process as the "poetical projection of the metaphoric axis onto the metonymic" ("The Structure of Allegorical Desire," *October* 12 [1980]: 50–51).

40. DH, 27. ¡Poderes de la luz, poderes de la tiniebla, sedme fieles amigos, alumbradme! (*Pone los brazos en cruz. Abriendo sus propios brazos, la monja iluminada se le acerca, junta las palmas de sus manos a las del Peregrino, y sella su boca de un beso que es como un soplo; luego se aparta de él y vuelve a sus éxtasis.*) Que mi boca pronuncie la palabra justa, la palabra presentida, que mi mano inicie el gesto deseado. Es una hermosa mujer. Quiero darle consuelo.

41. *DH*, 30. Esposa sin marido, casada sin hijo . . . ¡condenada! ¿Cómo llamarlo, si no?

42. Doña Tristeza exemplifies the sense of rebellion and thirst for freedom that typically characterize Gómez-Arcosian heroines and heroes. Perhaps, for this reason he has lent her his own last name. He comments, "For me the character of Doña Tristeza—and this is much more apparent in the new text—is a feminist character, *avant la lettre, comme on dit en français*, and what that means is that she is a women who does not submit to rules, who wants to change them, and who is capable of committing any type of subversive action in order to achieve her goals" (Interview with Feldman).

43. *DH*, 32. ¡Gime, gime como un vendaval, azota mi carne endurecida por la falta de fe, vence mi resistencia, desgárrame . . . !

44. Ibid. *La Iluminada cubre con un paño litúrgico el coito sagrado. Se oyen las ráfagas violentas del vendaval, el gemido lúbrico de las mujeres, la risa etílica de Madre Asunta. . . . Las mujeres se arrastran por las sombras del alba.*

45. *DH*, 42. ¡Quisiera apresar este milagro, y acunarlo en mi seno! ¡Robártelo!

46. *DH*, 52, 54. Su mercé me da miedo y me hace feliz. . . . ¡Es el diablo! ¡Confesión! ¡Confesión!

47. *DH*, 57. Un milagro como en el que a mí me crece cada día no puede darse a menudo entre los mortales . . . y menos en una misma localidad.

48. During the Renaissance, hysteria was often equated with diabolic possession. Cf. Marañón, *"Los alumbrados,"* 220–21.

49. *DH*, 76. Juntos, este santo y yo hemos sostenido *diálogos* espirituales que la estrecha mentalidad de las gentes de orden califica de herejías. Una necia palabra.

50. *DH*, 74. La ley del sacrificio . . . la ley del hombre. Estoy dispuesta a sufrirla.

51. *DH*, 87. (*Deteniéndose.*) Yo creo en la vida. A la vida no se le reza; se la lleva en el seno, se la alimenta de las propias entrañas, se la defiende. El Inquisidor impone una fé estéril, y manda rezar . . . porque sólo vive para dar la muerte. Me

ha acusado de soberbia. Injustamente. Es más facil para la conciencia calificar al rebelde de enemigo que reflexionar sobre su rebeldía; la conciencia es perezosa. La mía no, y le daré una prueba . . . que le ruego que acepte como prueba de humildad: inspirada por este Hijo mío, que está vivo, rezaré por el alma del Inquisidor, no por la del hereje. (*Sale definitivamente.*)

52. *DH*, 88. *como una moneda que tuviera dos caras idénticas.*

53. Ibid. ¿Cuánto dolor, cuánta sangre nos costarán todavía tu dolor y tu sangre? ¿Cuánta muerte nos costará tu muerte? . . . Si mi lengua fuera libre . . . te acusaría de asesino. Alguien lo hará . . . algún día.

CHAPTER 4. *LOS GATOS*

1. To make Him exist, only one way: invent Him. Inventing God is an obligation, painful, difficult, that demands innumerable daily sacrifices from us, of which the final result will be splendid: to have our hands filled with the emptiness of His Existence. . . . Let us say then that the invention of God, independent of its opportunity, is a logical necessity born out of the chaos of faith, just as the invention of Francoism was a logical necessity born out of the chaos of freedom (certain people call Francoism fascism, without realizing that fascism is a universal élan and Francoism an opportunistic usufruct).

2. *Los gatos* originally was to open on 20 October 1992 at Madrid's Teatro Albéniz, but when leading actor Héctor Alterio was stricken ill just a few days prior to this date, the production was postponed until 15 November, prompting journalist Begoña Piña to announce, "The writer Agustín Gómez-Arcos affirms that bad luck continues to pursue him in Spain" ("El escritor Agustín Gómez Arcos asegura que todavía le persigue la mala suerte en España: Se suspende el estreno de su obra *Los gatos* por enfermedad de Héctor Alterio," *Diario 16*, 20 October 1992, 64). Because of scheduling conflicts, the production was also moved from the Albéniz to the more prestigious María Guerrero (CDN). As a result, Alterio's unfortunate illness was also, ironically, a fortuitous occurrence.

3. Enrique Centeno, "Faldones de terciopelo," *Diario 16*, 12 November 1992, 69.

4. Strongly influenced by both Italian neorealist and Hollywood cinematic practices, Berlanga is especially renowned for his films *Bienvenido, Mr. Marshall* (1952) and *El verdugo* (1963).

5. Girard, *Violence*, 196.

6. For Bataille, transgression is an "inner experience" (*expérience intérieure*) occurring within the interior regions of consciousness and sparking a flux of contradictory emotions: desire is mixed with fear, anguish is intermingled with pleasure. His theory is underpinned by the notion (of Freudian origins) that all human beings are instinctively driven by an innate desire for excess—toward nonproductive expenditure (*la dépense*)—including sexual and religious ecstasy, collective celebrations of sacrifice and ritual, and conspicuous economic consumption. Although fear discourages the undertaking of a transgressive act, the fascination accompanying the idea of prohibition seems to encourage its realization, hence, the completed transgression incites, simultaneously, a stir of anguish over the infringement of an established rule and pleasure over the excitement of having victoriously traversed the boundary of a forbidden territory. This play between taboo and transgression reaches a climax at the decisive moment when a human being is on the verge of transcending a prohibitive frontier, when emotions are suspended in a sort of no-man's-land, hovering between the choice of surrendering toward an urge or repressing it. See Michèle

Richman (*Reading Georges Bataille: Beyond the Gift* [Baltimore: Johns Hopkins University Press, 1982]) for an examination of the philosophical and ethnological underpinnings of Bataille's essential theoretical notions; i.e., transgression, *expérience intérieure*, heterogeneity, sovereignty, *dépense*, boundary, excess, the sacred.

7. Bataille, *Erotism*, 93.

8. Philippe Sollers perceives an exterior manifestation of the isolated nature of discontinuous existence in the image of the contemporary urban landscape: "Consider, for example, the urban landscape that surrounds us now: an accumulation of superimposed and even rolling boxes that perpetuate corporal separation—a generalized staging of isolation" ("The Roof: Essay in Systematic Reading," in *Writing and the Experience of Limits*, ed. David Hayman, trans. Philip Barnard, with David Hayman, [New York: Columbia University Press, 1983], 103).

9. Bataille, *Erotism*, 61.

10. Ibid., 22.

11. Richard Schechner, *Performance Theory* (New York: Routledge, 1988), 208.

12. Stephen Greenblatt, "Loudun and London," *Critical Inquiry* 12.2 (Winter 1986): 332.

13. Regarding identification: Aristotle, in his definition of tragedy, refers to the emotional dualism of "fear and pity" that is inspired in the spectator through the cathartic effect of identification (*Theory of Poetry and Fine Art*, ed. and trans. by S. H. Butcher [New York: Dover, 1951], 33). Artaud, centuries later, manifests an appeal to the "cruelty and terror" that should be induced through the liberating experience of the theater spectacle (*The Theater and Its Double*, trans. Mary Caroline Richards [New York: Grove Press, 1958], 86). Brecht, on the other hand, rejects this empathetic, vicarious sort of theater experience. Brechtian alienation is realized through an initial degree of identification that is suddenly negated: what once was recognized as familiar and ordinary is subsequently defamiliarized and made to seem strange, striking, shocking (*Brecht on Theatre: The Development of an Aesthetic*, ed. and trans. John Willett [New York: Hill and Wang, 1964], 143–45, 192).

14. In "Violence in Modern Drama" (in *Reflections: Essays on Modern Theatre* [New York: Doubleday, 1969]), Martin Esslin presents a typology of five different forms of violence occurring in the theater spectacle and emanating from different directions. First, the most obvious form of violence is that which takes place between characters, such as the execution of the *alumbrados* in *Diálogos de la herejía*. Second, there is a form of violence which stems from the author or director and is directed toward the characters. Beckett's *Play*, in which he places his characters into urns that only allow for the protrusion of their heads, exemplifies this type of violence (physical and psychological), stemming from the author. Third, there is a form of violence that emerges from the realm of the spectator and is directed towards the characters on stage. Laughter is an example of this type of violation. Fourth, violence is directed from the author/director, toward the spectators; and fifth, from the characters, toward the spectators. During the 1960s, Peter Handke presented his play *Offending the Audience*, which portrays a literal representation of these final two notions of violence. In this play, the actors either barrage the spectators with insults or feign indifference with regard to their presence.

15. José Monleón, "*Los gatos* de Agustín Gómez-Arcos," *Primer Acto* 68 (October 1965): 53.

16. Javier Villán, "Sombría historia," *El Mundo*, 12 November 1992, 43.

17. *LG*, 9. *Salón de casa antigua, provinciana, inmovilizado en el tiempo: cuadros oscuros pintados por amigos o parientes con ramos de flores y antepasados, con gatos enredados en ovillos de lana, cuadros bordados con cañamazo, de dibujo desvaído*

por su vejez, flores de trapo viejas, vírgenes realistas, angelotes y santos de toda devoción revestidos con túnicas bordadas o pintadas, reclusos en hornacinas y campanas de cristal, con gesto mudo y único, gesto como parado en el aire carcelario que los rodea, muebles oscuros, tan rabiosamente españoles como incómodos, terciopelos oscuros, damascos oscuros, cortinas oscuras, aparatosamente oscuras, oscuro lujo nonacentista en trance de descomposición, aromas antiguos, aire antiguo, antiguas plantas de salón en macetones de escayola.... (All translations of *The Cats* were prepared by Lee Fontanella.)

18. *LG*, 48. entre recibir el cuerpo de Cristo y recibir el cuerpo de un hombre hay una gran diferencia.

19. *LG*, 63. A veces, la frontera entre el bien y el mal es mínima. Una sutileza.

20. "Autocrítica de *Los gatos*, que se estrena hoy," *ABC*, 24 September 1965, 79.

21. Cf. Ruiz Ramón, *Historia del teatro español. Siglo XX* on the esperpento (93–140).

22. Juan Emilio Aragonés, "*Los gatos* de Agustín Gómez-Arcos," in *Veinte años de teatro español (1960–1980)* (Boulder, Co.: Society of Spanish and Spanish-American Studies, 1987), 83.

23. All information regarding the staging of the 1965 production was obtained through my conversations with Mr. Gómez-Arcos and Lee Fontanella (a spectator who witnessed the première).

24. *LG*, 29. *El silencio y el aroma, espesos, borran casi completamente los contornos de los objetos. Como por arte de magia, en este espacio no subsiste un solo color que sugiera la posibilidad de otra época del año: es exactamente Semana Santa, y no puede pensarse en otra cosa. Incluso parecen haber surgido, en sitios donde no estaban, pesados damascos morados, morados Nazarenos de tamaño natural, Dolorosas moradas y traspasadas de puñales de plata ...*

25. A similar type of sacrilegious setting can be found in the works of Spanish writers, such as Rafael Alberti, Pérez Galdós, "Clarín," Valle-Inclán, Francisco Nieva, Fernando Arrabal, and in the films of Luis Buñuel and Pedro Almodóvar.

26. *LG*, 9.

27. Artaud, *Theater and Its Double*, 71. In *The Empty Space* (London: MacGibbon and Kee, 1968), Peter Brook incorporates Artaud's principles into his formulation of a "Holy Theater," in which the spectacle becomes a sacred experience of revelation and in which the invisible is suddenly made to appear visible. Brook interprets the Artaudian aesthetic as a search for this transcendent holiness: "He wanted that theatre served by a band of dedicated actors and directors who would create out of their own natures an unending succession of violent stage images, bringing about such powerful immediate explosions of human matter that no one would ever again revert to a theatre of anecdote and talk. He wanted the theatre to contain all that normally is reserved for crime and war. He wanted an audience that would drop all its defences, that would allow itself to be perforated, shocked, startled, and raped, so that at the same time it could be filled with a powerful new charge" (53).

28. Artaud, in his redefinition of the *mise en scène*, calls for the presence of a necessary violence (physical or psychical) in the theater—of erotic obsessions, savagery, and atrocious crimes.

29. Bataille, *Erotism*, 37–39.

30. *LG*, 17–18.

Angela. (Excitada.) Se han puesto a arañar el suelo debajo de la puerta. Saben que la comida está ahí. Ronronean como si fueran pequeñitos. Me gustaría que los vieras, Pura.

Pura. "Sobre el sexto mandamiento te pregunto: ¿quién lo guarda enteramente?"

Loli. "El que es casto en pensamiento, palabras y obras."

Pura. Castidad . . . No olvides nunca esa gloria del ser humano, ese estado de gracia, ese supremo orgullo . . .

Loli. Sí, señorita.

Angela. (*Cogiendo los despojos del suelo.*) Voy a ponérselos en la mirilla, a ver qué hacen.

Pura. "Peca con los malos pensamientos el que procura desecharlos?"

Loli. "No, señor; más bien merece, si con eso aparta las tentaciones."

Pura. Recuerda el Padrenuesto: No nos dejes caer en la tentación.

Angela. (*Feliz.*) Están desconcertados. ¿Los oyes maullar?

31. *LG*, 23–24.

Doña Rosa.—¡No!

Manuela. ¿No quiere dulces la señora?

Doña Rosa. Quiero dulces. Sigo siendo golosa. Además, los he comprado yo. Pero no quiero juntos el tenedor y la cuchara. Ni juntos ni revueltos. ¿O te parece mal?

Pura.— Manuela nada le parece mal, Rosa. Si tú no quieres comer los dulces con cuchara y tenedor, los comes sólo con cuchara, o si no con los dedos, y santas pascuas.

Doña Rosa. ¡Qué manía de juntarlo todo! En mi casa los tengo separados; unos en un cajón, otros en otro. Y para la luz, conmutadores, llaves . . . nada de enchufes. Así está el mundo, con tanta mezcla. Debe ser sexual.

Pura. ¡Vaya por Dios! Ahora va a resultar que la culpa de cómo está el mundo la tienen los tenedores, las cucharas y los enchufes.

Doña Rosa. Son símbolos, Pura.

32. *LG*, 14. Yo bajo aquí, y lo miro todo, objeto por objeto, y todo me recuerda lo que pudo haber sido mi vida. Miro el retrato de Paloma . . . y el balcón . . .

33. Gómez-Arcos develops this motif of confused double images in his first novel *L'agneau carnivore* (The Carnivorous Lamb), in which the transgressive (incestuous) relationship between two loving brothers functions as the ultimate metaphor for freedom. As the narrative progresses, a play of mirrors and interior duplication gradually establishes a complex network of parallels between the characterizations of the two brothers (Ignacio and Antonio) and their parents (Matilde and Carlos). When Ignacio looks in the mirror, he sees the face of his mother. Following her death, he begins to sense her presence invade his body and he perceives the world through her eyes. Also, in the same way that Antonio sodomizes Ignacio, Matilde, correspondingly, reminisces about the way in which Carlos would sodomize her (transgressively *expressing* himself within her) during their period of engagement. She declares, "that boy had fire. He didn't want to get me pregnant before we got married, but he had a burning desire to 'express himself in me' (185). (All translations of *The Carnivorous Lamb* pertain to William Rodarmor's published English version.) ("ce garçon-là était fougueux. Mais il ne voulait pas me mettre enceinte avant le mariage. Pourtant, il avait un très gros besoin de s'exprimer *en moi*" [222].) Furthermore, in describing his father, Ignacio paints a split image of two separate beings: "Father" and "Carlos." When Ignacio looks at Carlos, he sees Antonio's face, and he feels the same incestuous desire that his brother inspires. On one occasion, Ignacio even plants a wet kiss on Carlos's lips. Throughout the narrative, the images of Carlos, Father, Antonio, Ignacio, and Matilde become intermingled and transposed. In the final chapter, Ignacio summarizes this incestuous system of reincarnation and doubling:

Mother-me is named Matilde. Alive.
Father-Carlos is named my brother. Alive. (269)
{Maman-moi s'appelle Matilde. Vivant.
Papa-Carlos s'appelle mon frère. Vivant. (319)}

34. *LG*, 34. Un día la arañaron. Los gatos tienen uñas . . . (*Hacia Angela*) . . . como los hombres. Se le infectó la herida y murió de septicemia. No se pudo hacer nada
35. *LG*, 34–35. Se pusieron veneno en las uñas para corromperle la sangre. El veneno del odio, porque la odiaban. Venían chicos a visitarla, cada día, y entonces Paloma se olvidaba de ellos. Abría el balcón, y hablaba con unos y con otros. Le contaban cosas de la vida, y chistes, y hasta le decían algún piropo. Ella se ponía ahí, y yo aquí. Las dos nos reíamos. ¿Sabes?, los gatos se volvían inquietos, celosos. Ronroneaban alrededor de sus piernas—yo sé muy bien lo que querían los impúdicos—pero Paloma no les hacía caso. Yo tampoco. Llegaba primero uno, luego otro, luego otro, y después acercaban todos juntos. Y nosotras nada, como si no existieran. Por eso se vengaron: se sentían desplazados.
36. Bataille, *Erotism*, 25. See also Barthes, who comments, "We begin to recognize that the transgressions of language possess an offensive power at least as strong as that of moral transgression, and that the 'poetry' which is itself the language of the transgression of language, is thereby always contestatory" (*Sade, Fourier, Loyola*, 34).
37. *LG*, 45.

> ¿Dónde vas, Paloma Blanca,
> a deshoras de la noche?
> Voy en busca de mi hijo,
> me lo entierran esta noche.
> (*Maullan los gatos estremeciendo el ambiente.*)

38. *LG*, 47. Han desaparecido los elementos 'Semana Santa.' En la luz, en el color se cree adivinar una esperanza, como si motivos ajenos a las dos hermanas hubieran impuesto en la casa un clima tolerante. Se ve por el balcón que en la calle ha reverdecido algún árbol; su vigorosa vitalidad, quizás de efímero esplendor, parece penetrar en el salón hasta imponer una atmósfera distinta.
39. *LG*, 49–50.

Angela. Debió de comprar un paquete. (*Pura se calla.*) Sí; estoy segura de que es eso lo que hizo: fue a la papelería y compró un paquete. Lo que me gustaría saber es si fue de veinticinco o de cincuenta.

Pura. (*Un poco mosca.*) Dentro de pocos días te sacaré de dudas. Si la carta número veintiséis trae un sobre distinto, te diré: "Angela, fue un paquete de veinticinco."

Angela. (*Acusando su tono.*) Y yo te lo agradeceré. A mí esas cosas me preocupan, aunque parezcan tonterías. La gente tiene sus formas especiales de medir el amor, o la ausencia. Puede servirnos para averiguar si va a venir pronto o si tardará todavía.

40. *LG*, 67.

Angela. ¡Sigue! ¿Dónde fue? ¡Quiero saberlo todo! ¿Qué sentías?

Pura. Sentías calor, ¿verdad? Un calor sofocante . . . que te hacía vivir.

Angela. Calor . . . calor . . . ¡Sigue! Sigue tú, Pura.

Pura. Y . . . la sensación de estar descubriendo los misterios de la naturaleza.

Inés. Tía, por Dios . . .

Angela. ¿Qué misterios? ¿Qué misterios?

Pura. La suciedad, la liviandad, el placer, el pecado, la transgresión, todo eso que la gente llama los misterios de la naturaleza.

41. *LG*, 73. Servirá para Loli . . . dentro de un par de años. No es necesario que me dé prisa en terminarlo.

42. Gerardo Fernández, "Mi querida solterona," *Clarín* [Buenos Aires], 31 December 1992, 16.

CHAPTER 5. *MIL Y UN MESÍAS*

1. I felt that I was looking at the negative of a familiar photograph, and my chest tightened with despair. Wouldn't there ever be any real change in my life? Why was I forever encountering the clumsy copy of an eternal original? Or the faded original of a series of reproductions scattered at random? Was it a sickness of the family? The town? The whole country? I never found answers to all those questions, but ever since I was very young, I've suspected that Spain and life itself were nothing but the work of a copying machine that never broke down.

2. Interview with Feldman.

3. In addition to their holy character and artistic value, many of the *autos sacramentales* were composed with propagandistic intentions that were tied to the Counter Reformation. Because Protestants were known to reject the sacraments of the body of Christ, the *autos* provided the Catholic Church with a convenient instrument of didacticism and proselytism.

4. On Nieva's use of the *auto sacramental* genre, cf. Emil G. Signes, ("Francisco Nieva: Spanish Representative of the Theater of the Marvelous," in *The Contemporary Spanish Theater: A Collection of Critical Essays*, ed. Martha T. Halsey and Phyllis Zatlin (Lanham/New York/London: University Press of America, 1988).

5. Martin, Esslin, *The Theatre of the Absurd* (New York: Penguin, 1988).

6. In essence, the emergence of the theater of the absurd during the period following the Second World War, parallels the emergence of surrealism during the period following the First World War. Beckett, Genet, Ionesco, Pinter (and even Gómez-Arcos) are, in a sense, the artistic offspring of playwrights, such as Antonin Artaud and Alfred Jarry.

7. For a detailed account of the Tynan/Ionesco controversy, see Esslin, *The Theatre of the Absurd*, 100–05.

8. Ibid., 271–72.

9. In addition, there is the often-cited case of the 1957 staging of *Waiting for Godot* by Herbert Blau and Jules Irving's Theatre Workshop at the San Quentin penitentiary, in which the convicts interpreted Godot as the freedom "on the outside" that they were awaiting. See Esslin, *The Theatre of the Absurd* and *The Theatre of the Absurd Reconsidered.*

10. See Enoch Brater and Ruby Cohn's volume of essays for a reevaluation of the theater of the absurd. In his contribution to this collection, Benedict Nightingale notes, with regard to Harold Pinter, that "What some of his original critics 'dismissed as absurd rubbish,' he [Pinter] has said, actually embodied a 'political metaphor'" (*Around the Absurd: Essays on Modern and Postmodern Drama* [Ann Arbor: University of Michigan Press, 1990], 137).

11. On the absurdist dimension of Fernando Arrabal's theater, see Carlos Jerez Farrán, "El compromiso de la estética del absurdo en el teatro de Arrabal," *Revista Canadiense de Estudios Hispánicos* 14.2 (Invierno 1990): 277–91. On the theater of

the absurd and García Pintado, López Mozo, and Matilla, see César Oliva, *El teatro desde 1936*, Historia de la literatura española actual 3 (Madrid: Alhambra, 1989).

12. Michael Holquist, "Corrupt Originals: The Paradox of Censorship," *PMLA* 109.1 (January 1994): 15–16.

13. Patrice Pavis and Anne Ubersfeld present similar conceptions regarding the role of the spectator as a participant and producer of meaning in the reception of a *mise en scène*. Pavis, for example, employs the phrase "metatext of the *mise en scène*" to refer to the process by which the theatrical text is rewritten (internally) by the spectator as it is received in the form of a performance (*Languages of the Stage*, [New York: Performing Arts Journal Publications, 1982], 131–61). For Ubersfeld, the spectator is an essential component of the *mise en scène:* "The spectator is the recipient, he is the other at the end of the chain that is the spectacle, and in the final analysis, it is in him and through him that the spectacle is produced." (*L'école du spectateur (Lire le théâtre II)* [Paris: Éditions Sociales, 1981], 305.)

14. My employment of the term *scenic space* is derived from Ubersfeld's use of this term (*espace scénique*) to refer to the collection of signs emanating from the place occupied by the actors (that is, the "scenic place" [*lieu scénique*]) (*L'école du spectateur*, 52–58).

15. *MM*, Title page-1.

> *Acción: Hoy día, en una nación, o ciudad, o pueblo, que quizá no exista realmente, pero que participe de las características esenciales de nuestro mundo y nuestra civilización. Por supuesto, cada director podrá vestir a algunos personajes a la usanza y moda de la época que le convenga. Por ejemplo, El Gobernador podría salir constantemente vestido del siglo XVIII.*

> *Escenario: Un gran ciclorama, sobre el que se pueden proyectar las motivaciones que convengan. La mayor ausencia posible de elementos de attrezzo. . . .*

16. Ubersfeld, *L'école du spectateur*, 118. Cf. also Peter Brook, *The Empty Space* (London: MacGibbon and Kee, 1968).

17. Ubersfeld employs the term *theatrical space* (*espace théâtral*) to signify the combination of the scenic space and the spectator's space, plus the relationship between them (52–58).

18. *MM*, 3. comodamente instalado en el salón de mi casa con el whisky en la mano, . . . ya es otro cantar. . . . Dentro de mi casa quiero estar tranquilo. (*Confidencial*) Me gustan las mujeres elegantes y perfumadas, y los banquetes, y los homenajes, y los coloquios . . . como a ustedes.

19. *MM*, 12. Garantiza ocho horas de sueño. Los domingos y días festivos que no se proyecta una excursión, diez horas de sueño. Se levanta uno a tiempo del aperitivo y los oficios religiosos del mediodía. Es maravilloso. Allí están todos los amigos.

20. En casa me llaman Cary, con i griega

21. *MM*, 10–11. Ahora soy católica conservadora y tengo un maravilloso abrigo de visón. ¡Me siento tan protegida! En el Cielo y en la tierra! . . .

22. *MM*, 1. (*Muy amable, muy relaciones públicas*) Señoras, señores nos hemos reunido aquí para una despedida. Lucio se va. Lucio nos abandona. Nuestro querido Lucio, rebelde innato, esperanza y desesperación de la sociedad, producto de una civilización en alza y en crisis, nos deja hoy . . . posiblemente para siempre. Una tristeza. Una alegría. ¡Miren las caras de nuestra gente! ¡Alegría y tristeza!

23. Pavis, *Languages of the Stage*, 59–60.

24. *MM*, 3. Delante de él, nosotros; a su espalda, la frontera. Según sus propias palabras, la cárcel y la libertad.

25. *MM*, 5. Un hombre solo no teme a la verdad, porque la verdad está en el pensamiento, y el hombre solo piensa sin miedo. (*A los demás.*) Por eso le teméis todos al hombre solo, porque puede jugarse la vida por una idea, por una fé.

26. *MM*, 3. Uno se puede marchar con su propio cuerpo, con su pensamiento, con sus jadeos de asfixia, con sus ganas locas de respirar otro aire—ese aire maravilloso de más allá de la frontera—, uno se puede marchar con sus rebeldías que aquí se llaman lepra, o cáncer, o sueños, o coraje . . .

27. Ibid. Hermanos, volveré acompañado de mi verdad que ahora se humilla. Una verdad que será poderosa. Se vestirá de oro. La haré de raza judía . . . , lista, suave, razonable. ¡La convertiré en Dios! ¿Por qué no . . . otro dios? Y mi verdad será invitada a todos los cócteles, recibirá todos los homenajes, será la santa más venerada y la prostituta mejor pagada. . . .

28. Walter Benjamin, *The Origin of German Tragic Drama*, trans. John Osborne (London: New Left Books, 1977), 175.

29. *MM*, 12. Una ligera inquietud, un pequeño forúnculo—no especificado—en el orden divino de mi mandato, empieza a surgir en forma de esa cosa detestable que inventó usted (*Señala al Inventor 3*): la rebeldía. . . . En mis pesadillas hay un edificio que se derrumba de improviso, por algún fallo que concierne a sus cimientos. Y a mí me pilla dentro. Es espantoso. El edificio se parece a mi casa.

30. *MM*, 23. El té de las señoras," which, as he enigmatically proclaims, "No tiene nada y tiene mucho que ver con esta historia.

31. *MM*, 25.

Señora, Teresa, Jubilia. (*Cantando*)
> Una paloma
> del nido se fugó

Pobre. (*Coreando*)
> Pabú, Pabú,
> pabú, pabú.

Señora, Teresa, Jubilia. (*Cantando*)
> Una paloma coquetona
> repechugona.
> Jesús, qué horror,
> al nido no volvió

Pobre. (*Coreando*)
> Pabú, Pabú,
> pabú, pabú.

(*Hablando*) Moraleja: ved con qué facilidad pierde la casta paloma su honestidad.

32. On accumulation, cf. Craig Owens, "The Allegorical Impulse: Toward a Theory of Postmodernism: Part I," *October* 12 (1980): 67–86 and "The Allegorical Impulse: Toward a Theory of Postmodernism: Part II," *October* 13 (1980): 59–80.

33. *MM*, 26. ¡Todas! La de los treinta años, la de los cien años, la de los tres años, la del catorce, la del quince, la del dieciséis, y la que sólo duró seis días, por enfermedad de no sé quién, no recuerdo dónde.

34. *MM*, 22–25. Mis hijos serán normales. Como su padre. Como yo. Ninguno será diplomático, ninguno será militar, ninguno será play-boy, ninguno será cura, ninguno será marica, ninguno enviado especial, ninguno bailarín, ninguno listo, ninguno filántropo, ninguno soñador. Mis hijos serán como Dios manda. Tendrán su negocio, su oficina, su teléfono, su señora, su coche, su casa en las afueras, su querida. Su bar acostumbrado, su sábado de cana al aire, su domingo y su fiesta de guardar. . . .

35. In Gómez-Arcos's novel *Bestiaire* (1986), a similar situation occurs, but the process is reversed. Set in Paris during the 1980s, *Bestiaire* is a novel about individual freedom and the tolerance of difference: sexual, racial, cultural. It is also Gómez-Arcos's first novel whose concrete setting is anchored in a French historical reality. In contemporary Paris, Gómez-Arcos has found a very apt backdrop for the portrayal of his battle between order and anarchy, in that in France, as in many other countries, issues and controversies over sexual freedom, racial prejudice, and xenophobia have become part of the natural landscape. With Franco dead, Gómez-Arcos appears to have found, in the figure of Jean-Marie Le Pen and his National Front, a set of new living inspirations upon which to base his personification of taboo and sacred order.

Bestiaire's protagonist Denise Durand characterizes herself as a "soixant-huitarde modèle, c'est-à-dire héroïque" (a model sixty-eighter; that is, heroic), who, nearly twenty years after having participated in the student revolts of 1968 is still brooding over her defeat. Despite her French-bourgeois upbringing, she refuses to integrate herself into mainstream society. She is a devout anarchist who navigates the margins of Paris, both geographic and societal, consciously designing her own role as a outcast and plotting her strategy to wage a battle against all forms of established order— ecclesiastic, governmental, military. Disillusioned, following her *bataille soixantehuitièmaire* (in her view, the "Western revolt of the century"), Denise decides to commit a subversive act of treason against society (directed particularly against the right wing). Using her uterus as her weapon of choice, she devises a plan, based on a systematic inversion of the principles of Nazism. She conspires to use her feminine reproductive capacity, in combination with sperm cells drawn from men of the most diverse assortment of race and color that she can possibly find, in order to create a new, completely heterogeneous, ambiguous, diverse racial mixture. According to her calculations, the initial cataclysmic repercussions of her plan—her *théorie anarcho-belliqueuse*—will only affect the future of Paris and its environs, but she expects that in time, its destructive effects will extend throughout entire world. She finds her paternal ammunition in the bodies of three men from the "fourth world" whom she meets at her favorite night spot in the Parisian Latin Quarter: (1) René Fung, a Chinese-Frenchman (Chinese parentage, born in Montpellier); (2) an Aztec-Andalusian bastard, whose name, "Moctezuma Gómez," vaguely recalls the author of this novel; and (3) a sickly Tunisian (ravaged by tuberculosis), named "Mohamed." One evening, Denise arranges for her three unknowing accomplices to dine at her *chambre de bonne*. She prepares a packaged couscous dinner, uncorks a few bottles of cheap wine, and seduces all three in a roaring orgy of disorder and anarchy. To her surprise, however, her project of erotico-racial subversion produces disastrous results: three Aryan-looking, blond, *blue-eyed*, identical triplets are born. At first glance it is absolutely impossible to distinguish among them; hence, the name "Dominique" is given to all three: one male, one female, and "one who represents a sort of compromise between these two sexual tendencies."

36. *MM*, 29. *Hablará en lo que él considera un tono exquisito, pañuelo de encaje y rapé, énfasis dieciochesco, discursito de salón, de tal forma que las vulgaridades que dice quedarán más de manifiesto.*

37. *MM*, 30. *El mesías es una cosa que se espera, se espera, se espera . . . y nunca llega. Pero que algún día llegará. ¿Verdad que es bonito?*

38. Benjamin, *German Tragic Drama*, 182.

39. *MM*, 34. *¡Puterías! ¡Órdenes establecidos! Ahora estamos en otro orden, ¡el mío!*

40. *Os pido que os unáis a mí en esa tarea común de salvar a la nación, blá, blá, blá, blá, de inventar el progreso. . . .*

41. *MM*, 38.

42. *MM*, 44. Viniste sembrando la esperanza. No has hecho otra cosa que seguir el eterno juego de las clases, de las religiones, de las políticas. No has inventado nada nuevo. "¡Esperadme! ¡Regresaré!" Qué tontería. Te gustaba tu bella imagen heróica gritando "¡Esperadme!" Y las caras de los demás eran tu espejo. Sin embargo, sólo eres un pequeño criminal como tantos otros.

43. Jacques Derrida, "The Theater of Cruelty and the Closure of Representation," in *Writing and Difference*, ed. and trans. Alan Bass (Chicago: University of Chicago Press, 1978), 235.

44. Benjamin, *German Tragic Drama*, 166.

CHAPTER 6. *QUERIDOS MÍOS, ES PRECISO CONTAROS CIERTAS COSAS*

1. This long confession, spread over the history of the species, is the fruit of scraps of memory, of crises of Cassandra, of witnesses of victims, who all subscribe to the name of Prometheus, ravisher of fire and of life, swindler to his fellow men but himself vanquished. The gods, dictators, in the calm following the massacre, do not emerge at all, might they be unmercifully judged by such distress and oblivion for the persistent squandering of a kingdom of light. And through the final shadows, this abyss where the world darkened following the catastrophe.

2. Cf. Anthony Pasquariello, "Government Promotion, Honors and Awards: A Corollary to Franco Era Censorship in Theater," *Cuadernos de ALDEEU* 1 (January 1983): 67–81.

3. Just prior to his definitive leap into exile, he did perform a dramatic reading of *Queridos míos* for a group of friends at a private *soirée*. Present at this reading was actor/director Antonio Duque, who later would participate in several productions of Gómez-Arcos's plays in France and in the 1994 production of *Queridos míos* in Spain. According to Mr. Gómez-Arcos, a Norwegian translation of *Queridos míos* was staged in Oslo, Norway, in 1982.

4. My observations regarding the première and production of this play are derived from my own experience as a spectator.

5. Enrique Centeno, "Las cosas que nos prohibían," *Diario 16*, 9 December 1994, 44.

6. Javier Villán, "Con la verdad por delante: Gómez Arcos regresa con *Queridos míos, es preciso contaros ciertas cosas*," *El Mundo Magazine*, 11 December 1994, 64.

7. Centeno, "Las cosas que nos prohibían," 44.

8. *QM*, 17. *El escenario, es un ámbito especial que puede ser o convertirse en todo: palacio, cárcel, plaza pública, calle, campo, o cualquiera de las cinco partes del mundo, o cualquier nación, o cualquier ciudad, o cualquier casa.* (All translations of *My Dear Friends, It's Time We Get Certain Things Straight* were prepared by Lee Fontanella.)

9. In the 1994 production, there was an intermission.

10. Ahora es la antesala. Anoche fue el garaje. Luego será el salón del trono. ¿Lo comprendes?

11. *QM*, 11. *Los personajes saldrán detalladamente vestidos, cuidadosamente alhajados, adornados y peinados, de tal manera que su sola presencia indique sin lugar a dudas la época cronológica que viven en cada momento de su estancia en escena.*

12. Commenting on the image of the ruin, Benjamin observes the "common practice in the literature of the baroque to pile up fragments ceaselessly" (178). Owens draws a comparison between this strategy of accumulation and the practice of photo-

montage ("The Allegorical Impulse," I: 72). Angus Fletcher, as Owens indicates, equates this type of artistic construction with an obsessional neurosis (*Allegory: The Theory of a Symbolic Mode*, [Ithaca: Cornell University Press, 1964], 279–303).

13. *QM*, 18.

14. *QM*, 17–18. *Criados y comparsas pondrán a disposición de los actores, en el momento justo, los escasos elementos de attrezzo que necesitan para representar sus papeles, como si surgieran de la nada en el instante mismo en que los mencionan. Esto dará la impresión de una acción paralela e independiente del texto, aunque a su servicio. Los actores no hablarán ni verán directamente a estos criados de la escena, pese a que su comportamiento, en todo momento, deberá ser natural y realista.*

15. On the carnivalesque, see Peter Stallybrass and Allon White, *The Politics and Poetics of Transgression* (Ithaca: Cornell University Press, 1986).

16. The Cassandra theme has several precedents in Spanish literature. Most notably, Benito Pérez Galdós treats this theme in *Casandra*, his *novela dialogada* (1905) and eponymous theater piece (première, 1910). Nieva adapted and staged Galdós's play in 1983. Cf. Andrés Amorós, "Tres 'Casandras': de Galdós a Galdós y a Francisco Nieva," in *Actas del Segundo Congreso Internacional de Estudios Galdosianos* (Las Palmas, Canary Islands: 1979–80).

17. *QM*, 19. (*A gritos*) ¡Señoras y señores, piadosos, pecadores, hijos de España y de las Indias de España, en una palabra, cristianos, ha llegado el carro de Casandra, la adivina, lectora de manos y de naipes, lectora del corazón, visionaria de la fortuna y del destino, de la tempestad y la plaga, del oro y la calderilla . . . porque no todo el mundo ha nacido para la posesión del oro! ¡Acercaos! ¡Venid aquí! Por pocos céntimos yo abriré la entraña de esta sabia criatura, despejaré su mente y haré que su palabra ilumine vuestro futuro. . . .

18. *QM*, 20. Lo difícil es reconocer a la injusticia, saber cuáles son sus diversos camuflajes, bajo qué disfraces de orden o desorden, de paz o revolución se esconde. Por eso, queridos míos, es preciso contaros ciertas cosas. . . .

19. *QM*, 22. Producimos exactamente lo que comemos. Claro que, desgraciadamente, no podemos hacer comercio de exportación. Pero nos hemos resignado con la voluntad de Dios.

20. Jacques Derrida, "Plato's Pharmacy," in *Dissemination*, trans. Barbara Johnson (Chicago: University of Chicago Press, 1981), 127.

21. *QM*, 20. ¡Para eso os he traído a Casandra, la adivina! Para que no os equivoquéis! Por menos que le daríais a un mendigo, os dirá qué hierba os conviene más para curar el reúma, con qué pellejo de reptil convenceréis a la persona amada, con qué víscera de animal dañino alejaréis a la injusticia!

22. *QM*, 47–48.

Duquesa. Una especie de quiromante, o bruja, or estudiante, or judía, o negra prosélita de la palabra "no" vestida de greñas, peinada de harapos . . .

Todos. ¡Jesús, qué horror!

Duquesa. . . . que anda por los caminos del reino, por las calles de la ciudad, por las cafeterías, por los nightclubs, por los hipódromos y los campos de fútbol llamándolo al pan vino y al vino pan . . .

Todos. ¡Jesús, qué horror!

Duquesa. . . . descuartizando la pobre mentalidad de las gentes con un lenguaje impropio de nuestra civilización, almas como ciénagas, corazones como ciénagas, pensamientos cenagosos . . .

Todos. ¡Jesús, qué horror!

Duquesa. Un horror, querido.

23. Mary Douglas, *Purity and Danger: An Analysis of Concepts of Pollution and Taboo* (New York: Frederick A. Praeger, 1966), 95–99.

24. Ibid., 102.

25. *QM*, 23. ¡La injusticia! La boca llena con la palabra injusticia, como llena de sopas. ¿Y qué cara tiene la injusticia? Queridos míos, es preciso aclarar ciertas cosas. La injusticia, lo mismo que la mentira, sólo tiene una cara: el desorden. Todo lo demás es confusión, confusionismo.

26. *QM*, 147–48. Es mi secreto. Es mi búsqueda.

27. Interview with Feldman.

28. *QM*, 69–70. ¡No, no, no, no, no! . . . ¡No soy una mentira! . . . ¡Soy la verdad del hombre!

29. *QM*, 26. La verdad es sorda, y ciega, y muda. Y jorobada, y tullida, y leprosa, y talidomídica, y . . .

30. *QM*, 35–36. Queridos míos, es preciso acalaros ciertos matices. . . . Para las voces muertas no existe el silencio. Ni físico ni espiritual. Por eso es peligroso matar las voces, aunque alboroten. Así lo han comprendido los grandes gobernantes de la Historia.

31. Like the blue eyes, bread is also an ubiquitous motif in Gómez-Arcos's literature. The "Historia del pan" can be considered a minimalist rendering of *L'enfant pain* (The bread boy), a semiautobiographical novel that Gómez-Arcos originally wrote in Spanish before going into exile. The original Spanish version, entitled *El pan* (The bread), remains unpublished. The novel paints a grim portrait of the period immediately following the Spanish Civil War and of the suffering and sacrifice of a Republican family as seen through the eyes of an innocent child.

32. *QM*, 51. Santos corrompidos, verdades ultrajadas, aquí nazco y aquí muero, aquí como el mendrugo, aquí desfallezco, aquí me abro las venas, aquí grito mis palabras no tienen eco, cuarto cerrado, cuarto oscuro, aquí llamo a mis hombres y mis hombres están castrados, aquí nacen mis hijos castrados, raza de soledad, aquí no tengo canción, aquí no tengo pan. . . .

33. *QM*, 52. Si no traes dinero no puedo ser tu hijo, ni tu alimento ni tu tranquilidad.

34. *QM*, 53. y cogió el cuchillo, y cogió el fusil, y cogió la hoz, y la piedra y las uñas, y la rabia, y el recuerdo de Cristo, y el odio, y la sangre, y la herida abierta en el pecho, y las tripas fuera, y la lengua seca . . .

35. *QM*, 53. Ayer le hicieron la autopsia. Traía en la frente un trozo de alambrada, su corona de espinas. Una dama elegante dijo: Los estragos de la guerra.

36. *QM*, 131–32. Cuando ha de ser expuesta a la curiosidad ajena, se pule su piel, se abrillanta y se pone en el escaparate, de forma que parezca esplendorosa. Si está sana por dentro, miel sobre hojuelas. Y si tiene gusano es preferible disimularlo con el brillo exterior. Así es como se venden las mazanas.

37. *QM*, 54–55. ¿recuerdas?, aquella que hubo aquí mientras nosotras estábamos en Biarritz. Manchas de sangre que ahora, al haber pasado el tiempo, parecían manchas de otra cosa . . . , no sé, de vergüenza.

38. *QM*, 55. el hábito hace el monje

39. una de esas aburridas tardes de domingo de todas las épocas

40. *QM*, 94.

41. *QM*, 104–5. Los exilados son gallos con el pico cortado. Cuando sus cacareos llegan hasta nosotros, a través de la distancia, son ya voces viejas, que hablan de cosas viejas. Carecen de actualidad. Desentonan. Y aunque pudieran escarbar un poco en las heridas, hay una última solución: se censura la prensa extranjera, las publicaciones extranjeras. El exilio es el silencio.

42. *QM*, 119–120. Me he vestido de rey para ver si comprendes de una vez quién soy yo y quién eres tú. . . . Tú y yo somos dos poderes en pugna. El orden y el desorden. Mejor dicho; el desorden y el orden.

43. *QM*, 122. Un mundo de bocas que no piden pan, porque están satisfechas de pan. Bocas que canten.

44. *QM*, 128. Y yo, ¿qué debo hacer cuando el enemigo no tiene armas, sino palabras?

45. *QM*, 109. Casandra es otra cosa. Es una verdad.

46. *QM*, 141. Algo parecido a esto debería ser el mundo el primer día cuando el primer sol y la primera alborada, antes de convertirlo en parcelas y propiedades. Antes de levantar fronteras. . . .

47. *QM*, 144. ¡No mueras nunca! ¡Necesito que vivas! Todos los días que termine mi guerra, antes de acostarme, pensaré en ti. Pensaré: 'Ella vive. Yo también.' Déjame tener esa esperanza.

48. *QM*, 159–60. (*Al público*) Queridos míos, es preciso contaros ciertas cosas. No tengo padres. No tengo amigos. No tengo creencias. Ni destino glorioso. Ni sistema que me defienda. Ni enemigos que me respeten. Ni silencio donde hablar. No tengo nada. He nacido para que viva el error, la mentira, la falsedad, la injusticia. Son los hijos de mi carne, hijos predilectos, a través de los cuales he parido la guerra, la raza de Caín, la falsa paz. Y los busco. Dolorosa de espinas. Los busco porque salieron de mí y se me perdieron. . . .

49. *QM*, 166. Su voz no es solamente sonido. Es también enfermedad.

50. *QM*, 168. (*Con tono profesional.*) Ha sido muy sencillo. Una incisión limpia. Los nervios perfectamente degollados. El foco de infección, vulgo la lengua, duerme en la basura el sueño de los justos. Quiero decir el sueño de Luzbel. ¡Agua de rosas para lavarme la sangre de las manos!

51. *QM*, 170. ¡Señores y señoras, piadosos y pecadores, ciudadanos del mundo . . .

52. Derrida, "Plato's Pharmacy," 250.

53. *PPR*, 143–43. Le fait est qu'il avait la nostalgie de l'homme du passé et voulait en faire un portrait pour l'homme de demain.

54. *PPR*, 144. D'autres organisèrent des lieux de réunion, ouvrirent cafés, bistrots, échoppes et tavernes. Il surgit au bout d'un temps une vie sociale parallèle à celle préconisée par la Cité Future, marginale, pas du tout aseptisée, et très vivante.

55. *PPR*, 146. Les gens y vivent à leur manière, plus ou moins adaptés au monde actuel et pris entre deux feux: le passé qu'on ignore et le futur qu'on rejette. Oh non, pas comme des hors-la-loi: les lois, on les respecte, mais, plutôt comme des individus qui ne sont pas enclins à l'obéissance aveugle. Des gens libres . . .

56. *PPR*, 152. Corrupted saints, truth abused, here I am born and here I die, here like beggars' bread, here I grow weak and fall, here I open my veins, here I shout and my words have no echo, the closed room, dark room here I summon my men and my men are castrated men, here my castrated children are born, race of solitude, here I have no song, here I have no bread.

57. *PPR*, 156.

58. George Steiner, "Extraterritorial," in *Extraterritorial: Papers on Literature and the Language Revolution* (New York: Atheneum, 1971).

Chapter 7. *Adorado Alberto*

1. Ah, the bouquets of the Baroness! . . . Ineffable just as she. She would mix the orchids with the wild flowers, the roses with the chrysanthemums, the daisies with

the mimosas. One had the impression of a crossbreeding against nature, of an arrangement delivering some sibylline message, establishing once and for all the confusion of genres and species. False impression, because it was, rather, about an art: the art of ambiguity. A knowing touch of green among a yellow and a mauve would temper the masked antagonism of forms and colors, and each flower, so dazzling, so individualist as it were, would be blended into a harmonious whole, an ensemble of tones that seemed painted. Her grand masterpiece, the Baroness would smile and her smile would reproduce the strangeness of this floral ambivalence.

2. Salik also played the role of Mademoiselle Adèle in the original production of *Pré-papa* at the Café-Théâtre de l'Odéon.

3. Cf. also Phyllis Zatlin's commentary on these plays (*Cross-Cultural Approaches to Theatre: The Spanish-French Connection* [Metuchen, N.J.: Scarecrow Press, 1994], 77–78). My subsequent references to *Pré-papa* pertain to the French version since this is the only published version in existence at the present time.

4. Interview with Feldman. Gómez-Arcos is referring here to Miguel Arocena, then manager of the Café-Théâtre de l'Odéon.

5. Romero notes that the conference planners had originally envisioned an encounter with Spanish playwrights from the earlier generation (of the 1950s), such as Antonio Buero Vallejo, Lauro Olmo, and José Martín Recuerda, but when all three of these dramatists declined their invitations, the focus of the *Jornadas* was hastily changed to a younger, lesser known generation of playwrights. Romero also points out that many of the most prominent playwrights associated with the "new" Spanish theater"—among them, Ángel García Pintado, Manuel Martínez Mediero, and Jerónimo López Mozo—were not even apprised of the events taking place in Paris until well after the *Jornadas* had concluded. See also Oliva, *El teatro desde 1936*, 350–51.

6. Vicente Romero, "Teatro actual español en la Sorbona. Informe general," *Primer Acto* 152 (January 1973): 56.

7. Duque had served as assistant director for the 1969 dual production and had also directed plays by Ramón María del Valle-Inclán and Federico García Lorca at the Café-Théâtre de l'Odéon. Only Gómez-Arcos and Arrabal chose to present their plays in French. The other plays staged at the *Jornadas* were Arrabal's *Et ils passèrent des menottes aux fleurs*; León Felipe's *El payaso de las bofetadas*; Nieva's *Es bueno no tener cabeza*; Olmo's *Conflicto a la hora de la siesta*; and Romero Esteo's *Paraphernalia de la olla podrida, la misericordia y la mucha consolación*. For reviews of these plays, see Pérez Coterillo, "Teatro actual español en la Sorbona. Los espectáculos," *Primer Acto* 152 (January 1973): 60–67.

8. Ibid., 65

9. Ibid.; Romero, "Teatro actual español," 54.

10. Coterillo, "Teatro actual español. Los espetáculos," 65.

11. Pérez Coterillo also notes that *Et si on aboyait*, "the text that its author considers to be the final point—testament—of his theater of Iberian dimensions, has a perfect lucidity when it establishes in the midst of the religious, military, familiar or political features of our country, the conflict between the world of aberrant and castrating repression and of human maturity and lucidity, which has known how to free itself through the only road that has been possible, that of the incorporation of its own life and its own history and whose freedom becomes daring and liberating" (Ibid., 66).

12. Ibid.

13. I do not mean to imply here that Gómez-Arcos's pre-exilic work does not hold its validity when contemplated outside of these spatiotemporal limits. The successful

stagings of *Los gatos* in 1992 and of *Queridos míos, es preciso contaros ciertas* in 1994 confirm that his early drama continues to be both timely and relevant.

14. Interview with Feldman.

15. Interview with Marie-Louise Coudert, "Augustin Gomez Arcos," *L'Humanité Dimanche*, 15 June 1977. Je ne suis pas d'accord avec les idées traditionnelles au sujet des "racines" qu'un homme perdrait en changeant de place. C'est, à mon avis, une image folklorique et superficielle. Je pense qu'un être humain porte toujours ce qu'il est en lui-même. Où je me trouve, où j'irai, je serai moi. C'est-à-dire profondément espagnol. Mes racines espagnoles ne sont pas enfoncées dans tel ou tel endroit d'où elles ne peuvent s'extirper. Elles voyagent avec moi.

16. Michael Seidel, *Exile and the Narrative Imagination* (New Haven: Yale University Press, 1986), 2. Seidel examines the exilic condition as manifested in a series of novels by Daniel Defoe (*Robinson Crusoe*), Joseph Conrad (*Lord Jim*), James Joyce (*Ulysses*), Laurence Sterne (*A Sentimental Journey*), Henry James (*The Ambassadors*), and Vladimir Nabokov (*Pale Fire*). In a manner that parallels Seidel's approach, Jacques Derrida relates his concept of writing and difference to the process of exilic wandering in "The Question of the Book," an essay on the Jewish poet Edmond Jabès. Derrida draws an analogy between the written text and the exilic process of recreation (in *Writing and Difference*, ed. and trans. Alan Bass [Chicago: University of Chicago Press, 1978]).

17. Seidel, *Exile*, ix.

18. Ibid., 13. Seidel's allusion to Dante refers to the explanation the poet gave to his patron, Can Grande, with regard to the layering processes of narrative allegory. In so doing, Dante "cited the first line of Psalm 113 (Psalm 114 in the Protestant Bible) on the parting of the Red Sea at Exodus: 'in exitu Israel de Egyptó'" (8).

19. Judith Butler, *Gender Trouble: Feminism and the Subversion of Identity* (New York, Routledge, 1990), 6.

20. Interview with Feldman. In my personal interview with Mr. Gómez-Arcos, he denies any interest in "feminism" *per se*, which he considers an ephemeral notion: "I am only interested in what is everlasting. The transitory does not interest me at all. Feminism as well as political ideas and ideologies are all ephemeral things. I am more interested in the capacity of the individual."

21. On Freud's concept of bisexuality, see *Three Essays on the Theory of Sexuality* and *Civilization and Its Discontents*, in *The Standard Edition of the Complete Psychological Works of Sigmund Freud*, ed. James Strachey, 24 vols. (London: Hogarth, 1953–74).

22. Hélène Cixous, "The Laugh of the Medusa," trans. Keith Cohen and Paula Cohen. *Signs: Journal of Women in Culture and Society* (Summer 1976): 884. As Toril Moi points out, significant parallels exist between Cixous's notion of feminine writing and Derrida's notion of writing as *différance*" (*Sexual/Textual Politics: Feminist Literary Theory* [New Accents. New York: Routledge, 1985], 108–9).

23. Ambiguities of sex and gender occur with great frequency in Gómez-Arcos's novels (for example, *L'agneau carnivore, Maria Republica, Pré-papa, Bestiaire, L'homme en genoux* [The man kneeling], *L'aveuglon* [The little blind one], and *La femme d'emprunt* [The woman of artifice]).

24. *AA*, 1. *Al levantarse el telón, Alberto hace su número de travestí en un cabaret de París: un strip-tease en el que sólo desnuda sus manos. Actúa como si cantara alguna canción de doble sentido (la fuerza de la costumbre), pero no canta: dice un poema, acompañado por una música picaresca y vulgar. Naturalmente, el poema y la música son dos cosas absolutamente distintas, no inventadas para el mismo conjunto.*

25. Cf. Judith Butler, *Bodies that Matter* (New York: Routledge, 1993). See also Marjorie Garber, *Vested Interests: Cross-dressing and Cultural Anxiety* (New York: Routledge, 1992) on the metaphoric implications of cross-dressing.

26. *AA*, 1. *Rubia o morena, maquillada, glamorosa, mostrando todos sus aparentes encantos femeninos.*

27. *AA*, 2. *La música cesa. Alberto saluda. A continuación está en su camerino, quitándose la peluca, las pestañas, las uñas, etc., y poniéndose un pantalón, un bigote postizo, una bufanda . . . 'vistiéndose de hombre,' tal como deberemos verle en las escenas siguientes.*

28. *AA*, 1–2. Por ejemplo, tus manos. / ¿Sabes ya lo que buscan? / Si las dejas perdidas / se humillarán, buscando / un Dios que ya no existe. / O cortarán la flor. / O pegarán al niño. / O apretarán sin miedo / el gatillo /—sin miedo y sin piedad. / Y si son para eso / tus manos / córtatelas, y tíralas. / Porque es mejor que estén / en la boca de un perro / o en la basura / que siendo tu asesino / diario, mi asesino, / sin construir la vida, / construyendo la muerte. / O si tanto las quieres / tus manos, / dales quehacer de vida, / creación de quimeras, / realización de sueños, / casas, árboles, hombres, / amor que realizar, / cosas simples y hermosas / que hacer . . . / pero no les dés dioses / ni muerte: / Son tus manos.

29. *AA*, 2. ¡Adorado Alberto! Qué número tan divertido el de la chica que viene de provincias . . .

30. *AA*, 1. *sentada en una preciosa silla de mimbre, de playa o jardín, en pose de fotografía, vestida con elegancia veraniega a la moda de hace quince años. O quizá diez. (De todas maneras, debe ser un vestido que, a medida que cambie de adornos, se adapte a la moda de los últimos diez o quince años.)*

31. This situation, in which a dead person is endowed with characteristics normally reserved for the living, occurs in even more elaborate form in Gómez-Arcos's play *Interview de Mrs. Muerta Smith por sus fantasmas* (Mrs. Dead Smith's interview with her phantoms).

32. *AA*, 3. Mi adorado Alberto. Cuando alguien me preguntaba por qué te quería tanto, no podía contestar una sola palabra. Me quedaba como una tonta. No me bastaba con decir, "Le quiero porque es mi hijo." (*Ríe un poco.*) El amor de madre se comprende tan facilmente . . . No. Te quería por algo más. Por ti, Alberto. Por ti mismo.

33. *AA*, 8. Retratarle desnudito, con aquellos tirabuzones, en aquel cojín de satín. Supongo que los estarás pagando.

34. Mamá's unremitting love for her son and her validation of his ambiguous sexual identity are attributes that Gómez-Arcos continues to develop in his characterization of Matilde, the mother in his novel *L'agneau carnivore*. Matilde furtively dedicates her life to the pursuit of an anarchistic "cataclysm" that will serve as an ultimate act of defiance of the conventions of Franco's Spain. Eventually, when her sons Ignacio and Antonio engage in an incestuous love affair, she realizes that by engendering them she has, in effect, planted the seeds of her monumental explosion of dissent. From a very young age, the boys find themselves instinctively seduced by each other's presence. They begin sharing the same bed and mutually exploring all aspects of their sensuality. For the sake of appearances, Matilde denounces her sons' actions. Upon entering their room, an oasis transgression, she sniffs the air and bellows at her maid, "Clara! . . . Take those sheets off right away and put on clean ones! It smells of sulfur in here!" (15). Underneath her superficial condemnations, however, she secretly applauds her sons' erotic transgressions in that they represent a supreme gesture of cataclysmic anarchy. In a candid conversation with her husband Carlos (a Republican), Matilde discusses the implications of the boys' illicit affair:

"Now I understand, even if it seems pretentious to you, that in giving birth to them, I was bringing into the world a hunger for life beyond the margins of normalcy. And you were the one who engendered that fury for life in me. We weren't able to change the world, and the war you fought only plunged us forever into the absence of hope, which is worse than despair . . . But you and I, we made something different: two unnatural sons, as my friends would say. That's beautiful. A real achievement, and I'm proud of it. Are you sorry you won't have a grandson to rock in your arms?" (186). (Clara! . . . Otez-moi tout de suite ces draps et mettez-en des propres! Ça sent le soufre! [23]. . . . Je comprends, maintenant, même si cela te paraît prétentieux, que j'ai mis au monde, en eux, un besoin de vivre en marge des normes, contre nature, si tu veux. Et que c'est toi qui as engendré en moi cette rage d'exister. Nous n'avons pas pu changer le monde, et la guerre que tu as faite n'a servi qu'à nous installer pour toujours dans l'absence d'espoir, ce qui est pire que le désespoir. Mais nous, toi et moi, nous avons fait quelque chose d'autre: deux fils contre nature, comme diraient mes amies. C'est beau, ça. Toute une oeuvre. Et j'en suis fière. Tu regrettes de ne pas avoir la possibilité de bercer dans tes bras un petit-fils? [223]).

35. *AA*, 6. No vuelvas nunca, Alberto, no vuelvas. Ni siquiera a poner flores en mi tumba. Ni siquiera a decirme hola. Porque si vuelves, caerás en sus manos. (*Pequeña pausa. Sonriente:*) ¿Saben que Alberto nunca ha dicho 'adiós?' En realidad, nunca ha pensado en mi muerte. Siempre ha pensado en mi vida.

36. Doña Perfecta, the protagonist of Galdós's eponymous novel (1876) and theatrical adaptation (1896), implements her own personal code of morals in the name of the Catholic faith. There are additional parallels between *Adorado Alberto* and *Doña Perfecta* that are worthy of note. In Galdós's novel, Doña Perfecta arranges a marriage between her nephew Pepe Rey (who, like Alberto, has lived outside of Spain) and her daughter Rosario. Her plans, like those of Doña Julia, eventually backfire.

37. *AA*, 4. Lo importante es lo importante. Ya me confesaré, después.

38. *AA*, 8. [M]i querida hermana es tan hipócrita, tan fundamentalmente hipócrita, que ni siquiera se da cuenta de ello. No sé si ustedes lo han visto, pero está pisoteando todas sus creencias, sus principios morales, su Dios, por defender sus prejuicios sociales. Y todo porque mi hijo Alberto es . . . "así," y actúa como travestí en un cabaret de París. Ah, ¿les había dicho que el día que concebí a Alberto era un hermoso día de primavera, lleno de pájaros y flores, y que su padre era el hombre más hombre que nunca he conocido? Pues es verdad. Es histórico.

39. *AA*, 14. Doña Julia García tiene el orgullo de participar a todas sus amistades que su sobrino Alberto se casó ayer . . .

40. *AA*, 9. Nunca te permití que te pusieras fajas, ni que te afeitaras los sobacos, ni que te arrancaras los pelos del bigote, para que Alberto, hastiado al fin de tanta frivolidad, encontrara en ti a la mujer ideal, honesta. Mi pobre hermana daba un grito cada vez que te veía, como si viera al diablo. Decía que resultabas antiestética.

41. *AA*, 8. Sábanas color salmón pálido, de seda, que yo suponía que son lascivas, incitantes; en el balcón cinco plantas tropicales, de un verde que hace perder la cabeza y aquello que leí en mi libro de meditaciones, que era un pecado, y que incitaba al pecado: incienso oriental.

42. *AA*, 9. Alberto, que tiene unas manos maravillosas. Cogió unas tijeras, hilo y aguja y se puso a la obra. ¡Y mira!

43. *AA*, 10.

José-Mari. Había mucha gente . . . más que localidades. Un tumulto. Por eso pasó todo.

Julia. (Aterrada, santiguándose lentamente mientras habla.) Creo . . . que tengo que santiguarme. (*Mamá empieza a sonreír abiertamente.*)

José-Mari. El caso es que no cabíamos los dos en un solo asiento . . . (*Justificándose*) . . . aunque yo compré dos localidades . . . y Alberto se sentó directamente sobre mis rodillas . . . Dijo que estaba más cómodo. Doña Julia, no sé si fue el calor . . . o el perfume que llevaba . . . que no era colonia, sino perfume . . . o que la tela de su camisa era muy fina y yo le tenía abrazado . . . para que no se cayera cada vez que le gritaba a un jugador "¡Precioso chut, macho!" . . . el caso es que todo me empezó a crecer . . . a crecer . . . y se me quedó pequeño el pantalón.

44. *AA*, 13. Pobre Julia. Qué pena me das. ¿Sabes tú lo que es amor? No. Cuando de pequeña te hablaron del amor de Dios, y seguiste por ese camino, lo equivocaste todo. Y ya ves lo que hay en el número 5 del Amor de Dios: una casa de putas.

45. *AA*, 13. Cuando yo tenía a mi adorado Alberto en el vientre, y le sentía crecer día a día, mi amor no tenía límites. Amaba a su padre que me lo había engendrado, y a mi pequeñín que iba creciendo momento a momento dentro de mí. Pero nunca pude hablar de aquel amor en mis versos.

46. *AA*, 14 . . . si quiere casar a Alberto, ¡cáselo conmigo!

47. Ibid. Este mundo es un perro. . . . Este mundo moderno y corrompido es un perro. Y yo soy una perra. Y mi hermana la muerta es una perra. . . .

48. *AA*, 15.

Julia. . . . Pero más santa era tu madre. Santísima. Momentos antes de morir, después de comulgar . . .

Alberto. (*La mira, sin comprender.*)

Julia. . . . cogió mis manos entre las suyas y me dijo: "Julia, mi adorada hermana Julia, procura que Alberto se case. (*A Mamá le da un golpe de tos.*) ¿Qué será de él, sin una buena esposa que le cuide?"

Mamá. Ay, si los muertos pudieran hablar. (*Alberto se ha quedado triste, silencioso. Lentamente se sienta en el sofá.*) Adorado Alberto, no lo dije. ¡No lo dije!

Alberto. (*Después de una pausa.*) ¿Que Mamá comulgó?

Mama. ¡No!

Julia. Sí.

Alberto. Tita, ¿has mentido tú alguna vez?

Mamá. ¡Siempre!

Julia. Nunca.

Alberto. Entonces, Mamá comulgó. (*Mamá empieza a llorar desesperada, sin ruido.*) Moría . . . arrepentida. Arrepentida de una vida tan bonita como la suya.

49. *AA*, 16. Nos ha tocado el siglo veinte, pues siglo veinte.

50. Ibid. Alberto . . . Ahora que estás a punto de casarte, debo decirte un secreto que se le dice a todo muchacho la víspera de su boda, y que a ti te encantará: también las mujeres toman por el culo.

51. ¡No se las toques, aprovechada, lesbiana! ¡Albertito, cásate conmigo! ¡Ay que tetitas!

52. *AA*, 17. Alberto . . . (*La voz de José-Mari tiene dulzura, alegría, sorpresa, toda una serie de emociones nuevas.*) ¿Eres u . . . una mujer . . . con picha? (*Alberto ya no sabe ni lo que es, porque poco a poco le han ido convirtiendo en un monstruo.*)

53. In a similar manner, Gómez-Arcos's *L'agneau carnivore* ends in a marriage between the two brothers, Ignacio and Antonio, following the death of their mother. The ceremony is performed by their faithful servant Clara.

54. The image of the threesome as a chaotic mixture of sexual organs is somewhat evocative of the situation depicted in Gómez-Arcos's novel *Bestiaire* (1986), in which

three triplets attempt to establish a new world order. At first, it is absolutely impossible to distinguish one from the other; hence, the name "Dominique," a perfectly androgynous name which can apply to male, female, or any sort of intermediary hybrid, is given to all three. Eventually, they evolve into two heterosexuals (male and female) and one homosexual (in their mother Denise's words: "a sort of compromise between the two sexual tendencies "). In the triplets' journal, they refer to each other respectively as "Dominique-mâle," "Dominique-fente," and "Dominique-fesses," designations that express their erotic preferences. Viewed as a single entity, however, the triplets represent an hermaphroditic sexual hybrid, composed of a plurality of genders that are completely continuous with one another. See chapter 5, note 35, for more on this novel.

55. *AA*, 19. Este mundo moderno y corrompido es un perro. . . . Y mi director espiritual es un perro. Un perro que me dijo "Doña Julia, hija mía, case a su sobrino Alberto. Su vida es un escándalo." Un perro. Y a ese perro iré yo a decirle mañana por la mañana: "Padre, mi sobrino Alberto se ha casado . . . con un tío de veinticinco años como la copa de un pino." Y los principios morales, unos perros. Los prejuicios sociales, unos perros. La religión, una perra. Y ésos tres que se han ido, tres perros . . . tres perros con cuatro tetas, tres culos, un coño, dos pollas y dos pares de cojones. Lo sé de memoria. Perros, perros, perros, perros. Guau, guau, guau, guau. (*Se levanta.*) En fin. Es mejor terminar con los recuerdos.

CHAPTER 8. *PRÉ-PAPA*

1. My sublime decision: place myself in the margins of traditionally accepted ways and customs, live without identity papers, like a Martian.

2. Michael Ugarte, *Shifting Ground: Spanish Civil War Exile Literature* (Durham: Duke University Press, 1989), 4. Cf. also Paul Tabori, *Anatomy of Exile* (London: Harrap, 1972), on the written testimony of Spanish exiles and those of other nationalities.

3. In his essay "Censorship, Exile, Bilingualism: A Long Road to Freedom of Expression," Gómez-Arcos speaks of the rejection of his memory, which in his view, continues to persist even in the "new" democratic Spain: "Personally, up until now I have written and published ten novels in French: good or bad (although translated into several languages). This work is nonexistent for my country. The recent Spanish democracy ignores it and rejects it, as if it were an illegitimate child or (I've thought about it a lot) a terrorist act against the country where I was born and whose nationality I maintain with pride. As if my past and my memory did not belong to me, or . . . they were a common heritage shared with my fellow countrymen, which I have had the audacity to express in a foreign language." I quote, throughout, from the unpublished version of this essay. See note 34 in chapter one.

4. See the previous section on *Adorado Alberto* for a more detailed account of the staging and publication of these texts.

5. The novelistic version of *Pré-papa* is an exceptionally self-conscious allegorical narrative. It is structured as a fairy tale, within a fairy tale, within a fairy tale. . . . Gómez-Arcos also inserted a segment of his censored play *Queridos míos, es preciso contaros ciertas cosas* (My dear friends, it's time we get certain things straight) within the text of this novel. See the earlier discussion of *Queridos míos* in chapter 6 for more on the relationship between these two texts.

6. Gómez-Arcos's adaptation of Giraudoux's *La folle de Chaillot* (The madwoman of Chaillot) premiered in 1961, his translation of Clot's *La révélation* (The revelation) premiered in 1962, and his version of Giraudoux's *Intermezzo* premiered in 1963.

7. Ibid.

8. Ibid.

9. George Steiner, "Extraterritorial," in *Extraterritorial: Papers on Literature and the Language Revolution* (New York: Atheneum, 1971), 3.

10. Ibid., 11.

11. This situation is also present in Gómez-Arcos's novels. In *L'agneau carnivore* and *Bestiaire*, for example, he employs the theme of incest as a metaphor for all forms of transgression. The incestuous relationships that are at the center of these novels (brother with brother, brother with sister, children with parents, etc.) are analogous to the meshings of linguistic and cultural codes that characterize Gómez-Arcos's literary expression.

12. Raymond Gérome, *Pré-papa, L'Avant Scène Théâtre* 434 (1969): 37.

13. *PP*, 38. On dit qu'ils sont mariés, mais dans le fond, personne n'en sait rien: ce sont des étrangers

14. In the novelistic version of *Pré-papa*, John is characterized as a North American-born exile who works at a futuristic *Centre* as an "anatomical designer," battling new diseases. Mary is described as having been born in Europe. (Her real name is Marie but she changed it to the American spelling so that it would conform to her husband's nationality.)

15. *PP*, 43. des petits bourgeois. Une petite voiture, un petit appareil de télévision et un petit cocktail dans notre petit appartement chaque fin de mois . . . huit petits invités . . .

16. *PP*, 37. *Le sofa d'un cabinet médical où se trouve assis John et Mary Ferguson. Un pupitre de conférencier derrière lequel le Professeur Kedrova prépare son texte. Un prie-Dieu de confessionnal, en velours râpé.*

17. *PP*, 38. Le médecin est là pour qu'on lui expose les faits concrets. C'est à lui à décider.

18. In the novelistic version of *Pré-papa*, this lecture is depicted as a televised speech that is broadcast into John and Mary's living room.

19. In *Pré-papa*, the novel, Gómez-Arcos transfers this metaphoric treatment of space to a broader exterior landscape. The narrative is situated in a futuresque realm, a postwar *paysage d'apocalypse*, during the aftermath of a completely technological battle that only endured a matter of seconds but managed to reduce most of the world to dust. The new and orderly future is represented by the *Cité Future*, a city established in the midst of the apocalyptic *désert de la Catastrophe*, whose living environment is contained within a series of aseptic, green-house structures. The immaculate domes of the *Cité Future* shield it from contamination from nuclear dust. The *Cité Future* is controlled by an all-knowing research organization known as the *Centre*. The *Centre*'s computer, "le Videur, le Concierge" ("the Seer, the Concierge"), like the computer in Gómez-Arcos's novel *Maria Republica*, serves as a kind of surrogate deity. In contrast with this city of the future, the old—but also, orderly— past is represented by the *ville troglodyte* a place of traditional values and old-fashioned ways that languishes and decays in an atmosphere of radioactive dust particles. Complete disorder and anarchy are located along the *esplanade du Pendu* (Esplanade of the Hanged Man), a street that links the past world of the *ville troglodyte* with the space-age world of the *Cité Future*. The esplanade is inhabited by artists, free-spirits, and avid individualists, who reject the traditions of the past (religion, oppressive governments, sexual taboos), as well as the *Cité Future*'s starkly

pure, dehumanized, and oppressive system of mind-controlling computers. See my discussion of *Pré-papa* in chapter 6 regarding the relationship between this novel and *Queridos míos, es preciso contaros ciertas cosas*.

20. As Phyllis Zatlin points out, the fact that Professeur Kedrova is female and the nurse is male adds an additional twist to the gender reversals that are at work here (*Cross-Cultural Approaches to Theatre*, 77–78).

21. *PP*, 37. La consultation est annoncée pour neuf heures et il n'est qu'onze heures. Vous pouvez aller prendre l'apéritif. Le Docteur commence à se mettre du déodorant. Moi, il faut que j'aille réveiller le cancer, car il dort très tard. Environ quarante-cinq minutes.

22. *PP*, 38. Si l'Eglise avait un corps de police, je serais Inspecteur en chef.

23. *PP*, 37–38. Bonjour. Les athées on lâché un courant d'air dans les parages. Je me suis enrhumée. (*Personne ne lui répond.*) Je suis Mademoiselle Adèle. (*Aux Ferguson.*) Mariée, mais sans enfants. Veuve, mais sans amants. (*A tous, avec orgueil.*) Je suis ce que les moralistes appellent un individu exemplaire, le produit d'une société traditionnelle et parfaite qu'avec l'aide de Dieu, personne n'arrivera à abîmer. Du moins, aussi longtemps que je vivrai. (*Au Professeur, avec un sourire innocent.*) J'ai une santé de fer. (*Elle se dirige vers le prie-Dieu, sort de son sac un morceau de velours tout neuf, l'étend avec soin puis s'agenouille. L'infermier apparaît derrière le confessionnal.*) Oh Marie conçue sans péché.

24. *PP*, 39. Le monde entier n'est qu'un peché. Surtout la jeunese. Où allons-nous? Heureusement que je suis là, moi, pour confesser tout ça, commandement par commandement.

25. *PP*, 41. Depuis qu'ils sont mariés, ils ne cessent de commettre d'atroces péchés contre le sixième commandement. 'Tu ne forniqueras point.' In *Pré-papa*, the novel, Mademoiselle Adèle is John and Mary's neighbor, who lives in their apartment building and is continually observing their activities. She attends Mass several times per day and is described as an old woman from the generation that witnessed the apocalyptic Third World War.

26. *PP*, 37. Mesdames et Messieurs, nous avons ouvert l'espace. La vie commence pour l'homme. Désormais, le temps n'existe plus. Seul la conquête de l'universe. Une perspective merveilleuse.

27. *PP*, 39. L'homme en fin, s'appuyant sur la technique, a percé le ciel. Ce ciel, réservé pendent des siècles à Dieu et à ses anges, est maintenant notre domaine, un terrain ouvert à la vie nouvelle. Et en prononçant ces mots: 'vie nouvelle' la question surgit encore une fois: l'Homme est-il préparé pour commencer un voyage dont il ne connaît que le point de départ?

28. *PP*, 39. Je m'explique: y a-t-il rien de plus métaphorique que l'existence de Dieu? . . . Lorsqu'une chose nous fait peur, nous fabriquons un mystère autour, une métaphore.

29. *PP*, 39. Emportera-t-il, pour cette mission fabuleuse, les mêmes bagages qu'il avait emportés au cours de ses découvertes antérieures?

30. *PP*, 39–40.

> *Professeur.* Faisons une synthèse. Qu'est-ce que l'homme avait emporté avec lui lors de ses découvertes antérieures? Un système immuable. Un système basé sur la religion, la patrie, la famille, le pouvoir, les intérêts économiques, les préjugés sociaux et raciaux, et une quantité ridicule de langues et de règles grammaticales qui ne servent à rien.
>
> *Adèle.* (*criant.*) Tout ça, c'est dépassé maintenant. Les journaux le disent.
>
> *Professeur.* (*furieuse.*) Taisez-vous, folle! (*Elle continue.*) Résultat? La faim, la guerre, la maladie, l'incompréhension . . . Inutile de procéder à une analyse minutieuse des systèmes coloniaux. Nous n'en avons plus le temps. Il suffit de prendre pour exemple n'importe

quel empire colonial. Ces voyages dictés par l'avidité, l'homme ne les a pas entrepris pour lui-même, avec une idée de pureté ou d'évolution. Ce n'est pas la recherche du futur que l'interessait. Il voulait seulement établir le passé. Lourd de crimes et d'inutilité.

31. Seidel invokes the image of Dorothy of *The Wizard of Oz* as an example of this process: "When, for example, Judy Garland as Dorothy in *The Wizard of Oz* looks down at her dog Toto and up at the beautiful Witch of the North standing over them and says, 'now I *know* we're not in Kansas,' her famous words only partially construe the principle upon which her boundary crossing is devised. For it is the metamorphosis of an all-too-familiar Kansas (in Technicolor) that sustains the action of the outland. Oz is a place over the rainbow whose boundaries are exilic but whose allegorical energies translate local fears and homegrown desires" (4).

32. Interview with Feldman.

33. For more on Gómez-Arcos's notion of anarchy, see the introduction to this study.

34. *PP*, 39. Elle, elle travaille tous les jours un peu plus, elle maigrit et elle boit. Personne n'y comprend rien. Elle n'était pas comme-ça avant de se marier. Et lui, il pâlit. Il a déja les yeux tout cernés. Et il grossit. Deux phénomènes opposés.

35. *PP*, 42. (*il cesse de rire et sur un ton très social, il s'adresse a John*). Mon petit chéri, vous êtes enceint ... enceinte. (*Il y a un silence.*) Tout à fait enceint. De trois mois.

36. John Money, and Anke A. Ehrhardt, *Man and Woman, Boy and Girl: The Differentiation and Dimorphism of Gender Identity from Conception to Maturity* (Baltimore: John Hopkins University Press, 1972), 164. In a seemingly offhand commentary, Spanish writer Juan Goytisolo draws a similar analogy between gender identification and his own situation as a writer living in exile (in France and Morocco), who felt compelled to choose between French and Spanish as his language of literary expression. When asked why he, unlike Gómez-Arcos, opted to continue writing in Spanish following his departure from Spain, he responds, "It is a question that is as difficult to respond to as that which concerns a person's sexual orientation; it is the language that chooses a person and, although we can decide about certain characteristics, we come into this world predetermined by a series of imponderable factors" (Interview with Karl Kohut, *Escribir en Paris* [Barcelona: Hogar del Libro, 1983], 92).

37. *PP*, 42. John, pourquoi m'as-tu fait une chose pareille? Durant trois mois, j'ai attendu que tu me fasses mère, et voilà que tu me fais père. Salaud!

38. *PP*, 43.

39. *PP*, 42. *avec un mélange de curiosité scientifique et de tendresse.*

40. *PP*, 43. Il est à moi. Je suis sa mère.

41. In *Pré-papa*, the novel, as John grows, Mary diminishes in size, losing more and more weight. Symbolically, she is slowly disappearing from the scene, gradually fading away from society. Finally, she commits suicide, plunging to her death through an open window.

42. Interview with Feldman. Es decir, creo que la humanidad como proyecto es infinitamente más importante que la diferencia de los individuos. La diferencia es una casualidad. De todas maneras, eso es absolutamente científico. Se hizo la diferencia entre los sexos porque las condiciones hacían que fuese necesario para que la vida continuase pero el sentido de la vida es otro. El sentido de la vida es una perpetuación. El día en que la vida ya no necesita los dos sexos separados para perpetuarse, los sexos se volverán a juntar o habrá cualquier otro tipo de evolución, cualquier otro tipo de mutación.

43. *PP*, 41. Un être particulier, avec un cerveau lavé de toute tradition, sans mémoire et avec un corps ouvert à la évolution. Un être appartenant à une race nouvelle ou bien la créer lui-même hors de la prison de nos limites, de nos préjugés.

44. *PP*, 44. Vous et vos descendants, vous serez la race nouvelle, la vie nouvelle. Cela ne vous semble-t-il pas merveilleux?

45. "Censorship, Exile, Bilingualism."

46. *PP*, 44. Ce monde moderne et corrompu est un chien.

Chapter 9. *Interview de Mrs. Muerta Smith por sus Fantasmas*

1. Is there anything more metaphoric than the existence of God?

2. Even Gómez-Arcos himself noted the apparent irony of this situation, in which his play, written in 1972, was staged at a "center for new scenic tendencies." In his program notes, he makes the following apology to his audience: "Oh, you will also have to pardon the fact that I have been included in a program of new theatrical tendencies, even though I carry many years upon my shoulders: this means (I suppose) that either I am too modern or that our theater continues to be too antiquated, go figure; in any case, it is not my fault."

3. Juan Antonio Vizcaíno, "Gómez Arcos vuelve a la escena española tras más de 20 años de ausencia," *El País*, 25 February 1991, 31.

4. Enrique Centeno, "Una justa recuperación," *Diario 16*, 25 February 1991.

5. Eduardo Haro Tecglen, "La señora se pudre," *El País*, 25 February 1991, 31.

6. This defiant blend of religious and scatological imagery is also found in the work of contemporary Spanish director Almodóvar, whose film *Entre tinieblas* was (according to Mr. Gómez-Arcos) loosely inspired by a reading of his novel *Maria Republica*. Another noteworthy correspondence is found in the contemporary *tableau* photography of Andres Serrano of the United States. Many of Serrano's photographs portray religious images and icons that have been submerged in bodily fluids. In his most famous piece, *Piss Christ*, a crucifix is set in a Plexiglas tank of urine.

7. Mary Douglas, *Purity and Danger: An Analysis of Concepts of Pollution and Taboo* (New York: Frederick A. Praeger, 1966), 115.

8. Mikhail Bakhtin, *Rabelais and His World*, trans. Hélène Iswolsky, foreword by Krystyna Pomorska, prologue by Michael Holquist (Bloomington: Indiana University Press, 1984). Cf. Peter Stallybrass and Allon White (*The Politics and Poetics of Transgression* [Ithaca: Cornell University Press, 1986]), who note that Bakhtin anticipates by approximately three decades the principles of symbolic anthropology.

9. Bakhtin, *Rabelias*, 317.

10. Ibid., 18. Bakhtin also examines the process by which this material bodily principle of degradation manifests itself in the realm of popular language, forming the basis for a large number of verbal abuses, curses, and oaths. Traditional debasing gestures—for example, the tossing of excrement and the drenching with urine—are directly related to popular linguistic expressions, such as "I shit on you." Nevertheless, this fundamental artistic principle of degradation—this downward motion, which orients the grotesque perspective toward the underworld (the bowels of earth and body)—does not imply an exclusively negative connotation; rather, it also embraces the positive (carnivalesque) concepts of regeneration and renewal. The lower material bodily stratum is the zone where death and life metaphorically converge, for not only is this region associated with bodily waste; it is also the area of fertility and reproduction (148).

11. On the relationship between parody and allegory, see Brain McHale, *Postmodernist Fiction* (New York: Routledge, 1987), 145. On the shift in focus from work to frame, see Craig Owens, "The Discourse of Others," and "From Work to Frame, or, Is Their Life After 'The Death of the Author'?" in *Beyond Recognition: Representation, Power, and Culture*, ed. Scott Bryson, Barbara Kruger, Lynne Tillman, and Jane Weinstock (Berkeley: University of California Press, 1992).

12. As Owens points out, the science fictive genre is a twentieth-century allegorical form, as are the Western and the gangster saga ("The Allegorical Impulse: Toward a Theory of Postmodernism: Part II," *October* 13 [1980]: 74).

13. *IMM*, 18. *Cabina de hibernación del vehículo espacial de Mrs. Muerta Smith. Impresión de templo dedicado a un culto especial, único en su género.* All quoted passages pertain to the 1991 edition of the text.

14. Javier Villán, *"Interview de Mrs. Muerta Smith por sus fantasmas:* Beligerancia y oportunidad," *El Mundo*, 25 February 1991, 45.

15. Regarding the notion of theatrical "ghosting," see Herbert Blau, *Take Up the Bodies: Theater at the Vanishing Point* (Urbana: University of Illinois Press, 1982), 195–247.

16. *IMM*, 23.

17. Interview with Feldman.

18. *IMM*, 38. Hecho. (*Anuncia con tono oficial:*) Hoy día, la cirujía avanza a pasos agigantados. Mrs. Muerta Smith, conocida millonaria americana, embajadora política de los Estados Unidos en casi todos los países del mundo, ha festejado sus noventa y cinco años haciendo sustituir su viejo clítoris por uno nuevo y casi recién nacido en materia plástica, fabricación japonesa. . . .

19. *IMM*, 40. *espléndida mujer de oro sin vida, estatua, símbolo, mecano o autómata, el seno izquierdo rojo escarlata.*

20. *IMM*, 51. *Lentamente se acerca a la mesa-altar que el perro ha preparado, paño blanco bordado de liturgia, recipiente de oro para las hostias sagradas, cáliz de oro para el vino sagrado. Ella misma sacerdote, consagra el alimento divino, oración interior, exterior frío y ceremonioso. Ausencia de la música. Luz hiriente.*

21. Linda Hutcheon, *The Politics of Postmodernism* (New York: Routledge, 1989), 98–99. Hutcheon distinguishes between modernist parody (an apolitical mode that assumes closure and artistic autonomy), and postmodernist parody (which, on the contrary, endeavors to deconstruct the idea of artistic independence by exposing the politicized nature of representation). See also idem, *A Theory of Parody: The Teachings of Twentieth-Century Art Forms* (London/New York: Methuen, 1985).

22. Hutcheon, *Politics*, 98.

23. *IMM*, 52–53. Perro, *en Periodista, sacando su bloc de notas.*—. . . La conocida embajadora plenipotenciaria de los Estados Unidos de América, . . . embajadora del Hombre, se prepara física y espiritualmente, para tener una entrevista con Dios. Ha llegado la hora de que el ser humano, ansioso de poseer otros horizontes, conozca al fin a su Creador y se explique con El. La Tierra no tiene arreglo. ¡Arreglemos el Cielo!

Mrs. Muerta Smith, sencilla mujer de oro y chinchillas, toma su desayuno, simple y frugal. Hostias consagradas y vitaminadas.

24. *IMM*, 53. Los Estados Unidos de América, a pesar de determinadas falsas apariencias, son profundamente católicos.

25. *IMM*, 54. nuestros químicos inventaron las hostias vitaminadas. Una composición equilibrada de toda las vitaminas.

26. *IMM*, 55. Una especie de enorme celo evangelizador.

27. Ibid. Mis compatriotas, ahora, son menos cachondos, pero más religiosos.

28. A similar parodic subversion of the Eucharist, of the rite of communion, and of the Catholic Mass in general can be found in the theater of Francisco Nieva in such plays as *La Paz* and *Coronada y el toro*. Cf. Emil G. Signes, "Francisco Nieva: Spanish Representative of the Theater of the Marvelous," in *The Contemporary Spanish Theater: A Collection of Critical Essays* (Lanham/New York/London: University Press of America, 1988).

29. Terry Eagleton comments on the liturgy of the Eucharist and its relationship to discourse, "The bread and wine of the liturgy operate as a discursive language, like any other human product used as sign: they are shared out, handled, exchanged, passed round, in a visible, concrete, durational interchange of symbols. But the eating of the bread is a participation in the body of Christ; a communion of being established through a discursive communication of sign" (*Body as Language* [London: Sheed and Ward, 1970], 29).

30. Here, I am drawing upon René Girard's concept of sacrificial ritual (*Violence and the Sacred*, trans. Patrick Gregory [Baltimore: Johns Hopkins University Press, 1977]).

31. *IMM*, 60. Perro, ¿Cómo será? . . . ¿Será un soplo? ¿Una ameba? ¿Un grito de luz? ¿Será nada?

32. *IMM*, 64–65.

Perro, en Dios. Huele bien . . .

Mrs. Muerta Smith. ¡Naturalmente, Señora! Es usted misma que yo como.

Perro, en Dios, lanza un grito. ¿Yo misma? ¡Caníbal! (*Al Angel*.) ¡A ella! El Angel ladra, amenazador.

Mrs. Muerta Smith. Pero, cálmese, Señora. Es sólo en metáfora que yo como a la Señora.

33. *IMM*, 60. ¡Pero yo tengo un nombre, Yo!
34. *IMM*, 67.

Perro, en Dios. Salgo a dar mi paseo. Yo le llamo "paseo cenital": bonito, ¿no?

Mrs. Muerta Smith. Charming!

Perro, en Dios. Y cago.

Mrs. Muerta Smith. ¿Perdón?

Perro, en Dios. ¡Cago! A derechas y a izquierdas, cuando encuentro un sitio que me gusta. Es un placer modesto.

35. *IMM*, 68. Y todo eso estando a régimen. Imagina si comiera todo lo que me apetece. ¡Jesús, Jesús!

36. Although this reference to the "Smith's" of Utah seems to recall the Smith family that founded the Mormon Church, Gómez-Arcos recently confessed, in a personal conversation, that he was entirely unaware of this coincidence when he wrote *Interview de Mrs. Muerta Smith*.

37. Interview with Feldman.

38. *IMM*, 75. No sé por qué razón las ideas, en la Tierra, se han descompuesto. Y el olor de podrido forma parte incluso de la naturaleza del perfume. Sin embargo, nuestro sentido del olfato no se ha atrofiado. Invivible. Lo que siempre fue lógico hoy es anacrónico. Los hombres se revuelven contra sí mismos, incansablemente, como si la especie humana fuese un error. Un error lamentable.

39. *IMM*, 80. Arranqué de mi vida todos los sueños, para que sólo quedara El como sueño de mi vida. Y El es sólo un fantasma.

40. *IMM*, 82. ¡Teta izquierda y roja, crece, crece conviértete en algo más rojo y más grande que el Universo entero, que todo lo creado! ¡Desborda, envenena, oh sagrado símbolo de la revolución, avanza como la gangrena!

41. Ibid. *Mrs. Muerta Smith comienza su danza de pecado, lúbrica, bíblica, cáliz sagrado en las manos, cáliz fálico que acaricia las más secretas partes de su cuerpo sin vida. . . . Mrs. Muerta Smith ofrece un puñal a Doble Nick blanco, coge, una hostia, hace el gesto eucarístico de la elevación y Doble Nick blanco apuñala la hostia.*

42. *IMM*, 86. Actualmente yo me ocupo en construir el socialismo. Me apasiona. Un mundo sin pecados tradicionales. La posibilidad de la sorpresa. De pecados completamente originales, quizás. ¡Y otra vez la mierda del hombre en todo su apogeo!

43. Owens, "The Allegorical Impulse: Part II," 80.

Epilogue

1. A world where your passage will be a promenade. Not a conquest. Not a massacre. Not an irrational exploitation. A promenade.

2. *MR*, 254–55. / Là-haut, dans l'air brûlé / un oiseau insolite / Chante / Une chanson ancienne / Oubliée / Mais qui petit à petit leur revient en mémoire / A tous / Et qu'ils reprennent. / Un seul mot / Republica / Semble se réveiller dans toutes les bouches, / dans tous les souvenirs. / La mémoire les travaille, / Quelle joie / — pensent-ils— / se rendre compte enfin / que nous pleurions un cadavre / qui n'a jamais existé, / un cadavre qui n'a jamais cessé d'être vivant. / Alors, anesthésiés et soldats, / tous les hommes enfin réveillés / commencent à faire des projets, / à penser à demain. / Car demain / est un mot vivant lui aussi. / Vivant. / laissons-les parler de la vie. / C'est le plus beau sujet de conversation / Que peuvent avoir les hommes.

Appendix B

1. A reference to the *café-théâtre* de l'Odéon and its manager Miguel Arocena.

2. A reference to the text that is analyzed in chapter 3 of this study.

3. A reference to the novel *L'aveuglon.*

4. This excerpt from *The Carnivorous Lamb* is drawn from William Rodarmor's Translation (Boston: Godine, 1984).

5. A reference to the novel *Mère Justice.*

Bibliography

WORKS BY AGUSTÍN GÓMEZ-ARCOS

The orthographic renditions Gómez-Arcos's name tend to vary depending on the publication. For instance, English publications generally omit the accents from his name, many French publications instinctively add a *u* to Agustín, and the use of hyphens is extremely irregular. In citing the title of each entry, I have maintained the original spelling.

Plays (listed in order of composition)

Doña Frivolidad.

   Unpublished ts. 1955.

Unos muertos perdidos.

   Unpublished ts.

Verano.

   Unpublished ts. Fundación Juan March: Madrid, December 1959.
   "Título primitivo": *Santa Juliana.*
   Later converted into *L'enfant miraculée* (novel).

Historia privada de un pequeño pueblo.

   Unpublished ts.

Elecciones generales.

   Subtitle: *Farsa política disparatada.*
   Unpublished ts. Madrid, December–January 1959–1960.
   Premio: Primer Festival Nacional de Teatro Nuevo 1960.
   Staged: 1960 (Madrid).

Fedra en el Sur.

Unpublished ts.

El tribunal.

Unpublished ts.

El rapto de las siamesas.

Unpublished ts.
Written in collaboration with Enrique Ortenbach and Adolfo Waitzman

Balada matrimonial.

Unpublished ts.

El salón.

Unpublished ts.

Prometeo Jiménez, revolucionario.

Unpublished ts.

Diálogos de la herejía.

Unpubished ts. 1962.
Published version (censored): *Primer Acto* 54 (June 1964): 26–53.
Unpublished new restructured version: Paris, 1980.
Premio Nacional Lope de Vega 1962 (subsequently annulled).
Finalist: Premio Calderón de la Barca.
Staged: 1964 (Madrid).

Los gatos.

Written: 1963.
Published: Madrid: Sociedad General de Autores de España, 1994.
Finalist: Premio Nacional de Literatura Dramática, 1994.
Staged: 1965 (Madrid), 1992 (Madrid), 1993 (National tour of Spain and travel to Buenos Aires).

Mil y un mesías.

Unpublished ts. Madrid, 1966.

Queridos míos, es preciso contaros ciertas cosas.

Written San Cugat del Vallès, 1966.
Published: Madrid: Centro Dramático Nacional, 1994.
Premio Nacional Lope de Vega 1966.
Dramatic Reading: 1966 (Madrid).
Staged: 1982 (Olso), 7 December 1994–22 January 1995 (Madrid).

Adorado Alberto.

Unpublished ts. Paris, Fall 1968.
Staged: 1969, 1972, and 1973 (Paris) as *Et si on aboyait?*

Pre-papá.

Unpublished ts. Paris, Fall 1968.
Published in French: *Pré-papa.* Translated by Rachel Salik. *L'Avant-Scène Théâtre* 434 (1969): 37–44.
Later converted into *Pré-papa ou Roman de fées* (novel).
Staged: 1969, 1972 and 1973 (Paris) as *Pré-papa.*

Cena con Mr. & Mrs. Q.

Unpublished ts. Paris, 1972.
Staged: 1972 (Paris) as *Dîner avec Mr & Mrs Q.*

Sentencia dictada contra P y J.

Unpublished ts. Paris, September 1970.
Re-edited version: Unpublished ts., 1993.

Interview de Mrs. Muerta Smith por sus fantasmas.

Written: Paris, 1972.
Bilingual French/Spanish edition: *Interview de Mrs Morte Smith par ses fantômes / Interview de Mrs. Muerta Smith por sus fantasmas.* Translated by Rachel Salik. Arles: Actes-Sud, 1985.
Spanish edition: Introduction by Moisés Pérez Coterillo and Lola Santa-Cruz. Teatro 15. Madrid: *El Público*/Centro de Documentación Teatral, 1991.
Staged: 1986–87 (Toulouse, Charleroi, and Paris) as *Interview de Mrs Morte Smith par ses phantômes*, 22 February 1991 (Madrid).

Spanish adaptations/translations of French plays (listed in order of composition)

La loca de Chaillot.

Translation of Jean Giraudoux's *La folle de Chaillot.*

Unpublished ts. Madrid, 1961.
Staged: 1962, 1989 (Madrid).

La revelación.

Translation of René-Jean Clot's La révélation.
Unpublished ts. Madrid, 1962.
Staged: 1962 (Madrid).

Intermezzo.

Translation of Jean Giraudoux's Intermezzo.
Unpublished ts. Madrid, 1963.
Staged: 1963 (Madrid).

Adaptation of a Norwegian children's musical

La villa de los ladrones.

by Thorbjorn Egner
Unpublished ts. Madrid, 1963.
Staged: 1963 (Madrid).

Novels (listed in order of composition)

El pan.

Unpublished ts. Madrid.
Later reworked in French as L'enfant pain.
Finalist, Premio Formentor (Seix Barral).

L'agneau carnivore.

Paris: Stock, 1975.
Seuil "Points Roman," 1985.
Prix Hermès 1975.

Maria Republica.

Written 1975.
Paris: Seuil, 1983.
Liste Goncourt 1983.

Ana Non.

Paris: Stock, 1977.

Stock "Livre de poche," 1980.
Téléfilm, France, 1980s.
Prix de Livre Inter 1977
Liste Goncourt 1977
Nominated: Prix Deux Magots 1978.
Prix Roland Dorgelès 1978
Prix Thyde-Monnier de la Société des Gens de Lettres 1978.

Scène de chasse (furtive).

Paris: Stock, 1978.
Finaliste: Prix Goncourt 1978.

Pré-papa ou Roman de fées.

Paris: Stock, 1979.

L'enfant miraculée.

Paris: Fayard, 1981.

L'enfant pain.

Paris: Seuil, 1983.
Seuil "Points Roman," 1987.

Un oiseau brûlé vif.

Paris: Seuil, 1984.
Gómez-Arcos's Spanish translation/adaptation: *Un pájaro quemado vivo.* Madrid: Debate, 1986.
Finaliste: Prix Goncourt 1984.

Bestiaire.

Paris: Le Pré aux Clercs, 1986.
Liste Goncourt 1986.

L'homme à genoux.

Paris: Julliard, 1989.
Prix Européen de l'Association des Écrivains de Langue Française 1990.

L'aveuglon.

Paris: Stock, 1990.

Gómez-Arcos's Spanish translation/adaptation: *Marruecos*. Madrid: Monda-
    dori, 1991.
Premier Prix du Levant, 1991.

Mère Justice.

Paris: Stock, 1992.
Prix Littéraire du *Quotidien du Médecin* 1992.
Liste Goncourt 1992.

La femme d'emprunt.

Paris: Stock, 1993.

L'ange de chair.

Paris: Stock, 1995.

Poetry collection

Ocasión de paganismo.

Barcelona: Agustín Gómez-Arcos, 1956.

Short story

"El último Cristo."

Unpublished ts.
Premio Nacional.

Essay

"Censorship, Exile, Bilingualism."

In *Critical Fictions: The Politics of Imaginative Writing*, edited by Philomena
    Mariani. 220–22. Seattle: Bay Press, 1991. (Published and altered version of
    paper delivered at Critical Fictions Symposium, Dia Art Foundation, New York
    City, 12 May 1990.)

Selected interviews

"Agustin Gomez-Arcos et *La femme d'emprunt*: Roman d'une métamorphose."
    Ouest France 8 October 1993.
"Entretien avec Agustin Gomez-Arcos: *L'enfant pain*." *Wallonie*, 1 July 1983.
Gómez-Arcos, Agustin. Interviewed by Marie-Françoise Allain. "Agustin Gomez-
    Arcos: 'je suis un maquisard!'" *Les Nouvelles Littéraires*, 13 September 1979.

———. Interviewed by Jean-Claude Bologne. "Agustin Gomez-Arcos, du sacré au sensuel." *Gai Pied Hebdo*, 24–30 September 1983, 38.

———. Interviewed by Léa Chapignac. "Agustin Gomez Arcos: A propos de son dernier roman *Scène de chasse (furtive)*." *Rouge*, 13 November 1978.

———. Interviewed by José Benito Fernández. "Voy a contaros ciertas cosas . . . : Entrevista con Agustín Gómez Arcos." *Quimera* 117 (1993): 49–55.

———. Interviewed by Pierre Canavaggio. "Un homme de *Caractères*: Agustín Gomez-Arcos ce soir sur A2." *Panorama du Médecin*, 5 October 1990, 21.

———. Interviewed by Josefina Casado. "Agustín Gómez Arcos en Francia o El vacío político que dejan las dictaduras." *Liberación*, 14 January 1985, 1–2.

———. Interviewed by Ramon Chao. "Goncourt 78. Gómez Arcos, Finalista: un español que novela en francés." *Triunfo*, 25 November 1978, 58.

———. Interviewed by Francisco Correal. "Agustín Gómez-Arcos, Dramaturgo y novelista: 'El cine no lo considero un arte.'" *Diario 16*, 8 May 1993, 28.

———. Interviewed by with Marie-Louise Coudert. "Augustin Gomez Arcos." *L'Humanité Dimanche*, 15 June 1977.

———. Interviewed by Jean Duvignaud. "Agustin Gomez-Arcos: 'Je n'ai plus le mal du pays.'" *Nouvelles Littéraires*, 14 April 1977, sec. lettres.

———. Interviewed by Sharon G. Feldman. "Agustín Gómez-Arcos in New York." New York City. 14 May 1990.

———. Interviewed by Feliciano Fidalgo. "Agustín Gómez Arcos, escritor: 'El fútbol es un coñazo.'" *El País*, 11 December 1994, 56.

———. Interviewed by Brigitte Giraud. "Gomez-Arcos, Hors Tout." *Lyon Libération*, 21 May 1990, Culture, 6.

———. Interviewed by Karl Kohut. *Escribir en París*. Barcelona: Hogar del Libro, 1983. 128–55.

———. Interviewed by Rosa Montero. "Agustín Gómez Arcos: El creyente de la palabra." *El País*, 6 October 1985, suplemento dominical, 4–10.

———. Interviewed by Moisés Pérez-Coterillo. "Agustín Gómez Arcos: 'El pensamiento es más arriesgado (y más cauto) que la noticia.'" *Turia de Madrid*, 9/6 December 1994, 27–29.

———. Interviewed by Begoña Piña. "El escritor Agustín Gómez-Arcos asegura que todavía le persigue la mala suerte en España." *Diario 16*, 20 October 92, 64.

———. Interviewed by Yann Plougastel. "Entretiens de l'été: Agustin Gomez-Arcos: 'Dans mes livres, on n'entend pas mon accent.'" *Événement du Jeudi*, 28 August–3 September 1986, 68[?], 71.

———. Interviewed by Vicente Romero. "Entrevista con un autor casi olvidado: Agustín Gómez Arcos." *Primer Acto* 148 (September 1972): III–IV.

———. Interviewed by Pierrette Rosset and Francoise Ducout. "Avec l'accent." *Elle*, 4 December 1978.

———. Interviewed by Lola Santa-Cruz. "Agustín Gómez-Arcos: El teatro es subversión." *El Público* 84 (May–June 1991): 30–32.

———. Interviewed by Jean-Yves Tournie. "Michel del Castillo et Gomez-Arcos: Le maître de ballet et l'idéologue." *Indépendent*, December 1984.

———. Interviewed by Javier Villán. "Agustín Gómez Arcos, Dramaturgo y novelista: 'Soy republicano y como escritor, apátrida.'" *El Mundo*, 7 December 1994, 74.

Other

"Autocrítica de *Los gatos*, que se estrena hoy." *ABC* [Madrid], 24 September 1965, 79.

"Autodefensa." *Primer Acto* 54 (June 1964): 22. (Re: Diálogos de la herejía).

Program Notes. *Diálogos de la herejía.* Teatro Reina Victoria. Madrid: May 1964.

Program Notes. *Los gatos.* Teatro Marquina. Madrid: September 1965.

Program Notes. *Interview de Mrs. Muerta Smith por sus fantasmas.* Sala Olimpia. Madrid: February 1991.

Program Notes. *Queridos míos, es preciso contaros ciertas cosas.* Teatro María Guerrero/Centro Dramático Nacional. Madrid: December 1994.

English translations

Ana No. Translated by John Becker. London: Secker and Warburg, 1986.

A Bird Burned Alive. Translated by Anthony Cheal and Marie-Luce Papon. London: Chatto and Windus, 1988.

The Carnivorous Lamb. Translated by William Rodarmor. Boston: Godine, 1984. New York: Plume, 1986.

The Cats. Translated by Lee Fontanella. Unpublished ts. Madrid, 1965.

Mrs. Dead Smith's Interview with her Phantoms. Translated by Sharon G. Feldman. Unpublished ts. Austin, 1990.

My Dear Friends, It's Time We Get Certain Things Straight. Translated by Lee Fontanella. Unpublished ts. Madrid, 1966.

ARTICLES AND SELECTED REVIEWS OF GÓMEZ-ARCOS'S WORK
Page numbers are given where available.

Adorado Alberto (Et si un aboyait?)

Pérez-Coterillo, Moisés. "Teatro actual español en la Sorbona. Los espectáculos." *Primer Acto* 152 (January 1973): 60–67.

L'agneau carnivore

"*The Carnivorous Lamb.*" *New York Times Book Review,* 4 May 1986, 43.

"*The Carnivorous Lamb.*" *Publishers Weekly,* 31 August 1984, 421.

Delacour, Marie Odile. "Á la troisième republique espagnole." *Libération,* 12 November 1976.

"Fiction: *The Carnivorous Lamb.*" *The Listener* [London], 1 May 1986, 35.

Gascón-Vera, Elena. "Los reflejos del yo: Narcisismo y androginia en Agustín Gómez-Arcos." *Cuadernos de ALDEEU* 7.1 (1991): 31–52.

"Gomez-Arcos, Agustin. *The Carnivorous Lamb.*" *Booklist,* 15 February 1985, 822.

"Gomez-Arcos, Agustin. *The Carnivorous Lamb.*" *Library Journal,* 15 February 1985, 180.

Keates, Jonathan. "Archetypes of Ambiguity." *Observer Magazine* (Sunday Supplement to the *London Observer*), 20 April 1986, 24.

Latour, Bruno de. "*L'agneau carnivore* d'Augustin Gomez Arcos: Un univers clos." *Quotidien de Paris*, 28 October 1975.

Mainil, Jean. "L'inceste: Un 'Agneau carnivore'?" *Romance-Notes* 31.3 (Spring 1991): 257–65.

Manguel, Alberto. "Nothing Exceeds like Excess." *Village Voice*, 16 April 1985, 46.

McCulloch, Jeanne. "*The Carnivorous Lamb.*" *New York Times Book Review*, 17 March 1985, 26.

Rechy, John. "A Story Daring in its Passions." *Los Angeles Times Book Review*, 30 December 1984, 7.

Stuewe, Paul. "Fiction: *The Carnivorous Lamb.*" *Quill and Quire* [Canada], August 1985, 49.

Williams, Arnold. "In Defiance of Franco: *The Carnivorous Lamb, Extramuros.*" *San Francisco Review of Books*, May 1985, 9–10.

Ana non

Andejean, Cristian. "*Ana non.*" *Esprit* 5 (1977): 124–30.

Baroche, Christiane. "Un concentré d'indignation permanente." *Quinzaine Littéraire*, 16 July 1977.

Codaccioni, Anne. "*Ana Non.*" *Nouvelles Affiches de Marseille*. 23–26 October 1977.

Coppermann, Annie. "*Ana Non.*" *Les Echos*, 27 June 1977.

Florenne, Yves. "Le réalisme épique de Gomez-Arcos." *Le Monde*, 17 June 1977, 19, 21.

Gateau, Jean-Charles. "Letters espagnoles: La longue marche d'Ana Non." *Gazette de Lausanne*, 5 June 1977.

K., V. "Agustin Gomez-Arcos 3ᵉ prix Roland-Dorgelès." *Le Figaro*, 16 December 1977.

Kanters, Robert. "La vieille femme et la mort." *Le Figaro*, 31 July 1977.

Poirson, Alain. "Figures de femmes." *L'Humanité*, 15 September 1977.

Pons, Anne. "Le rendez-vous espagnol." *Le Point*, 25 April 1977.

R., P. "La naissance d'Ana." *Elle*, 13 June 1977.

L'aveuglon

Bichelberger, Roger. "L'infirmité d'un môme." *Républicain Lorrain*, 28 September 1990.

Brincourt, André. "A. Gomez-Arcos: Voir ou ne pas voir, telle est la question." *Le Figaro*, 22 October 1990.

Chemin, Anne. "L'enfant-symbole d'Agustin Gomez-Arcos." *Le Monde*, 31 August 1990, livres / idées, 13.

Cortan, Gérard de. "Gómez-Arcos: La terre ne ment pas." *Quotidien de Paris*, 10 October 1990.

Lequeret, Elisabeth. "Un roman hispano-marocain: La rage de vivre." *Jeune Afrique*, 24–30 October 1990, 63.

Leroux, Luc. "Le Marrakech des estropiés." *Le Provençal*, 30 September 1990.

Mobailly, Dominique. "Agustin Gómez-Arcos nous peint un monde sans pitié dans le cadre de Marrakech: *L'aveuglon.*" *La Vie*, 13 August 1990.

Bestiaire

"En Bref. La première sélection du Goncourt." *Le Monde*, 20 June 1986.

Caballero, Oscar. "Cerca de doscientas novelas compiten por los grandes premios de la 'rentrée' literaria francesa." *La Vanguardia*, 9 September 1986, cultura, 39.

Cessole, Bruno de . "Bonjour les monstres." *Le Point*, 28 April 1986.

"Los 'desfiles' editoriales: Francia presenta sus ofertas bibliográficas." *El País*, 4 September 1986, libros, 12.

Ezine, Jean-Louis. "Trois zèbres dans une litière." *Nouvel Observateur*, 20 June 1986.

Diálogos de la herejía

Aragonés, Juan Emilio. "*Diálogos de la herejía* de Agustín GómezArcos." In *Veinte años de teatro español (1960–1980)*. Boulder, Co.: Society of Spanish and Spanish-American Studies, 1987. 62–65.

Domenech, Ricardo. "*Diálogos de la herejía* de Agustín Gómez-Arcos." *Primer Acto* 54 (June 1964): 51–52.

Feldman, Sharon. "Agustín Gómez-Arcos's *Diálogos de la herejía* and the Deconstruction of History." *Gestos* 18 (Noviembre 1994): 61–80.

Llovet, Enrique, Elías Gómez Picazo, and Alfredo Marquerie. "Tres críticas de la prensa diaria a *Diálogos de la herejía.*" *Primer Acto* 54 (June 1964): 24–25.

Monleón, José. "Los mitos embalsamados." *Primer Acto* 54 (June 1964): 17–18.

Mollá, Juan. "*Diálogos de la herejía.*" In *Teatro español e iberoamericano en Madrid 1962–1991*, edited by Luis T. González-del-Valle. Boulder, Co.: Society of Spanish and Spanish-American Studies, 1993. 11.

Morera, José María. "Reflexiones de un director después de un estreno polémico: *Diálogos de la herejía.*" *Primer Acto* 54 (June 1964): 23.

Valdivieso, L. Teresa. "El intertexto como principio configurativo en el teatro de Fernando Arrabal y Agustín Gómez-Arcos." In *Teatro español contemporáneo: Autores y tendencias*, edited by Alfonso de Toro and Wilfried Floeck, Kassel: Reichenberger, 1995. 167–90.

Elecciones generales

Marquerie, Alfredo. "*Elecciones generales*, de Gómez-Arcos." *ABC*, 6 April 1960, 63.

L'enfant pain

"Agustin Gomez-Arcos: *L'enfant pain.*" *Fête*, 8–12 November 1983, 43.

Benoot, E. "Esplendida Andalucia [*sic*]." *Standaard* [Amsterdam], 24–25 September 1983.

Bernstein, Michèle. "Un goût étrange venu d'ailleurs." *Libération*, 26 May 1983, 25.

"*L'enfant pain*: Agustin Gomez-Arcos." *Tribune de la Vente*, July-August 1983, 85.

"*L'enfant pain* d'Augustin Gomez-Arcos." *Lutte Ouvrière*, 10 September 1983.

"*L'enfant pain* par Augustin Gomez-Arcos." *Humanité Dimanche*, 1 July 1983, romans.

"Entretien avec Agustin Gomez-Arcos." *Wallonie*, 1 July 1983.

Fily, Jean-Pierre. "Lectures brèves." *Bretagne à Paris*, 22 April 1983.

Gazier, Michèle. "Le pain de la guerre." *Télérama*, 6 April 1883, livres.

"Gomez-Arcos (Agustin): *L'enfant pain*." *Bulletin Critique du Livre Français*, March 1984, littératures ibériques et latino-américaines.

"Gomez-Arcos (Agustin): *L'enfant pain*." *Culture et Bibliothèques pour Tous, Union Nationale: Notes Bibiographiques*, June 1983.

"Gomez-Arcos (Agustin): *L'enfant pain*." *Info-Livres*, September 1983, 44.

"Humiliés et offensés." *Journal de Genève*, 25 October 1987.

Limoges, Michel. "C'est Noël, faites-vous un cadeau: Choisissez de lire." *Courrier de Saone et Loire*, 20 December 1983.

"Des livres en supplément de bagage." *Cosmopolitan*, August 1983.

Lozi, J. "Un rayon de soleil dans des cieux écrasants." *Dernières Nouvelles d'Alsace*, 30 April 1983, dernières nouvelles des livres.

Morelle, Paul. "L'amour de l'Andalousie: Quand Clément Lépidis et Agustin Gomez-Arcos font la même peinture d'un même pays." *Le Monde*, 26 August 1983, romans.

———. "Celui qui ne peut pas oublier." *Panorama du Médecin*, 15 September 1983, 26.

Pelegrin, Benito. "*L'enfant pain* par Agustin Gomez-Arcos." *Esprit*, October 1983, 295.

Plantureux, Chantal. "*L'enfant pain* par Augustin Gomez-Arcos." *La Vie*, 9 June 1983.

Ricaulmont, Jacques de. "Romans de désenchantement: Agustin Gomez-Arcos: *L'enfant pain*." *Spectacles du Monde*, November 1983, 112.

Rudel, Christian. "Au bout de la faim." *Croix*, 30 July 1983, 17.

Trudel, Clément. "L'Espagne rouge, blanche et noire." *Le Devoir*, 25 June 1983.

La femme d'emprunt

C., P. "La femme d'emprunt, d'Agustin Gomez-Arcos: Les plumes de la paonne." *Panorama du Médecin*, 27 September 1993.

Cortanze, Gérard de. "*La femme d'emprunt* d'Agustin Gomez-Arcos." *Le Figaro Magazine*, 11 September 1993.

Lequeret, Elisabeth. "Gomez-Arcos, baroque toujours." *Jeune Afrique*, 16–22 September 1993, 67.

M., L. "Il ou elle." *Art et Culture* [Brussels], October 1993.

Los gatos

Aragonés, Juan Emilio. "*Los gatos* de Agustín Gómez-Arcos." In *Veinte años de teatro español (1960–1980)*. Boulder, Co.: Society of Spanish and Spanish-American Studies, 1987. 83–84.

Blanco, Miguel Angel. "Lo mío es un cabreo constante." *Ideal* [Almería], 27 November 1992.

"Carmen Portaceli estrena esta noche *Los gatos*, de Agustín Gómez Arcos: Héctor Alterio, una mujer de los 50, en el María Guerrero." *Diario 16*, 10 November 1992, 48.

Centeno, Enrique. "Faldones de terciopelo." *Diario 16*, 12 November 1992, 69.

Feldman, Sharon. "*Los gatos:* Gómez-Arcos's Spectacle of Sacrifice." *Estreno: Cuadernos del teatro español contemporáneo* 23.1 (Primavera 1995): 38–44.

Fernández, Gerardo. "Mi querida solterona." *Clarín* [Buenos Aires], 31 December 1992, 16.

Fernández Torres, A. "Otra opportunidad: *Los gatos*, vuelve a los escenarios tras veinticinco años." *El Mundo*, 13 November 1992, E3.

Freire, Susana. "Héctor Alterio es un gato que maúlla contra el autoritarismo." *La Nación* [Buenos Aires], 3 June 1993, espectáculos.

Galindo, C. "*Los gatos*, una reflexión sobre el pasado de Agustín Gómez Arcos." *ABC*, 6 November 1992, 96.

Haro Tecglen, Eduardo. "Injusticia mal reparada." *El País*, 12 November 1992, 34.

Hera, Alberto de la. "Resulta increíble." *Ya*, 14 November 1992, cartelera.

Hernández, Esteban. "Agustín Gómez Arcos: 'El teatro debe ser transgresor.'" *El Mundo*, 10 November 1992, cultura, 50.

López Sancho, Lorenzo. "*Los gatos* y la cara y cruz de la intransigencia hasta el crimen." *ABC*, 12 November 1992, espectáculos.

Llovet, Enrique. "Estreno de *Los gatos* en el Teatro Marquina." *ABC*, 27 September 1965, 91.

Marín, Ana. "Madrid se llena de 'maullidos.'" *Ya*, 10 November 1992, 44.

Martínez, D. "Agustín Gómez Arcos: 'En España se valora mucho la cultura de escaparate.'" *Voz de Almería*, 26 November 1992.

———. "Héctor Alterio y Paco Casares interpretan a dos mujeres en la obra *Los gatos* de Gómez-Arcos." *Voz de Almería*, 27 November 1992.

Monleón, José. "*Los gatos* de Agustín Gómez-Arcos." *Primer Acto* 68 (October 1965): 53–54.

Piña, Begoña. "El escritor Agustín Gómez Arcos asegura que todavía le persigue la mala suerte en España: Se suspende el estreno de su obra *Los gatos* por enfermedad de Héctor Alterio." *Diario 16*, 20 October 1992, 64.

———. "La intolerancia de los cincuenta." *Guía de Madrid*, 6 November 1992.

Portaceli, Carme. *Los gatos*. Program Notes. Teatro María Guerrero. Madrid: November 1992.

Torres, Rosana. "Héctor Alterio y Paco Casares interpretan a dos beatas intolerantes: *Los gatos*, de Gómez Arcos, llega a Madrid." *El País*, 6 November 1992.

Vilches de Frutos, Ma Francisca. "La temporada teatral española 1992–1993." *Anales de la Literatura Española Contemporánea* 20.3 (1995): 463–502.

Villán, Javier. "Sombría historia." *El Mundo*, 12 November 1992, 43.

Vizcaíno, Juan Antonio. "Nuevos rumbos: Con la llegada de la crisis, los dramaturgos toman la palabra para reflejar críticamente la sociedad." *El País*, 6 February 1993, Babelia, 4–5.

L'homme à genoux

"Agustin Gomez-Arcos: *L'homme à genoux*." *Vendredi: L'Hebdomadaire des Socialistes*, 8 September 1989.

Bernstein, Michele. "Gomez-Arcos. A votre bon cœur." *Libération*, 31 August 1989, 5F.

Cortanze, Gérard de. "Gomez-Arcos: L'envers du décor." *Quotidien de Paris*, 4 October 1989.

Haddad, Martine. "Roman: Agustin Gomez-Arcos: *L'homme à genoux.*" *Jeune Afrique*, 30 October 1989.

"*L'homme à genoux.*" *Cité*, 30 November 1989, culture, 64.

"*L'homme à genoux.*" *Événement du Jeudi*, 5–11 October 1989, lettres.

"*L'homme à genoux.*" *Livres*, November 1989.

"*L'homme à genoux.*" *La Vie: Hebdomadaire Chrétien d'Actualité*, 7–13 September 1989.

"*L'homme à genoux.*" *Vendredi Samedi Dimanche*, 7 September 1989.

"*L'homme à genoux* par Agustin Gomez-Arcos, chez Julliard.*" Arts et Métiers Magazine*, January-February 1990.

Maricourt, Thierry. "Note de lecture: *L'homme à genoux.*" *Le Monde Libertaire* [Paris], 26 October 1989, expressions.

"Roman étranger: *L'homme à genoux*: Augustin Gomez-Arcos." *Librairie, L* September 1989.

Roussel, Eric. "L'autre Espagne." *Tribune Médicale*, 7 October 1989.

Interview de Mrs. Muerta Smith por sus fantasmas

Armiño, Mauro. "Recuerdo de un pasado." *El Sol*, 27 February 1991.

Castellano, Manuel. "*Interview de Mrs. Muerta Smith por sus fantasmas:* Teatro y verdad bajo sospecha." *Reseña* 216 (April 1991): 20.

Centeno, Enrique. "Una justa recuperación." *Diario 16*, 25 February 1991.

Feldman, Sharon. "Sanctifying the Scatological and Debasing the Divine: Postmodernist Allegory and Gómez-Arcos's *Interview de Mrs. Muerta Smith por sus fantasmas.*" *España Contemporánea* 8.1 (1995): 21–42.

Fernández Torres, A. "Desagravio incompleto: El CNNTE estrena una obra de Agustín Gómez Arcos. *Metrópolis* (*El Mundo*), 1 March 1991, 69.

Galindo, Carlos. "Interview de Mrs. Muerta Smith por sus fantasmas, experiencia teatral de Agustín Gomez Arcos." *ABC*, 2 February 1991, 84.

Green, Pere. "Julieta Serrano, Actriz: Mujeres al borde de todos los peligros." *El Observador*, 25 February 1991.

Haro Tecglen, Eduardo. "La señora se pudre." *El País*, 25 February 1991, 31.

Idoeta, Nerea. "Carme Portaceli dirigeix una obra de Gómez Arcos a Madrid." *Diari de Barcelona*, 25 February 1991.

Larrañeta, Pablo. "Teatro contra los bombardeos." *Tiempo*, 25 February 1991, 145.

López Negrín, Florentino. "Interview de Mrs. Muerta Smith por sus fantasmas: Gómez Arcos, en el Olimpia." *El Independiente*, 25 February 1991.

López Sancho, Lorenzo. "'Mrs. Muerta Smith y sus fantasmas,' demasiado tarde." *ABC*, 1 March 1991.

M. H. "Gala y Gómez-Arcos, el teatro de los literatos: Las entrañas podridas de una sociedad decadente." *El Independiente*, 22 February 1991, espectáculos, 35.

Martín-Lunas, Milagros. "Una 'muerta' muy viva: Julieta Serrano, pasión teatral." *Metrópolis* (*El Mundo*), 8 March 1991.

Pérez Coterillo, Moisés. "Breve interrupción de una ausencia." Introduction to *Interview de Mrs. Muerta Smith por sus fantasmas*, by Agustín Gómez-Arcos. Teatro 15. Madrid: *El Público*/Centro de Documentation Teatral, 1991. 9–12.

Piña, Begoña. "Símbolo de una sociedad podrida." *Diario 16*, n.d.

Podol, Peter. Review of *Interview de Mrs. Muerta Smith por sus fantasmas*, published by *El Público*/Centro de Documentación Teatral *Estreno* 19.1 (Spring 1993), 49.

S., R. "Estrena Gómez-Arcos una fábula antibélica." *Epoca*, 3 March 1991.

Santa-Cruz, Lola. "Agustín Gómez-Arcos." Introduction to *Interview de Mrs. Muerta Smith por sus fantasmas*, by Agustín Gómez-Arcos. Teatro 15. Madrid: *El Público*/ Centro de Documentation Teatral, 1991. 13–15.

———. "La mortaja del Tío Sam." *El Público* 84 (May-June 1991): 26–29.

Valdivieso, L. Teresa. "El intertexto como principio configurativo en el teatro de Fernando Arrabal y Agustín Gómez-Arcos." In *Teatro español contemporáneo: Autores y tendencias*, edited by Alfonso de Toro and Wilfried Floeck. Kassel: Reichenberger, 1995. 167–90.

Villán, Javier. "*Interview de Mrs. Muerta Smith por sus fantasmas:* Beligerancia y oportunidad." *El Mundo*, 25 February 1991, 45.

Vizcaíno, Juan Antonio. "Gómez Arcos vuelve a la escena española tras más de 20 años de ausencia." *El País*, 25 February 1991, 31.

———. "Ideologías ensangrentadas: La obra de Agustín Gómez Arcos vuelve a representarse en España." *El País*, 22 February 1991, En cartel, 6.

Zatlin, Phyllis. *Cross-Cultural Approaches to Theatre: The Spanish-French Connection.* Metuchen, N.J.: Scarecrow Press, 1994. 78–80.

Maria Republica

"Agustin Gomez-Arcos: *Maria Republica*." *Lutte Ouvrière*, 17 September 1983, 193.

Florenne, Yves. "Un ex–voto espagnol." *Le Monde*, 4 June 1976.

Madelin-Rondeau, Noëlle. "Livres en poche." *Républicain Lorrain*, 3 November 1983.

"*Maria Republica*." *Action Laïque*, October 1984.

"*Maria Republica*, Agustin Gomez-Arcos, Points Seuil." *Magazine Littéraire*, November 1983, 143.

Maricourt, Thierry. "*Maria Republica*—Agustin Gomez-Arcos." *CPCA*, July-August 1984, 17.

Saint-Pierre, Isaure de. "Agustin Gomez-Arcos, la putain et le franquisme." *Quotidien de Paris*, 27 April 1977.

Mère Justice

Barland, J.-R. "Agustin Gomez-Arcos: La vengeance d'une mère. *Le Provençal Dimanche*, 19 April 1992.

Carrasco, Candide. Rev. of *Mère Justice*. *The French Review* 67.1 (October 1993): 163–64.

Fossey, Jean-Michel. "Un roman-réquisitoire de Gomez-Arcos: La réalité du racisme au quotidien." *Liberté des Livres*, 19 May 1992.

Freneuil, Martine. "De la fiction à la réflexion avec Gomez-Arcos et Paul Guimard." *Quotidien du Médecin*, 22 September 1992.

Morand, Élisabeth. "Agustin Gomez-Arcos: Un beau roman, fort et pudique, sur le racisme: *Mère Justice.*" *La Vie*, 23 April 1992.

Mourthé, Claude. "*Mère Justice* d'Agustin Gomez-Arcos." *Le Figaro Magazine*, 4 July 1992.

Romain, Maxime. "Le combat d'une mère." *La Marseillaise*, 10 April 1992.

Sissung, Maud. "Histoire d'un crime ordinaire." *Jeune Afrique*, 18 June 1992.

Un oiseau brûlé vif

"Agustin Gomez-Arcos: *Un oiseau brûlé vif.*" *Républicain Lorrain*, 4 November 1984.

"Agustin Gomez Arcos: Peintre du franquisme quotidien." *Le Monde*, 30 November 1984.

Allain, Marie-Françoise. "*Un oiseau brûlé vif* d'Agustin Gomez-Arcos: Les fascismes rampants." *Le Monde Diplomatique*, January 1985.

Bell, Ian. "Whodunnit, Gringo? *Glasgow Herald*, 16 April 1988.

Bourgeade, Pierre. "*F* Livres." *F*, September 1984, 98.

Brincourt, André. "Les temps cramoisis d'Augustin Gomez-Arcos." *Le Figaro*, 2 November 1984, 22.

Buss, Robin. "Fascists in the Bed." *Times Literary Supplement* [London], 30 November 1984, 392.

Clavel, André. "Les femmes intolérables d'un andalou parisien." *Matin des Livres*, 11 September 1984.

Cunningham, Valentine. "Neapolitan Ice Cream." *Observer* [London], 10 April 1988.

David, Jean. "Gomez Arcos: Un roman écrit au lance-flammes." *Vendredi Samedi Dimanche*, 11–17 August 1984, 62.

"Enfance espagnole." *Humanité Dimanche*, 8 February 1985.

Favarger, Alain. "A. Gomez-Arcos: L'Espagne face à la dictature." *Liberté* [Fribourg, Switz.], 29 September 1984.

Fernandez-Recatala, D. "*Un oiseau brûlé vif.*" *Révolution*, 11 September 1984, 53.

"Franco et après." *Elle*, 29 October 1986, 64.

"Gomez-Arcos (Agustin): *Un oiseau brûlé vif.*" *Bulletin Critique du Livre Français*, December 1984.

Goury, Gérard-Humbert. "*Un oiseau brûlé vif.*" *Biba*, November 1984.

Kearns, Gloria. "Un oiseau brûlé vif: L'âcre Arcos." *Continuum* [Montreal], 19 November 1984.

Lovell, Moira. "Skilful [sic] but brutal." *Natal Witness*, 29 November 1988 [Cape Town].

Nye, Robert. "Man out of mind." *Guardian* [London], 8 April 1988.

"*Un oiseau brûlé vif.*" *Biba*, November 1986.

"*Un oiseau brûlé vif.*" *Progrès*, 2 December 1984.

"*Un oiseau brûlé vif* d'Agustin Gomez-Arcos." *Le Figaro Magazine*, 8 September 1984.

"*Un oiseau brûlé vif* par Agustin Gomez-Arcos." *Valeurs Actuelles*, 12 November 1984.

Pache, Jean. "Augustin Gomez-Arcos: *Un oiseau brûlé vif.*" *24 Heures* [Éd. nat. et vaudoise, Lausanne], 6 October 1984.

Paugam, Jacques. "*Un oiseau brûlé vif* d'Augustin Gomez-Arcos." *Panorama du Médecin*, 3 October 1984.

"Les petites phrases." *Matin des Livres*, 4 September 1984, 21.

Profumo, David. "Stories of Strange Lives in Strange Lands." *Sunday Times* [London], 22 May 1988, G6.

"La rentrée littéraire." *Le Point*, 10 September 1984, 146.

Ribais, Yak. "Cruel." *Contre Ciel*, February 1985, 78.

Pré-papa (novel)

D., L. "*Pré-papa* d'Agustin Gomez-Arcos: Une jolie fable futuriste." *Le Matin*, 2 October 1979.

Garzarolli, Richard. "Augustin Gomez-Arcos: *Pré-papa ou roman de fées.*" *Tribune de Lausanne*, 29 October 1979.

Murol, Constance. "*Pré-papa.*" *Le Figaro*, 28 October 1979.

Schmidt, Joël. "De vie et d'amour." *Réforme*, 1 December 1979.

Pré-papa (play)

Gérome, Raymond. *Pré-papa. L'Avant Scène Théâtre* 434 (1969): 37.

Pérez-Coterillo, Moisés. "Teatro actual español en la Sorbona. Los espectáculos." *Primer Acto* 152 (January 1973): 64–66.

Queridos míos, es preciso contaros ciertas cosas

Centeno, Enrique. "Las cosas que nos prohibían." *Diario 16*, 9 December 1994, 44.

Galindo, Carlos. "Agustín Gómez-Arcos, un autor un busca de la utopía perdida. *ABC Internacional*, 20 December 1994, 33.

Haro Tecglen, Eduardo. "La doncella y el mal" *El País*, 9 December 1994, 30.

Portaceli, Carme. "*Queridos míos* . . . , en el María Guerrero." *ABC*, 8 December 1994, 114.

Torres, Rosana. "Gómez Arcos recibe grandes honores de dramaturgo con 30 años de retraso." *El País*, 7 December 1994, 36.

Villán, Javier. "Entre Franco, Sófocles y Felipe. *El Mundo*, 9 December 1994, 80.

———. "Con la verdad por delante: Gómez Arcos regresa con *Queridos míos, es preciso contaros ciertas cosas.*" *El Mundo Magazine*, 11 December 1994, 64.

Scène de chasse (furtive)

Boisriveaud, Juliette. "*Scène de chasse (furtive).*" *Cosmopolitan*, November 1978, 16.

Bourboune, Mourad. "*Scène de chasse (furtive):* Un livre d'Agustin Gomez-Arcos . . . y Goya." *Demain l'Afrique*, 4 December 1978.

Fouchet, Max-Pol. "*Scène de chasse (furtive)* d'Agustin Gomez Arcos." *Vendredi Samedi Dimanche*, 4 November 1978.

Rinaldi, Angelo. "Gómez-Arcos: L'ingenu et les roublards." *L'Express*, 2–9 December 1978, 76–77.

Poirson, Alain. "La peur au ventre des bourreaux." *L'Humanité*, 9 November 1978.

Pons, Anne. "Arènes sanglantes." *Le Point*, 9 October 1978.

La villa de los ladrones (Translation/Adaptation of a Norwegian children's musical by Thorbjorn Egner).

Llovet, Enrique. "Estreno teatral: *La villa de los ladrones*." *ABC*, 19 November 1963, 81.

General

Allain, Marie-Françoise. "Outrages non posthumes au drapeau rouge-jaune-rouge de l'Espagne franquiste." *Le Monde Diplomatique*, April 1981, politique et littérature, 12.

Aragonés, Juan Emilio. *Teatro español de posguerra*. Temas españoles 520. Madrid: Publicaciones Españolas, 1971. 88.

Armiño, Mauro. "Extranjero en su patria." *El País*, 3 December 1994, Babelia, 7.

Brochard, Gilles. "La panoplie du parfait écrivain." *Plumes*, October 1993.

"Del Castillo—Gomez-Arcos: Espagne plurielle." *Indépendant*, 10 December 1984.

Duncan, Ann. "Agustín Gómez-Arcos." In *Beyond the Nouveau Roman: Essays on the Contemporary French Novel*, edited by Michael Tilby. New York: Berg, 1990. 151–76.

García, Ángeles. "Un intelectual alejado del poder." *El País*, 30 June 1985.

———. "El último creador en el exilio." *El País*, 30 June 1985.

Gascón-Vera, Elena. "Los reflejos del yo: narcisismo y androginia en Agustín Gómez Arcos." *Cuadernos de ALDEEU* 7.1 (April 1991): 31–52.

Nourissier, François. "Lisez-vous le 'franpagnol'?" *Le Figaro Magazine*, 4 November 1978.

Miralles, Alberto. *Aproximación al teatro alternativo*. Damos la palabra 3. Madrid: Asociación de Autores de Teatro, 1994. 16.

Monleón, José. "Gómez-Arcos: La honesta herejía." *Primer Acto* 238 (March-April 1991): 132–44.

———. "Premio Nacional de Literatura Dramática." *Primer Acto* 256 (November-December 1994): 4–5.

Oliva, César. *El teatro desde 1936*, 324326. Historia de la Literatura Española Actual 3. Madrid: Alhambra, 1989. 222, 224, 226, 233, 322, 324–26, 350, 434, 445.

Pérez-Stansfield, María Pilar. *Direcciones del teatro español de posguerra*. Madrid: José Porrúa Turanzas, 1983. 157, 310

"Signatures." *Midi Libre*, 10 December 1984.

Sorel, Andrés. "Literatura sí. Policías no." *Liberación*, 14 January 1985, cultural liberación, 1–2.

Valdivieso, L. Teresa. "El intertexto como principio configurativo en el teatro de Fernando Arrabal y Agustín Gómez-Arcos." In *Teatro español contemporáneo: Autores y tendencias*, edited by. Alfonso de Toro and Wilfried Floeck. Kassel: Reichenberger, 1995. 167–90.

Villanueva, Antonia S. "Agustín Gómez-Arcos: 'La realidad española no ha cambiado mucho con la democracia.'" *Voz de Almería*, 10 January 1987.

———. "Novela y teatro, formas de expresión literaria de Agustín Gómez-Arcos." *Voz de Almería*, 10 January 1987.

"Yo, cuando escribo teatro, hago la guerra." *Diario 16*, 30 June 1985.

Zatlin, Phyllis. Cross-Cultural Approaches to Theatre: The Spanish-French Connection. Metuchen, N.J.: Scarecrow Press, 1994. 76, 77–80, 83, 112, 191, 212.

———. "The Return of the Prodigal: The Theatre of Gómez-Arcos." *Hispanic Journal* 16.1 (Spring 1995): 55–63.

OTHER REFERENCES

Abellán, Manuel L. *Censura y creación literaria en España (1939–1976).* Temas de Historia y Política Contemporánea 9. Barcelona: Península, 1980.

———. "La censura teatral durante el franquismo" *Estreno* 15.2 (Fall 1989): 20–23.

———, ed. *El exilio español de 1936.* 6 vols. Madrid: Taurus, 1976–78.

Amorós, Andrés. "Tres 'Casandras': de Galdós a Galdós y a Francisco Nieva." In *Actas del Segundo Congreso Internacional de Estudios Galdosianos.* Las Palmas, Canary Islands: 1979–80. 69–102.

Applewhite, James. "Postmodernist Allegory and the Denial of Nature." *Kenyon Review* 11.1 (Winter 1989): 1–17.

Aragonés, Juan Emilio. *Teatro español de posguerra.* Temas españoles 520. Madrid: Publicaciones Españolas, 1971. 88.

Aristotle. *Theory of Poetry and Fine Art.* Edited and translated by S. H. Butcher. New York: Dover, 1951.

Artaud, Antonin. *The Theater and Its Double.* Translated by Mary Caroline Richards. New York: Grove Press, 1958.

Bakhtin, Mikhail. *Rabelais and His World.* Translated by Hélène Iswolsky. Foreword Krystyna Pomorska. Prologue by Michael Holquist. Bloomington: Indiana University Press, 1984.

Barrajón, Jesús. *La poética de Francisco Nieva.* Ciudad Real: Diputación Provincial de Ciudad Real, 1987.

Barthes, Roland. *Image / Music / Text.* Translated by Stephen Heath. New York: Hill and Wang, 1977.

———. "The Metaphor of the Eye." In *Critical Essays,* translated by Richard Howard. Evanston: Northwestern University Press, 1972.

———. *Sade, Fourier, Loyola.* Translated by Richard Miller. Berkeley: University of California Press, 1989. Trans. of *Sade, Fourier, Loyola.* Paris: Seuil, 1971.

Bataille, Georges. *Erotism: Death and Sensuality.* Translated by Mary Dalwood. New York: Walker and Company, 1962. San Francisco: City Lights Books, 1986. Trans. of *L'érotisme.* Paris: Minuit, 1957.

———. *Histoire de l'œil.* Paris: Jean-Jacques Pauvert, 1979.

———. "The Notion of Expenditure." Translated by Allan Stoekl. In *Visions of Excess,* 116–29. Trans. of "La notion de la dépense." *La Critique Sociale* 7 (January 1933): 7–15. (Reprint in *Œuvres complètes.* Vol. 1. 302–20.)

———. "The Psychological Structure of Fascism." Translated by Carl R. Lovitt. In *Visions of Excess,* 137–60. Translation of "La structure psychologique du fascisme." *La Critique Sociale* 10 (November 1933): 159–65, and 11 (March 1934): 205–11. (Reprint in *Oeuvres complètes.* Vol. 1. 339–41.)

———. *Visions of Excess: Selected Writings, 1927–1939.* Edited by Allan Stoekl. Translated by A. Stoekl, Carl R. Lovitt, and Donald M. Leslie, Jr. Theory and History of Literature 14. Minneapolis: University of Minnesota Press, 1985.

Bataillon, Marcel. *Erasmo y España*. Translated by Antonio Alatorre. Rev. 2d ed. Mexico City: Fondo de Cultura Económica, 1966. Trans. of *Érasme et l'Espagne*.

Beckett, Samuel. *Play. The Collected Shorter Plays of Samuel Beckett*. New York: Grove, 1984. 145–60.

Benjamin, Walter. *The Origin of German Tragic Drama*. Translated by John Osborne. London: New Left Books, 1977. Trans. of *Ursprung des deutschen Trauerspiels*. Frankfurt am Main: Suhrkamp Verlag, 1963.

Blau, Herbert. *Take Up the Bodies: Theater at the Vanishing Point*. Urbana: University of Illinois Press, 1982.

Brater, Enoch and Ruby Cohn, eds. *Around the Absurd: Essays on Modern and Postmodern Drama*. Ann Arbor: University of Michigan Press, 1990.

Brecht, Bertolt. *Brecht on Theatre: The Development of an Aesthetic*. Edited and translated by John Willett. New York: Hill and Wang, 1964.

Brook, Peter. *The Empty Space*. London: MacGibbon and Kee, 1968.

Buero Vallejo, Antonio. "Obligada precisión acerca del imposibilismo." *Primer Acto* 15 (July-August 1960): 1–6.

Butler, Judith. *Bodies that Matter*. New York: Routledge, 1993.

———. *Gender Trouble: Feminism and the Subversion of Identity*. New York, Routledge, 1990.

Cabo, Ángel. *José Martín Recuerda: Génesis y evolución de un autor dramático*. Granada: Diputación Provincial de Granada, 1993.

Caillois, Roger. *L'homme et le sacré*. 2nd ed. Paris: Gallimard, 1950.

Camp, André. "L'actualité théâtrale." *L'Avant-Scène Théâtre* 434 (1969): 46.

Camus, Albert. *Le mythe de Sisyphe*. Paris: Gallimard, 1942.

Carlson, Marvin. *Theories of the Theatre: A Historical and Critical Survey, from the Greeks to the Present*. Ithaca: Cornell University Press, 1993.

Carravetta, Peter. *Prefaces to the Diaphora: Rhetorics, Allegory, and the Interpretation of Postmodernity*. West Lafayette: Purdue University Press, 1991.

Casaux, Manuel P. "La censura y otros demonios." *Primer Acto* 184 (April-May 1980): 90–91.

Cixous, Hélène. "The Laugh of the Medusa." Translated by Keith Cohen and Paula Cohen. *Signs: Journal of Women in Culture and Society* (Summer 1976): 875–93. Trans. of "Le rire de la Méduse." *L'Arc* (1975): 39–54.

Connor, Steven. *Postmodernist Culture: An Introduction to the Theories of the Contemporary*. Oxford/New York: Blackwell, 1989.

Cowan, Bainard. "Walter Benjamin's Theory of Allegory." *New German Critique* 22 (Winter 1981): 109–22.

Cramsie, Hilde. *Teatro y censura en la España franquista. Sastre, Muñiz y Ruibal*. American University Studies. Series 2. Romance Languages and Literatures, vol. 9. New York: Peter Lang, 1984.

de Man, Paul. *Allegories of Reading*. New Haven: Yale University Press, 1979.

———. "The Rhetoric of Temporality." In *Blindness and Insight: Essays in the Rhetoric of Contemporary Criticism*. 1971. 2d ed. Theory and History of Literature 7. Minneapolis: University of Minnesota Press, 1983. 187–229.

Derrida, Jacques. "Edmond Jabès and the Question of the Book." In *Writing and Difference*. Edited and translated by Alan Bass. Chicago: University of Chicago Press, 1978. 64–78.

――――. "Plato's Pharmacy." In *Dissemination*, translated by Barbara Johnson, 61–171. Chicago: University of Chicago Press, 1981.

――――. "The Theater of Cruelty and the Closure of Representation." In *Writing and Difference*, 232–50.

Domènech, Ricardo. "*Diálogos de la herejía* de Agustín Gómez-Arcos." *Primer Acto* 54 (Junio 1964): 51–52.

――――. "El teatro desde 1936." In *Historia de la literatura española*. Vol 4. Madrid: Taurus, 1980.

Douglas, Mary. *Purity and Danger: An Analysis of Concepts of Pollution and Taboo*. New York: Frederick A. Praeger, 1966.

Eagleton, Terry. *Body as Language*. London: Sheed and Ward, 1970.

――――. *Exiles and Émigrés: Studies in Modern Literature*. New York, Schocken, 1970.

Edwards, Gwynne. *Dramatists in Perspective. Spanish Theatre in the Twentieth Century*. New York: St. Martin's Press, 1985.

Eliade, Mircea. *The Sacred and the Profane: The Nature of Religion*. Translated by Willard R. Trask. New York: Harcourt Brace Jovanovich, 1987.

Esslin, Martin. *The Theatre of the Absurd*. 3d ed. 1980. New York: Penguin, 1988.

――――. "The Theatre of the Absurd Reconsidered." In *Reflections: Essays on Modern Theatre*. New York: Doubleday, 1969. 183–91.

――――. "Violence in Modern Drama." In *Reflections: Essays on Modern Theatre*. New York: Doubleday, 1969. 163–78.

Facio, Angel, coordinator. "Mesa redonda." *Primer Acto* 184 (April-May 1980): 104–15

Fernández, Angel. "Mirada a las cunetas." *Primer Acto* 184 (April-May 1980): 120.

Fineman, Joel. "The Structure of Allegorical Desire." *October* 12 (1980): 46–66.

Fletcher, Angus. *Allegory: The Theory of a Symbolic Mode*. Ithaca: Cornell University Press, 1964.

Foucault, Michel. "A Preface to Transgression." In *Language, Counter-memory, Practice*. Edited by Donald F. Bouchard. Translated by Donald F. Bouchard and Sherry Simon, 29–52. Ithaca: Cornell University Press, 1977. Trans. of "Préface à la transgression." Hommage à Georges Bataille. Spec. issue of *Critique* 195–96 (1963): 751–70.

Freud, Sigmund. *Civilization and Its Discontents. Standard Edition* 21: 64–145.

――――. *Three Essays on the Theory of Sexuality. The Standard Edition of the Complete Psychological Works of Sigmund Freud*. Edited by James Strachey. 24 vols. London: Hogarth, 1953–74. 130–243.

Frye, Northrop. *Anatomy of Criticism*. Princeton: Princeton University Press, 1957.

Garber, Marjorie. *Vested Interests: Cross-dressing and Cultural Anxiety*. New York: Routledge, 1992.

Gala, Antonio. "Respuesta a José Monleón." *Primer Acto* 184 (April-May 1980): 92–93.

García Lorenzo, Luciano. *El teatro español hoy*. Barcelona: Planeta, 1975.

――――, ed. *Documentos sobre el teatro español contemporáneo*. Madrid: Sociedad General Española de Librería, 1980.

García Templado, José. *El teatro español actual*. Madrid: Anaya, 1992.

Girard, René. *Violence and the Sacred*. Translated by Patrick Gregory. Baltimore: Johns Hopkins University Press, 1977. Trans. of *La violence et le sacré*. Paris: Bernard Grasset, 1972.

Goytisolo, Juan. *Disidencias*. Barcelona: Seix Barral, 1977.

———. Interviewed by Karl Kohut. *Escribir en Paris*. Barcelona: Hogar del Libro, 1983. 77–102.

———. Presentación crítica of *Obra inglesa de Blanco White*. 1972. Barcelona: Seix Barral, 1982.

Greenblatt, Stephen J., ed. and preface. *Allegory and Representation: Selected Papers from the English Institute*. Baltimore: Johns Hopkins University Press, 1986.

———. "Loudun and London." *Critical Inquiry* 12.2 (Winter 1986): 326–46.

Halsey, Martha T., "Introduction to the Historical Drama of Post-Civil-War Spain." *Estreno* 14.1 (Spring 1988): 11–12, 17.

Halsey, Martha T. and Phyllis Zatlin. *The Contemporary Spanish Theater: A Collection of Critical Essays*. Lanham/New York/London: University Press of America, 1988.

Handke, Peter. *Offending the Audience*. In Kaspar *and Other Plays*, translated by Michael Roloff. New York: Farrar, Straus and Giroux, 1969.

Heras, Guillermo. "Sobre autocensuras y metalenguaje." *Primer Acto* 184 (April-May 1980): 98–99.

Hinchliff, Arnold P. *The Absurd*. London: Methuen, 1969.

Holquist, Michael. "Corrupt Originals: The Paradox of Censorship." *PMLA* 109.1 (January 1994): 14–25.

Holt, Marion P. *The Contemporary Spanish Theater (1949–1972)*. Boston: Twayne, 1975.

Honig, Edwin. *Dark Conceit: The Making of Allegory*. Chicago: Northwestern University Press, 1960.

Hunter, Lynette. *Modern Allegory and Fantasy: Rhetorical Stances of Contemporary Writing*. New York: St. Martin's Press, 1989.

Hutcheon, Linda. *The Politics of Postmodernism*. New York: Routledge, 1989.

———. *A Theory of Parody: The Teachings of Twentieth-Century Art Forms*. London/New York: Methuen, 1985.

Huxley, Aldous. *The Devils of Loudun*. London: Chatto and Windus, 1961.

Ilie, Paul. *Literature and Inner Exile: Authoritarian Spain 1939–75*. Baltimore: Johns Hopkins University Press, 1980.

Ionesco, Eugène. *Notes and Counter-Notes: Writings on the Theatre*. Translated by Donald Watson. New York: Grove, 1964.

Jansen, Sue Curry. *Censorship: The Knot that Binds Power and Knowledge*. Oxford: Oxford University Press, 1988.

Jerez Farrán, Carlos. "El compromiso de la estética del absurdo en el teatro de Arrabal." *Revista Canadiense de Estudios Hispánicos* 14.2 (Invierno 1990): 277–91.

Krauss, Rosalind E. "Grids." In *The Originality of the Avant-Garde and Other Modernist Myths*. 9–22. Cambridge: MIT Press, 1985.

Lewis, C. S. *The Allegory of Love: A Study in Medieval Tradition*. 1936. Reprint New York: Oxford University Press, 1972.

Lindenberger, Herbert. *Historical Drama: The Relation of Literature and Reality*. Chicago: University of Chicago Press, 1975.

Longo, Robert. *When heaven and hell change places*. Galerie Hans Mayer, Düsseldorf, November 1992-March 1993.

Lyotard, Jean-François. *The Postmodern Condition: A Report on Knowledge.* Translated by Geoff Bennington and Brian Massumi. Minneapolis: University of Minnesota Press, 1984.

Madsen, Deborah L. *The Postmodernist Allegories of Thomas Pynchon.* Leicester: Leicester University Press, 1991.

Malla, Gerardo. "En torno a las censuras." *Primer Acto* 184 (April-May 1980): 100–3.

Marañon, Gregorio. "Los alumbrados y el espíritu español." *Primer Acto* 54 (Junio 1964): 19–21.

McGlynn, Fred. "Postmodernism and Theater." In *Postmodernism—Philosophy and the Arts,* edited by Hugh J. Silverman, 137–54. New York: Routledge, 1990.

McHale, Brian. *Postmodernist Fiction.* New York: Routledge, 1987.

Mediero, Manuel Martínez. "'Qué verde era mi valle'" *Primer Acto* 184 (April-May 1980): 94–97.

Melville, Stephen. "Notes on the Reemergence of Allegory, the Forgetting of Modernism, the Necessity of Rhetoric, and the Conditions of Publicity in Art and Criticism." *October* 19 (1981): 54–92.

Miller, Arthur. *The Crucible.* 1967. London: Heinemann, 1982.

Miralles, Alberto. *Aproximación al teatro alternativo.* Damos la palabra 3. Madrid: Asociación de Autores de Teatro, 1994.

———. "Epílogo. De la agonía a la esperanza y se van a cumplir cinco años." *Primer Acto* 184 (April-May 1980): 121–23.

———. "Los lunes del María Guerrero." *Primer Acto* 184 (April-May 1980): 116–17.

Moi, Toril. *Sexual/Textual Politics: Feminist Literary Theory.* New Accents. New York: Routledge, 1985.

Money, John, and Anke A. Ehrhardt. *Man and Woman, Boy and Girl: The Differentiation and Dimorphism of Gender Identity from Conception to Maturity.* Baltimore: John Hopkins University Press, 1972.

Monleón, José. *Cuatro autores críticos: José María Rodríguez Méndez, José Martín Recuerda, Francisco Nieva, Jesús Campos.* Granada: Gabinete de Teatro, Secretaría de Extensión Universitaria, 1976.

———. "Historia y drama histórico durante la Dictadura." *Estreno* 14.1 (Spring 1988): 5–6.

———. "Nuestra generación realista," *Primer Acto* 32 (March 1962): 1–3.

Nägele, Rainer. *Theater, Theory, Speculation: Walter Benjamin and the Scenes of Modernity.* Baltimore: Johns Hopkins University Press, 1991.

O'Connor, Patricia W. "Government Censorship in the Contemporary Spanish Theatre." *Educational Theatre Journal* 18 (1966): 443–49.

———. "Torquemada in the Theater: A Glance at Government Censorship." *Theatre Survey* 14.2 (1973): 33–45.

Oliva, César. "Breve itinerario por el último drama histórico español." *Estreno* 14.1 (Spring 1988): 7–10.

———. *Disidentes de la generación realista (Introducción a la obra de Carlos Muñiz, Laura Olmo, Rodríguez Méndez and Martín Recuerda.)* Murcia: Departamento de Literatura Española, Universidad de Murcia, 1979.

———. *El teatro desde 1936.* Historia de la literatura española actual 3. Madrid: Alhambra, 1989.

Oliva, César, and Francisco Torres Monreal. *Historia básica del arte escénico*. Madrid: Cátedra, 1990.

Ortega y Gasset, José. *Velázquez*. Madrid: Austral, 1970.

Owens, Craig. "The Allegorical Impulse: Toward a Theory of Postmodernism: Part I." *October* 12 (1980): 67–86. (Reprint in *Beyond Recognition: Representation, Power, and Culture*.)

———. "The Allegorical Impulse: Toward a Theory of Postmodernism: Part II." *October* 13 (1980): 59–80. (Reprint in *Beyond Recognition: Representation, Power, and Culture*.)

———. *Beyond Recognition: Representation, Power, and Culture*. Edited by Scott Bryson, Barbara Kruger, Lynne Tillman, and Jane Weinstock. Berkeley: University of California Press, 1992.

———. "The Discourse of Others: Feminists and Postmodernism." In *The Anti-Aesthetic: Essays on Postmodern Culture*, edited by Hal Foster, 57–82. Seattle: Bay Press, 1983. (Reprint in *Beyond Recognition: Representation, Power, and Culture*.)

———. "Representation, Appropriation, and Power." *Art in America* 70.5 (May 1982): 9–21. (Reprint in *Beyond Recognition: Representation, Power, and Culture*.)

———. "From Work to Frame, or, Is There Life After 'The Death of the Author'?" In *Beyond Recognition: Representation, Power, and Culture*. 122–39.

Paso, Alfonso. "Los obstáculos para el pacto." *Primer Acto* 12 (January-February 1960): 7–8.

Pasquariello, Anthony. "Government Promotion, Honors and Awards: A Corollary to Franco Era Censorship in Theater." *Cuadernos de ALDEEU* 1 (January 1983): 67–81.

Pavis, Patrice. *Languages of the Stage*. New York: Performing Arts Journal Publications, 1982.

Pérez, Janet. "The Game of the Possible: Francoist Censorship and Techniques of Dissent." *Review of Contemporary Fiction* 4 (Fall 1984): 22–30.

Pérez-Coterillo, Moisés. "Teatro actual español en la Sorbona. Los espectáculos." *Primer Acto* 152 (Enero 1973): 60–67.

Pérez-Stansfield, María Pilar. *Direcciones del teatro español de posguerra*. Madrid: José Porrúa Turanzas, 1983.

Phillips, Elda María. *Idea, signo y mito: El teatro de José Ruibal*. Madrid: Orígenes, 1984.

Quilligan, Maureen. *The Language of Allegory*. Ithaca: Cornell University Press, 1979.

Richman, Michèle H. *Reading Georges Bataille: Beyond the Gift*. Baltimore: Johns Hopkins University Press, 1982.

Rojas, Fernando de. *La Celestina*. Edited by Julio Cejador y Frauca. 2 vols. Madrid: Cátedra, 1972.

Romero, Vicente. "Teatro actual español en la Sorbona. Informe general." *Primer Acto* 152 (January 1973): 52–58.

Rosen, Charles. "Walter Benjamin and His Ruins. *New York Review of Books* 27 October 1977, 31–40, 17 November 1977, 30–38.

Ruiz Ramón, Francisco. Historia del teatro español. Siglo XX. Madrid: Cátedra, 1977.

———. "Pasado/Presente en el drama histórico." *Estreno* 14.1 (Spring 1988): 22–25.

Ruggeri Marcheti, Magda. *Il teatro di Domingo Miras. Con l'edizione di "El doctor Torralba."* Rome: Bulzoni, 1991.

Russell, Ken, dir. *The Devils*. With Oliver Reed and Vanessa Redgrave. Great Britain, 1971.

Salvat, Ricard. "Teatro actual español en la Sorbona. El comienzo de una nueva sensibilidad." *Primer Acto* 152 (January 1973): 59–60.

Sastre, Alfonso. "A modo de respuesta" *Primer Acto* 16 (September-October 1960): 1–2.

———. "Teatro imposible y pacto social." *Primer Acto* 14 (May-June 1960): 1–2.

———. "Teatro de la realidad." *Primer Acto* 18 (December 1960): 1–2.

Schechner, Richard. *Performance Theory*. New York: Routledge, 1988.

Seidel, Michael. *Exile and the Narrative Imagination*. New Haven: Yale University Press, 1986.

Serrano, Virtudes. *El teatro de Domingo Miras*. Prologue by Francisco Ruiz Ramón. Murcia: Universidad de Murcia, 1991.

Signes, Emil G. "Francisco Nieva: Spanish Representative of the Theater of the Marvelous." In Halsey and Zatlin, *The Contemporary Spanish Theater: A Collection of Critical Essays*. Edited by Martha T. Halsey and Phyllis Zatiln. Lanham/New York/London: University of America, 1988. 147–61.

Simon, Joan. "Double Takes." *Art in America* 8 (October 1980): 113–17.

Smith, Paul H. "The Will to Allegory in Postmodernism." *Dalhousie Review* 62 (1982): 105–22.

Sollers, Philippe, "The Roof: Essay in Systematic Reading." In *Writing and the Experience of Limits*, edited by David Hayman, translated by Philip Barnard, with David Hayman, 103–34. New York: Columbia University Press, 1983. Trans. of "Le toit: Essai de lecture systématique." *Tel Quel* 29 (Spring 1967): 26–46.

Sontag, Susan. "The Pornographic Imagination." In *Styles of Radical Will*. 1966. New York: Farrar, Straus and Giroux, 1969.

Spariosu, Mihai. "Allegory, Hermeneutics, and Postmodernism." In *Exploring Postmodernism*, edited by Matei Calinescu and Douwe Fokkema. Amsterdam/Philadelphia: John Benjamins, 1987.

Stallybrass, Peter and Allon White. *The Politics and Poetics of Transgression*. Ithaca: Cornell University Press, 1986.

Steiner, George. "Extraterritorial." In *Extraterritorial: Papers on Literature and the Language Revolution*. New York: Atheneum, 1971. 3–11.

Stoller, Robert. *Sex and Gender: On the Development of Masculinity and Femininity*. New York: Science House, 1968.

Suleiman, Susan Rubin. "Transgression and the Avant-Garde. Bataille's *Story of the Eye*." In *Subversive Intent: Gender, Politics, and the Avant-Garde*. Cambridge: Harvard University Press, 1990. 72–87.

Tabori, Paul. *The Anatomy of Exile*. London: Harrap, 1972.

Tebar, Juan. *Fernando Fernán Gómez, escritor*. Madrid: Anjana, 1984.

Toro, Alfonso de, and Wilfried Floeck, eds. *Teatro español contemporáneo: Autores y tendencias*. Kassel: Reichenberger, 1995.

Ubersfeld, Anne. *L'école du spectateur (Lire le théâtre II)*. Paris: Éditions Sociales, 1981.

Ugarte, Michael. *Shifting Ground: Spanish Civil War Exile Literature*. Durham: Duke University Press, 1989.

Ulmer, Gregory L. "The Object of Post-Criticism." In *The Anti-Aesthetic: Essays on Postmodern Culture*, edited by Hal Foster. Seattle: Bay Press, 1983. 83–100.

Valle-Inclán, Ramón del. *Luces de Bohemia*. Madrid: Espasa Calpe, 1974.

Van Dyke, Carolynn. *The Fiction of Truth: Structures of Meaning in Narrative and Dramatic Allegory*. Ithaca: Cornell University Press, 1985.

Wellwarth, George E. *Spanish Underground Drama*. University Park and London: The Pennsylvania State University Press, 1972.

———. *Teatro español underground*. Prologue by Alberto Miralles. Hoy es Siempre Todavía. Madrid: Villalar, 1978.

Whiting, John Robert. *The Devils*. New York: Hill and Wang, 1961.

Wolin, Richard. *Walter Benjamin: An Aesthetic of Redemption*. Berkeley: University of California Press, 1993.

Zatlin, Phyllis. Cross-Cultural Approaches to Theatre: The Spanish-French Connection. Metuchen, N.J.: Scarecrow Press, 1994.

———. *Jaime Salom*. Boston: Twayne, 1982.

Index

All works written by Agustín Gómez-Arcos are indexed, as well as all other names of persons cited in this study. Italicized numbers refer to pages with illustrations.